EIGHTEENTH-CENTURY
EUROPE

EIGHTEENTH-CENTURY EUROPE

LEONARD W. COWIE

FREDERICK UNGAR PUBLISHING CO.
NEW YORK

First published 1963
Reprinted 1964
First American edition 1964
by arrangement with the original publishers

Printed in Great Britain

PREFACE

THE aim of this book is to provide a clear and simple survey of the history of Europe in the period between 1715 and 1815. The author has concentrated upon supplying information about the development of the main issues of this century. The narrative has been made as simple and intelligible as possible so that a broad view of European affairs will not be obscured by the inclusion of over-much detail. The book is chiefly concerned with the outstanding questions in the relations of the various powers and the leading figures who took part in the events of the time. The internal history of separate countries is considered where it is important in relation to European history as a whole. This has inevitably meant that much space is given to France, the French Revolution and Napoleon, but developments in other countries, such as Prussia and Russia, are not neglected. At the same time, such matters as population, religion and thought, social and economic developments, war and diplomacy, are surveyed in the introductory chapters.

The use of footnotes is confined to indicating complementary passages in the book so that repetition is avoided and the chapters are linked together.

An indication of the many writers on this period to whom the author is indebted would be too lengthy to include. The bibliography consists largely of the leading authorities in English, which may be used for further information on particular topics.

CONTENTS

LIST OF MAPS

I · EIGHTEENTH-CENTURY EUROPE

The States of Europe

FOR the political history of Europe, the eighteenth century is commonly taken to be the period between the death of Louis XIV in 1715 and the defeat of Napoleon in 1815, the years which followed the Treaty of Utrecht and culminated in the Treaty of Vienna. It begins and ends with the frustration of an attempt to dominate the Continent by its leading power, and between lie the events which brought about the French Revolution and its aftermath. What the Renaissance was to the fifteenth century and the Reformation to the sixteenth, the French Revolution was to the eighteenth century. Like these two great earlier movements, it arose from events in previous centuries and affected all the countries of Europe despite their different national developments.

These countries, indeed, still possessed a large common background. They had inherited together much from the past, while political and economic interaction, the sharing of ideas and imitation of institutions, was constant. Before considering the history of the leading European states during this period, this common background must be understood, and this first requires a knowledge of the origin and boundaries of these states, the distribution of population among them and the religious outlook of their peoples.

The political map of Europe in 1715 was that produced by the Treaty of Utrecht, which ended the War of the Spanish Succession in 1713. Though France had been defeated, she obtained better terms than had seemed possible at one stage in the War. She was accorded her frontiers of 1697, so that, except for a few towns on the eastern frontier, she kept the earlier acquisitions made by Louis XIV – Artois and most of Flanders, Valenciennes and Cambrai, Alsace and Franche Comté, besides Cerdagne and Roussillon on the Spanish border. The kingdom was territorially larger than fifty years before and strategically more compact. In addition, she still held valuable colonies in North America and the West Indies. She was still able to take an active and warlike part both in Europe and overseas in the eighteenth century, but she had paid a high price for her successes and placed a strain upon her largely antiquated system of government which was to destroy it three-quarters of a century after Louis XIV's death.

The role played by France in international affairs during the greater part of the eighteenth century was not, therefore, as striking as might have been expected from the strength given her by the size of her population and natural resources. Throughout the reigns of Louis XV and Louis XVI she suffered numerous military reverses in contests with her rivals in Europe. Outstanding victories were nullified by serious setbacks, and between 1715 and 1789 her place among the nations of Europe declined. Two new nations in eastern Europe, Prussia and Russia, strengthened their positions, while in the west, Britain exerted a decisive superiority over France in the hard-fought conflict for colonial and commercial prizes. The Revolution of 1789 gave France a new system of government and national aspirations which revived her power. During the almost continuous warfare of the period between 1792 and 1814, French rule was extended over a large part of the Continent; but the gains were ephemeral, for Napoleon's defeat at Waterloo in 1815 ended forever this imperial aspiration.

A main contestant in the period of warfare which ended with the Treaty of Utrecht had been Spain, which had fought three wars to defend the Netherlands against Louis XIV, but had been dependent upon allied subsidies and even armies. While at the beginning of the seventeenth century she had been generally recognized as the strongest European power, now she was far gone in decline. The opening years of the eighteenth century found the great powers contending for the succession to her former proud and independent heritage. She lost the Netherlands and her Italian provinces; she kept her overseas dominions only because her European rivals could not agree about their division. The establishment of Philip V upon the Spanish throne in 1700 was followed by a period, lasting some seventy years, which produced many important reforms and a considerable regeneration of the country; but Spain could no longer be the chief antagonist of France. Now, bound to her by a Bourbon family compact, she was largely dependent upon her.

This family compact replaced the older one between the Spanish and Austrian Habsburgs. The death of Charles II in 1700 had brought the Spanish branch of the family to an end,

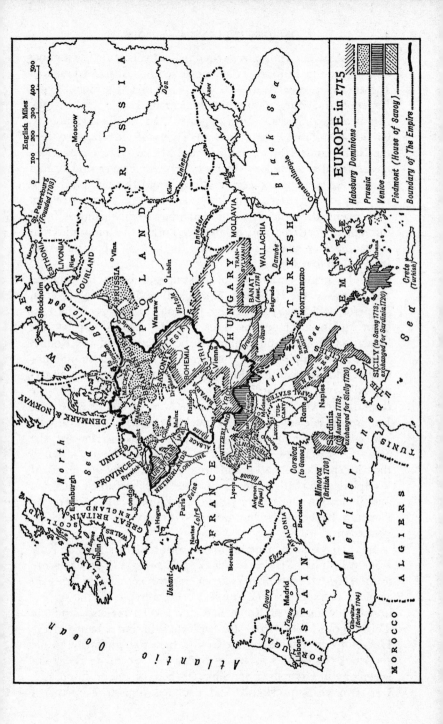

EUROPE in 1715

Habsburg Dominions
Prussia
Venice
Piedmont (House of Savoy)
Boundary of The Empire

English Miles
0 100 200 300 400 500

RUSSIA
Moscow
Don
Azov
Black Sea
Dnieper
Kiev
Dniester
Constantinople
St. Petersburg (Founded 1703)
Narva
ESTHONIA
LIVONIA
Riga
COURLAND
Vilna
POLAND
Warsaw
Vistula
Lublin
MOLDAVIA
TRANSYLVANIA
WALLACHIA
Danube
BANAT (Aust. 1718)
HUNGARY
Belgrade
Save
MONTENEGRO
TURKISH EMPIRE
RAGUSA
Adriatic Sea
Athens
Crete (Turkish)
Stockholm
Baltic Sea
SWEDEN
PRUSSIA
Stettin
SILESIA
BOHEMIA
Dresden
AUSTRIA
Vienna
Drave
STYRIA
SWEDEN
Oder
BRANDENBURG
MECK.
Hanover
SAXONY
Ratisbon
BAVARIA
TYROL
SWITZERLAND
PIEDMONT
Turin
PAPAL STATES
Rome
NAPLES
TWO SICILIES
Naples
SICILY (to Savoy 1713; exchanged for Sardinia 1720)
SARDINIA (to Austria 1713; exchanged for Sicily 1720)
Corsica (to Genoa)
TUSCANY
Florence
Lucca
Modena
Genoa
Mediterranean Sea
DENMARK & NORWAY
North Sea
UNITED PROVINCES
Ryswick
AUSTRIAN NETHERLANDS
Utrecht
Cologne
Mainz
Rhine
LORRAINE
ALSACE
FRANCE
Paris
La Hogue
Seine
Loire
Nantes
Lyons
Rhone
Avignon (Papal)
Bordeaux
Garonne
GREAT BRITAIN
SCOTLAND
Edinburgh
WALES
ENGLAND
London
IRELAND
Dublin
La Bogue
Ushant
Atlantic Ocean
SPAIN
Madrid
Tagus
Douro
Ebro
CATALONIA
Barcelona
Minorca (British 1708)
Gibraltar (British 1704)
PORTUGAL
Lisbon
MOROCCO
ALGIERS
TUNIS

but the Austrian Habsburgs remained with increased dominions
and prestige in Europe. They possessed the Austrian Lands of
Upper and Lower Austria, Styria, Carinthia, Carniola, Tyrol,
Breisgau and Burgau and the Bohemian Lands of Bohemia,
Moravia and Silesia. In 1699 they had obtained Hungary,
Croatia and Transylvania; and the Treaty of Utrecht gave them
the Netherlands, Naples, Sardinia and Milan. Their possessions
now formed a dominion which ranked with France and Britain
among the strongest powers of Europe, and the eighteenth century was to see a determined effort made by administrative reform
to overcome the difficulties and weaknesses from which it suffered
through its scattered and isolated territories, the many different
nationalities among its subjects and the lack of a natural centre
from which to rule them.

Besides being Archdukes of Austria and Kings of Bohemia
and Hungary, the Habsburgs also held the office of Holy Roman
Emperor, which was an elective position. Since 1356 the Em-
peror had been chosen by those German princes who became
known as Electors and claimed to be successors of the Roman
Senate in an empire which considered itself the western inheritor
of the old Roman Empire; but from 1440, almost uninter-
ruptedly, only the head of the House of Habsburg had worn the
Imperial crown. In 1715 the boundaries of the Holy Roman
Empire still enclosed nominally much territory in central Europe.
This included Germany, though without Prussia in the east; the
Swiss Confederation and the Dutch Republic, having asserted
their independence, had been formally excluded by the Treaty of
Westphalia in 1648. The Habsburgs' own hereditary Austrian
and Bohemian lands were within the Empire, and so were the
Austrian Netherlands, but neither Hungary nor their Italian
possessions.

In 1756 Voltaire made his well-known remark about the Holy
Roman Empire – '*Ce corps qui s'appelait et qui s'appelle encore
le saint empire romain n'était en aucune manière ni saint, ni
romain, ni empire.*' The Empire's claim to represent the ancient
imperial authority of Rome had never been realized, and the
Thirty Years' War (1618–48) frustrated the last attempt of the
Habsburgs to establish an effective Imperial authority, while
Frederick the Great's seizure of Silesia in 1740 made Habsburg
hegemony in Germany impossible. When, therefore, Francis II,
who two years previously had declared himself Emperor of

Austria, was compelled by Napoleon's policy in Germany to relinquish the title of Holy Roman Emperor in 1806, he was deprived of little more than an empty title.[1]

During the eighteenth century the machinery of government of the Holy Roman Empire remained, though to little purpose. The Diet, composed of delegates representing the members of the three Colleges of Electors, Princes and Imperial cities, met at Ratisbon, but it had become merely an assembly of envoys from practically independent states, and its decisions had little effect. The Imperial Chamber sat at Wetzlar on the Lahn, but only un-important cases were brought before it, and it had no means of enforcing its decrees. The ten administrative Circles still existed, but were unable to implement Imperial decisions. An effective Imperial army, drawn from contingents sent by the Circles, hardly existed. Across the boundaries of the Circles ran those of the German states, divided in religion, and each determined to assert its own authority.

The rulers of these German states included monarchs of Euro-pean importance, like those of Austria and Prussia, eight electoral princes, 94 spiritual and lay princes, 103 counts, 40 prelates and 51 imperial free cities. In all, there were in eighteenth-century Germany some 300 separate political entities, each supposed to hold its territory from the Emperor, but all enjoying practical sovereignty. Outstanding among these states was Prussia, which had developed from the Electorate of Brandenburg in the north-east of Germany. It had gained Cleves, Mark and Ravensburg in the west in 1614 and Prussia in the east in 1618. To these dominions had been added East Pomerania, Halberstadt, Cammin and Minden in 1648, Magdeburg in 1680 and Guelders in 1713, while since 1701 the Elector of Brandenburg had possessed the additional title of King of Prussia. These possessions were all German, but they were scattered, and in the eighteenth century the Prussian rulers set out to unite them by extending their territory.

Besides Germany, another part of Europe which remained dis-united was the Italian peninsula. Here the Treaty of Utrecht substituted an Austrian domination for the Spanish domination which had existed since the Treaty of Cateau-Cambrésis of 1559. Austria received Milan, Naples and Sardinia. The eighteenth century was to bring changes in her Italian territory, but she was to maintain her superiority in the peninsula (except during the

[1] P. 367.

years of Napoleonic conquest) until the nineteenth century brought about a united Italy. Across the centre of the peninsula were the Papal States; but the most important Italian state was the kingdom of Piedmont, which had developed from the duchy of Savoy in the previous century and possessed an Italian dynasty. The Treaty of Utrecht granted her Sicily, which she exchanged with Austria for Sardinia in 1720. She was destined to take the lead in the movement for Italian unification, but there was no sign of this during the eighteenth century.

The Treaty of Utrecht also gave Austria the southern Netherlands, which had belonged to Spain. The other half of the Netherlands, the Dutch Republic, had experienced years of great power and influence in the first half of the seventeenth century, when its people had founded trade routes across nearly all the known world, established an empire greater than that of Venice in her prime and pioneered the economic institutions of capitalism. Later in the century, however, Holland was to decline steadily. She fared badly in economic competition with England and was crippled by her wars with France. By the end of the War of the Spanish Succession, she had survived as an independent state, but with power and prestige seriously impaired. The outbreak of the War of the Austrian Succession found her still weaker, and the Treaty of Aix-la-Chapelle came only just in time to save her from disaster. The end of Dutch influence upon European events was recognized after the First Treaty of Versailles in 1756, when France accepted her neutrality in the coming struggle.

In eastern and northern Europe in 1715 the largest state was the kingdom of Poland, which still extended from the Dnieper to the Vistula and from the Dniester to the Baltic. Yet, although so large, she was also among the weakest of European countries. Lack of natural frontiers, a variety of races among her inhabitants and defects in her constitution and administration combined to make her powerless against her stronger neighbours. She had lost territory steadily in the second half of the seventeenth century and ceased to be a state in the eighteenth century. The question of the partition of the Spanish Empire, which had brought about war in the later seventeenth century, was replaced early in the eighteenth century by the question of the partition of Poland as a matter of grave European consequence.

The eighteenth century opened upon the decline of another

Baltic power, Sweden. In the previous century she had been one of the largest European states, possessing about twice as much territory as she does today; but the Treaty of Nystadt with Russia, which ended the Great Northern War (1700–21), deprived her of most of her lands on the other side of the Baltic, leaving her with only Finland and part of West Pomerania. The Swedish attempt to dominate the Baltic had been thwarted; her position as a great power was over. She could no longer fight a major war or aspire to international importance.

In place of Sweden, Russia had become the leading power in the Baltic and the north of Europe. During the seventeenth century, she had begun to take the first steps towards the goal of becoming a western nation, a process which was rapidly accelerated during the momentous reign of Peter the Great (1682–1725). St. Petersburg took the place of Moscow as the capital of the country, western ideas and techniques were encouraged, the power of the nobles was curbed, the Church brought under the Czar's control, the army trained by foreign officers, and Russia gained a Baltic coastline from Riga to the Gulf of Finland. Despite the hatred of Russian conservatives for Peter's work and the series of mediocre rulers who immediately followed him, his achievements were largely sustained and made possible the successful reign of Catherine the Great (1762–96). Russia was now a prominent European power, increasingly able to exercise a decisive influence in international questions – within ten years after Peter's death in the disputed Polish Succession, within forty years in the outcome of the Seven Years' War and within ninety years in the overthrow of Napoleon.

The rise of Russia coincided with the decline of Turkey, which continued steadily during the eighteenth century. In 1715 the Turkish Empire in Europe possessed territory about as extensive as France or Spain, covering all the Balkan peninsula and northwards beyond it as far as the lower Danube and including the whole of the delta on the Black Sea and north of it the coastal plain of Bessarabia and Jedisan as far as the estuary of the Dnieper. The Treaty of Karlowitz in 1699, however, when both Austria and Russia made territorial gains at her expense, marked the end of Turkey's three-hundred-year-long period of expansion. Her neighbours had now passed to the offensive. Russia sought to establish herself on the Black Sea, while Austria tried to advance down the Danube. Their ambitions aroused growing fears among other European powers, especially Britain and France, and brought into being a new phase in the Eastern Question. The problem henceforward presented to Europe by the Turkish Empire was no longer to resist its aggression, but to agree upon the division of its provinces.

The Population of Europe

Any estimate of the population of Europe in the eighteenth century must be based upon inference or even guesswork. Reliable figures are almost entirely absent before 1800. Sweden and Finland had systems of registration by parishes which from 1750 yielded quite trustworthy figures; but generally in Europe contemporaries knew little about the population of their countries. In England, a Bill for Registering the Number of the People, introduced into Parliament in 1753, was only passed in the House of Commons amid violent opposition as a 'project totally subversive of the last remains of English liberty' and a 'Frenchified inquisitorial bill' and was rejected by the House of Lords. We know that the population of eighteenth-century England was increasing more rapidly than ever before, but most contemporaries thought it was declining – Horace Walpole suggested it was due to excessive drinking. Arthur Young was one of the few who discerned a rising population.

Nor do the elementary resources of eighteenth-century administration enable taxation and other figures to be taken as a satisfactory guide to population. In 1788, for instance, an Irish revenue-commissioner found that lax tax-collectors had omitted no less than 200,000 households from the latest returns for the hearth-tax in the island. According to Dr. Kuczynski it is likely that about 80 per cent of the population of the world in 1800 is not known to within a margin of 10 per cent either way. Neither Britain nor France began real census-taking until the beginning of the nineteenth century, and these first censuses were still imperfect. The British census of 1831, for instance, gave the acreage of England twice over with a discrepancy as large as Berkshire.

Dr. Kuczynski has estimated that Europe's population in 1700 was perhaps 118,000,000 and in 1770 about 152,500,000. Professor Willcox puts it at about 140,000,000 in 1750 and 187,000,000 in 1800 or 21·2 and 22·4 per cent of the population of the whole world; but Dr. Carr-Saunders suggests that this should be 19·2 and 20·7 per cent. It does seem certain, at any rate, that the population of most European states, after a period of staying almost stationary, was now beginning to increase markedly.

Actual figures for the rate of this increase are largely speculative, but in all countries for which any sort of estimate can be made a growing population is indicated before 1770. There are three countries – England, Sweden and Norway – for which the information allows estimates of the average annual rates of increase in percentages of total population for both the earlier and middle decades of the century. In each of these countries, the rate for the earlier period is low, Sweden being the highest with 0·36 per cent; but it is much higher in each for the later period, reaching 0·8 per cent in Norway between 1750 and 1770. In Finland, Austria and Prussia, for which estimates relating to the middle period alone are possible, the rate corresponds roughly to that in the same period for the three countries already mentioned. For France, it is possible to estimate only the rate for the whole period from 1701 to 1770, and it is low – 0·18 per cent; but for Russia between 1721 and 1763 it is high – 0·73 per cent. Despite fragmentary data, there is little doubt that Europe's rate of growth in population became more rapid during the century, and the average rate of increase for the continent as a whole between 1700 and 1800 was about 0·68 per cent. The present-day annual increase of the world's population has been estimated at 1·7 per cent.

The reasons for this increase during the eighteenth century are not clear. It is certainly true that famine, plague and war, which for three centuries had kept the population of Europe in check, no longer exerted the same effect. Scarcity, however, remained, and even plague made one last onslaught early in the century in Germany (where estimates suggest that a third of the population of the province of Prussia and 18,000 people in Königsberg alone died in 1709) before retreating eastwards; and an epidemic is estimated to have killed 80,000 in Brittany in 1741. Moreover, there was an almost complete ignorance of hygiene in this period. Smallpox, typhus and children's diseases killed many each year. England, which was in advance of the Continent in hygiene and had no further plague after 1666, still had in this century a normal death-rate of 41 per 1,000 (compared with an average of 13·7 today); and in London it was probably over 50 in the first half of the century, though falling to about 30 by the end.

In all countries, the urban death-rate was so high that many statisticians believe that the towns only maintained their numbers from the countryside. In Berlin it seems to have been 40 or more at the beginning of the century and not to have fallen below 30 at the end. Other suggested figures range from 50 for Vienna to half that rate for Coburg. The larger the town, the higher the death-rate seems to have been.

The birth-rate was high in both urban and rural areas, ranging from 30 to 60 per 1,000 from country to country, but infant mortality was everywhere heavy. Between a third and a fifth of all children died in their first year. Most families seem to have had at least four children and commonly six or more, but only two or three usually survived early infancy. Rousseau decried the confidence placed by parents in the future – 'Of all the children that are born, only half at most attain to fourteen years, and it is probable yours may not reach the age of manhood.' Necker estimated that of the whole French population, a quarter died before the age of three, a quarter between three and twenty-five and a quarter between twenty-five and fifty.

Nevertheless, the most likely cause of the increase in population does seem to have been a gradual rise in the expectation of life and not any extraordinary increase in fertility. Diet improved as trade multiplied the variety of foodstuffs. Improvements in medical knowledge and skill, particularly in midwifery, slowly reduced the high death-rate among mothers in childbirth and very young children. This improved knowledge found social expression in the establishment of infirmaries, hospitals and lying-in charities in the towns. In the towns, also, though their sanitation remained primitive, life became healthier and death-rates gradually fell. In 1730 three of every four children born in London probably died before they were five years old, but a hundred years later the situation was almost reversed, while the French death-rate seems to have fallen from 39 to 29 per 1,000 between 1780 and 1820.

Estimates of the population of England and Wales, based upon records of baptisms, marriages and burials, put it at about 5,500,000 in Queen Anne's reign. It seems to have increased slowly to about 6,000,000 by 1740 and then to have grown more rapidly until it reached about 7,500,000 in 1770 and 8,000,000 in 1790. The census figures were 8,872,980 for 1801 and 10,163,676 for 1811. Scotland's population in 1700 was about 1,000,000, and its census figures for 1801 and 1811 were

1,599,068 and 1,805,699.   Ireland had about 2,000,000 people
in 1700; its first census (in 1811) gave a total of 5,937,856.

The population of France, after being probably stationary or
even declining in Louis XIV's reign, grew markedly in the
eighteenth century.   In 1715 it was no more than 19,000,000; by
the middle of the century it perhaps approached 22,000,000; and
by the time of the Revolution it was probably 26,000,000.   The
first French census in 1801 gave the country a population of some
24,000,000, and in 1811 it was 28,000,000.

The population of Spain, after probably falling from 8,000,000
to 6,000,000 in the previous century, does not seem to have grown
in the first part of this period by much more than 500,000, mainly
owing to the inadequacies of the country's farming.   In 1748 a
contemporary made a rather high estimate of 7,500,000 for the
population, but he also said that 2,000,000 people were on the
verge of starvation and 72,000 square miles of good farming land
were entirely uncultivated. In Charles III's reign (1759–88), however, the population is said to have risen by 1,500,000; and it may
have been about 10,500,000 at the end of the century.   The population of Portugal remained below 3,000,000 throughout the
century.   Italy's population may have increased from 11,000,000
in 1700 to over 16,000,000 in 1770.

Changes in the territory of the Austrian Habsburgs make com-
parisons difficult.   In 1700 their population may have been about
25,000,000; figures for 1800 give 11,000,000 for the territories
within the Empire and 16,000,000 for those outside.   The population of Germany, which may have been reduced by the Thirty
Years' War from about 21,000,000 to rather less than 15,500,000,
had probably more than reached the former figure again by the
end of the eighteenth century.   The scattered possessions of
Prussia contained perhaps 2,000,000 people in 1700, Prussia itself
having less than 500,000.   Conquest brought increased population, but at a cost.   One in nine of the Prussian population may
have perished in the Seven Years' War (1756–63); Frederick the
Great himself said that he had lost about 500,000 out of a total
population of 4,500,000.   By the end of the century, however,
the population may have been 6,700,000, an increase due partly
to long-encouraged immigration and partly to greater prosperity.
A conservative estimate suggests that 16–20 per cent of the
whole Prussian population were immigrants since 1640 or their
descendants.

The vast unexplored territory of Russia makes estimates of her population difficult, but it seems that it was about 12,000,000 at the beginning of the period, and in 1797 a figure as high as 36,000,000 was used in an official registry of people on crown and noble lands. This increase came about through both territorial acquisition and natural causes. The social composition of the country was indicated by the fact that it was held that of this 36,000,000 some 34,000,000 were serfs of whom nearly 20,000,000 were on private estates and the rest on crown estates.

The two most urbanized European countries were England and France. France continued to have more large towns than England throughout the century; but London was unique. While in 1700 Paris was the largest city in Europe, London steadily overtook it from the middle of the century. By about 1740 London's population exceeded 500,000, and the figures in 1801 and 1811 were 864,845 and 1,009,546, while Paris at the end of the century had just over 500,000 inhabitants. Other English towns made advances. Bristol, the next largest city, may have grown from about 30,000 to 50,000 between 1700 and 1750, and Liverpool strikingly advanced from about 5,000 to 26,000 in the same time. Scotland's largest town, Glasgow, which had a population of about 12,000 in 1700, had quadrupled this on the eve of the American War of Independence.

Yet while London had, even in 1801, nearly ten times the population of the next largest English town, Paris never approached this proportion, though it was easily the largest French town. France had several towns larger than the leading English provincial towns. Lyons and Marseilles, each with over 100,000 inhabitants, were considerably greater throughout this period than any towns in the English provinces. By the end of the eighteenth century, the largest English provincial towns were Manchester, Liverpool, Birmingham and Bristol with populations ranging between 90,000 and 60,000, but Bordeaux and Rouen were still larger than any of them. Leeds was the only other English town with more than 50,000 inhabitants, but France had also Nantes, Lille and Toulouse. There were only five English towns with between 30,000 and 50,000 inhabitants – Sheffield, Plymouth, Portsmouth, Norwich and Newcastle-upon-Tyne; but eight in France – Amiens, Angers, Orleans, Besançon and Caen in the north, Nîmes, Montpellier and Béziers in the south. Not until the nineteenth century did England become a land of big towns.

The largest Habsburg towns at the end of the century were Vienna (226,000), Milan (119,000), Brussels (80,000), Prague (75,000) and Antwerp (60,000). In Holland, Amsterdam, though Dutch commercial supremacy had been lost to England, still had a population of about 200,000. The largest German town by this time was Berlin, which had grown steadily from about 60,000 in 1720, 120,000 in 1760, 140,000 in 1775, 150,000 in 1785 to 170,000 in 1800. This increase was due not only to the development of trade and industry and the influx of French and Dutch immigrants, but also to the growth of the Prussian army and the mounting political importance of the city. In 1783 it was estimated that it contained about 33,000 garrison troops with their families, 15,000 officials and their families, together with 10,000 personal attendants on these and the court, so that a total of about 58,000 in the city were directly dependent on the Prussian king's will. At the end of the century, there were seven other Prussian towns with a population of 20,000 or more – Warsaw (67,000), Königsberg (60,000), Breslau (57,000), Danzig (36,000), Potsdam (26,700), Magdeburg (26,300) and Halle (20,000). Outside of Prussia, there were only five German towns of this size – Munich (50,000) and Mannheim (23,000) in Bavaria, Dresden (50,000) and Leipzig (33,000) in Saxony, and Mainz (30,000) whose Prince-Archbishop was the premier spiritual elector of the Empire. The many German ducal courts, modelled upon the magnificence of Versailles, were insignificant establishments in small towns. Weimar in Goethe's time had about 8,000 inhabitants.

Russia possessed two considerable cities. Ancient Moscow had 150,000 people early in the century and 250,000 when occupied by Napoleon in 1812. Peter the Great's newly constructed St. Petersburg, which was a swamp in 1700, had 75,000 inhabitants in 1725, the year of his death, while a census taken by the police in 1789 gave the city's population as just under 218,000 of whom about a fifth belonged to the military establishment and a sixth were foreign-born. The total number of urban dwellers increased from 328,000 in 1724 to 1,300,000 in 1796, but they were still only about 4 per cent of the total population of European Russia, and as late as 1785 there were only five towns in the whole country with populations of over 30,000. Eastwards across the European continent the urban units became scarcer and scarcer until there were none in the steppes.

Urbanization, therefore, was comparatively slow in Europe in the period. Contemporaries, indeed, expected it to be so. When London had a population of 700,000, David Hume held that there was 'a kind of impossibility' that it should grow much further. The population of all states increased more rapidly in the countryside than in the towns, sometimes, in fact, up to the limits of current means of production, but the general density of population was nowhere large. Germany, for instance, was predominantly poor and rural throughout the century. It has been estimated that in the country as a whole in 1800 only a quarter of the population lived in agglomerations with populations over a thousand, while the average number of persons to the square kilometre was just 72 on the fertile soil of Württemberg, 50 in Saxony with its manufactures and a bare 30 in Prussia, though this was over twice what it had been in that kingdom in 1700. The figure for England was 65 and for France 69, which represented increases merely of $1\frac{4}{5}$ and $1\frac{1}{6}$ in the same period.

Eighteenth-century Frenchmen prided themselves on their large towns. In the middle of the century, when Warsaw was approaching a population of 60,000, *philosophes* complained that Poland had no large town; but at that time French provincial capitals like Rennes, Dijon and Grenoble had little more than 20,000 inhabitants, and by the time of the Revolution the total French urban population was 2,500,000 at the most. In fact, during the last decades of the *ancien régime* France suffered from acute and growing rural over-population, which was unrelieved by agrarian or industrial revolutions.

Such a situation led French writers to question current ideas about population. The predominant mercantilist theory of commerce held that a large population was always advantageous to a state. Adam Smith wrote, 'The most decisive mark of the prosperity of any country is the increase of the number of its inhabitants', while Frederick the Great said in a letter to Voltaire, '*Je regarde les hommes comme une horde des cerfs dans le parc d'un grand seigneur et qui n'ont pas d'autre fonction que de peupler et remplir l'enclos.*' Conditions in France, however, brought about a recognition of the connexion between population and food-supply. Mirabeau stated in *L'Ami des Hommes*, '*La mesure de la subsistence est celle de la population,*' *and* Rousseau held, '*Il y a pire disette pour un état que celle des hommes.*' When, therefore, an English clergyman, Thomas Malthus, maintained in his essay on population, published in 1798, that there is a natural tendency for population to increase faster than the means of subsistence and argued the necessity of checks on population in order to reduce vice and misery, his ideas received considerable European support.

In the next century, industrialization with its demand for labour was to change the situation and, by making children profitable, encourage early and prolific marriages, but during this period increasing population brought serious problems in Europe and especially in France. Nevertheless, the fact that France had long been the most populous European state did much to account for her position on the Continent. Lorraine became part of France in 1766 and Corsica in 1768, but in 1789 France still lacked Savoy, Nice and the papal city of Avignon, and yet with this smaller territory, her large and increasing population joined with her wealthy natural resources and long-established national unity to enable her to dominate the Continent. France in 1789 had about three-fifths of her present population, but her relative position in Europe was very different. Today France's population is less than that of Germany, Britain or Italy. Even if Russia be excluded, France is, therefore, only the fourth largest power in Europe. In the eighteenth century, on the other hand, France's population was relatively large and compact. Germany and Italy both had a considerable total population, but were merely territories divided into a number of states, each with a population much less than that of France. The motley collection of territories and peoples of the Habsburgs could rival France in population, and the backward Russian Empire seems to have equalled France's numbers by about 1789, but neither of them, nor indeed any other single state, could surpass the French position in Europe. Not until the nineteenth century did industrialism and the achievement of national unity among her rivals bring this about.

Religion in Europe

The division of the countries of eighteenth-century western Europe between the Roman Catholic and Protestant faiths had been practically completed in the previous century, and, indeed, the religious divisions recognized by the Treaty of Westphalia in 1648 have remained substantially unchanged ever since. The events of the Reformation and Counter-Reformation had made the Protestant mainland surprisingly compact. It could roughly be enclosed by a line drawn from the Hague to Berne and then along the Bavarian and Bohemian boundaries to Reval (Tallin) in Estonia. Such a demarcation is only approximate since it includes the archbishopric of Cologne and the considerable Roman Catholic minority in Holland, and outside of this area must be added the surviving Huguenots in France, the completely Lutheran Scandinavian countries and Britain, where the Roman Catholics had become a small minority. In eastern Europe, the Orthodox Church was dominant in Russia and the Balkans and had adherents in eastern Poland and parts of the Habsburg dominions.

Papal political influence in European affairs was negligible by this time. Spiritual sanctions now had no place in international affairs, and peace treaties were made without reference to the Papacy. The Roman Catholic Church continued to exercise a strong influence, in countries where it was established, through its religious orders, its control of education and the devotion of the people; but its efforts were weakened by a general tendency for its hierarchy to be drawn largely from the aristocracy. This was to be seen even in the Papal States where Pope Benedict XIV in 1746 reconstituted the Roman nobility as a closed caste of 187 families. It was at its worst in the French Church whose bishops were all noblemen and often notoriously worldly in character, appointed by the crown under the terms of the Concordat of Bologna of 1516. Nevertheless, the French Church possessed an unrivalled pre-eminence in Roman Catholicism. In prestige it was superior to any other Church in western Europe, and though in the eighteenth century it neither advanced nor maintained the spiritual vigour and intellectual vitality it had shown in the great French religious revival of the previous century, it entered this period uniquely distinguished through its previous character and achievements.

A considerable degree of religious intolerance and persecution still persisted, particularly in the earlier part of the century. The severe laws against the Huguenots remained in force in France, and as late as 1775 a General Assembly of the Clergy asked Louis XVI to enforce them; but since their enforcement depended upon local *intendants,* the general picture was of semi-tolerance alternating with outbreaks of fanaticism, such as the two scandalous acts of injustice in the 1760's which aroused Voltaire – the cases of Calas and the Chevalier de la Barre.[1] Persecution was

[1] P. 34.

more severe in central Europe with its legacy of past religious strife. Repression of Polish Protestants produced the 'blood-bath of Thorn' in 1724, when a religious tumult was followed by the execution of Calvinist rioters and town-officials.[1] In the Habsburg dominions, the persecution of Bohemian Protestants continued, and Hungarian Protestants were placed under severe disabilities. When the Archbishop of Salzburg in 1728 expelled 20,000 Protestants from his domain at three days' notice, similar expulsion followed in other places in Austria. No Swedish subject might leave the Lutheran Church, nor were Roman Catholics allowed to reside in the country. In England, Roman Catholics enjoyed a practical toleration, but a parliamentary measure designed to relieve them of certain legal disabilities provoked the Gordon Riots in 1780 in London.

The spirit of the age, however, increasingly told against religious uniformity and repression. Reaction, exhaustion and indifference set in after the fervour and controversy of the previous century; religious torpor, materialistic values and moral laxity followed. 'Enthusiasm' was decried and 'reason' exalted; the new ideas of the time were hostile to tradition and authority. Past wars of religion seemed to prove the futility of attempting to enforce conformity to one faith or another. Eighteenth-century writers urged that each man should be free to profess whatever religious belief he chose, and their readers in English country-houses and French *salons* admired their humanitarianism and rationalism. There was a growing dislike also of ecclesiastical interference in politics and of clerical immunities and privileges as inconsistent with contemporary ideas of government and society.

Such developments deprived western Christianity of much of its traditional position in the life of the State and had serious consequences for it. In general, Protestantism proved itself more tolerant and flexible in meeting the new conditions. Several Roman Catholic countries experienced acute difficulties in the relations of Church and State, a notable consequence of which was suppression by the Papacy, under compulsion, of the Jesuits.[2] Moreover, the ideas which found expression in the French Revolution produced also open repudiation of Christianity. Many who sympathized with the Revolution regarded Christianity as an outworn, reactionary superstition from which it was the duty of reformers to free mankind in the new era of enlightenment; and

[1] P. 279. [2] Pp. 121–2.

Napoleon, while retaining an outward allegiance to the Church, accorded the Pope scant respect and treated with him entirely along political lines.[1]

Yet at the same time, there were developing within different parts of Christianity new movements which were to exercise an important influence in the future. As the pressure of uniformity grew less, old suppressed tendencies could revive, notably those of the medieval separatist monastic congregations and of individual humanists and mystics. This tendency was represented in France by Jansenism, which did not survive Louis XIV's onslaught upon it; but the German Pietists and the Moravian Brethren, the Methodists and the Evangelicals in England were examples of these voluntary fellowships which penetrated the thought and life of eighteenth-century Christianity and prepared the way for the religious revival in Europe in the opening years of the next century.

[1] Pp. 356–7.

II · THE ENLIGHTENMENT

The Influence of England

LORD BALFOUR once stated that 'for the purposes respectively of science, philosophy and theology' the eighteenth century began with the publication of Newton's *Principia* (1687), Locke's *Essay Concerning Human Understanding* (1690) and Toland's deistical work, *Christianity Not Mysterious* (1696). It was not mere parochialism that made Lord Balfour name three English writers to mark the intellectual beginnings of the century which was to be the age of the Enlightenment. This century of rationalism was supremely the century of England's influence, and its origins go back to the scientific, philosophical and theological movements in which these three writers took a leading part.

The seventeenth century had been an age of scientific thinkers, and the seal was set upon their work by Sir Isaac Newton (1642–1727), the greatest of them all. His main contribution to the development of scientific ideas was his principle of universal gravitation, which he set out in his *Philosophiae Naturalis Principia Mathematica*. René Descartes (1596–1650) had outlined a mathematical interpretation of nature. 'Give me extension and motion,' he said, 'and I will construct the universe.' Newton proceeded to do this. He proceeded not by induction, but by way of analysis, not by abstraction and definition, but by observation and experience. He saw no contrast between experience and thought. Presupposing order and regularity in the physical universe, he stated this through principles or laws expressed in mathematical terms. The apparent attraction of the earth on bodies at its surface, as well as the course of the planets round the sun, could be explained, he showed, by the one assumption that every particle of matter attracts every other particle of matter with a force proportionate to the product of the two masses and inversely proportionate to the square of the distance between them.

In this way, Newton provided a complete and coherent system of dynamics. As he himself claimed, he 'subjected the phenomena of nature to the laws of mathematics' and so provided a clear and positive meaning' to the universal order of the heavens. His coherent system of the universe was formed on the principle that the earth might be in motion; it made it possible to explain how the earth kept in motion. Moreover, he had performed the unprecedented task of explaining the material world, for he made it possible, by means of relatively few fundamental laws, to determine, in principle at least, the properties and behaviour of every material body in the universe and with a degree of precision and simplicity hitherto unimagined. The whole universe, indeed, despite its multiplicity of facts, seemed to be subject to one unifying system of law.

The effects of the Newtonian synthesis extended beyond the realm of physical science in the eighteenth century. It was natural and, indeed, almost inevitable that those who admired its achievements should seek to apply its methods and principles as widely as possible. Alexander Pope's well-known couplet expressed their confident belief:

> Nature and nature's laws lay hid in night:
> God said, Let Newton be! And all was light.

Not only was the mechanical model of the Newtonian system imitated in other sciences such as biology, where purely mechanical explanations are now known to be insufficient, but also in all that related to the social life of men. Since men were objects in nature no less than stars or stones, it was believed that their interaction could be studied and explained and accommodated in much the same way. President Woodrow Wilson observed in an essay that the first American political writers 'speak of the "checks" and "balances" of the Constitution and use to express their idea the simile of the organization of the universe and particularly of the solar system'.

So 'nature' and 'natural law' became the keywords of the age, to which were added 'reason' and 'rational'. The rational study of nature was expected to reveal its laws. Reason, therefore, could answer all questions and solve all problems. Above all, by explaining to men their true, natural character, it would enable them to turn their back on all their mistakes and crimes in the past and create a society which was wholly just, virtuous, rational and happy.

This was the purpose of John Locke (1632–1704), the most important figure in English philosophy, even though others have surpassed him in genius. The son of a Puritan country lawyer, he saw the Civil War as a boy in Somerset and in the 1650's at Oxford experienced the rule of Puritan saints. During the course of his life, his active interests included medicine, and his writings on economics, politics and religion expressed the leading ideas of those later years of the seventeenth century when Whig society rejected the violent enthusiasm of the revolutionary Puritans, which had characterized the 'good old cause', in favour of political aims based upon a rational appraisal of human conduct in the light of the abstract law of a mechanistic universe. Locke said that for himself it was 'ambition enough to be employed as an under-labourer clearing the ground a little and removing some of the rubbish that lies in the way of knowledge'; but his influence was great.

In *An Essay Concerning Human Understanding*, most of which he wrote while in exile in Holland between 1683 and 1689, Locke undertook by 'historical plain method' a systematic investigation 'into the original certainty and extent of human knowledge, together with the grounds and degrees of belief, opinion and assent'. His main conclusion was that the real existence to which knowledge extends are self, God and the world of nature. Of the first we have an intuitive knowledge, of the second a demonstrative knowledge and of the third a sensitive knowledge. 'God has set some things in broad daylight', Locke considered; but of others we have only 'the twilight of probability', and with that we have to be content.

An Essay Concerning Human Understanding expounded the philosophy of which Locke's two tractates on toleration and government were the application. The sceptical conclusions of his *Essay* led him to plead toleration. His attitude was expressed in the opening paragraph of *A Letter Concerning Toleration* – 'Absolute liberty, just and true liberty, equal and impartial liberty, is the thing we stand in need of.' He insisted that oppression harmed the individual and occasioned seditious activity, but freedom from political tyranny and religious dogmatism would promote personal happiness and social harmony. Since he regarded the Churches as voluntary societies, which men may freely join according to their own conception of the way they should seek their personal salvation, he held that the State had no concern with religion and should tolerate all forms of beliefs and worship which do not endanger the safety and well-being of the civil society. Locke did not include in his plea for toleration papists and atheists, stating that neither would be good citizens, the former because they owed allegiance to a foreign and hostile potentate, the latter because 'the taking away of God dissolves all', including bonds of fidelity. Otherwise the State has no right to demand conformity from its citizens.

Locke maintained, indeed, that political power exists 'only for the public good.' *A Treatise of Civil Government* contains his famous dictum, 'He who attempts to get another man into his absolute power does thereby put himself into a state of war with him.' Locke believed as a historical fact that the establishment of human societies on earth was somehow preceded by a condition of natural anarchy. He did not consider this 'state of nature' as completely intolerable as had Thomas Hobbes (1588–1679), who described human life in such a condition as 'solitary, poor, nasty, brutish and short'. For Locke, this condition was sociable and happy and enjoyed the great advantage of complete freedom. Its disadvantage was the absence of a clear and settled law, a known and impartial judiciary and an executive power to make and enforce law. So Locke imagined members of primitive communities combining to form societies to obtain these necessities by establishing a legislative body to secure for men life, property and the maximum liberty and also entrusting executive authority to a sovereign who should be, however, subordinate to the law and so, ultimately, to the legislature.

Locke was careful to point out, however, that men had 'natural rights' and insisted that a community did not surrender all these to a government established by itself, but only those necessary for communal existence. Men still possessed especially their rights to life, liberty and property, and if the sovereign of a society violated these rights at any time, it was the duty of the citizens to expel that sovereign and appoint another. So Locke, through his insistence upon such a right of rebellion, upheld the Whig conception of the Glorious Revolution of 1688, which had already taken place when his *Treatise of Civil Government* appeared.

The rationalistic approach to politics was repeated in religion. Mark Pattison has described rationalism in England in the first half of the eighteenth century as 'a habit of thought ruling all minds'. The centre of gravity in religion shifted from authority to reason. The group of influential philosophical divines known as Cambridge Platonists emphasized the indwelling of God in the mind, since 'the spirit in man is the candle of the Lord'. Such liberal theologians, who were opprobriously called Latitudinarians, did much to prepare the way for the religious temper of England in the eighteenth century; and their greatest preacher, John Tillotson, Archbishop of Canterbury (1691–4), proclaimed 'The Laws of God are reasonable, that is, suitable to our nature and advantageous to our interests.' Locke himself in his *Reasonableness of Christianity* (1695) was sceptical of any claim to revelation or inspiration. 'Reason,' he said, 'must be our judge and guide in everything,' though he meant this to apply only to men of his own social class and not such as 'the day-labourers and tradesmen, the spinsters and dairy-maids'. They must be instructed in doctrine, for 'the greatest part cannot know, and therefore they must believe'. He thought that the essentials of Christianity might be reduced simply to belief in God and in Jesus as Messiah and a resolute effort to live according to the teachings of Jesus, all else being left to the judgement of educated men.

Locke strongly influenced subsequent developments of Deism, the system of natural religion which originated in England at this time and was marked by an opposition to revealed religion, particularly Christianity. The Deists believed in a personal God, the Creator of the universe, but regarded Him as detached from the world to which He had made no revelation. The classical exposition of Deism is John Toland's *Christianity Not Mysterious,* though he himself was not an original thinker. Brought up a Roman Catholic, he attributed the mysteries of Christianity to the intrusion of pagan conceptions and the machinations of priestcraft; he asserted that neither God Himself nor His revelation is above the comprehension of human reason. 'I prove first,' he wrote, 'that the true religion must necessarily be reasonable and intelligible. Next I show that these requisite conditions are found in Christianity.' Nevertheless, like other eighteenth-century writers, he treated religion as being a system of ideas and a code of moral precepts, while the essence of Christianity is personal communion with God, salvation from sin and the redemption of the world through the Incarnation.

Deism was never widely accepted in England and had very little final effect on English thought, but it exercised considerable influence abroad, especially in France and Prussia. Perhaps its most important influence was upon Freemasonry, which was founded in England early in the eighteenth century and became a stronghold of Deism. Freemasonry spread from England to many other countries. In France, Italy and other Roman Catholic countries the Masonic Lodges were openly hostile to the Church and religion generally, but in England, Germany and other Protestant countries, they mostly professed an undogmatic Christianity. With its emphasis on reason, virtue and human brotherhood, Freemasonry achieved rapid popularity and counted among its members many prominent men of affairs and rulers, from Frederick the Great to George Washington.

The Enlightenment

The consummation of the rational influences, which originated in England, is to be found in the movement commonly known as the Enlightenment. The phrase was first used in England about 1865 (after the German *Aufklärung*) to designate the spirit and aims of the French *philosophes* of the eighteenth century with the implied charge of shallow and pretentious intellectualism and unreasonable contempt for tradition and authority. Nowadays it is used rather in a neutral, technical sense with the indication that the ideas of Newton, Locke and the Deists underwent a change of character and impact when transferred to the Continent.

By the beginning of the eighteenth century, England (like the Dutch Republic) had already experienced both her religious reformation and her bourgeois political revolution. She was now essentially a commercial commonwealth, controlled by a modern-minded oligarchy which practised a measure of self-government and toleration. The English thinkers could feel, therefore, that on the whole they lived under conditions favourable to the ideas and way of life which they upheld, and they themselves enjoyed freedom from active obstruction in their work and did not suffer the prohibition of their writings.

In the countries which had not undergone similar religious and political changes, however, these same English ideas became revolutionary and seditious. The Empress Maria Theresa banned the teaching of English in Austrian universities 'because of the dangerous character of this language in respect of corrupting religion and ethical principles'. The French *philosophes,* as Professor Cragg has observed, 'were members of the middle class, believing in order and security, and wanting a stable society. The idea of a disordered universe was abhorrent to them.' They lived, however, in a country where the privileges of feudalism and medieval religion remained almost undiminished, with the arbitrary intolerance which this involved. This fact inevitably affected their outlook and the implications they drew from the new English ideas.

The story really began with a widespread invasion of English ideas into France in the first half of the eighteenth century. This originated with the writings of Huguenot refugees settled in England, who assimilated the political outlook of their new country and took the lead in spreading a knowledge of English philosophy and institutions into France. Then there followed a change in the attitude of French opinion towards England. In the seventeenth century England had seemed to be a land of civil war and regicide, religious turmoil and Puritan iconoclasm, but now she had accomplished the bloodless Glorious Revolution, and through her sea-power, William III's tenacious diplomacy and Marlborough's campaigns had led the Grand Alliance which defeated Louis XIV and become the leading colonial and commercial power. England was also admired as a pioneer in agricultural method and scientific progress.

The admiration of English things spread rapidly, and during the decade 1740–50, although these years were almost entirely occupied by war with Britain, attained such heights that it gave rise to the derisive term '*l'anglomanie*'. French society was devoted to everything that had an English air – horses, saddles, carriages, clothes, china and methods of sanitation. Five o'clock tea became the mode, fashionable young people affected to speak French with a slight English accent, and some noblemen replaced the formal French gardens of their châteaux by lawns and landscaping in the English manner. More seriously, French writers began to cross the Channel to investigate conditions in England; and in Paris the *Club des Entresols*, the members of which were mostly lawyers, met to debate political principles, and especially English ones, under the heading of '*le bien public*', from its foundation in 1724 until its suppression in 1731 by Cardinal Fleury.

As the eighteenth century progressed, the thought of the Enlightenment, though English in origin, became increasingly French in character. The basic concepts shaped by Newton, Locke and Toland were publicized by Diderot and Montesquieu, Voltaire and Rousseau. During the century, despite her growing military and naval, financial and colonial failure, France's cultural supremacy remained almost unchallenged. A brilliant social and intellectual life was concentrated in Paris and Versailles; current ideas were freely discussed in the *salon*; the *philosophes* were talented men of letters who believed in the popular diffusion of knowledge. French had succeeded Latin as the universal language of the upper classes of Europe. Frederick the Great, though a German national hero, was always entirely French in both language and culture; Catherine the Great of Russia also wrote in French. French books were read everywhere in Europe. Many were published abroad, especially in England, Holland, Germany and Switzerland; partly because of French censorship, but partly also because of the general European demand for French writings. However great the inroads of *anglomanie,* the common knowledge of the French language alone ensured that French culture dominated eighteenth-century Europe.

The contrast between the Enlightenment in England and in France was marked. The English writers were able to discuss their ideas freely and even met with public sympathy on some points, but the French writers had to face the constant possibility of persecution and imprisonment. The main reason for the contrast seemed to lie in the different nature of the ecclesiastical establishment in the two countries, and so the attitude of the writers towards Christianity itself differed markedly. The English writers wished to reject what seemed to them its grosser superstitions and retain what they saw as admirable in it; the French writers were driven by oppression to 'cite the Divinity itself at the bar of reason.' Indeed, Professor R. G. Collingwood defined the Enlightenment on the Continent in these terms – 'By the Enlightenment is meant that endeavour, so characteristic of the eighteenth century, to secularize every department of human life and thought. It was a revolt not only against the power of institutional religion but against religion as such.'

Another characteristic of the French writers of the Enlightenment is to be found in their attitude towards the existing régime in their country. The English writers generally accepted the British constitution and conformed to its laws and conventions, but the French writers expressed disenchantment with the *ancien régime*; they compared it unfavourably with English institutions and violently attacked it with every weapon of invective, ridicule and ribaldry. When, therefore, the French Revolution broke out, their constant undermining had destroyed the self-confidence and prestige of the old order. The French monarchy was abolished, and France, instead of England, became the revolutionary state of western Europe.

The French Encyclopaedia

The new secular knowledge was systematized in France in the famous *Encyclopédie ou Dictionnaire raisonné des sciences, des arts et des métiers*. This in itself is an example of the French development of an English conception, for the undertaking originated when the bookseller Le Breton invited Denis Diderot (1713–84), who had already been condemned by the Parlement of Paris and imprisoned for his philosophical writings, to edit an expanded, translated version of the *Cyclopaedia* published by Ephraim Chambers in 1728. In Diderot's hands the character of the work was transformed. He enlisted nearly all the important French writers of the time as contributors, and, as well as a compendium of useful information, produced an exposition of the ideas of the *philosophe* party.

For some twenty years Diderot persevered in his task despite constant discouragements and dangers. The sale of the *Encyclopaedia* was again and again prohibited, and its editor always ran the risk of imprisonment or exile. It was denounced by the Archbishop of Paris in an official pastoral. The *Conseil du Roi*, unwilling to suppress altogether such an important work, made an unsuccessful attempt to transfer control of it to the Jesuits. Diderot's co-editor, Jean d'Alembert, resigned rather than continue to endure the strain and indignity of being constantly subjected to the threats, insults and abuse of the *Encyclopaedia*'s opponents. Le Breton, fearful of further persecution, deceitfully mutilated some of the articles almost beyond recognition.

Nevertheless, his undaunted energy, varied knowledge and ability to rally his fellow-workers enabled Diderot to complete his vast undertaking. The first volume appeared in 1751. By the time the seventh appeared in 1757, the list of two thousand original subscribers had been almost doubled. All the seventeen massive, stoutly-bound folio volumes of letterpress had been completed by 1765, and the eleven lavishly illustrated volumes of plates were published in 1772.

The articles discussed in alphabetical order all questions of philosophy and religion, literature and aesthetics, politics and political economy, theoretical and technical science. The main object was to express the sceptical, rationalist attitude of the *philosophes*, but this was done in a skilful, deceitful way. Articles which might be suspected of expressing subversive opinions, such as 'Soul', 'Freedom of the Will', 'Immortality' or 'Christianity', were carefully orthodox in their exposition, but articles on various subjects which were not likely to be suspected presented quite different views, supported by arguments, while hidden references, readily comprehensible to the initiated reader, made clear the connexion between the two types of articles. Radical statements, which could not safely be expressed openly, were put forward allegedly as an objective exposition of the beliefs of others. A notable example of this ruse was D'Alembert's article on 'Geneva' in the seventh volume. 'The Genevese clergy', he wrote, 'have exemplary customs', which include a readiness to tolerate others and a lack of dogmatism; he also insinuated that theology was the ally of superstition by the comparative statement that 'there are few countries where the theologians and ecclesiastics are more hostile to superstition'.

Among the most notable contributors to the *Encyclopaedia* were, besides Diderot and D'Alembert themselves, Voltaire, Montesquieu, Turgot, Necker and Mirabeau (the father of the more famous Mirabeau of the Revolution). They hardly formed an organized, harmonious party, for they sometimes quarrelled among themselves and disowned each other's articles. Their purpose was to bring about a fundamental change in contemporary ways of thought rather than spread a definite system of knowledge. In fact, they were more in agreement about what they opposed than what they believed. They were particularly united in implacable opposition to the French Church, and the reason for this, as they saw it, as a recent writer has said, 'can perhaps best be summarized in two words – Dogma and Sin'. The Encyclopaedists found it offensive that the members of any institution should claim a monopoly of truth, and they resented that these members should ever be ready to apply to them such emotive terms as atheism, impiety and blasphemy, all of which implied a right to censorship and suppression. Almost equally repugnant to the Encylopaedists was the Church's teaching about sin because it involved a view of the inherent wickedness of human nature which they could not accept. Inspired by the great advances made in the human knowledge of the physical world, they believed it possible not so much to change human nature as to understand it and with this knowledge to channel human morals and behaviour towards rational ends. It was this devotion to the cause of liberty and reason which united the Encyclopaedists, however much they might differ about the implications of the cause.

Montesquieu

The *philosophe* who made the most serious attempt to achieve a comprehensive study of human society was the Baron de Montesquieu (1689–1755), who was trained as a lawyer and succeeded his uncle as President of the Parlement of Bordeaux from 1716 to 1726 when he sold the office. A member of the *Club des Entresols*, his interests in political and social institutions led him to travel for three years; he went to Vienna, Venice, Rome, Switzerland, Holland and England. His visit to England was made under the guidance of Lord Chesterfield, whom he had met in Italy, and he stayed there from 1729 to 1731, mixing with statesmen and writers, frequenting the Houses of Parliament, studying Locke's writings and analysing the British constitution. He thus became familiar with the ideas of Locke and his Whig disciples and with the British constitutional practices which grew up in the early eighteenth century under their influence. The contrast between Louis XV's obscurantist autocracy and George II's tolerant constitutionalism impressed him deeply during these years. Hitherto he had thought that republicanism was the only form of government which would respect liberty and public opinion, but now he saw the possibilities of this under a 'mixed constitution'.

The results of Montesquieu's travels and researches was his monumental *De l'Esprit des Lois*, which, though published anonymously in 1748 and quickly put on the Roman Index, achieved twenty-two editions in under two years. It was divided into thirty-one books and contained in all 595 chapters. He himself indicated the originality of the work by prefixing to it the epigram '... *Prolem sine matre creatam*'. His analysis of the forms and principles of government went further than that of any writer since Aristotle. The originality of his studies lay in relating these to the varying manner and customs of mankind, but the result was, as has been said, 'a splendid failure', for he misunderstood the essential character of these differences. He explained their evolution as due to differences in climate and geography. In common with other thinkers of the Enlightenment, he thought of men as part of nature and so looked to the facts of the natural world for an explanation of the various ways in which they ordered their political affairs. His answer was based upon his belief that human life was regulated by geographical and climatic conditions in the same way as was the life of plants. A modern historian would certainly recognize a close connexion between a national culture and its natural environment, but would consider that its character was determined, not by the facts of that environment in themselves, but by the response of a people to them, which would depend upon what sort of people they were. Montesquieu's approach, though it drew attention to the importance of such considerations, was too uncritical to be of real value.

In the analysis of human governments, Montesquieu divided them into three classes – despotism, based on tyranny; monarchies, based upon a legislative balance between a sovereign and his people; and republics, based on the virtue of their citizens. Before his visit to England, his republicanism had largely consisted of a rather unrealistic regret for the decline of the ancient virtue of the Roman people, but now England was to him 'une nation dans le monde qui a pour objet direct de sa constitution la liberté politique', and he recommended her 'mixed constitution' as the best form of government for the European kingdoms of his day.

Mainly through the influence of Locke, Montesquieu attributed much of the success of the British constitution in safeguarding individual freedom to the recognition that the powers of government were of three distinct kinds – executive, legislative and judicial – which should be separately exercised by different persons. He imagined that this existed more markedly in the British constitution than it actually did, but no other conception of any philosophe writer had a more practical effect. It inspired rationalist critics of the oppressiveness of the ancien régime and stimulated the constitutional claims made by the Parlement of Paris just before the outbreak of the Revolution, while it exercised a decisive influence upon the framing of the constitution of the United States of America and the attempts at constitutional monarchy in revolutionary France.

Voltaire

If Montesquieu may be said to have achieved most in practical results among the philosophes, the most famous and influential during his own lifetime was François Marie Arouet (to which he himself added the name of Voltaire), who was born in 1694 and died in 1778. He was not himself an original thinker, but he did more than anyone else to increase the prestige of the new empiricism and gain it a wider understanding. His mother belonged to the lesser nobility, and his father was a distinguished, influential lawyer, who had him educated at a Jesuit school and repeatedly tried to make him study law. Voltaire, however, was determined to have a literary career. He became a poet, dramatist, essayist, historian, novelist, philosopher and scientific amateur, whose fame rested upon his polemical genius and unequalled power of ridicule.

Voltaire made his way into the society of the Temple, a famous circle of free-thinkers, formed by nobles, writers and even clerics in Paris. Here his wit, irony, scepticism and literary ability were both admired and developed. Between 1716 and 1718 satirical verses against the Regent, the Duc d'Orléans, led first to his banishment from Paris and then to his imprisonment for eleven months in the Bastille. So far, however, he had been still no more than a dilettante, interested mainly in himself and only distinguished by his greater cleverness from innumerable other *beaux esprits* in the French capital at that time. This he remained until a quarrel with a prominent nobleman, the Chevalier de Rohan, brought about his return to the Bastille, from which he was released only on the condition of going into exile in England, where he remained from 1726 to 1729.

The effect on Voltaire of his stay in England was profound and decisive. He owed much to the influence of the gifted Henry St. John, Viscount Bolingbroke (1678–1751), whose Jacobitism had excluded him from political life. Bolingbroke was a Deist and an associate of men of letters. He introduced Voltaire to the English Deists and to Pope, Swift and other writers. Voltaire was also strongly attracted to Locke's philosophy and began to study Newton's astronomical physics. Above all, he was impressed by the unique political and religious freedom which existed in England, where constitutional government obtained, religion was subject to the State, the nobility participated in public life and were not hostile to fresh ideas, traders were not despised, and writers, philosophers and scientists enjoyed high social and ecclesiastical esteem instead of suffering official suspicion. What he learnt and saw in England gave Voltaire an aim in life.

Henceforward, throughout his exhausting and exciting career, he maintained a keen interest in science, an indignant opposition to despotism and an active concern for the happiness of others and for social reform.

Five years after his return from England, Voltaire published his revolutionary *Lettres philosophiques* (also called *Lettres sur l'Angleterre*), which were his impressions of aspects of English life framed so as to be an attack on the institutions and conventions of contemporary France.   His praise, criticisms and omissions were all significant.   The first four letters give an account of life with a Quaker family, members of a sect that pays more attention to the simple moral and spiritual precepts of Christ than to dogma and ritual and is yet tolerated in England.   In subsequent letters the British nobility are described, not by emphasizing their splendid country houses and estates, but rather their patronage of literature and encouragement of inoculation against small-pox. Similarly, George II's coronation is ignored, but Newton's burial at the public cost in front of the choir of Westminster Abbey is described to illustrate the prestige accorded to scientists in England.

The purpose of the *Lettres* was recognized only too clearly in France.   Voltaire himself stated that he wished to reduce the French Church '*à l'état où elle est en Angleterre*', to secure that religious toleration which he admired in England as much as he disliked the cooking, contrasting England's a hundred religions and one sauce with France's one religion and a hundred sauces. He had to retire for a time over the frontier into Lorraine, and the Parlement of Paris had the *Lettres* burned by the public hangman as '*contraire à la religion, aux bonnes mœurs et au respect dû aux puissances*'.

For the rest of his life, Voltaire experienced alternating favour and disfavour in France according to the arbitrary decisions of the French government.   From 1750 he was in enforced exile from Paris and, after staying three years with Frederick the Great in Berlin, he purchased estates on the borders of France and Switzerland so that he could speed from one to another to escape French or Swiss officials.   Not until the last year of his life did he return to Paris, when he was honoured by the *Académie Française* and acclaimed by enthusiastic crowds; but the Church never forgave him and refused him a decent burial at the end.

With his contemporaries, Voltaire shared a great admiration

for '*le sage Locke*' as the true originator of the Enlightenment. In his *Lettres philosophiques* he wrote, 'Many a philosopher has written the tale of the soul's adventures, but now a sage has appeared who has, more modestly, written its history. Locke has developed human reason before men, as an excellent anatomist unfolds the mechanism of the human body. Aided everywhere by the torch of physics, he dares at times to affirm, but he also dares to doubt. Instead of collecting in one sweeping definition what we do not know, he explores by degrees what we desire to know.'

From the works of Newton and Locke, Voltaire deduced theological conclusions which they themselves had not made. Newton, though not orthodox, had been a conforming Churchman and become interested in the millenarian prophecies of the Books of Daniel and Revelation; Locke had accepted the authority both of reason and the Bible. English writers saw no conflict between the authority of science and religion, but Voltaire held that Newton's discoveries undermined much orthodox Christian dogma and the authority of the Scriptures. Personal feeling added violence to his attacks on traditional theology, and he was, indeed, not free himself from the bias he attributed to theologians. Montesquieu remarked, '*Voltaire . . . est comme les moines, qui n'écrivent pas pour le sujet qu'ils traitent, mais pour la gloire de leur ordre. Voltaire écrit pour son convent.*' His 'convent' was the philosophical circle in Paris.

The fallacy of Voltaire's sweeping criticisms of the beliefs of the Bible, on the grounds that they were inaccessible to rational proof, would be recognized today. He did not realize that theological and empirical may be different and yet entirely valid in their own fields. The distinction between different disciplines was only gradually recognized. To some extent Voltaire assisted the recognition of this distinction by insisting that there were certain areas in which ecclesiastical authority and coercion were not legitimate. His popularization of Newtonian analysis attracted many to whom his attacks on Christianity were repugnant and largely made it an integral part of the thought of all educated Frenchmen by 1750. As an interpreter and popularizer of 'English ideas', he was more interesting, incisive and eloquent than their original authors.

Voltaire's bitter hatred of traditional authority combined with his generous avowal of toleration to make him an opponent of injustice and persecution.   His wrath was aroused by extreme examples of the sporadic incidents which had replaced consistent religious repression in France.   One was the case of Jean Calas, a Huguenot tradesman, who in 1762 was broken on the wheel by order of the Parlement of Toulouse on the cruel and irrational charge of having murdered his eldest son (who had hanged himself) because he had contemplated conversion to Romanism. Voltaire, throughout four years, made the exposure of this act of injustice his main concern to such effect that in the end the *Conseil du Roi* in Paris reversed the verdict.   The other notorious case followed soon afterwards when the youthful Chevalier de la Barre was executed at Abbeville in 1766 on charges of sacrilege which rested on little more than suspicion.   Voltaire tried in vain to secure the reversal of this verdict, but in this case, as in the previous one, he gained much popular support.   The spirit of religious persecution was dying in France, and the publicity he gave to these two manifestations of intolerance hastened the process.   He expressed his own views in a widely read *Traité sur la Tolérance*, in which he insisted upon the right of the individual to freedom of expression and opinion provided it did not disturb public order.

It was in the year of the execution of Calas that Voltaire began with the slogan, '*Ecrasez l'infâme*' ('Crush the infamous thing'), his direct attack upon the Roman Catholic Church as the representative of privileged and persecuting orthodoxy.   He did not, however, accept atheism, since he upheld the argument against it from design, strongly urging a deistic religion (*Théisme*) and holding that belief in the existence of God and personal immortality were necessary for the proper conduct of human affairs – '*Si Dieu n'existait pas, il faudrait l'inventer*'.   Some of his contemporaries, therefore, who believed that the ideas of the Enlightenment made any form of religion impossible, said of him, '*Voltaire est bigot; il est déiste*'.   Voltaire also retained a regard for the human personality of Jesus Christ, but most of contemporary Christianity seemed to him backward and barbarous and destined to perish in face of the mature rationalism of the Enlightenment.

In his later years, however, Voltaire's brilliant optimism and faith in progress were replaced by a profound pessimism in the face of the power of evil in the world, which seemed to him, moreover, to deny the Christian conception of a good and omnipotent

God. In his famous philosophical novel, *Candide*, published in 1759, he described in a short space with his usual devastating wit the caprices of nature, the irresponsibilities of governments and the incapabilities of ordinary humanity and ended with the epicurean aphorism that for those who were wise, '*Il faut cultiver notre jardin*', rather than engage in public affairs.

Rousseau

The reaction from the earlier liberating rationalism of the Enlightenment is further represented by Jean-Jacques Rousseau (1712–78), the son of a French refugee Huguenot family at Geneva. Though brought up a Calvinist, he became for a time a Roman Catholic in 1728 under the influence of Mme. de Warens, his benefactress and later his mistress. Rousseau saw the inadequacy of logic and reason alone, but his *Emile* in 1762 expounded only an indefinite religion of reverence for God and love for mankind, the forerunner of the humanistic liberalism of the nineteenth century. While most of the *philosophes* belonged to the wealthy bourgeoisie and shared their political aims, Rousseau – who was a vagabond in early life – came from a lower social class. The ideal of equality before the law, so strongly desired by the other writers of the Enlightenment, was not enough, therefore, to satisfy him, and in his writings appear the first aspirations of his class for social and economic equality.

Rousseau's greatest political work, *Du Contrat Social*, was also published in 1762. He did not hold with Locke that the basis of the State was an original contract between king and people, but that the contract was rather imposed by the wealthy with the defence of property as its object. Hence, '*L'homme est né libre et partout il est dans les fers*' (that is to say, is everywhere subject to government). The remedy, Rousseau believed, was the destruction of these chains and the establishment of a form of government which would ensure that the 'general will' of the people was sovereign. In other words, a new 'social contract' must be made.

In considering how this might be done in practice, Rousseau devised a theoretical constitution such as the age loved. He idealized the ancient city of Rome and the modern Swiss cantons. Such small communities of citizens, deciding their affairs together, provided a direct democracy in which the general will always prevailed in a way impossible in a representative democracy. 'The English people,' Rousseau wrote, 'is free only during the election of its Members of Parliament. As soon as they are elected, it is a slave, it is nothing.' Yet his conception of the social contract advocated the sacrifice of the individual to the State in a sort of democratic despotism, for he envisaged each associate as handing over himself and all his rights to the whole community, thereby subordinating his liberty to the tyranny of the majority.

Though often obscure and self-contradictory, *Du Contrat Social* has passages of indisputable power. 'The importance of Rousseau's writings,' M. S. Anderson has suggested, 'lay not so much in what he said as in the tone in which he said it.' Rousseau was at his formidable best when he seemed to be on the verge of madness. He was passionate, challenging and sensitive; David Hume said, 'He was born without a skin'. The quality of his influence on future events has been questioned. The State he envisaged was purely an ideal; he himself said it was not intended to bear any relationship to the facts of actual political experience; but his ideas had their adherents among the leaders of the French Revolution, notably the Jacobins between 1791 and 1793 and Robespierre in particular.[1] On the one hand, he may be said to have influenced the emotional desire to secure a more simple and primitive society and the predilection for abstract ideas and ideal constitutions, which had a strong effect in the second half of the century; on the other hand, he may also have supplied the passion and violence which animated the Revolution, and encouraged the envy of the poor and unsuccessful for the riches and power enjoyed by others, which was to become a powerful force in the evolution of modern Europe.

The Influence of the Enlightenment

'The eighteenth century,' Sir Isaiah Berlin has said, 'is perhaps the last period in the history of western Europe when human omniscience was thought to be an attainable goal.' Newton had expressed the hope in the Preface to his *Principia* that all the laws which would eventually be found to govern the universe would be reducible to mathematical laws governing matter and motion or perhaps, more generally, to the laws of physics. In other words, he thought that mechanistic determinism would probably be found universally true. The unparalleled success of the scientific movement, in which Newton was the greatest figure, gave the

[1] P. 325.

men of the Enlightenment a supreme confidence in the power of the human mind and rational thought. To them everything appeared much clearer than it ever had done to previous or subsequent thinkers. They were convinced that the rational scheme, on which Newton had so conclusively demonstrated the physical world to be based, could be applied to human personality and human society.

The effect of their outlook was to make the eighteenth century a period of progress, achievement and promise. It is true that the influence of the Enlightenment was limited. The new ideas had little effect in some countries, such as Italy, Spain and even Germany. In all countries only a small educated minority was influenced, but it was an expanding minority. The new middle classes, whose heyday was to be the nineteenth century, were gaining economic and political liberties which enabled them to abrogate political and ecclesiastical censorship of thought and enter upon the inheritance established by earlier thinkers and writers. And in face of the new rationalism, sensibility and humanitarianism, a growing number of age-long superstitions, injustices and inefficiencies were swept away. Perhaps most striking was the general acceptance for the first time by society of a humanitarianism, which gradually made effective its protests against practices possessing the support of very ancient tradition, such as judicial torture, cruel punishment of criminals, flogging in schools, brutality towards the sick and indifference towards the sufferings of others.

The limitations and weaknesses of the Enlightenment are indicated by its very name. For the men of the Enlightenment, the growth of the new scientific spirit was the central point of history. They held that before then all had been darkness and superstition, error and deceit. Humanity had languished intellectually for countless generations in the most childish errors on all sort of crucial subjects until it was redeemed by the simple scientific discoveries of the late seventeenth century.

Consequently, they had no real idea of cause and effect in human history. It was, for instance, the historians of the Enlightenment who adopted the absurd notion that the Renaissance was the result of the Turkish capture of Constantinople in 1453 and the consequent flight of Greek scholars westwards. Their assertion of the 'rights of man' was equally unhistorical, for these were 'natural rights', based on abstract reason rather than human

history.   Edmund Burke said of the thinkers of the Enlightenment, 'They are so taken up with their theories about the rights
of man that they have totally forgotten his nature.'   Indeed, the
tragic paradoxes of human life were beyond their rational faith.
Voltaire recognized Pascal as a dangerous enemy of the Enlightenment because his awareness of this element in man's existence
led him to insist upon religious faith as the only source of hope.
It is not surprising that later in this period there was a reaction
against the Enlightenment, a religious revival and a Romantic
movement in literature.

Yet the Enlightenment also achieved much.   There followed
upon it the triumph of the empirical and scientific spirit, an unprecedented ethical and humanitarian advance and a growth
of religious toleration and democratic government.   That these
gains have not all been maintained in following generations
emphasizes the words of Albert Schweitzer – 'Only a world-view
that accomplishes all that rationalism did has a right to condemn
rationalism.'

III · SOCIAL AND ECONOMIC CHANGE

The Aristocracy

THE eighteenth century was to end with a Revolution which struck hard at the idea of a privileged order in the State, but during the preceding period the social prestige of the landowning aristocracy was very high in western Europe. Almost everywhere, except in Britain and Holland, its members enjoyed important legal privileges, which included rights of jurisdiction, immunity from certain degrading or severe punishments and exemption from some taxation. Its feudal origins as a class with important military functions still governed the traditions and ambitions of many of its families, who, despite the changed nature of eighteenth-century warfare, continued to supply most of the officers of nearly all Continental armed forces and also administrative officials for the government of many countries.

The French aristocracy, as might be expected in this age when France maintained so much of her importance in Europe, exerted an especially considerable influence, even though its position was somewhat different from that of the aristocracy in other lands. Its way of life, its châteaux and its tastes were still imitated by the aristocracy elsewhere. Moreover, recent historians have emphasized the paradox that it was making successful efforts to retain and even increase its position in the administration of the *ancien régime* during the very years leading up to the Revolution which was to destroy once and for all its entire place in society.

The old French aristocracy, it must be realized, did not form a uniform class. Talleyrand declared in his memoirs, '*Au lieu d'une noblesse, il y en avait sept ou huit: une d'épée et une de robe, une de cour et une de province, une ancienne et une nouvelle, une haute et une petite*'. Only the comparatively few *noblesse d'épée* were descended from the old feudal families. All the other groups had been ennobled more recently. They belonged to families which had been bourgeois a generation or so earlier and had obtained noble rank by buying official posts in the higher administration and the law courts, or positions in municipal councils or *lettres de noblesse*, which raised them into the ranks

39

of the lesser aristocracy.   Moreover, there were other differences
of rank and position, between an exalted *duc et pair* and a more
lowly *comte* or *marquis,* between a landless *hoberau* living in the
provinces on his remaining feudal dues and a rich nobleman with
a fine *hôtel* in Paris and a place at court.   These differences did
not coincide with those between the older and newer nobility, and
yet there had long been intermarriage between the families of
these groups.

The old *noblesse d'épée* had suffered a severe decline during
the seventeenth century in both economic and political power.
Many had practically severed their connexion with the land;
their estates were mortgaged or sold to wealthy bourgeois.   Even
the minority, who still drew substantial rents and feudal dues
from their estates, were often impoverished through debts and
extravagance, and only a few were saved by marrying daughters
of the new nobility.   The political power of the old nobility had
been destroyed by Richelieu, Mazarin and Louis XIV.   Ever
since the collapse of the second Fronde in 1653, they had been deliberately excluded from the government of the State in favour of
bourgeois administrators; and all important nobles were attracted
to the court, first at Paris and then at Versailles, where their submission was ensured by their desire for official posts, sinecures and
pensions to relieve their financial needs.

By the eighteenth century, indeed, possible careers for the
noblesse d'épée were very few.   A small number of rich noblemen could seek to make money by agricultural improvements on
their estates or investing capital in new industrial ventures, but all
forms of commerce were denied them as unbecoming for their
order.   For most, the choice, as Mirabeau scornfully expressed it
in his memoirs, was '*porter les armes ou valeter à la cour*'.
French defeat in war reflected the favouritism accorded to
courtiers in the army, yet the extravagance of military life brought
financial disaster to many aristocratic officers.

Since the end of the Middle Ages many old noble families had
lost a large proportion of their estates, but the *noblesse de robe*
established their new nobility on considerable holdings of land.
Indeed, between the fifteenth century and the Revolution they
reconstituted and even increased the aristocracy's share of land.
They secured estates and exploited feudal dues as men of affairs.
Whenever they could, they added to their estates; these they
sometimes cultivated themselves, but more usually they let them

out to *métayers*.[1] The new nobility were also largely behind the seizure of common lands and elimination of communal grazing rights and inspired much of the so-called *réaction seigneuriale* of the eighteenth century.[2] The unpopularity such actions brought upon them was further increased by the exemptions from taxation, which they enjoyed as noblemen, and the rising rents which accompanied the inflation of the period.

The *noblesse de robe* had come into being as a new administrative nobility, created to supplement and even replace the old landed and military *noblesse d'épée* in undertaking the complex social and financial problems which now dominated the government of France. Though despised by the older nobility and without much access or influence within the court or the royal family, it grew in wealth and importance during these years. From it came many of the Secretaries of State who directed most of the various administrative departments of the central government in the last era of the *ancien régime* – Chauvelin, Maurepas, Machault and the D'Argenson brothers. Others of the *noblesse de robe* were *intendants*, each of whom acted as a royal agent supervising all local justice, administration and finance in one of the thirty-four *généralités* into which the country was divided. Many had acquired or inherited government and judicial posts sold by the monarchy in its need for administrators and funds.

Of particular importance was their domination of the *cours souveraines* and especially the thirteen *parlements* – Paris, Toulouse, Grenoble, Bordeaux, Dijon, Rouen, Aix-en-Provence, Rennes, Pau, Metz, Besançon, Douai and Nancy, the last being established only in 1775. These were great conservative and largely hereditary legal corporations, which functioned mainly as high courts of justice, hearing appeals from inferior courts. The most important was the Parlement of Paris with an area of jurisdiction including half the kingdom. From the time of the Regency of Philippe d'Orléans to the outbreak of the Revolution, the new nobility used such positions of authority to attack the crown's power until they finally destroyed both it and themselves.

Indeed, one of the most notable aspects of French history between 1715 and 1789 was the return of the aristocracy to political importance after its eclipse in the previous century and its lengthy, persistent contest with the crown aimed at both preserving its privileges and obtaining supremacy in the government of the

---

[1] Pp. 44-5.   [2] Pp. 45-6.

country. Its members succeeded in strengthening their hold on all the leading positions in the State. Although royal ministers and Secretaries of State continued to be appointed mainly from the *conseillers d'état, maîtres des requêtes* and other high administrators, such men were practically all members of families which had risen from bourgeois origin into the aristocracy several generations earlier. By the second half of the eighteenth century noble birth was almost essential for any important administrative post. There was no repetition of the accession to power of bourgeois administrators, such as Colbert and Louvois, in the previous century.

Similarly, in the reign of Louis XVI every *intendant* was an aristocrat. A few came from the old feudal nobility, but the majority belonged to families which had been ennobled for a century or rather more. The same was true of the *parlements* and other *cours souveraines*. Nearly all the posts in these bodies had been held for several generations by the same families, originally bourgeois but now ennobled. Several *parlements* during the eighteenth century tried to prevent bourgeois aspirants joining them and did at least make it difficult for any but the sons of noblemen to do so. Again, a royal decree of 1781, insisting that future officers must possess certificates of four generations of noble birth, sought to monopolize commissions in the army for the nobility.

It is a strange fact, therefore, that the Revolution, which was to obliterate the aristocracy's privileges and abolish their political authority, was largely precipitated by their action. The way for the middle-class revolution of the Third Estate and the subsequent town and peasant revolutions was prepared by the previous *révolte nobiliaire*. This was because only the privileged aristocratic orders were able to challenge royal power and try to curtail the monarchical absolutism created by Louis XIV. The most effective steps taken against the monarchy were not the work of the *noblesse d'épée*, but of the judges of the *parlements*. From the fifteenth century these bodies had claimed the *droit de remonstrance*, the right to control the legislation by refusing to register royal edicts unacceptable to them. Louis XIV in 1672 had deprived them of this right, but they regained it in 1715 and made increasing use of it.[1] Indeed, the whole judiciary, once bourgeois and allied with the crown against the nobility, had be-

[1] Pp. 153, 154.

come, through purchase of titles and marriages with the old nobility, aristocratic in outlook and determined to maintain noble privileges. '*Elle avait été bourgoise et royaliste,*' wrote Joseph Barnave, a prominent spokesman of the Third Estate in 1789; '*elle devint noble, féodale, refractaire.*' In such circumstances, the eighteenth century saw the once politically ineffective French nobility able to assert itself in the State.

The social life of the contemporary French court nobility was closely imitated by the nobility in many states of western Germany. Here a number of the princes received subsidies from France or hired mercenaries to the great powers, which enabled them to found splendidly elaborate courts, establish French ballet and Italian opera and erect such palaces as the Zwinger in Dresden, built between 1709 and 1719 for Augustus II, King of Poland and Elector of Saxony, or Bruchsal, the residence after 1722 of the Prince-Bishops of Speyer. The colonnades and wings, pavilions and orangeries of such palaces showed the inspiration they owed to Versailles.

Very different was the position in Prussia, where the nobility spent their lives in the service of the State. Here there was no new nobility, leisured and wealthy. The Prussian aristocracy was a feudal class, living upon its lands and dependent upon the labour and payments in kind of its serfs. Until the reforms of Stein in 1807, it could not engage in trade or sell its land to burgesses.[1] Many were so poor that commissions in the army or administrative posts were the only means of avoiding comparative destitution. Such men were in no position to assert themselves against the government, and the rulers of Prussia were able to take advantage of their condition. During the reigns of Frederick William I (1713–40) and Frederick II (1740–86), it was insisted that the noblemen must enter the employment of the State and especially serve in the officer-corps of the army, so that they came to regard this service as their natural, honourable career.[2]

The same idea of a nobility serving the State for life was also envisaged in Russia during the reign of Peter I (1682–1725), who wished to have a nobility enjoying wealth and social prestige in return for their national responsibilities. In 1714 he gave legal recognition to the hereditary nature of all estates, but at the same time abolished the old Muscovite custom of inheritance, which

---

[1] P. 377.   [2] P. 136.

allowed estates to be divided, and replaced it by a system of entail
so that only the eldest son inherited land and the younger ones
had to find employment; and in 1722 he classified all military
and civil posts into fourteen grades and announced that even
noblemen must begin in the lowest and obtain promotion.   The
Russian nobility, however, were to assert their independence.   In
1730 young noblemen received permission to begin their State
service in a noble cadet corps; in 1736 they were granted the
right to terminate the service to the State after only twenty-five
years; and in 1762 they obtained from Peter III the power to
resign from it whenever they chose.   The effect of this success in
securing release from the obligation of service must not, however,
be exaggerated.   In fact, they nearly all continued to serve since
it was the only way of achieving rank and possible fortune.

The Peasantry

Most of the people in eighteenth-century Europe were still
peasants, but their conditions of life varied considerably from one
part of the continent to another.   This depended not only upon
economic circumstances, but also the extent to which the status of
serfdom with its attendant disabilities still operated or had been
modified over the course of time.

In France, where they formed about 80 per cent of the population, the condition of the peasants and the amount of land they
held differed from region to region.   In fact, the French peasantry really consisted of a number of social classes.   Rather less
than a twentieth of them actually owned their land, which formed
a proportion varying from 22 to 70 per cent of all land in different
parts of the country.   There may have been an increase in the
total amount of land they owned in the decades before the Revolution, but since they were the largest single group of landowners,
most individual holdings were small.   Just under a quarter of the
peasants were tenant-farmers, some of whom were rich enough
to have large farms and produce for the market.   Perhaps a half
were *métayers*, men without capital who rented a little land and
received stock, seeds and tools from their landlords to whom they
had to give half their annual produce.   Under a quarter were
landless labourers, and about a twentieth were serfs, bound to the
land, performing feudal duties and with no right of bequest over
their holdings.

Métayage was most common in the west, centre and south of

France.   Serfdom persisted mainly in one or two eastern provinces.   Voltaire in his last years campaigned against its existence,
particularly on certain Church lands, and in 1779 Louis XVI
was persuaded to abolish it on royal lands and express the wish
that noble and ecclesiastical landlords would do the same, but
it survived, to be abolished by the National Assembly in 1789.

Although by the eighteenth century, French peasants, unless they
were serfs, could sell, exchange or bequeath their land as they
chose, they still nearly all had to pay, as well as the rent for their
holding, feudal dues to the *seigneur* or lord of the manor.   These
also varied from region to region and even from manor to manor.
Since they had been fixed in amount centuries earlier and not
been raised to meet higher prices, the money dues were not usually
very burdensome, but the payments in kind were more serious,
for they deprived peasants of a part of their crops which they
could ill-afford to lose, especially in years of scarcity and high
agricultural prices.   Other feudal obligations were oppressive
enough.   Peasants had to use their lord's mill, wine-press and
bakery, which was often expensive and vexatious.   The *droit de
chasse*, a system of game laws, placed their crops at the mercy of
huntsmen.   *Justice seigneuriale,* the lord's right to judge his
tenants, survived sufficiently to make justice always slow for peasants and often unobtainable.

The maintenance and resuscitation of these remnants of the
manorial system was the object of the *réaction seigneuriale*, which
was not a new process, but seems to have gained fresh strength
in the eighteenth century.   This was partly because the old
nobility, many of whom were impoverished or ruined by extravagance in Paris or at court, wished to make as much money as
possible from the peasants on their land.   Even more it was because the new aristocracy, among whom were judges and administrators with legal knowledge, were determined to secure a profit
from the capital invested in their estates and were more capable
men of business than the old nobility.   There was a similar inspiration behind the enclosure of common lands and the taking
away of grazing rights from the peasants.   This movement, although not so widespread in France as in contemporary England,
was on the increase in the decades before the Revolution with the
beginnings of agricultural improvement.   Such aspects of the *réaction seigneuriale* had to be accompanied with at least a show of
legality, and so in the last years of the *ancien régime* landlords all

over the country perused the seigneurial archives with the aim of rediscovering and enforcing old feudal rights. Consequently, the events of the year 1789 were to include the burning of the archives in many aristocratic châteaux (and often of the châteaux themselves).

Besides feudal dues, French peasants had also to pay ecclesiastical tithes and, still more, heavy direct and indirect taxes. The burden of taxation was inevitably heavier in times of war, but its incidence, owing to the incoherence of the administrative system, varied also with classes and provinces. The most important direct tax was the *taille*. Since the clergy and the nobility were exempt from it, and many members of the middle-classes also managed to secure exemption, it fell mainly on the peasantry. In the *Pays d'Etats*, those provinces which had their own estates, the *taille* was *réelle*, levied on land; in the rest of France, the *Pays d'Elections*, it was *personnelle*, levied on personal income. The *taille personnelle* bore most heavily on peasants and was more subject to noble exemption than the *taille réelle*.

Two other direct taxes had been introduced towards the end of Louis XIV's reign – the *capitation*, a graded tax on all classes except the poorest, and the *dixiéme*, an income tax of 10 per cent. Again, there were provincial differences in the incidence of both these taxes; although both had been intended to apply to all sections of the community in proportion to their wealth, they were largely evaded by the nobility. Indeed, there is no doubt that in all direct taxation the exemption won by the privileged orders and even by inhabitants of towns ensured that the main burden always fell on the peasantry.

In addition, there were indirect taxes – the *aides* on wines and spirits and, above all, the *gabelle* or salt-tax, which also was levied differently in various regions. While some provinces were exempt from the tax, it was lowest in the provinces known as the *Pays de Petite Gabelle* and highest in the *Pays de Grande Gabelle*, where salt was also a government monopoly and everyone had to buy a fixed quantity, which commonly brought special hardship upon the peasants. Other burdens which fell almost entirely on the peasants were service in the *milice*, reserve troops recruited by lot, and the *corvée royale*, an annual period of work on the roads, which by 1789, however, was generally commuted into some form of money payment.

The French peasantry of the eighteenth century were certainly more fortunate than most other Continental peasants. The greater part of the period was a time of agricultural prosperity in France. There were no such devastating famines as had ravaged the countryside in the previous century and no such rural insurrections as the revolts of the *va-nu-pieds* in 1630 and 1639. Nevertheless, the standard of living of most of the French rural population was low, and their wages remained below the long-term rise in prices of the century. This was partly due to rural over-population, but still more to the backwardness of French agriculture, especially compared with that of contemporary England. Moreover, the last decade before the outbreak of the Revolution was a period of agricultural depression. This sharpened the rural tensions between peasants and landowners, already acerbated by the *réaction seigneuriale*, and culminated in bad harvests and mounting bread-prices in 1788 and 1789, which influenced the events of 1789 and 1790, particularly since urban wage-earners were also embittered by the high cost of food. 'The deficit,' Arthur Young wrote a day after the Bastille had fallen, 'would not have produced the revolution but in concurrence with the price of bread.'

Throughout French rural society in the eighteenth century ran deep social divisions. These were not only between the privileged orders and the peasants, but also between peasant and peasant, between wealthy landowners or tenant-farmers and landless or almost landless labourers, between whom came the majority of struggling small landowners and *métayers*. By 1789, however, both monarchy and privileged classes had earned the united hostility of all the rural classes. The cause is to be found in the financial burden borne by a comparatively primitive agriculture and a low level of production. Though large and small peasant landowners, *métayers* and tenant farmers and landless labourers were divided by many rival interests, all resented the disproportionate share of direct and indirect taxes levied upon them by the crown and the tithes and feudal dues imposed by the clergy and nobility. The burning of manorial archives and rural châteaux and the murder of some noblemen and their families were but the prelude to the abolition of these long-standing, increasingly hated exactions.

The condition of the peasants in western Germany was much the same as in most of France. The nobility of the small states in this part of the country had been ready to cede land and rights to their serfs in return for money payments to enable themselves to spend most of their time in the local capital and court. Consequently the peasants usually paid money dues, were personally free, did little work on the manorial estates and held their land on a hereditary basis, while the jurisdiction of their landlords over them was confined to minor cases. They could also sell their produce in the towns, owned their buildings and implements and could generally dispose of their land freely.

East of the Elbe, on the other hand, where the peasantry formed three-quarters of the population, German serfdom was much more severe. In Brandenburg and Saxony, the value of servile labour for the landlords had been increased by the devastation of the Thirty Years' War and, still more, by the serious shortage of labour which it produced. Also towns were fewer in the east than in the west, so that lack of markets prevented the peasants paying their dues in money. The nobility of East Prussia, the Junkers, usually themselves farmed their extensive estates and exercised both civil and criminal jurisdiction over their serfs, who were bound to the soil, unable to marry or learn a trade without permission, and forced to work on the manorial estates under the overseer's switch for at least three days a week.

In other countries of central and eastern Europe, most of the peasantry were similarly unfree and subjected to heavy servile burdens. In the Habsburg provinces, where the nobility possessed considerable additional power and the authority of the central government was hard to enforce, serfdom was generally onerous. Many peasants still lived under the unchanged conditions of medieval villeinage, paying dues in kind, performing weekly work and giving a share of their harvest to their lord, who had exclusive jurisdiction over them and whose permission was required if they wished to leave the land, marry or place their children in new occupations. Also, in some parts of the Empire, a system existed which obliged the children of peasants, on reaching the age of fourteen, to work in the lord's house or on his land for a period varying from three to seven years.

Most of the Russian peasants were serfs on private estates and were very much under the power of their masters. Serf dues in rent, commonly consisting of both cash and kind, were usual in the less fertile north, but labour dues were normal in the southern black-earth areas. The landowner could, however, frequently change the dues of serfs, demand extra labour from them and their wives and children at harvest and other times, flog them whenever he chose and sell them with or without their land and even apart from their families. Moreover, the general effect of Peter the Great's policy of developing the resources of Russia and making the nobility serve the State was to worsen the position of the peasants. He made landlords responsible for collecting the poll tax from their serfs and obtaining recruits for the army from their estates and so greatly increased their authority over their serfs. In addition, Peter made great use of serf labour in establishing mining and manufacturing enterprises; and thousands of industrial serfs laboured in mines or factories controlled by state or private undertakings under a system similar to slave labour in the ancient Roman world. The trend in Russian serfdom initiated by Peter continued in this period, and the power of masters over their serfs was increased.[1] Russia, indeed, was the one European country where the legal position of serfs definitely worsened during the eighteenth century.

Polish serfs, who were seven or eight million in number, lived in a similar condition of subjection to the nobility. The years of war in the seventeenth century had added to their burdens. The population had fallen and grain production decreased. The nobility in many places took advantage of the situation to increase the weekly work required from their serfs and even sometimes to take away part of their holdings to add to the manorial domain. In addition, all serfs were completely bound to the soil and amenable to feudal jurisdiction which included, until 1768, the right to inflict the death penalty.

Serfdom was universally condemned by the liberal thinkers of the Enlightenment; the personal dependence of peasants upon a landlord and his power to inflict punishment upon them was a shocking evil in their eyes. And agrarian reformers condemned the servile system of forced labour as inefficient. Yet the impetus of the French Revolution was needed before effective steps were taken to free the serfs of the Continent, and even then not much progress was made until the nineteenth century. In Prussia a proposal made by the government in 1723 to limit the control exercised by landlords over the marriage of peasant girls on their estates was nullified by Junker opposition, and an attempt made by Frederick II in 1763 to give the peasantry greater security of tenure met with the same fate. Serfs on the Prussian royal estates

[1] Pp. 264-6.

were freed in 1798 and the following years, but the rest were only
freed between 1807 and 1810 and then at the price of concessions
which included the surrender by the peasant of a third of his
holding to his landlord.[1]   In other parts of Germany, the peasants lost even more of their land.   Even in western Germany,
where the peasantry had only to be freed from feudal dues and
given independence in their holding of land, these concessions
were granted only after the French Revolution.   In the Austrian
Empire, Joseph II's enlightened policy secured great reforms for
the peasants.[2]   Yet even here serfdom was completely abolished
only in 1848.   Complete emancipation of the Russian serfs did
not come until 1861.

The Middle-Classes

While the social prestige of the aristocracy remained high and
the majority of the population of western Europe were still peasants in the eighteenth century, yet contemporary political and
economic forces were gradually changing the structure and composition of society.   These forces tended to develop urban
middle-classes, which became ever more powerful and numerous,
though the factors which brought this about were not the same
nor as potent in all parts of the Continent.

In France where, as in England and Holland, there was considerable industrial and commercial progress, the traders and
manufacturers grew in wealth and numbers, especially during
the great expansion of French colonial trade which took place
in the years after the Peace of Paris in 1763.   Such men became
a class of capitalist directors of economic undertakings.   Some
exploited coal and iron mines, forges and foundries; but most
controlled the *manufactures* of glassware, paper, leather-goods
and tapestries, which they operated on the domestic system in the
countryside to avoid the guild-regulations of the towns.   Their
agents supplied raw materials to the work-people in their own
homes, paid them at piece-rates and collected and sold the
finished products.   So were produced the tapestries of Brittany
and Maine, the silks of Lyons and the woollen goods of Picardy,
Normandy, Flanders and Languedoc.   In the sea-ports the corresponding class were the *armateurs*, capitalist magnates, who
owned, equipped and provided with crews the merchant-ships
engaged in trading or privateering on the high seas.

[1] P. 377.   [2] Pp. 101, 246–7.

A distinguishing feature of these rich French manufacturers, however, was their readiness to invest their profits in land and hereditary legal and administrative positions, which brought them both financial gain and social prestige. The result was that, as the century advanced, many of them no longer sought to enrich themselves further through the productive economic effort which had first brought them wealth and importance, but were rather *vivant noblement*, as the current phrase expressed it.

Moreover, under the *ancien régime* the largest fortunes were not made by merchants and manufacturers, but by those who benefited from the system of tax-collection and the crown's continual financial needs. Known collectively as *financiers*, the most important were court-bankers, like Samuel Bernard (1651–1739), already wealthy under Louis XIV, government contractors, such as Joseph Pâris–Duverney (1684–1770) and his three brothers, and the forty *fermiers-généraux* (sixty after 1755), who every six years bought from the government the right to collect the indirect taxes. Below them were the numerous *receveurs*, *fermiers*, *régisseurs* and others profitably engaged in the financial affairs of the State.

Besides this *haute bourgeoisie* of merchants and financiers, there was also in France a *petite bourgeoisie* who remained outside the privileged orders. These were the minor officials of the royal bureaucracy, the professional administrators of the great departments of state, the numerous lawyers, doctors, chemists, engineers, writers, lower army officers, traders, bankers and their clerks. The eighteenth century saw a great increase in their numbers and wealth, and they formed a social group which actively staffed the administration and the professions, but could not attain the higher posts in Church or State through lack of *noblesse* or enough money to buy it. Particularly, since their educational standards were rising rapidly, they felt increasingly humiliated by their subordinate position and ready for drastic social and political change. The ideas of Rousseau strongly appealed to this class. For a time in this century, they supported the *parlements* against the crown, but in the last days of the *ancien régime* they realized that their interests differed, and the inevitable split occurred.

In central and eastern Europe, where economic development was much less considerable, the numbers of the middle-classes were mainly increased, not by successful industrialists and traders, but rather by the appointment of more and more administrators, especially in the later part of the century. The best known of these were the bureaucrats of the Prussian crown, particularly the members of the seventeen provincial boards who practically governed the country during the eighteenth century. Even during the reign of the powerful, able Frederick II, Prussian adminstrative officials possessed considerable powers of initiative and responsibility, and these grew during the century. Prussian military successes after 1740 hastened the development of a full-time, professional bureaucracy in the Habsburg dominions, which began when Maria Theresa appointed district officers in her own provinces.[1]

Agrarian Revolution

The agriculture of eighteenth-century Europe was almost exclusively primitive and self-sufficient and was, indeed, to remain so until well into the next century. Agricultural methods had advanced little beyond medieval standards, and the main object on small-holdings and large estates alike was to produce all that the owners with their families and dependants needed for their upkeep. Any resultant surplus was sold in whatever markets were available, but farming to supply commercial demand was not paramount.

While the century lacked statistical skill to estimate agricultural output accurately, it has been reckoned that throughout the period the port of Danzig exported annually only about as much corn as could be grown on 100,000 acres, although it had the whole of the eastern corn-lands of Germany as its hinterland. As late as 1850 the European agricultural population as a whole consumed two-thirds of its total production of food, the remaining third comprising not only exports, but also supplies for the towns. Smaller eighteenth-century towns, indeed, grew so much food themselves that they needed little from the countryside, and many of the inhabitants of larger towns had considerable gardens and vineyards beyond the suburbs or kept cattle and pigs on common-land and in the woods.

Among countries where agricultural improvements had been made, the Netherlands were pre-eminent. An English writer of Polish origin, Samuel Hartlib, in his *Discours of Husbandrie used in Brabant and Flanders*, published in 1652, considered that

[1] Pp. 241–2.

the standards of Dutch farms and those in Flanders and neighbouring parts of Germany, which had come under their influence,
were the highest in Europe. There, expensive land and high
wages combined with urban requirements to produce a specialized
agriculture, which devoted much land to garden crops and dairy
products for the towns and even exports to the Rhineland and
England. Attention to breeding and stall-feeding with fodder-
crops secured larger cattle than elsewhere; the fertility of the land
was improved by constantly ploughing in clover and other crops.
Although eventually surpassed by England in agricultural pro-
ductivity, the Netherlands probably retained the lead into the
nineteenth century.

Arthur Young defined the 'Norfolk system of husbandry',
which became so famous in the late eighteenth century, as having
seven main points – enclosure by agreement, the use of marl and
clay, a proper rotation of crops, the culture of hand-hoed turnips,
the growing of clover and ray grass, long leases and large farms.
It is now known that this system was of Dutch origin and was first
practised in north-west Norfolk in the closing years of the previous
century. It was well established on the Walpole estates at
Houghton Hall some years before 1700 and continued to be
practised throughout Sir Robert Walpole's time. Indeed, it has
been said that had Walpole lost his struggle in 1730 with Viscount
Townshend (1674–1738) and retired to his estates, he would
doubtless be known to posterity as 'Turnip Walpole'.

Similarly, Thomas William Coke, of Holkham, Earl of
Leicester (1752–1842), was certainly an efficient and successful
landlord, but the gross rental of his estates in Norfolk was about
doubled between 1776 and 1816 and not increased four, nine
or ten times, as is sometimes stated. He was not a worker of
miracles, who brought fertility to a sandy waste, for agricultural
progress was a feature of the Holkham estates during the whole of
the eighteenth century, and wheat had been grown in Norfolk as
early as the sixteenth century. Men like him are largely famous
because their work coincided with the rise of popular agricultural journalism, embodied in the pages of Arthur Young,
William Marshall and their circle, so that their names were
chronicled while those of their predecessors had gone unrecorded.

Enclosures began in England on a large scale in the second
half of the eighteenth century through the combined effect of
increasing population, the need for corn exports to pay for

expanding trade with the colonies and the Continent, the growth
in the non-food-producing proportion of the population caused
by the Industrial Revolution, the demand for a higher standard of
living, and the food-shortage, rise in prices and drain on manpower brought about first by the Seven Years' War and then by
the Revolutionary and Napoleonic Wars. The effect of these
factors was felt within a period of forty to fifty years, and they all
demanded more food-production and so enclosures, without
which the new agricultural developments could not be employed.

The later years of the eighteenth century formed, therefore, the
period when the enclosure movement got under way. Between
1760 and 1800 Parliament passed nearly 5,000 Enclosure Acts;
but the rapidity of this movement, again, must not be exaggerated. The common fields of large villages were soon enclosed,
but vast stretches of waste remained unenclosed much longer,
especially in the north of England. In 1773 Arthur Young, a
zealous advocate of enclosure, said, 'You may draw a line from
the north point of Derbyshire to the extremity of Northumberland, of 150 miles as the crow flies, which shall be entirely across
waste lands.' By 1800 over 200,000 acres of waste had been enclosed in the two northern counties of Northumberland and
Durham, but here and in other parts of the country enclosures
were still proceeding during the first half of the nineteenth
century.

It would seem, therefore, that the Agrarian Revolution in
England was much less cataclysmic than has been commonly
supposed. It was a slow process, evolutionary rather than revolutionary, and the changes connoted by such a phrase came
more gradually than the name implies and over a longer period
than some historians have believed, since important changes in
estate management, usually attributed to the last quarter of the
eighteenth century, had been introduced earlier and sometimes
much earlier. Enclosures also took place over a fairly long
period. Nevertheless, it remains true that in the later years of the
century, English farming was considerably more productive than
in most parts of the Continent. In Silesia, for instance, between
1770 and 1780 wheat gave an average crop of 5.6 fold and rye
5.2 fold, while in England wheat and rye already produced ten-
fold crops, and some other crops did even better in comparison
with those in Silesia.

English agrarian reformers agreed in blaming the prevalent

system of land tenure for the backwardness of Continental agriculture. Arthur Young regarded the French aristocracy's relation to the land as parasitic. 'A Grand Seigneur', he wrote in his
Travels in France in 1787, 'will at any time and in any country
explain the reason of improvable land being left waste'; and he
denounced *métayage* as 'a miserable system that perpetuates
poverty'. He was shocked by the low yield of the agricultural
land as a whole and the prevalence of the open-field system. He
described the fertile arable region of northern France as 'lying
under the unprofitable neglect of open fields and disgraced with
the execrable system of fallowing'.

Modern historians consider that Arthur Young's strictures were
too severe on French agriculture in the last years of the *ancien
régime*. It is difficult to generalize about the entire country.
Farming was much better in Normandy, where customary law
allowed enclosures and techniques of cultivation were relatively
advanced, than in backward Lorraine, barren and poverty-
stricken Brittany and even the Ile-de-France. Similarly, the
obligation of individual peasants to follow a traditional system of
crop rotation was strictly enforced in eastern France, but much
less so south of the Loire. Moreover, France had its own agricultural reformers and publicists, some of whom were strongly
inspired by the example of farming *à l'anglaise*, and the government made some efforts to bring about changes. These efforts,
coupled with the actions of the *réaction seigneuriale*, did bring
about some adoption of improved methods, enclosure of holdings
and ending of common rights on the land.

Total agricultural production in France was probably greater
than in any other European country, but the methods of farming
as a whole were very backward compared with those in England.
The working of much of the tillable land by small peasant pro-
prietors, an inequitable system of inheritance, scarcity of working
capital, inadequate transport and marketing facilities, numerous
restrictions on internal trade, ignorance and technical backwardness, all told against change and produced a large measure of
stagnation in the farming of pre-Revolutionary France. During
Louis XV's reign there were said to be normally 30,000 beggars
in Paris, many of them ruined peasants or landless labourers, who
had flocked to the city from the countryside which could not
support them.

More vigorous were the efforts made by the rulers of Prussia to improve agriculture in their kingdom. From 1685 onwards religious refugees from France and Holland were settled in the thinly-populated eastern districts, where they were later joined by emigrants from such southern states as the Palatinate and Württemberg. Frederick William I gained new land for cultivation by extensive draining and the deepening of rivers in the area of the Havel; he also improved roads to facilitate the transport of farm-produce. These efforts were continued by Frederick the Great, who carried out a large drainage scheme in the Oder and Warthe marshes, an area of some 300,000 acres, and similarly reclaimed sandy wastes and moorlands. In this way nearly 300 new villages were created in Pomerania, Brandenburg and the marshes, mostly on regained land. He also made great efforts to introduce the latest English methods of agriculture and new crops, the most important of these being the potato, which was first grown in the 1740's, but not much eaten until about 1770, when there might have been a famine without it, and which in time became a more important staple article of rural diet than bread. Both landlords and peasants, however, resisted the changes in agricultural techniques which he wished to make, such as enclosures, and he met with comparatively little success in this respect.

Industrial Revolution

The Industrial Revolution, a term coined by the French economist, Auguste Blanqui, in 1837, probably describes more accurately industrial development in Britain than the Agrarian Revolution does agricultural development. It is true that there were few large towns in England until the nineteenth century, and that it was not until the second quarter of that century that industrial change began markedly on the north-east coast of England and made it one of the chief centres of economic power in the country. Nevertheless, development was more rapid in industry than in agriculture, and inventions and improvements had a more revolutionary effect.

The early start of the Industrial Revolution in Britain, compared with the rest of Europe, was due to a number of economic and social circumstances. The country possessed abundant coal and iron resources as well as navigable rivers and outlets to the sea. It enjoyed political stability and religious toleration, the security of an island position and naval power, an absence of internal customs barriers and medieval economic restrictions, and a general readiness to invest in commerce and industry. The wars stimulated the making of munitions, and expanding overseas trade demanded an increasing variety and number of manufactured goods, as also did the growing population and the rising standard of living. The activities of Sir Isaac Newton and other members of the Royal Society had established a scientific movement in the seventeenth century, which was continued by chemists like Joseph Priestley (1733–1804) and Joseph Black (1728–99), the results of whose experiments were of important practical application in British industry. In some other European countries at this time, some of these circumstances also obtained, but in Britain alone they combined to give her a lead in industrialization which she maintained well into the nineteenth century.

An early aspect of the Industrial Revolution was the invention of new techniques to meet contemporary requirements. The iron industry, for instance, could not satisfy the demands of war and peace as long as it depended upon the disappearing forests of the Sussex Weald and other old areas. Between 1709 and 1750 Abraham Darby and his son devised a means of using coke instead of charcoal in smelting ore into pig-iron and in converting pig-iron into the cast-iron suitable for smaller articles; but not until 1784 did Henry Cort free the forging of the purer and less brittle wrought-iron from dependence on charcoal by discovering a puddling or stirring process which separated from the molten metal the carbon impurities which had hitherto prevented the use of coke here. These inventions enabled the output of British iron to be increased from 20,000 tons in 1740 to 156,000 tons in 1800.

Other early improvements took the form of mechanical inventions which were mainly labour-saving devices demanded by the limited skilled or semi-skilled labour force then available to manufacturers. These devices, in fact, could often be operated by children instead of men and women. They occurred notably in the textile industry, which developed more rapidly than others in the eighteenth century. In 1733 John Kay invented, for weaving wide lengths of cloth, a flying shuttle, which was knocked across the loom by hammers worked by one man instead of being passed by hand from one weaver to another. A device which similarly saved labour in spinning came thirty-five years later when James Hargreaves produced the spinning jenny, named after his wife, which enabled a hundred threads of yarn to be spun simultaneously by several vertically-installed spindles.

Later inventions utilized new forms of power, and these made possible an increase of manufacturing production. Water-power was the first to be used extensively to drive machinery. In the textile industry, about the same time as Hargreaves invented the jenny, Richard Arkwright devised a water-frame with water-driven rollers to draw out the fibres into loose bands, which were then wound into thread by spindles. This operated much more rapidly than hand-fed spindles, but could only be used to produce coarse cotton-thread. In 1779, however, Samuel Crompton combined the spinning jenny and the water-frame in a machine which he called a mule. This was both water-driven and could produce fine thread, hence making possible the fashionable ladies' muslin-dresses of the period. This use of water-power led to the establishment of hundreds of textile-mills on the Lancashire and Yorkshire moors along the banks of the Pennine streams.

Steam-power was first used in the mines to pump water out of workings which became deeper as the demand by industry for coal increased. By 1760 the atmospheric engine of Thomas Newcomen (1663–1729) was used for this purpose in many pits, and British output of coal increased from about 2,500,000 tons in 1750 to 10,000,000 tons in 1800; but the greatest growth of coal-mining was delayed until the next century and with it, therefore, the development of industries dependent upon supplies of coal.

The use of steam-power to operate machinery in industry was made possible through the improvement of the Newcomen engine by James Watt (1736–1819); he patented this in 1769 and formed a partnership with Matthew Boulton (1728–1809) in 1774 to manufacture it. This gradually led to the replacement of water-power by steam, not only in the textile-mills, but also in other industries where water-driven machinery had been adopted, such as blast-furnaces, iron-works and the famous pottery established by Josiah Wedgwood (1730–95) at Etruria in Staffordshire, which exported china to all European countries and the colonies. By 1800 there were some 300 steam-engines in use in British industry.

The development of machinery and new forms of power led to the growth of the factory-system in Britain. At the end of the century, it had become general in cotton-spinning and also in the iron industry. Matthew Boulton's iron-works employed 700 people and much machinery, and the Carron Iron Works in Scotland, founded in 1759 by John Roebuck, was by now the greatest munition-works in Europe and has been described as the 'portent of a new type of undertaking'. Yet on the Continent, small charcoal furnaces lingered into the middle of the next century. England, indeed, entered the new industrial age at least half a century before other countries. The measure of this was displayed when Napoleon tried to deprive Europe of British goods through his Continental System.[1]

Nevertheless, some of the large French industries, especially iron and cotton, grew considerably in the eighteenth century and notably during its last decades. Industrial production had been increased by hand-machines introduced from England, and the use of the steam-engine was already beginning in the mines. Despite the unreliability of the statistics, it seems that until well after the Treaty of Paris of 1763 the output of these industries was greater than that of their English rivals, as might be expected, indeed, when the French population was three or four times the size of the English; but these French industries were generally technically less advanced and did not succeed in adopting British methods. One reason for this was the inability of the coal industry to expand. Though its output was multiplied several times during the eighteenth century, it was not organized on a large scale and lacked capital and labour. By the end of the century, the French output of coal was probably only a twentieth of that of Britain.

The general industrial development of France before the Revolution was hindered by two factors. One was that most manufacturers were still organized in a system of guilds, which were hostile to technical improvements and the new liberal principle of unrestricted competition. Industries requiring a considerable labour-force could not be established in the countryside to avoid it, and neither the factory-system nor English inventions were adopted in the textile industry on a large scale under the *ancien régime*. Turgot tried to suppress the guilds in 1776, but they were not abolished until 1791. The other factor, which was derived from the country's social history, lay in the eagerness with which wealthy industrialists invested their capital in land and hereditary legal and administrative posts rather than in trade and

[1] Pp. 369–70.

industry, and also in the unparalleled importance accorded in the State to the *financiers*.[1]   No English industrialist, not even Arkwright or Boulton or Wedgwood, enjoyed the social status or political influence of a great French nobleman, banker or tax-farmer.

The years after the Revolution, however, did see a more considerable development of French industry.   It was assisted by the demands and territorial gains of the wars of the period.   It was also assisted by the economic policy of Napoleon.   The rate of expansion, however, was still slow compared with that of England, and in the end his military policies proved to be incompatible with economic progress.[2]

Germany was very backward in industrialization in the eighteenth century compared with Britain and France and even with Holland.   The first Watt steam-engine was installed in the country only in 1785.   The domestic system prevailed, machinery was little used, and coal and iron had yet to be mined extensively. During the reign of Frederick II (1740–86), however, an attempt was made to increase the output of Prussia.   For the King, the purpose of industry was to augment the national revenue and secure a favourable balance of trade.   Prussian manufacture of commodities for the home market was not yet realizable on a large scale, nor did he desire it.   He sent administrators to England to learn the new industrial methods and purchase machinery for the state-owned mines, copper-mills, cannon foundries and saltworks; and he encouraged such manufactures as sugar-refineries, porcelain-works, embroideries, silk and velvet fabrics, which exported about a third of their products abroad.   Their output was not large, but Prussia was started on the way towards industrialization.

Much more remarkable was the rise of Russia as a European industrial power during this period.   She did not achieve this primarily through the employment of new techniques and machines, but rather because of her importance as a producer of metals, of which most notable were copper and, still more, iron. Particularly spectacular was the development of the ironworks of the southern Urals by Peter the Great.   Throughout his reign, government support, large and easily-felled forests, the labour of industrial serfs, the need for munitions during the war with Sweden, all assisted its continuous expansion.   After Peter's

[1] Pp. 50–1.   [2] Pp. 360–1.

death and the coming of peace with Sweden, its growth continued, though not so rapidly, and it became more marked in Catherine II's reign (1762–96). By 1800 this area was producing 80 per cent of Russian copper and iron; most of it was exported to the countries of western Europe, some of which were experiencing a shortage of wood for smelting. Britain, where this shortage had been most serious, imported an annual average of nearly 26,000 metric tons even as late as the 1790's.

The Physiocrats

In asserting government influence in industry and encouraging exports, the Prussian and Russian governments were acting in accordance with the ideas of mercantilism, the system of official economic regulation which for more than two centuries had been followed by the leading states of Europe. Mercantilism assumed that national wealth could be increased if the State encouraged its means of production and protected them from foreign competition. This notion had operated during the Middle Ages, when production was on a municipal basis, and in the words of a writer on mercantilism, 'the government of each separate town controlled the enrichment of that town as a whole'. Municipal and guild regulations in each medieval town had regulated its manufactures and protected them from outside competition. In the sixteenth century, when the rising power of the State had eclipsed the individual importance of the towns, mercantilism now aimed at a similar regulation of economic affairs on a national basis.

The seventeenth century had been the great age of mercantilism in western Europe and especially in England, Holland and France, where in its varying forms it had resulted in considerable industrial and commerical progress. On the other hand, mercantilism was only beginning in the early eighteenth century to secure any considerable adoption in central, southern and eastern Europe. In Germany, Russia and Spain, economic advance had been considerably less marked, and the middle-classes consisted of bureaucrats rather than prosperous manufacturers and merchants. Consequently, rulers in this part of Europe adopted the economic regulation and control of mercantilism in the hope of gaining the power and prosperity which it appeared to have brought to other countries.

The eighteenth century in western Europe, however, saw a

reaction against mercantilism. Now it became commonly regarded as false in conception and harmful in practice. This view
was expressed in France in the economic doctrines of François
Quesnay (1694–1774) and his followers, who were known as the
Physiocrats. They preceded and inspired the Scottish political
economist, Adam Smith (1723–90), although differing national
circumstances made them regard agriculture as the source of a
country's wealth while he insisted upon the importance of
industrial and commercial enterprise.

Nevertheless, whatever their differences of emphasis and outlook, both the Physiocrats and Adam Smith agreed in condemning the economic restrictions and regulations inherited from
medieval and mercantilist policies. The Physiocrats were themselves a product of the Enlightenment, for they believed in a
natural order of economic society as opposed to the artificial controls of guilds and government regulations. Any interference
with the natural development of economic life they rejected on
principle, not only as contrary to the individual's natural right to
personal freedom, but also because they considered it economically pernicious. The spirit of unfettered individual competition
and eagerness to acquire wealth must, they believed, be upheld
for both moral and economic reasons. One of the less well-known
Physiocrats, Vincent de Gournay (1712–59), summarized the
political programme of his school in the well-known words,
'Laissez faire, laissez passer'.

Such a slogan essentially appealed to the middle-classes. It
represented their attitude to as much as their attack on feudal
privilege and ecclesiastical authority. They wanted economic
equality as much as they wanted civil equality. The plea of the
Physiocrats for natural liberty and their argument that national
wealth was to be obtained apart from the acts of government, and
often in defiance of the State, were in conformity with the
interests of the bourgeois capitalists in their contests with the landowning classes. At the same time, Physiocratic ideas were also
used by Enlightened Despotism to assist in the establishment of a
theoretical basis for its form of government.[1]

[1] Pp. 92–3.

IV · OVERSEAS COMMERCE AND COLONIZATION

Changes in International Trade

SOME fifty years before the opening of the eighteenth century the general pattern of European trade was still much what it had been in the Middle Ages. It was, that is to say, primarily an exchange of regional products within Europe and an international trade in luxuries rather than necessities. The bulk commodities of northern Europe – timber, naval stores and corn – were exchanged for the produce of southern and western Europe – English wool, Dutch herrings, Flemish cloth, Spanish wool and silver, French and Portuguese salt, Mediterranean wines, oil and fruits. The discoveries of the new oceanic routes had not brought about any essential change in Europe's international trade. Though the western countries had been introduced to tobacco, potatoes and other important new commodities, the old luxury commodities – spices, ivory, silk, bullion and other costly goods – still accounted for the most substantial part of the trade.

From about the middle of the seventeenth century, however, the volume of international trade began to increase and continued to increase in a revolutionary manner in the eighteenth century. This was partly due to better conditions of oceanic transport with the suppression of piracy and the development of marine insurance, the slow increase in the size of ships and the improvement of port facilities. It was also partly due to the growing volume and variety of goods brought into international trade by the technological developments and increased production of the Industrial Revolution. It was due still more to the rapid expansion of trade between European countries and settlements in America, Africa and Asia. It became steadily more evident that this was where the greatest commercial wealth was to be obtained, and the maritime nations exerted themselves to secure as large a share as they could in the new colonial trade.

European profits on many colonial re-exports were immense. Already essential in the economic life of Spain and Portugal, they came to provide the most valuable part of English, French and Dutch trade.   India and, to some extent, south-eastern Asia were regions where advantageous commercial undertakings were possible, but the main direction of economic expansion was westwards.   The Atlantic trade, in which the West Indian islands played a particularly important part, was highly esteemed and inevitably provided a constant source of dispute between Britain, France, Holland and Spain, the European states with colonies in that area.   In this struggle, shipping and the ability to protect it emerged as an important factor for success or failure among the contestants.

In the first half of the seventeenth century, a large part of the total volume of European seaborne commerce was managed by the Dutch.   They flourished primarily as exchangers of merchandise, through their maritime achievements and superior business methods, and favourable circumstances brought them the opportunity of handling much of Europe's trade.   They pioneered the economic institutions of capitalism – the national bank, the stock exchange and the chartered company, and their trade routes extended across nearly all the known world.

The revolutionary increase in the volume of international trade, which began in the second half of the seventeenth century, was marked, however, by a change in the relative importance of the leading commercial states.   Holland was unable to maintain its pre-eminent position, and Dutch trade, though it remained considerable, gradually declined.   There were several reasons for this.   Holland was without sufficient natural resources to enable her to produce industrial goods for the export markets, and when foreign manufacturers learnt her business methods, she could not compete with them solely as carriers.   To this was added the effect of tariffs, navigation laws and similarly protective measures adopted by England and France and even by smaller countries like Sweden, which undermined the Dutch as middlemen in European trade.   Then the wars of the later seventeenth century revealed the grave weaknesses of the Dutch strategic position because their vital sea-routes through the English Channel and to the Baltic were exposed to British naval attack, while their land frontiers were vulnerable to French military strength.   Finally, Holland was incapable of maintaining a lead in the all-important Atlantic commerce.   The ever-increasing flow of British colonial products, such as raw cotton, sugar and tobacco, were almost completely sent to England to be processed and re-exported. Consequently, while Holland continued to be an important financial centre in world trade, the central market of European commerce steadily moved westwards to England. By 1739 it was thought that twice as many ships discharged their cargoes in London as in Amsterdam.

Holland was overtaken by France and Britain as great commercial states, and the eighteenth century was marked by rivalry between these two countries for commercial supremacy in all the chief areas of world trade (at the same time as colonial conflict was taking place between them).[1] Nowhere was this rivalry more continuous than on the American side of the Atlantic, particularly during the first part of the century in the Caribbean. Here lay the greater bulk of the vast Spanish Empire upon which the mother country still relied for bullion to finance her own purchases in Europe and with which France was now linked by the Bourbon family compact. At the Treaty of Utrecht Britain had obtained the *Assiento* or exclusive contract for supplying slaves to the Spanish colonies and the right to send an annual ship to Porto Bello, but this breach in the commercial monopoly which Spain had for two centuries asserted in the New World far from satisfied English traders. Smuggling continued and ostensibly brought about war in 1739.[2]

Supremely valuable were the West Indies. Their products – sugar, tobacco, cotton, dyewoods and indigo – made both France and Britain originally rate them higher than their colonies on the American mainland. Each country hoped in the War of 1744 to ruin its rival's West Indian islands and destroy their competition in the European market. The same was true in the Seven Years' War (1756–63), but to a lesser extent, for by the middle of the century the growing population of her thirteen American colonies and their consequent greater value as potential markets was making Britain esteem them more. So when peace was at last made in 1763, Britain took Canada, but allowed France to keep her West Indian islands, although the War had been marked there by French naval reverses and a total disruption of French commerce.

Another important area of Anglo-French commercial rivalry was India and south-eastern Asia. The Dutch were able to retain their hold on the Malay archipelago, but their trade with

---

[1] Pp. 74 ff.   [2] P. 76.

the Indian mainland declined, and here the struggle for economic supremacy was between Britain and France. The supremacy of the Dutch in the Malay archipelago led to the concentration of English commercial interests on the mainland, where by the end of the seventeenth century their East India Company had established four factories at Surat, Bombay, Madras and Calcutta. The first half of the eighteenth century saw the Company with expanding trade and revenues as well as the beginnings of territorial aggrandisement. Its exports of textiles, tea, coffee and saltpetre doubled, and its annual fleet grew from eleven to twenty ships, which were also larger than those of the Dutch.

The French came later to India. The *Compagnie des Indes Orientales*, formed in 1664 by Colbert, failed to develop despite the acquisition of Pondicherry as a base in 1683. Not until Law reorganized the enterprise under a new *Compagnie perpetuelle des Indes* in 1719 did trade make much progress, and within thirty years an annual convoy of thirty ships was supplying the French market with Indian produce. So far French economic policy here was apparently confined to commercial objectives; the few forts built were to safeguard trade. Dupleix, who became Governor-General of the French Indies in 1741, brought a new policy of territorial expansion across southern India to promote both imperial and commercial aims, but he failed, and the Treaty of Paris in 1763 destroyed the French hope of supremacy in India. The English East India Company, now unopposed, went on to reach within a few years the apex of its prosperity.

During the first years of the eighteenth century, many people in Britain regarded France as a very serious commercial competitor. She had a larger population, produced more in certain important industries and manufactured finer luxury goods, such as tapestry, furniture, silks and porcelain. Above all, French exports and re-exports enjoyed a favourable balance of trade over her imports, which was regarded as synonymous with economic well-being for the greater part of this period.

Nevertheless, French commerce suffered from a fundamental, even if undetected, weakness. As far as the statistics can be considered reliable, they seem to show that, while Britain continually maintained her favourable balance of trade throughout the century, France fell away from this position, despite the quintupling of her foreign commerce between 1716 and 1789. Unlike Britain, her commerce was not founded upon the manufacture of widely-demanded utilitarian goods such as cloth and hardware. Her ability to supply her West Indian islands with essential slaves, manufactures and food was outmatched by smugglers from Holland, Britain or New England. Most serious was French naval weakness, the causes of which went far back into her history. The lengthy dynastic contests and Continental campaigns of the past had produced an emphasis upon land warfare, while the comparative economic self-sufficiency enjoyed by much of the country told against a realization of the influence of sea-power.

Britain, on the other hand, augmented the initial natural advantage offered by her island position through a deliberate policy of sea-power. Naval strength was needed to protect her colonial shipping in the West Indies as well as her cargoes of exports and re-exports to markets in the Baltic and the Mediterranean, and this need increased as her trade routes grew longer. To protect her growing seaborne commerce, therefore, Britain relied upon a strong navy and, from the seizure of Gibraltar in 1704 from Spain to the retention of Malta, Ceylon, Mauritius and the Cape of Good Hope after the War ending in 1815, achieved the creation of an organized system of strategically-placed naval bases.

Without sea-power it would have been impossible for Britain to enforce the system of regulation and protection embodied from the time of the Commonwealth in the Navigation Acts, which compelled the export of certain valuable colonial products to Britain and gave British manufacturers an advantage in colonial markets, besides restricting the participation of foreign ships in British commerce. It is impossible to ascertain the contribution these Acts made to the growth of British trade; it may be that their effect was to sacrifice the interests of European trade to those of colonial trade. Commercial circles in England were confident of the desirabilty of these Acts, a confidence which was only slightly shaken by the fundamental criticisms of them first made in the 1740's, and not until the nineteenth century was the soundness of their underlying principle seriously challenged.

Undoubtedly another reason for the growth and soundness of British commerce in the eighteenth century was the development of British industry and the nature of that development. No longer was the export of cloth to Europe the most important part of British trade. Metal goods, pottery and paper had become common exports in the seventeenth century, while from about

THE WORLD
in 1713

English
French
Spanish
Portuguese
Dutch

Spitzbe

GREENLAND

Arctic Circle
Iceland

SCOTLAND
IRELAND
Plymouth
La Rochelle
PORTUGAL
Azores
Madeira
Mogador
Canaries

NORTH

New Albion

San Francisco

AMERICA

VIRGINIA

Bermudas

California

NEW
SPAIN
Mexico

Florida

Bahamas

Cuba

HISPANIOLA
SAN DOMINGO

WEST
INDIES

Jamaica

Cadiz

PORTUGAL
SPAIN
Morocco

Cape Verde Is

GUINEA
Sierra Leone   Gold
Coast

Cartagena
NEW
GRANADA
QUITO
Guayaquil

Trinidad

R. Amazon

PERU
Callao
Lima
Arica

BRAZIL

SOUTH

Ascension

St Helena

R. Pisagua

AMERICA

Rio de Janeiro

Valparaiso
Juan Fernandez

River Plate

Tristan da

Falkland Is
Magellan's Straits
Tierra del Fuego
Cape Horn

W. 120   90   60   30   O

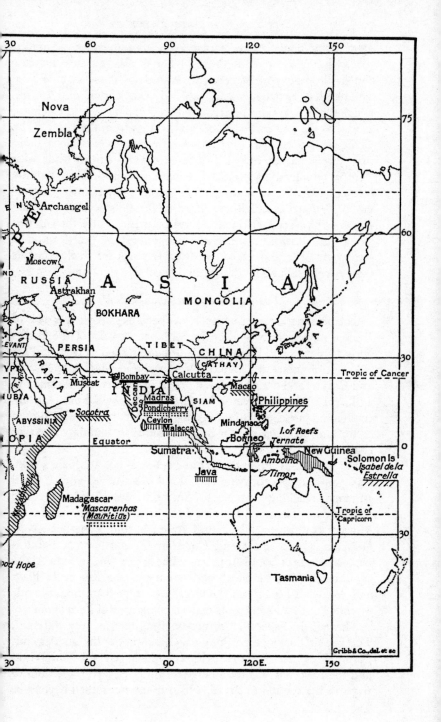

1700 cotton goods gained a place and from about 1720 woollen goods declined in importance. There was notable increase also in the re-export of colonial products. These included the 'enumerated' articles, sugar, tobacco, raw cotton and indigo, which the Navigation Acts reserved for shipping only to England, as well as tea and coffee, spices and textiles from the East. The Clyde received in 1724 over four million pounds of tobacco, more than three-quarters of which it re-exported. British trade with Europe remained and, indeed, expanded considerably, but the colonial and African markets were becoming increasingly important. Perhaps as much as a third of Britain's oceanic shipping was by 1753 engaged in trade with America. By then it was clear that British commercial prosperity was based upon a greater number and variety of manufactures for world-markets than either Holland or France had been able to attain.

Earlier European Colonization

The first period of European overseas expansion was one of Iberian monopoly, which began with the exploits of the Portuguese explorers and Spanish *conquistadores*, such as Diaz and Da Gama, Columbus and Balboa, Vespucci and Magellan, Pizarro and Cortez, and ended with the defeat of the Spanish Armada in 1588. By then the Spanish Empire was, in fact, the only existing colonial empire, since it had taken over the Portuguese Empire in 1580, and no other nation had succeeded in founding overseas colonies.

Except for the Philippines, annexed in 1569, all Spain's colonies were in South America, the West Indies and Central America, reaching into North America from Florida across to California. The main Spanish dominions on the mainland were Mexico, comprising all Central America, and Venezuela, New Granada, Quito, Peru and Chile on the northern and south-western coasts of South America, while across the southern Andes lay Buenos Aires on the broad estuary of the Rio de la Plata and Asuncion farther up the river, and from there Spanish rule extended until it touched the eastern boundaries of Peru again.

The widely-dispersed Portuguese Empire was very different. The largest Portuguese colony was Brazil in South America, but Portugal was too small to develop colonies in both the New World and the East and was too interested in her eastern possessions to pay much attention to Brazil, which it had not settled beyond its coastline. Around the African coast, the Portuguese had founded forts and trading-posts while pioneering the discovery of the direct sea-route to the east. On the western coast they were established in the Gulf of Guinea, trading in gold and slaves; on the eastern coast they had Delagoa, Mozambique and Mombasa. They had Ormuz, key-port to the Persian Gulf, and settlements along the western coast of India, the most important being Goa. They were also established in Ceylon and Bengal, traded with China and Japan, and, above all, possessed the Spice Islands, clustering around Borneo and Celebes. This was the empire, essentially a trading empire, which was incorporated with the Spanish Empire by Philip II.

The seventeenth century, however, brought no further Spanish and Portuguese colonial growth. Both empires were on the defensive. The Portuguese Empire regained its independence in 1640, but it suffered severely and, indeed, almost disintegrated. The Portuguese had lost their strength and initiative and were overtaken by more active nations with larger financial and maritime resources. The potential wealth of this empire attracted them, and by the end of the seventeenth century they had deprived it of its most important possessions. On the other hand, the vast Spanish provinces of the New World remained intact with the loss of only a few outlying possessions, such as Jamaica, taken by England in 1655; but Spain seemed to retain them largely through the forbearance of the rest of Europe. Her rivals wanted to increase their trade rather than extend their colonies, while France supported her politically.

This situation determined the nature of the colonial conflict in the first half of the eighteenth century. It was partly between Spain and those nations which wished to participate in the trade of the Spanish Empire. It was also partly between the various maritime powers to decide which was to benefit from Spain's weakness, and this contest resolved itself into an Anglo-French struggle.

Although England's Elizabethan seamen had led the way in challenging the monopolistic claims of the Spanish Empire, the Dutch made the first successful attacks upon it and were its most determined opponents until about 1650. By this time they had established an empire many times the size of their own small country and a trade which brought them great wealth. In the east they had Java, Sumatra, Borneo and the Spice Islands,

Ceylon and settlements on the Indian mainland, and Formosa. As calling-stations on the route to the east, they had secured the Cape of Good Hope, St. Helena and Mauritius. In the west they had acquired Curaçao and other Caribbean islands, established a sugar colony in Guiana, conquered much of northern Brazil from the Portuguese and planted the small but prosperous colony of New Netherlands on the North American mainland.

During the second half of the seventeenth century, however, Dutch expansion had come to an end, and she began to lose colonies. Portugal, after regaining her independence from Spain, asserted her complete control of Brazil in 1654; Formosa was lost to Chinese refugees from the Manchus in 1661; and the English in 1664 conquered the colony of New Netherlands and renamed it New York. Thereafter, the Dutch retained most of their possessions, but in the colonial history of the eighteenth century remained in the background, satisfied with the valuable empire they had gained in the past.

The French had founded two colonies in North America almost at the same time as the first English settlement on the mainland. These were Acadie on the coast in 1605 and Canada, with Quebec as its centre, in the St. Lawrence valley in 1608. Under Louis XIV there was a remarkable expansion of French rule in Canada. Fur traders and Jesuit missionaries penetrated beyond the Great Lakes to the Mississippi, De la Salle reached the Gulf of Mexico in 1682, Louisiana was occupied in 1697, while to the north trading posts were established as far as Hudson Bay. Emigration was encouraged by Louis XIV's great minister, Jean-Baptiste Colbert (1619–83), but French occupation along these frontiers still remained sparse; it was never consolidated as in the thirteen English colonies on the Atlantic. Agriculture was subsidiary to the fur-trade as the main occupation, and the quest for pelts had resulted in a dispersed white population and few important centres of settlement. At the beginning of the eighteenth century, French colonization in North America was largely represented by a few scattered forts, migrant fur-traders and occasionally a small village of white farmers and fur-traders.

The French had also secured tropical colonies. By the end of the seventeenth century they were firmly established in the West Indies. Their islands included St. Christopher, held jointly with the English, Martinique, Guadeloupe, Grenada, the Windward Islands and St. Domingue, the western part of Hispaniola.

Frenchmen had emigrated more freely to these islands than to Canada. About a thousand immigrants a year came from France. By 1685 their population was said to be 52,000, of whom about two-thirds were negro slaves. A flourishing sugar trade had developed, the number of French ships engaged in it rising from four in 1662 to over 200 in 1683.

Colbert had wanted France to rival and even destroy Dutch commercial power in the East Indies, but little had been achieved in the seventeenth century. After the formation of the *Compagnie des Indes Orientales* in 1664, two islands in the Indian Ocean, Bourbon (Réunion) and Ile de France (Mauritius), were occupied as naval bases, and factories were established at Surat and Bantam. This was followed by the most important step, the purchase of the village of Pondicherry in 1683, which by the end of the seventeenth century had a population of 50,000. These were, however, results which fell short of Colbert's hopes, and the inadequate finances of the Company restricted its activities. The French had made a beginning in India, but little more.

The most considerable British possessions in the New World in 1715 were the colonies on the North American mainland, which were still confined to a narrow coastal belt stretching from the river mouths of Maine in the north to the borders of Spanish Florida in the south, and the southernmost colony of these old thirteen – Georgia – was not founded until 1733. Acadie had been secured at the Treaty of Utrecht, and it became Nova Scotia, the name given to it by James I. The Treaty had also recognized British possession of Newfoundland and the Hudson Bay Territory, where the Hudson's Bay Company had, despite French hostility, maintained forts in which factors exchanged English goods for furs taken by native trappers. The Red Indian tribe of the Iroquois had been recognized as being under the protection of the British crown, which was understood to bring the boundary of the colony of New York to Lake Ontario. Practically, however, the English communities in America, after a century of settlement, were still centred on tide-water; but an era of expansion was at hand.

Britain also had valuable colonies in the West Indies. St. Christopher in 1623 was the first island to receive English settlers, though it was not definitely declared an English colony until the Treaty of Utrecht. The uninhabited island of Barbados was occupied in 1627, and other settlements followed in the Bahamas,

Nevis, Montserrat, Antigua and British Honduras, while the Commonwealth government captured Jamaica in 1655. From about 1640 sugar-growing had become the mainstay of their economy. By 1700 Barbados, though no larger than the Isle of Wight, possessed a population much greater than that of Virginia and exported more in value than all the English colonies on the American mainland together. It was only natural, therefore, that British opinion at this time should regard these islands as more precious than either the American mainland colonies or the trading factories in India where, in fact, the field of future development and contest lay.

The Anglo-French Overseas Contest

As A. T. Mahan said of the War of the Spanish Succession (1701–13), 'Before that war England was one of the sea powers. After it she was *the* sea power, without any *second*.' Britain indeed, seemed to be placed in an unchallenged position, at least for some time to come. The French navy had been almost destroyed; the Spanish navy had nearly all rotted away in harbour; and the Dutch, England's chief maritime rivals in Stuart times, had been exhausted by the strain of land defence during Louis XIV's wars and could no longer attempt to be a leading naval and colonial power.

For twenty-five years after the Treaty of Utrecht, Walpole and Fleury maintained peace in Europe between Britain and France, but acute commercial and colonial rivalry continued, for the issue between these two states, now isolated as the main contestants for overseas power, was still undecided. Though Britain exploited the advantage she had won in the War and steadily extended her trade in all directions, France seemed on the whole to be gaining the advantage, particularly in North America, where she was able to take advantage of circumstances favourable to herself. At the same time as her ally, Spain, was making an effort to put her own colonial effort in shape and also to create a naval force in European waters, France rebuilt her navy and entered upon new colonial schemes.

A cardinal aim of French policy in North America was to unite by a chain of fortified posts the two colonies of Canada and Louisiana. Shortly before his death, the great engineer, Sébastien de Vauban (1633–1707), had been commissioned by Louis XIV to build the fort of Louisbourg on Cape Breton Island at the mouth of the St. Lawrence.   Other forts now followed – Crown Point on Lake Champlain, Frontenac and Fort Niagara on Lake Ontario, St. Charles and Fort Rouge (Winnipeg) on Lake Winnipeg and Fort Chartres on the Mississippi.   If the French could establish firmly this crescent-shaped line along the St. Lawrence, the Great Lakes, the Ohio and the Mississippi, this alone would prevent the English colonists penetrating into the interior.   Moreover, the French might be able to advance past Lake Champlain and the Hudson valley to the Atlantic, so splitting the English colonies into two groups and making their conquest possible.

The English colonists, therefore, had to capture the key French forts and overwhelm the line of colonies if they were to obtain any security.   No fixed frontiers separated the settlements of the two nations, but the outposts of each side crept nearer to each other. It was a life-and-death struggle, fought mercilessly.   Because the French were explorers and traders, they had the advantage of knowledge of the countryside and friendship with the Indians, while the English farmers and settlers were often ignorant of the border territory and had gained the hatred of the Indians through seizing their lands.   So the French were able to hire bands of Indian savages, who raided English settlements with fire and slaughter.   When the English sought to emulate this policy, they provided rum as a stimulant which eventually proved more palatable to the Indians than the rival French firewater, brandy. Natural routes for attack by the French and their native allies from the St. Lawrence were provided by the waterways of the Penobscot, Kennebec, Connecticut and Hudson.   Brutal incidents took place along these rivers and on the shores of Lake Champlain.   Colonial border-warfare had been almost continuous for years, and the absence of hostilities in Europe did nothing to diminish it.

Though rivalry in the New World was destined to bring about a renewal of open warfare between Britain and France, the first of the chain of events which caused this occurred, not along the Anglo-French colonial frontiers in North America, but in the waters of Spanish America.   Ever since Elizabethan times, the supposed wealth of tropical America had lured English adventurers and traders there.   During the earlier years of the eighteenth century, in Britain high hopes had been placed upon the South Sea Company, formed in 1711 to trade with the Spanish colonies and ultimately with the rich lands thought to await discovery in the Pacific beyond. These hopes were increased when the commercial concessions obtained at the Treaty of Utrecht were assigned to the Company; but they were disappointed. The Company was a victim of inadequate geographical and financial knowledge which produced similar results in other countries at this time. It promised large profits which it never made, and in 1720 the fraudulent booming of its shares caused the scandalous 'South Sea Bubble'. The Company's operations continued, however, and so did those of English smugglers who ran cargoes from Jamaica into Caribbean ports.

The Spanish authorities tried hard to confine trade to the terms of the Treaty of Utrecht.[1] Their *guarda-costas* stopped every English ship they met to search it for contraband goods. This produced incidents, one of which finally led to war. The representatives of the British merchant class in Parliament brought about hostilities with Spain by exploiting the case of a West Indian shipmaster, Captain Robert Jenkins, who claimed he had been mutilated by the Spaniards and exhibited a cut-off ear preserved in a bottle of spirits to support his story. So Walpole was forced into the War of Jenkins's Ear in 1739. Once again the object of the British merchants was to secure unrestricted participation in the trade of the New World.

The British war-plan was to seize the ports on both coasts of Spanish America. Porto Bello, on the Panama isthmus, was captured by Admiral Vernon, but could not be held. Cartagena was invested by the strongest British expedition that had ever gone to the West Indies; the venture failed through tropical fevers and the inexperience of its commanders. Anson was sent round Cape Horn to attack the coast of Chile and Peru, but lost all his ships except one through storms and was reduced to taking prizes. Though he arrived home with treasure worth £1,250,000 after his heroic four-year voyage round the world, he had lost four-fifths of his men and inflicted no permanent damage upon the enemy.

By 1743 the War of Jenkins's Ear had become merged with a general European conflict, the War of the Austrian Succession. This brought into prominence a new field of Anglo-French overseas conflict – India. Both the English and French East India Companies had been forced by native troubles to fortify their factories, and in the Carnatic province their respective headquarters, Madras and Pondicherry, lay close together on the same

[1] P. 175.

coastline; but the two Companies had agreed not to fight each other in previous wars and had united to defeat attempts by Denmark, Sweden and the short-lived Ostend Company to share in Indian trade.   This situation was changed, however, by Joseph François Dupleix (1697–1763), who in 1741 became Governor-General of the French Indies.   He saw that the collapse of the Mogul Empire, following the death of the last great Emperor in 1707, made it possible to secure the help of Indian princes against the English, now that the trading interests of the two countries had begun to clash.   When the War of the Austrian Succession broke out, the French also secured local naval supremacy and captured Madras in 1746, but could not take advantage of their success because of the two British naval victories off Cape Finisterre.   When the Treaty of Aix-la-Chapelle ended hostilities in 1748, Madras was exchanged for Louisburg, which Britain had taken in 1745.[1]

The Treaty of Aix-la-Chapelle was in its colonial as in its European aspects nothing more than a truce.   In America and in India the possessions of both Britain and France remained unchanged. So also did their ambitions and resentments, and the events of the 1740's had only increased them.   In both these overseas areas Anglo-French rivalry seemed more than ever to be insoluble without further conflict; and this time the contestants soon drifted into unofficial war in both areas.

It was not long before the disappointed Dupleix renewed the contest in India, though there was peace in Europe.   In 1750 he made a native claimant the puppet-ruler of the Carnatic in return for his formal recognition of French suzerainty in southern India. The British had their own claimant, but he was besieged in Trichinopoly by his French-assisted rival.   The situation was saved for the British by Robert Clive (1725–74), who by a daring dash from Madras occupied and held Arcot, the capital of the Carnatic, for over fifty days in 1751 until the besiegers had to retire.   This proved to be the turning-point of the struggle.   He won further victories and gained increasing Indian support for the British before returning in 1753 to England, where he was popularly hailed as a victor.

Dupleix was still ready to struggle on, but his government, which was weak and preoccupied with events in America, would not give him adequate support.   Neither would the directors of

[1] P. 213.

the French Company, who were interested only in peaceful trade. So Dupleix was recalled in 1754. The British were now stronger and the French weaker in India, but the future of the great sub-continent was still undetermined.

The decision came with the fighting which accompanied the Seven Years' War in Europe. The French made ready an expedition for India in 1756, but before it arrived, a native prince, the Nawab of Bengal, took Calcutta and committed the atrocity of the Black Hole, in which many of his prisoners died. Clive sailed with a punitive expedition against the Nawab, who was an ally of the French, and in 1757 overthrew him at the Battle of Plassey, an event which, Lord Macaulay said, 'decided the fate of India'. The East India Company now ceased to be merely a trading corporation, for all Bengal, with a native population twice that of England, passed under its control. Meanwhile, the French expedition had reached the Carnatic. Its commander, the Comte de Lally, after unsuccessfully besieging Madras, was defeated by Sir Eyre Coote at Wandewash in 1760 and retreated to Pondicherry, which he had to surrender the next year. The French were now without possessions in India. At the Treaty of Paris in 1763, they regained their factories, but none of the adjoining territory; the British remained the virtual rulers of the two vast provinces of the Carnatic and Bengal and had none to dispute their possession. Their East India Company not only practically monopolized the commerce of India, but had entered through pressure of circumstances and the initiative of its officials upon a process of territory conquest which it could not reverse.

During this time, a similar conquest had been proceeding in North America. Here also the period between the wars was marked by actual hostilities. To connect the two great water-ways they held – the St. Lawrence and the Mississippi – the French had to occupy the Ohio. In 1749 a French expedition passed down its course from Canada, built Fort Duquesne and claimed possession of the region, a claim which was asserted successfully against both Virginian colonists under George Washington in 1754 and British troops under General Braddock the next year. The French seemed to have the upper hand and to be potentially in possession of North America.

When the Seven Years' War began, the greatest British effort was made in North America, where Pitt's admirals and generals conquered Canada by a planned three-fold attack. General

Forbes in 1758 took Fort Duquesne, 'the key to the great un-
bounded west'; General Wolfe captured Louisbourg in 1758 and
sailed up the St. Lawrence to take Quebec the next year; and
General Amherst advanced up the Champlain valley from the
south and took Montreal in 1760. Weakness at sea, a decisive numerical inferiority in North America and a continual
threat of food shortage in Canada had made the French defeat
inevitable.

By the Treaty of Paris, France ceded to Britain the whole of
Canada and the disputed territory between the Alleghany
Mountains and the Mississippi. Britain restored to France the
three finest of the several West Indian islands which she had also
conquered from her – St. Lucia, Martinique and Guadeloupe –
and retained only the less important islands of Tobago, St.
Vincent and Dominica; she restored to France her slaving-posts
at Gorée in Africa, which supplied labour for the sugar-planta-
tions, but kept those in Senegal. This recovery by France of
most of her possessions in the Caribbean did not offset the effect
of the gain by Britain of the whole of the settled areas of North
America from the Atlantic coast to the Mississippi. Here also
the Anglo-French struggle for supremacy was over.

Britain won the colonial struggle because she had an island
position and built a navy which protected her trade and enabled
military aid to be sent to her colonies in wartime, while France
had land-frontiers to defend and was deprived of naval supremacy through concentration upon military power. Britain also
had a class of wealthy landowners and merchants who recognized
the values of commerce and colonies, but the French aristocracy
and middle-classes cared more for court favour and official posts.
Even Voltaire could not share the English outlook here. 'You
know,' he wrote of England and France, 'these two nations are
at war for a few acres of snow in Canada, and that they are
spending more on this fine war than all Canada is worth. It is
beyond my poor capacity to tell you whether there are more mad-
men in one country than in the other.'

Pitt strongly criticized the terms of the Treaty as being less
than what Britain might have obtained.[1] Nevertheless, her gains
in territory, trade and prestige were greater than she had made in
any previous war. Two huge territories seemed inevitably destined to be developed by her. The sea-power and maritime trade

---

[1] P. 232.

THE WORLD
in 1810

English
French
Spanish
Dutch
Russian
Danish
Portuguese

SPITZBE

GREENLAND

Davis Str.
Frobisher B.

Arctic Circle

Iceland

SCOTLAND
IRELAND
Plymouth
La Rochelle

PORTUGAL

Labrador

Newfoundland

NORTH

San Francisco
New Albion
California

AMERICA

NEW
SPAIN
Mexico

Florida

Cuba

Azores
Madeira
Mogador
Canaries

Cape Verde Is

VIRGINIA

Bermudas

Bahamas

HISPANIOLA
SAN DOMINGO

Jamaica

WEST
INDIES
Trinidad
Guiana

GUINEA
Gold
Coast

Cartagena
NEW
GRANADA
QUITO

Guayaquil

PERU

Lima
Callao
Arica

R.Pisagua

SOUTH

A.Amazon

BRAZIL

Sierra Leone

Ascension

St Helena

AMERICA

Valparaiso
Juan Fernandez

River Plate

Rio de Janeiro

Tristan da

Falkland Is
Magellan's Straits
Tierra del Fuego
Cape Horn

W. 120

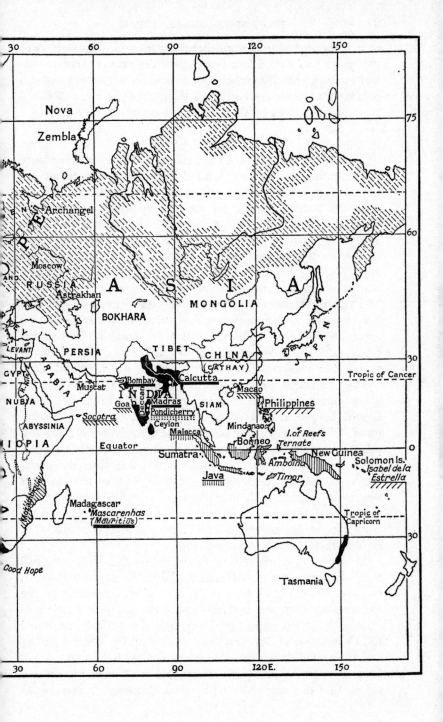

of a large part of the world belonged to her.   Through Pitt's
policy, she was now definitely committed to pursue overseas aims
and interests as well as maintain her position in Europe; and this
continued to be so, even although the first empire she established
was to be disrupted by the American Revolution.

The American Revolution

The causes and events of the American War of Independence
belong rather to American and British than to European history, but its nature and consequences had a considerable effect
upon the latter.   During the controversy which preceded the
outbreak of hostilities, both sides argued from conflicting principles.   The British government maintained the undoubted legal
right of the King in Parliament to exercise supreme authority over
every British subject whether he be in England or the colonies
and insisted that to resist this authority was treason and rebellion.
The American colonists, on the other hand, who had inherited
English political traditions, took their stand on equally convincing
constitutional right.   American lawyers appealed to Magna
Carta, and Burke stated that nearly as many copies of Black-
stone's *Commentaries on the Laws of England*, published in
1765–9, had been sold in America as in Britain. The Bill of Rights
of 1689 had condemned 'levying money for or to the use of the
Crown by pretence of prerogative without consent of Parliament'.   The Americans considered that this privilege of all British
subjects not to be taxed without the consent of their elected representatives should apply to themselves, but they were not represented in the Parliament at Westminster, so they took as their
slogan 'no taxation without representation'.   The American victory seemed, therefore, to be a triumph for those principles of the
British constitution which had attracted the admiration of
eighteenth-century thinkers in Europe.

Moreover, in effecting their revolution the Americans justified
themselves in terms of the radical philosophy of the eighteenth
century.   The representatives of the colonies, meeting as the
Continental Congress at Philadelphia on 4th July 1776, proclaimed 'a decent respect to the opinion of mankind' and issued
the Declaration of Independence, drawn up by Thomas Jeffer-
son, the second paragraph of which opened with the words – 'We
hold these truths to be self-evident: That all men are created
equal; that they are endowed by their Creator with certain un-

alienable rights; that among these are life, liberty and the pursuit of happiness. That, to secure these rights, governments are instituted among men, deriving their just powers from the consent of the governed; that, wherever any form of government becomes destructive of these ends, it is the right of the people to alter or abolish it, and to institute a new government, laying its foundation on such principles, and organizing its power in such form as to them shall seem most likely to effect their safety and happiness.'

The Declaration of Independence was, therefore, to quote Professor Faulkner, 'an appeal to the liberal thought of Europe'. It spoke in the language of Locke, Montesquieu and Rousseau. It accepted the right of revolution by people against a tyrant and dissolved the contract with the sovereign formally and with a careful list of grievances. So the social contract theory of the European political philosophers was made the official basis of the new confederation under the inspiration of the same intellectual influences which were to produce the Declaration of the Rights of Man adopted by the French Constituent Assembly in 1789.[1]

Nowhere, indeed, was the effect of the American Revolution more marked than in France. When the colonies revolted against Britain, widespread public sympathy for their cause combined with the desire to revenge the loss of Canada and India to make French opinion overwhelmingly anxious to support the rebels. French arms, supplies and money were sent to them with official connivance, and the young Marquis de Lafayette (1757–1834) and other volunteers crossed the Atlantic to fight for the cause. When the British army under General Burgoyne surrendered at Saratoga in 1777, France entered into an alliance with the new republic and declared war on Britain. The formation of the League of Armed Neutrality in 1780 by the Baltic Powers, in opposition to Britain's policy of naval blockade, further embarrassed her. The Treaty of Versailles, which ended the War in 1783, restored to France only the small West Indian islands and Senegal in Africa lost by her in the Seven Years' War, but Britain's loss of her American colonies was a considerable consolation. As Professor Cobban has said, 'No one as yet supposed that the price to be paid for American independence was a French revolution.'

[1] P. 316.

One reason why this was so was that the French alliance with the Americans introduced into France ideas of democratic government which had been developing in the American colonies, Britain, Switzerland, the Austrian Netherlands and the Dutch Republic, but had hitherto had very little influence in France. The *philosophes* had not been democrats, but now democratic and republican ideas became respectable and fashionable in French society. Typical of the young French noblemen who fought for American independence was the Comte de Ségur, and he wrote: 'I was far from being the only one whose heart palpitated at the sound of the growing awakening of liberty, seeming to shake off the voice of arbitrary power.' The simple manners and plain, homespun suit of Benjamin Franklin, the envoy of the American insurgents in Paris, aroused enthusiasm in polite circles; and the translation into French of the constitutions adopted by the new states of the Union (and especially Massachusetts and Virginia) popularized the idea of a written constitution and a declaration of the rights of citizens as a security against governmental abuse of power. One of the liberal parties called itself '*les américains*', and for many Frenchmen the white settlers of the transatlantic republic represented the ideal, natural man living without a hereditary monarchy, a landed aristocracy or an established priesthood, but free to lead his own life and choose his own rulers. After the fall of the Bastille, its key was sent to George Washington as a token that a victory had been won over tyranny in France too.

Another reason why the American War of Independence contributed towards the outbreak of the French Revolution was that it completed the bankruptcy of the French crown. Louis XIV had accomplished the development of a great military and bureaucratic system of government, larger and more far-reaching in its activities than that of other European states; but it exhausted French resources because they were not adequately organized and modernized to maintain it. The old feudal liberty was not eliminated, but expensively bribed by fiscal exemption and grants of pensions from the royal revenue; the government of the country was made more costly by the property rights of officials in their posts. The consequent reduction in the crown's income, added to the cost of the court and constant wars for over a century, ruined royal finance. To raise money without taxing the privileged orders, the crown resorted to the widespread sale of posts and titles to the *bourgeoisie* and heavier and heavier taxation upon the poorer people. Moreover, the system of taxation was such that the government failed to obtain more than a proportion of its yield. The *gabelle*, for instance, brought in sixty million livres, but cost twenty million to collect and required the employment of about fifty thousand troops and agents to combat smuggling. The government was also compelled, therefore, to resort to continuous borrowing. After the Seven Years' War, when the national income was more than 472 million livres a year, 236 million livres, or a half of the income, was needed to pay the interest on debts; and this despite the fact that the crown had defaulted by reduction of interest or repudiation of debt five times already in the century.

Such was her financial position when France participated in the American War of Independence at a cost of 1,200,000 livres. This made an extremely difficult situation practically insoluble. Each new *Contrôleur Général* sought to solve the problem, but none could do anything of lasting effect under the circumstances.[1] Every war fought by France in the eighteenth century had produced a severe financial crisis. Now the last, the American War of Independence, combined with food-shortages and political disturbance was to cause a revolution.

The New British Empire

For Britain, the loss of the American colonies meant the abandonment of a dominion from Hudson Bay to the Gulf of Mexico soon after it had been created by Pitt's genius. This radical alteration in the composition of her overseas empire did not, however, mean the end of her position as an imperialist, colonizing power. She still possessed her Canadian colony, West Indian islands and provinces in India. The remaining years of the eighteenth century saw the consolidation of these possessions and the beginnings of a new expanding empire.

The United Empire Loyalists, who moved northwards rather than accept American rule, initiated a new English Canada alongside the conquered French province; and in 1791, within eighteen years of the conquest of the colony, both parts – Upper and Lower Canada – were granted legislative assemblies. In India, the Company's rule prospered under the governorships of two outstanding men. From 1773 to 1784 Warren Hastings

[1] Pp. 306 ff.

established a just and efficient system of administration in the Company's territory; and from 1798 to 1805 the Marquess of Wellesley quadrupled the area of British territory, made the most important princes the Company's vassals and placed the Great Mogul of Delhi under British protection.   By 1818, when the power of the Mahratta princes was broken, Britain had become the sovereign ruler of India.

Meanwhile, before the end of the American dispute, Captain James Cook (1728–79) had made his remarkable voyages in the Pacific which were to bring Britain possession of both Australia and New Zealand; the establishment in 1788 of the penal settlement at Botany Bay in New South Wales marked the beginning of their colonization.   And the retention by Britain of some of her conquests in 1815, notably the Cape of Good Hope, was another stage in the construction of the new empire which was already taking the place of that disrupted by the American Revolution.[1]

[1] P. 385.

V · ENLIGHTENED DESPOTISM

European Monarchy

THOUGH republicanism was established in the United States of America and in France during the later years of the eighteenth century, monarchy was still regarded as the normal form of European government in this period. Moreover, in its various forms on the Continent it was absolute monarchy, the result of past developments which had strengthened the position of most rulers and apparently made them more secure than ever. At the beginning of the century, the most powerful seemed to be the French monarchy as established by Louis XIV, symbolized to opponents of monarchical absolutism by the notorious *lettre de cachet*, which enabled it to order arbitrarily exile or imprisonment without trial or sentence. While subsequent years brought about an undermining of the position of the French monarchy, Louis XV was making no unconstitutional claim when he stated in 1766: 'In my person alone resides sovereign power . . . I alone possess complete and untrammelled legislative authority.'

Kingship remained a divine or at any rate a divinely-instituted office. Sovereigns still wielded their powers as vice-gerents of God. They continued to think of themselves as reigning, in the words of the thirteenth-century jurist, 'under God and the law', and this idea contained a considerable element of truth. In most countries the theoretical limits to the power of the king were vague and uncertain, and there was no effective check to this power from the traditional assemblies of the estates.

Moreover, there seemed, in the first part of the century at any rate, to be no alternative to kingly rule. This was suggested by experience rather than argument. The European republican exceptions to monarchy – Holland, Switzerland and some German and Italian states – were small, less well governed and less effectively led than the great kingdoms. The failure of Oliver Cromwell to establish the Commonwealth in England seemed to emphasize the general indispensability of monarchy as a system of government in important states; and the fatal disunity and weakness which accompanied the limitation of monarchical power in Poland suggested that to be effective kingship must be powerful.

Europe's monarchies were an inheritance from her pre-industrial condition of society in which kingship was normal and universal. Then kings seemed to have performed three main roles, which they still substantially exercised in the eighteenth century, though already important changes were taking place in their function. First, the king was a warrior. George II was destined to be the last British sovereign to command in person an army in the field, when he was present at the Battle of Dettingen in 1743, but among the delusions suffered by George III when he went mad was a belief that he had led his troops at Waterloo as kings had done in warfare in the past. Second, the king was a priest. The important part of a medieval coronation service was not the crowning of the king, but the anointing of him with oil to consecrate him to a semi-ecclesiastical position as 'protector of the holy Church of God'. And, third, the king was a law-giver. This meant according to medieval ideas that he acted as the fountain of justice to interpret an already existing, God-given fundamental law.

In the eighteenth century, kings continued to hold and exercise these functions in varying degrees and remained remote, awe-inspiring and fundamentally mysterious figures to most of their subjects; but events were bringing about a change of emphasis in the way their traditional role was regarded. In war, the king had now to plan and organize for the success of his forces rather than lead them in battle; he was the director of the national effort demanded by the increasing scale and complication of the nature of warfare. Louis XIV no longer went to war in person or wore the costume of a fighting-man; he rode in a coach rather than on horseback, wore a wig and carried a walking-stick; and he spent regular hours at work in his study and at council meetings. Again, the religious events of the sixteenth century in both Protestant and Roman Catholic countries increased the power of the State over the Church so that the king became in effect the ruler of the Church instead of its protector, and in countries which were divided in religion he was expected to prevent religious strife. Finally, the king came to act as a law-maker instead of a law-interpreter, to rule his country by personal decree, as emphasized by a revival of the study of Roman law with its well-known axiom, '*Quod principi placuit, habet legis vigorem*'.

These changes of interpretation were accompanied by tendencies from about 1500 onwards which strengthened the power of most European kings. There was the revival of aristocracy in the sixteenth and seventeenth centuries. It was a transformed aristocracy. No longer was it a feudal, warlike class, often contending for power with the crown. It was now a nobility of service, associated successfully with the king in the government of the country by the gift of offices, titles and land. Then there was the rise and expansion of the middle-classes in the seventeenth and eighteenth centuries. In the countries of north-western Europe, England and Holland, where oceanic trade became so important, the middle-class was mainly capitalist and rose to power so fast that it overwhelmed the monarchy; but in the landlocked states of eastern Europe, Prussia and Poland, where the middle-class was professional and bureaucratic, it remained much weaker, and the nobility was correspondingly more powerful. Forming a sort of geographical bridgehead between these two groups of countries was France, where the crown had to contend with both *noblesse* and *bourgeoisie*. The Revocation of the Edict of Nantes in 1685, which struck at the Huguenot trading classes, may be said to mark to some extent the triumph of the crown over such bourgeois resistance as existed in France, but in the eighteenth century the French monarchy failed to solve the problem presented by a revived aristocracy, and so the Revolution came. A final way in which the power of some European kings was strengthened lay in their ability to organize and encourage the economic, colonizing and nationalist forces which were surging up out of the depths of society. James I of England was vainly advised by Francis Bacon to do this and so secure himself on the throne; Gustavus Adolphus of Sweden and Louis XIV of France were both ready, in their different ways, to undertake the task. Kings who succeeded in exploiting these forces could unite all groups among their subjects under their rule, but if they failed, then their whole position was placed in jeopardy.

These changes in European kingship had a twofold implication. They demanded a life of incessant activity on behalf of the State from the king. 'What is the use of a king shut up in a box?', Gustavus Adolphus is said to have replied to his officers when they rebuked him for exposing himself to danger at the Battle of Lützen in 1632, at which he was later killed. Yet at the same time the absolute king had to occupy a remote, unique position in society if he were to retain his dominance. Hence the magnificent setting and the elaborate court hierarchy and ceremonial of Louis XIV's Versailles, which was widely imitated by other Continental monarchs.   In fact, however, these twofold implications proved mutually inconsistent and the tension produced a strain which sometimes manifested itself in the marked psychological aberrations in the characters of monarchs subjected to it.

The king at Versailles was really enclosed in a box and needed an administrative system to accomplish his rule.   The new absolutism was that of monarchy rather than kingship.   In place of part-time, amateur administrators, who were either ecclesiastics or hereditary noblemen remunerated with land, rulers came to have whole-time, expert officials, drawn from the aristocracy or middle-classes, and then some bureaucratic organization, which tended to assume the form either of the French system of departments of state or of the Habsburg system of administrative councils.

Monarchical absolutism was still justified by the doctrine of the divine right of kings.   This was a doctrine which had originated to strengthen the assertion of their authority by secular rulers against the claims of the Papacy.   It generally regarded the king as God's agent entrusted with the duty of disciplining his sinful people and so to be obeyed unquestioningly and completely by them.   It also maintained that certain dynasties had been destined to rule from the time of Adam; James I sought to justify the accession of the *parvenu* House of Stuart to the English throne in this way, though he could not persuade either his parliaments or his people to accept the idea.   In fact, the general doctrine of the divine right of kings by the seventeenth century found more favour in court circles than among political thinkers and by the eighteenth century had become so difficult to justify in intellectual terms that as the years passed it was asserted with ever less confidence.

Monarchy was also justified by representing the relationship between a ruler and his subject as analogous to that of a father and his family.   This was the view put forward by the strongly royalist political writer, Sir Robert Filmer, in his *Patriarcha* (published posthumously in 1680), which Locke later attacked. One of the titles of the Russian czars, the last of the Continental despots to survive, was 'Little Father', and the czardom long continued to retain popular loyalty despite wars, intrigues and palace revolutions. In the eighteenth century, the idea of the king as the father-figure of his people was still generally acceptable. 'The true image of a free people, governed by a patriot king,' wrote the sophisticated Lord Bolingbroke in 1738, 'is that of a patriarchal family.' The family was then a much larger unit than today, for it included both the household and many dependent relatives, and the head of a family ruled with a correspondingly greater authority, which included the unquestioned right to chastise both his children and his servants. 'Good order must be had in the kingdom as in the home,' said a contemporary writer; 'therefore, the sword must be in the prince's hand no less than the rod in the parent's hand to be used by both discreetly and for the upholding of authority and justice.' It was consequently natural for people still to compare the position of an absolute monarch to such a domestic figure.

Enlightened Despotism

The eighteenth century saw the rise of a form of monarchy known as Enlightened Despotism, which represents the final form of European absolutism. None of the rulers who are generally considered to be examples of Enlightened Despotism ever themselves used the term, but the expression '*Despotisme éclairé*' and '*Despotisme légal*' appear in the writings of the Physiocrats from about 1760 onwards, and Diderot was the first to use the term itself in his letters. Enlightened Despotism was a type of government closely affected by the ideas and particularly the political ideas of the Enlightenment. It was the last phase in the history of the hierarchical system of government and society which had come down from the Middle Ages, and it was adopted because the traditional justifications for this system of government were now losing ground. The doctrine of divine right was losing adherents. The effectiveness of the comparison with fatherhood to uphold monarchical absolutism was diminished because, as Edward Gibbon wrote: 'the domestic discipline of our ancestors has been relaxed by the philosophy and softness of the age'. Above all, contemporary thinkers had already begun to dispute the rightness and expediency of the existence of the traditional classes and privileges of Continental absolutism. They sought to alleviate the inadequacies and hardships of this social system, but they lacked the courage to arrive at the full consequences of their

ideas and advocate the destruction of the existing social order
and governments based upon it.

Enlightened Despotism's main ideas came into being in France
in the 1760's as a political development from the economic beliefs
of the Physiocrats.[1] This was because the natural order of the
Physiocrats did not, in fact, exist. It had been destroyed by
centuries of economic control, and a policy of *laissez faire* was,
therefore, not immediately possible. On the contrary, absolute
power seemed necessary in the State to secure the return of the
natural order, the removal of all that obstructed the free growth
of productive forces and the undoing of those who sought through
self-interest or prejudice to maintain the existing situation. This
power, however, must not be capricious, but 'legal', which meant
it should be submitted to a rational law harmonizing enlightened
thought with the practical political measures necessary to accomplish it.

The wielder of such power would be the Enlightened Despot,
whose role should be solely '*de reconnaître, de proclamer et de
faire respecter le droit naturel et d'assurer l'ordre naturel*'. To
enable this to be done, the Physiocrats held that the executive
power of the State had to be exercised, entire and undivided, by
a fully sovereign monarch. So completely did they believe in the
inevitability of the triumph of the Enlightenment, through its
acceptance by all intelligent men, that though they insisted upon
the right of freedom of speech, they urged hereditary kingship
without any qualifications and emphatically opposed the idea of
parliamentary control or some such division of governmental
powers familiarized by Montesquieu.

The theoretical basis of Enlightened Despotism, therefore,
looked for support from many of the ideas current in Europe as
a result of the Enlightenment. Yet, as Pirenne has observed,
Enlightened Despotism contained nothing particularly novel in
its conception of state-government. Although it was sometimes
regarded as superseding the traditional patriarchical view
of monarchy, it was really a fresh version of this old idea, the
only difference being that the conduct of the ruler, as the father
of his country, which had hitherto been swayed by his heart,
should now be guided by his reason. It was also essentially a
development of the old doctrine of divine right. Royal power
was now regarded as a sacred trust (or, at any rate, a rational

[1] Pp. 61–2.

engagement) which gave the ruler serious responsibilities. He was responsible for the welfare of his subjects, and this still justified infringements of their individual liberty and demanded their implicit obedience to him.

Moreover, in practice Enlightened Despotism was not very radical. The Physiocrats in the 1760's and 1770's had difficulty in convincing even the thinkers of the Enlightenment of its merits, and in their own country they could not secure any significant implementation of their ideas. One of their number, Turgot, secured control of French economic policy as *Contrôleur Général des Finances* for twenty months, but he could not substantiate any important measure of reform against the opposition of the privileged classes and wealthy *bourgeoisie*, and Louis XVI was no Enlightened Despot.[1] Several European monarchs, however, have been represented as being influenced to some extent by the ideas of Enlightened Despotism in the second half of the eighteenth century, especially between 1763 and 1792, and their claim to the title of Enlightened Despot must be examined.

Catherine II of Russia

One illustration of the change in the nature of European monarchy after the feudal period may be found in the fact that some of the most successful absolute rulers of important states in these later times were queens, and notable among them in the eighteenth century was the Czarina Catherine II of Russia, who reigned from 1762 to 1796. As a German princess who had had a French governess, she was in touch with European thought and interested in the Enlightenment and established contacts with its French adherents, including supporters of the idea *Despotisme éclairé*. Her favourite authors included Locke, Diderot, Voltaire and Montesquieu. She corresponded with Voltaire; she welcomed Diderot to St. Petersburg, where he professed to find in her *'l'âme de Brutus avec les charmes de Cléopâtre'*, and she purchased his library for the Hermitage palace. These contacts, however, suggest an importance which they were far from actually having for they had practically no effect upon Catherine's rule in Russia.

It was in accordance with the ideas of the Physiocrats that Catherine within a fortnight of her accession abolished most of

[1] Pp. 304-6.

the state monopolies in the sale of commodities, which her predecessor, the Czarina Elizabeth, had farmed out to private individuals. She also continued the efforts of earlier administrators
to establish internal free trade in the empire, and towards the end
of her reign a foreign observer even held that Russia had fewer
restrictions upon trade than any other European state. Nevertheless, Catherine's policy of economic liberalism was limited in its
effects. Governmental patronage and encouragement continued
to be extended in industry to noblemen, who employed ascribed
serf labour, while the restrictions of the manorial system upon a
flexible supply of free labour greatly impeded the development of
free enterprise on the lines of western Europe. The foundation
by Catherine of an Imperial Free Economic Society in 1765
seemed to uphold her attachment to Physiocratic principles, but
when the society offered a prize for an essay on the condition of
the peasant, the advocacy by the prize-winning essay of the
establishment of peasant-proprietors in Russia was so unacceptable to her that she forbade its publication.

Her political liberalism was similarly limited. In the early
years of her reign, to minimize the unfortunate impression
created abroad by the *coup d'état* which had brought her to the
throne, she announced that she would summon in Moscow a
representative Legislative Commission (*Zemstvo*) to prepare a new
codification of the laws. For their guidance she drew up an Instruction (*Nakaz*), the main ideas of which were certainly those of
thinkers of the Enlightenment, much of it being derived from
Montesquieu's *Esprit des Lois*. It was very advanced and
impressively humane as a statement of abstract principles and
proposed reforms, which included insistence upon the equality of
all in the sight of the law, an emphasis upon the prevention of
crime rather than the infliction of punishment and the complete
prohibition of torture. It achieved, however, nothing. The
Zemstvo, for which she had composed it, met briefly and fruit-
lessly only once in 1767. No social or legal progress was made,
and no attempt was made to abolish cruel punishments or torture,
such as breaking on the wheel and flogging with the hide-thonged
knout.

In secularizing the lands of the Russian Church in 1764,
Catherine was acting in accordance with the spirit of the age of
Enlightenment; but there were also Russian precedents to lead
her to do this. It had been proposed by her husband, Peter III,

in 1762.[1] Still more, by depriving the clergy of their financial independence and making them paid servants of the State, it was a step which completed a process begun by Peter I.

The comprehensive reform of the structure of local government, which Catherine instituted later in her reign, had also been anticipated in proposals made during the reign of the Czarina Elizabeth. Between 1775 and the end of her reign, Catherine replaced the twenty vast and unwieldy units of local administration by fifty smaller provinces, each with a population of about 350,000 people and sub-divided into districts of about 25,000. Each province was headed by an imperial governor, who was assisted by centrally-appointed collegiate boards of officials performing legal and administrative functions. The districts had similar boards which were elected locally. These reforms won considerable praise from liberals outside Russia. Even such an experienced traveller as Archdeacon Coxe wrote: 'By the new code this enormous power of the lords is reduced to restrictions more consonant to the humane principles which distinguish all the regulations of the present empress.'

In fact, however, this was not so. As only the local nobility were allowed to form assemblies for electoral purposes, the new local boards were dominated by their representatives. Moreover, the new nobility gained complete control over their serfs, whose right of appeal was abolished; and her reign was noted for its considerable number of wealthy serf-owners, many enriched by her bounty, who were exacting in their right to enforce labour-dues and extensively maintained discipline by flogging. The rights of the landowning nobility in local administration were strengthened by Catherine's charter of the nobility in 1785. Besides recognizing their position in the local assemblies, this confirmed their other privileges such as exempton from military service, personal taxation, corporal punishment and the billeting of troops, as well as reasserting their right to be tried by their peers. The charter also emphasized their responsibilities – to compel their serfs to pay the poll tax and secure the required number for service in the army. In this way, the Russian nobility, linked to the crown by privilege and serving as its agents, assisted the progress of Catherine's absolutist rule.

Catherine the Great, therefore, though she was to Voltaire the '*Sémiramis du Nord*', was hardly an Enlightened Despot. As

[1] P. 260.

Richard Charques has said, 'Enlightenment in Catherine was not much deeper than her vanity; despotism, on the other hand, was implicit in her ambition'. She was only prepared to encourage the ideas of the age of reason if she could control them; when she could not, she suppressed them. Even in the *Nakaz*, she pronounced herself so strongly in favour of absolutism that when Diderot read it he wrote that the Empress of Russia was certainly a despot because, whatever the true end of her government, it made all liberty and property depend on one person. The theoretical abstraction in the *Nakaz* remained no more than a fashionable tribute to French thought, which won for her from the *philosophes* the title of '*législatrice*' to her great satisfaction. Such practical reforms as she did introduce into Russia concealed a despotic purpose behind their liberal façade.

Frederick II of Prussia

Professor Fritz Hartung has held that the first of the Enlightened Despots was really Frederick the Great of Prussia, the admirer of Voltaire. It is true that his conception of the nature of the State was without originality. Even his well-known definition of a prince as the '*premier domestique du peuple*' has its origins in antiquity. Nevertheless, Frederick was the first monarch not only to use these words, but also to put them into practice in several notable ways throughout his reign from 1740 to 1786.

One way was through his religious policy, which displayed a tolerance unusual at the time. This was due partly to his scepticism towards the dogmas of all Christian Churches as revealed in his own definition of his toleration – 'Everyone in this kingdom shall go to heaven in his own way'; but it was due also to the Prussian tradition of religious toleration which Frederick William, the Great Elector, had been led by circumstances to adopt a century earlier.[1] When Britain and Prussia concluded the Convention of Westminster in 1756, French and Austrian observers feared that a new day of confessional alliances, and so of religious wars, was at hand, but Frederick regarded such concepts as obsolete and assured the Marquis d'Argenson, the French Foreign Minister, that no one, not even women, would now become fanatical about Luther or Calvin. His attitude towards religion was entirely that of expediency. He claimed to be the Pope of

[1] Pp. 182–3, 186–7.

the Lutherans and was pleased that 'a Protestant prince is far more master in his own state than a Catholic one'; he gave asylum to French Jesuits to counteract the influence of the pro-Austrian Jesuits of Silesia; and he tolerated Jews for their economic activities. His general attitude he summarized in his *Testament* of 1768 – 'It matters not to the State what metaphysical dominate men's minds; enough that everyone behaves as a good citizen and patriot.' Frederick's religious policy did more to increase his prestige in the sight of his enlightened contemporaries than his military exploits ever did. 'Your majesty will do the human race an eternal service in extirpating this infamous superstition [Christianity]' Voltaire wrote to him.

The principles of the Enlightenment were also fully reflected in the improvement which Frederick fostered in the adminstration of justice. The way in which he expounded legal questions in his political testaments indicates that he recognized the right of his subjects to speedy trials and impartial verdicts in the law-courts. He relied much upon expert advice, especially that of the jurist, Samuel von Cocceji, who was given a free hand in the reform of legal procedure. Delays and abuses were remedied, and law became more uniform throughout Prussia and more impartial and equal for all classes, though cases concerning the State were placed beyond the capacity of the ordinary courts. The training of legal officials was improved, while Frederick, who distrusted lawyers, maintained a constant watch over the whole legal system. The completion of Cocceji's work came with the codification of Prussian law by the great Silesian jurist, Karl Gottlieb Svarez, in the *Corpus Juris Fridericanum*, which did not, however, come fully into operation until after Frederick's death.

Finally, the influence of enlightened thought is to be seen in Frederick's financial administration. Much of Prussia had long been administered directly by the King almost as though it were a private estate. Frederick acknowledged the principle that the King was only the administrator of the wealth of the country, not its owner, and had therefore no right to dispose of it arbitrarily. In contrast to his father's practice, he subordinated the interests of the royal budget to the common interest of the country; and he appointed French financial officials to organize the collection of taxes on French lines and retain a proportion of the proceeds as their payment.

At the same time, there were limits to Frederick's position as an

Enlightened Despot. Towards commerce, industry and the development of Prussian resources, he adopted a strongly mercantilist policy.[1] He failed to display any interest in education. And his views on the existing divisions of Prussian society were conservative. Its division into nobles, townsfolk and peasants suited his policies, and he wished to preserve it. He appointed the officers of his army solely from the nobility, whose numbers he also increased in administrative posts, thereby adding to their importance in much the same way as his later contemporary, Catherine II of Russia. In addition, early and very tentative efforts towards improving the position of the peasants were abandoned because of opposition from the landed nobility.[2] Yet Frederick's achievements as an Enlightened Despot are undeniable, despite such limitations, and may perhaps be said to represent the summit of eighteenth-century absolutism in this respect.

Joseph II of Austria

'Joseph II,' Dr. Padover has said, 'was the eighteenth century's epitome of political reform as Voltaire was of polemical literature.' He was certainly the most significant of the Enlightened Despots, being imbued with the beliefs of the Enlightenment and practising them on a revolutionary scale. Though he became Holy Roman Emperor in 1765, he was only co-regent with his mother, Maria Theresa, until her death in 1780. Maria Theresa and her Chancellor, Count von Haugwitz, made an important beginning with reforms affecting central administration, local government, finance, education and religion, so laying the foundations for many of Joseph's measures;[3] but he longed to be in power himself to carry out more drastic reforms to promote the happiness of the people, and he was to have only a brief decade of sole rule to do this.

In seeking to realize his programme, Joseph's methods were wholly those of monarchical absolutism. His position, he considered, gave him complete sovereign power which he was entitled to exercise arbitrarily in accordance with '*le bon sens et la réflexion*'. For him none of the traditional restraints upon policy, '*les thèses tirées du siècle passé et d'un usage de cent années*', had any vitality. He refused to recognize the separate constitutions of the several dominions within his rule and accord-

---

[1] P. 60.   [2] Pp. 49–50.   [3] Pp. 237 ff.

ingly would not submit to the traditional Hungarian coronation ceremonies. He considered that his possessions formed a German state. 'I am Emperor of the German *Reich*,' he said, 'therefore all other states which I possess are provinces of it.' He emphasized the subordination of the ruler to the State and his duty to administer properly the national wealth as belonging to the State and not to himself, but he was ready to give account of his rule only to God and would not permit his estates to share in his power.

His political principles combined with his own personal character to induce him to bring about a concentration of governmental power in his person and organize the administration of his territories as uniformly as possible without regard for their old frontiers and legislative assemblies, their varying laws and traditions or their peoples of many races and languages. The whole of his dominions, including even the Austrian Netherlands and Lombardy, were proclaimed to consist of a single state divided into thirteen districts, each of which was placed under the rule of a governor. Diets were to be called only on the Emperor's express orders, and municipal and county liberties were rescinded. German was to be the only official language. In 1787 a penal code and in 1788 a code of criminal procedure were promulgated, to be applied in every part of the Habsburg dominions. Class distinctions before the law were abolished and legal costs reduced; torture was prohibited and the death penalty reserved for fewer crimes; many religious courts were abolished and marriage became a civil contract. The revision of the system of courts included the establishment of appellate tribunals which were made subject to a final supreme court at Vienna. As against this, the number of crimes against the State were sharply increased, and there was little mitigation of the brutal treatment of prisoners.

Joseph's religious policy was truly enlightened, though it was not initiated by him. Measures of ecclesiastical reform had already been introduced during the reign of Maria Theresa, but Joseph went further. Faithful to the spirit of the Enlightenment, he granted religious toleration and insisted upon the supremacy of the State over the Roman Catholic Church. His Edict of Toleration of 1781 permitted the private exercise of their religion to Lutherans, Calvinists and Greek Orthodox and improved the condition of the Jews. Deists, however, were not tolerated, the punishment for professing Deism being two dozen strokes of the cane.

The Roman Catholic Church was deprived of its privileged position and placed under a control by the State which was more vigorous than that to which Napoleon submitted the French Church in 1801. It involved the rearrangement of the administrative organization of the Church so as to conform to the boundaries of the different provinces in the Habsburg dominions and a large increase in the number of parishes. It also involved far-reaching changes in ecclesiastical institutions, especially monasteries. He suppressed 606 out of 2,000 monasteries and convents and abolished the small diocesan seminaries, replacing them by great central institutions in Vienna, Budapest and other cities, staffed by professors known to be favourable to his own principles. Papal bulls were put under civil control, while episcopal dispensations were to replace papal faculties for marriages in cases of consanguinity.

For his religious policy, Joseph was hated by the Ultramontanes, ridiculed by the freethinkers and designated 'my brother the sacristan' by Frederick the Great of Prussia. It was also the most unpopular of his reforms among the people, and Joseph was amazed at 'the ridiculous enthusiasm, especially among women' shown in Vienna for Pope Pius VI when he made his visit in 1782 to the Emperor in a vain effort to check his ecclesiastical measures.[1] Nevertheless, Josephinism, as it came to be called, was to be of considerable importance in Austrian history, continuing in force until a concordat was signed with the Papacy in 1855.

The dissolution of the Jesuit schools, which was also part of Joseph's religious policy, was accompanied by an attempt to initiate a comprehensive system of secular education aimed at producing 'respectable moral citizens'. Provincial communities were compelled to establish elementary schools and make every effort to enforce compulsory attendance at them; and their better pupils were to go on to the grammar schools and universities. It was typical of Joseph's policy that all educational institutions were subjected to strict state control and typical of his character that he issued numerous decrees regulating their discipline and teaching. Girls were not to wear stays or use cosmetics at school; teachers were forbidden to discuss religious questions with

[1] P. 123.

their pupils; and in higher education the emphasis in the curriculum was to be upon the practical arts and the medical and juridical faculties. Mirabeau's comment upon such measures of control was that even the souls of the students were to be put into uniform.

Joseph's agrarian reforms have been called the 'most spectacular reform of the whole age of the Enlightenment'. He made important changes in the condition of the serfs through two series of edicts.[1] Between 1781 and 1785 he abolished their personal bondage and endowed them with legal personality, making it possible for them to marry, migrate, take employment and educate or apprentice their children without the approval of their manorial lords; the *Robot*, the labour rent due from the serfs to their lords, remained, but was regulated and could be commuted for rent in kind or money. Then he turned to the question of their rights over their land. Maria Theresa had already carried out a register of all peasant and noble land-holdings; Joseph now set out to improve the peasants' economic position. It has been estimated that, even after his first series of agrarian reforms, the average peasant paid 10 per cent of his income in tithe to the Church, 29 per cent in dues to his lord of the manor and 34 per cent in taxation, leaving him only 27 per cent for the support of himself and his family. Joseph abolished the tithe and introduced a single land-tax so as to leave the peasant about 70 per cent of his earnings. He also gave the peasants security of tenure, forbidding the nobility to take their land, and made it possible for them to purchase their holdings by easy payments. These measures were similarly accompanied by paternal regulations, which ordered the peasants to adopt improved farming methods, encouraged them to breed more horses and less cattle, and forbade them baking gingerbread as bad for the digestion !

As a whole, Joseph II's work must be regarded both as a remarkable achievement of the philosophy of the Enlightenment and a sign of the strength of the structure of the Habsburg government. He interfered with everything, great and small, important and unimportant. During the decade in which he was sole ruler, he issued over six thousand orders and decrees and made over eleven thousand laws. His policy, particularly his religious, political and agrarian reforms, met with increasing opposition from his subjects. Joseph was unable to overcome

---

[1] Pp. 246–7.

this opposition, partly because of his own impatient, stubborn character and inability to delegate authority, but still more because his Enlightened Despotism was hostile to the outlook and interests of important classes and peoples in his dominions.

Joseph could not appreciate any justification for resistance to his policy. His mental rigidity and dogmatism made him incapable of compromise; he has been called by a biographer 'the Ignatius Loyola of the idea of the absolute State'. It seemed to him foolish when the Estates of Brabant revolted in 1790 because he proposed to grant them what the French people were simultaneously and violently demanding as their rights. He could not understand that his attempt to make his dominions into '*une province égale dans toutes les dispositions et charges*' was contrary to tradition and incompatible with the inner structure of the Habsburg monarchy. Consequently the nobility defended their privileges, the peasantry maintained their superstitions, and Joseph's possessions were torn by a series of rebellions. The strongest resistance, which culminated in revolt, was in Hungary where the nobility, in claiming their traditional rights and social privileges, received much national support which had been roused by hostility to the abrogation of the ancient constitution and the recognition of German as the official language. Even in Bohemia, the Imperial nobility who had been established by the Habsburgs as an act of conquest after the Thirty Years' War, could represent their hostility to reform as an act of Czech patriotism.

Unrest in the Netherlands and Hungary and his unfortunate Turkish war compelled Joseph, shortly before his death, to revoke many of his great reforms, and others were abolished by his successor, Leopold II. Of his agrarian reforms, the *Robot* was fully restored almost at once, and the single land-tax was abolished, but the rest of his measures remained in force. Joseph died uncompromising to the end, but insisting that his failure was complete. Professor Temperley has described him as 'one of the most tragic failures of history'. This is so, judged by the disrupted condition of the Habsburg monarchy at his death and the contrast between his efforts and achievements, though on a longer view his reforms had lasting results.[1]

In 1831 Von Moltke, the Prussian field-marshal, said of Joseph: 'This Austrian emperor, to whom history still owes rehabilitation,

[1] Pp. 245–8.

attempted to achieve by means of the authority and power vested in him what the French Revolution only obtained after many years of blood and terror.' It was, in fact, largely because he attempted a single-handed revolution that he failed. His revolution lacked the support of a revolutionary class. Napoleon came to power in France after a great revolution and was able to base his regime on the support of the peasants. Joseph condemned the French Revolution, saying, 'I am a king by profession.' Here he revealed the self-contradiction of his policy. His aims could have been consummated only by a revolution which would at the same time have destroyed his dynasty.

The Failure of Enlightened Despotism

Nor did Enlightened Despotism achieve any more permanent successes in other countries under Habsburg rule. In the most important regions of Italy – Lombardy and Tuscany – it had the same characteristics and produced the same tensions. Thus in Tuscany, the Grand Duke Peter Leopold, the younger brother of Joseph II, ruled from 1765 to 1790, during which time he freed economic enterprise from guild control and internal dues, abolished torture and the death penalty and the confiscation of a criminal's property, restricted the judicial rights of the landlords and gradually abolished serfdom. Even though he was circumspect in his policy, by the time he left the Duchy to succeed Joseph on the Imperial throne reaction had set in against it among the Tuscan people, who resented it as a 'cold wind from the north'.

In both the kingdoms of the Iberian peninsula, Enlightened Despotism in the second half of the eighteenth century was marked by the effort of a ruler to bring the life of the country into line with contemporary economic progress and assert the supremacy of the State over the Church. Charles III, King of Spain from 1759 to 1788, imposed restrictions on ecclesiastical privilege and expelled the Jesuits, as well as attempting to develop natural resources and encourage trade.[1] In Portugal, the Marquis de Pombal, chief minister during the reign of Joseph (1750–77), founded trading companies to foster commerce and sought to stimulate agriculture, checked expenditure and corruption in the financial system, reduced the privileges of the nobility and, above all, expelled the Jesuits from the country.[2] The work of neither

[1] Pp. 116-7, 178-9.   [2] Pp. 115-6.

of these two men, however, produced permanent results, particularly in the economic sphere.

Enlightened Despotism, in fact, came into being in western Europe at the time when the strength of monarchical absolutisms was being weakened by the secularizing political theories of the *philosophes* of the Enlightenment. This inevitably meant that the confidence and creative energy of princes was really declining. It is a weakness in every absolutist system of government that it has to depend to a great extent upon the ability and character of the ruler and his ministers, but eighteenth-century Enlightened Despotism suffered from a particular flaw inherent in its condition. The Enlightened Despots tried to base their power upon the traditional patriarchical conception of government, to represent their system of rule as the fatherly tutelage of their subject-population; but this approach proved incapable of serious development because it was fundamentally inconsistent with the very essence of the Enlightenment.

For this reason, though Voltaire had admired Frederick the Great of Prussia, Enlightened Despotism was increasingly opposed by political thinkers (who were also coming to realize that its practical effect was to make the State more tyrannical and better able to raise taxes). Not that their defection in itself did much to weaken Enlightened Despotism, for they tended to content themselves with withdrawal from political affairs rather than taking the leadership in a struggle for political and spiritual liberty.

Perhaps a more serious weakness suffered by Enlightened Despotism at the end of the eighteenth century was that it was no longer based upon the facts of the situation, since by now Britain and the United States of America had developed very different and much admired systems of government. It was, therefore, no longer generally popular. The idea of the State as modelled upon the family was being replaced by the conception of it as a unit of business enterprise, rather like the highly-esteemed joint-stock company, and so the effective British and American legislatures seemed to represent a much better form of government. It would seem that in these circumstances, therefore, Enlightened Despotism was a waning of monarchical absolutism, a final phase in its history.

The postscript to this history was Napoleonism. The rational organization of Napoleon's regime offered an alternative to strong legislatures as a more up-to-date form of government. He partly counterfeited monarchical absolutism and partly anticipated modern administrative systems as well. His absolutism differed, not only from Enlightened Despotism, but also from the 'classical absolutism' of the whole period from the sixteenth to the late eighteenth centuries. The conditions determining the nature of his rule were the events of the French Revolution, which gave him the power to eliminate the surviving traditions of the *ancien régime*; absence of this power had been a grave weakness of the Enlightened Despots. Napoleon could be more thorough and ruthless, and his absolutism possessed a vital driving-force which had escaped previous dynasties.

Yet at the same time, Napoleon's revolutionary inheritance robbed him of the legitimacy, the appeal to tradition and the self-assured confidence of an established hereditary monarchy. His regime never enjoyed a sense of stability because he had ever to face the possibility of another political reversal in France. He attempted to meet this threat in several ways. He instituted the Legion of Honour and revived traditional titles to take the place of the old privileges and society of the *ancien régime* – 'men', he said, 'may be won over by toys'. He also initiated pseudo-parliamentary institutions designed to conceal his despotism. And he hoped to retain the favour of the people by a spectacular, successful foreign policy.[1]

Thus, although Napoleon adopted some of the characteristics of the traditional monarchical absolutism and resembled in some ways the Enlightened Despots, his rule was, in fact, neither of these. It was essentially a military dictatorship, brought about by war and reaction from revolution. When it went down in defeat, the next stage of liberal political development, that of middle-class democracy, was already beginning. The victorious allies in 1815 endeavoured to restore the 'legitimist' monarchies on the Continent. The kings crawled out again into the daylight like ants when a stone is lifted from their nest, as Shelley expressed it; but the old position could not be restored. Fresh revolutions and constitutions were to destroy this attempt at renewed absolutism on traditional lines. Enlightened Despotism had failed to save the old form of monarchy.

[1] Pp. 349 ff.

VI · CHURCH AND STATE

Hostility to Religion

THE eighteenth century, and especially the period from 1750 to 1815, was a time of recession and decline for Christianity in Europe. The vitality of the Reformation and Counter-Reformation was replaced by a marked decay and weakness in the life of Protestantism as well as Roman Catholicism. This made it difficult for both to meet the mounting threats to Christianity and ecclesiastical organization which, in several forms, were a feature of these years, when the intellectual currents of the Enlightenment, especially among the cultured classes of western Europe, produced growing atheism and anticlericalism.

Especially serious for the Roman Catholic Church were the divisions provoked by the question of Jansenism.[1] Originating in the Low Countries, it had gained considerable strength in France during the later seventeenth century. Royal persecution and papal condemnation did not secure the end of its influence. The resulting controversy made many doubt the nature of truth and led them to advocate religious toleration on the grounds that, since absolute truth had not been discovered, freedom to look for it should now be allowed. The influence of the Jansenists was not confined to France. They gained adherents and encouragement in other countries as well. In the words of Lord Acton, 'The suppression of the Jesuits was their work; they had a great part in the revolutionary reforms of such princes as Joseph II; and when the French Revolution broke out, they supported the confiscation of the property of the Church'.

To the activities of such anti-papal forces as the Jansenists were added in several European countries the determination of their rulers to secure the subservience of the clergy to themselves and their readiness to use ecclesiastical institutions for their own purposes. This tendency became more marked in the latter part of the century with the rise of Enlightened Despots, who all dealt with the Church in a masterful fashion; and the advent of the French Revolution and Napoleon brought still further difficult passages in the relations of Church and State.[2]

[1] Pp. 111-3.   [2] Pp. 113-5, 122-3, 354-7.

There was one branch of the ecclesiastical system of the Roman Catholic Church which monarchs and revolutionaries, atheists and reformers, Jansenists and Gallicans together with others inimical to the Church were united in attacking. This was the Society of Jesus. The reasons for such widespread hostility to it were several, some of them being bound up with the extraordinary success which it had obtained since its foundation by Ignatius Loyola in 1540. The founder's aims for the Society were to support the Papacy and the faith against heresy and do missionary work among the heathen. It did not take the Jesuits long to become firmly established in Europe as pastors, confessors and educators and to found successful missions in America, Asia and Africa. The Society's power, loyalty to the Papacy and international position did not commend it, however, to eighteenth-century rulers wishing to strengthen their own autocratic powers. In addition, since the sixteenth century Jesuits had been abhorred by many as teaching that the end justified the means, that the Pope had the right to excommunicate and depose sovereigns, and, further, were suspected of tolerating regicide, while in the seventeenth century Pascal had attacked them in effective and memorable terms for their lax casuistry. Now both Jansenists and thinkers of the Enlightenment disliked their constant concern for strict orthodoxy in doctrine. Finally, the wealth of the Society brought it unpopularity; in particular, the commercial enterprises upon which its members had embarked in some parts of the world attracted the resentment of competing commercial companies.

The result was a mounting wave of hostility against the Jesuits in the middle years of the eighteenth century. Within a period of twenty years, the Society was attacked by nearly every Roman Catholic ruler in Europe, and finally its suppression by the Papacy was secured in 1773.[1]

France, Monarchy, Republic and Empire

Before the Revolution, the French Church claimed the service of perhaps some 130,000 persons and on the whole was very wealthy through its possessions accumulated from the past and not taken from it by any Reformation. It owned much agricultural land, though this was not as widespread in the country as was once supposed. Its holdings were few in the west and,

[1] Pp. 121-2.

roughly speaking, became still fewer as one moved towards the south, where in some districts they only formed four per cent of the land.   Northwards, it was about 30 per cent in Picardy and as much as 60 per cent around Cambrai, but this was exceptional, and for the whole country the average may not have been much more than six per cent.   The Church had a further source of income in the possession of urban properties and also in drawing feudal dues and tithes.   The incidence of the latter as a burden of the peasantry varied, but on the average amounted to a twelfth.   All cereals were subject to such dues; the liability of other products, including even wine, depended upon the district. Sometimes the tithe was paid to the *curé* himself, but in other parishes it had been appropriated by a bishop, cathedral or monastery.   It is difficult to determine exactly the Church's total income.   Modern estimates range from about 60 million livres to nearly three times as much.

In addition, the Church enjoyed considerable immunities from taxation.   It was exempt, for instance, from the *taille*, though often, like the nobility, it paid indirectly, since the rents of its tenant-farmers were reduced on land liable to the tax.   The *clergé de France,* as distinct from the *clergé étranger* of recently-annexed provinces such as Flanders, Alsace and Lorraine, possessed the right to hold regular assemblies to decide the size of the *don gratuit,* the contribution they made to the treasury. These Assemblies of the Clergy usually met every five years, but sometimes more often in times of national emergency.   It has been reckoned that from 1715 to 1788 the average amount of a *don gratuit* paid by the *clergé de France* was not much more than three million livres, which was not a great proportion of their income, though it cost them more because they raised loans to make these payments and burdened themselves with an increasing heavy debt at high rates of interest.

There is no doubt that the clergy did not pay a fair share of taxation.   The free-thinking *philosophes* were quick to criticize this, but attempts by eighteenth-century French governments to curtail their privileges were persistently resisted by the clergy and the *dévot* party at court.   Machault's taxation proposals of 1749 were largely defeated by the refusal of the clergy to make any contribution in direct taxation.[1]   And the very last Assembly of the Clergy in 1788 secured from the government yet one more of

[1] P. 294.

the many confirmations of its privileges and voted less than a
quarter of the *don gratuit* requested by the treasury. So the
French clergy shared in the sustained attachment to exemption
from taxation which was one of the aspects of the aristocratic
revolt that destroyed the old monarchy.

These clerical privileges were all the more resented because of
the wealth and high social position of some of the clergy, who
were, however, only a small minority. Under the *ancien régime,*
the clergy, like the nobility, were regarded as forming a privileged
order of society which marked them off from the numerous Third
Estate or *roturiers.* By the eighteenth century this was, however, hardly more than a theoretical conception. Talleyrand
wrote with inside knowledge of the clerical profession in his
memoirs, '*L'Etat, quoique divisé en trois ordres, ne l'était réele-
ment qu'en deux classes: la class noble et la class plébienne; une
partie du clergé appartenait à la première et l'autre partie à la
seconde de ces deux classes*'. The French Church in the
eighteenth century reflected, as in every age, contemporary
society, its highest positions being increasingly filled from the great
noble families and the rest from the middle-classes and peasantry.

The growing monopoly of the highest ecclesiastical posts by the
sons of the French nobility was a continuation of a development
already apparent in the seventeenth century. At the outbreak of
the Revolution, only one of the 130 French bishops was a com-
moner, and most of the lucrative abbacies, priories and canonries
were held by the nobility. Talleyrand, who belonged to an old
aristocratic family and was Bishop of Autun when the Revolution began, wrote in his memoirs, '*Dans l'Eglise et l'épiscopat les
dignités les plus lucratives étaient devenues le partage presque
exclusif de la classe noble*'.

Many of the greater dioceses brought their occupant an annual
income of 100,000 livres or more, while in some it was twice or
even four times as much. Such wealthy bishops were commonly
non-resident and lived as worldly peers, hunting and enjoying the
court life at Paris or Versailles. Many had been ordained without a vocation because they were the younger sons of the nobility
or, like Talleyrand himself, unfit for a military career. Such
men brought discredit upon the episcopate, the changed character of which was emphasized by the absence among its members of
scholars and preachers like Fénélon, Bossuet and other great
figures of the previous century.

There was also a pious, conscientious minority among the bishops, though its members frequently offended contemporary ideas of tolerance by persecuting Jansenists and free-thinkers. In any event, they usually occupied the poorer, distant dioceses, which might have an income of 7,000 livres. They were not well known and hardly influenced the character of the Church.

Nor did all worldly bishops devote themselves to empty pleasures. A writer of the times divided the episcopate into '*administrateurs des sacrements*' and '*administrateurs des provinces*'. Typical of the latter was the Archbishop of Narbonne, who assisted agriculture and commerce and constructed roads and canals in his diocese. Others, such as Talleyrand himself and Cardinal Leoménie de Brienne, attained important posts in the State.

Such ambitious bishops were commonly on terms of close friendship with *philosophes* and themselves expressed rationalist views. When Brienne's supporters urged his appointment to the archbishopric of Paris, Louis XVI demurred, '*Non, l'archevêque de Paris doit au moins croire en Dieu*'. Similarly enlightened in outlook was Cardinal de Rohan, who was the main figure in the scandalous affair of the Queen's necklace in 1785.[1] Indeed, the prevalence of religious indifference, political ambition and unrestrained intrigue among so many French bishops at this time was yet another example of the way in which they succumbed to the outlook of the class and circumstances to which they themselves belonged.

After a period of reform during the religious revival of the seventeenth century, French monasticism gradually declined. The abbots and abbesses were commonly of aristocratic rank, and the headships of several hundred houses were held *in commendam* by noble laymen, who drew a third of the income of the monasteries of which they were the titular rulers though living at court. Many of the younger sons and daughters of noble families also found places as monks and nuns and enjoyed in comfortable living the wealth possessed by most religious orders. Monastic morale was low. The religious were aware of the growing hostility of the age to their vocation, especially from the *philosophes*, for whom the cloister symbolized the darkened superstitions of the past. Declining confidence in the monastic ideal was shown in several ways. Numbers were declining, canonical services

[1] P. 303.

were neglected, and some monks whitewashed over the religious frescoes in their churches and replaced wooden images by multi-coloured marble. So far was conventual discipline sometimes relaxed that visitors entered monasteries freely, monks went out at will, and mixed entertainments were held in refectories.

The French government intervened in 1766 by establishing a *Commission des réguliers*, which took drastic measures. It fixed the minimum age for taking vows at twenty-one for men and eighteen for women (since boys and girls had commonly been sent to religious houses by their families) and eased the return to secular life of those who had lost their vocation. It also closed within four years some 1,500 moribund or practically deserted n.onasteries and convents. These measures, however, far from restoring monastic standards, merely increased the wish of the indifferent for greater latitude.

The lower secular clergy, the *curés* and *vicaires*, were generally popular and in the countryside often lived the same life of poverty as the peasantry. In 1686 stipends were fixed at 300 livres for *curés* and 150 livres for *vicaires;* and despite the steep rise in prices these were raised in 1768 only to 500 and 200 livres. Moreover, the *décimes*, levied by the Assemblies of the Clergy to pay the *don gratuit*, fell most heavily on the lower clergy. The differences of origin, outlook and manner of life between the higher and lower clergy were deep and were embittered by episcopal abuses which oppressed the parish priests. The French historian, Pierre Sagnac, has claimed that the antagonism within the Church intensified in the eighteenth century virtually to the point of civil war. The lower clergy were ready to take the offensive against their detested leaders. The bishops silenced critics among them with *lettres de cachet*, but the resentments remained and had their effect in 1789, when the lower clergy soon threw in their lot with the Third Estate.[1] This desertion by them of the cause of the privileged orders was a consequence of the attitude of generations of noble-born bishops towards their inferiors.

Such religious fervour as still existed in the eighteenth-century French Church was generally attracted towards Jansenism. This movement took its name from Cornelius Jansen (1585–1638), Bishop of Ypres, who wrote the *Augustinius*, a long commentary on St. Augustine's theology, emphasizing the corruption

[1] P. 313.

and weakness of human nature and the irresistible character of
the grace bestowed by God upon the elect. His ideas were
publicized in France through the preaching of an intimate
friend, the Abbé de Saint-Cyran, Jean Duvergier de Hauranne
(1581–1643), and under his influence the Cistercian convent of
Port Royal des Champs became the centre of Jansenism, together with the *Solitaires*, the community of learned and pious
men associated with it. The Jansenists early drew upon themselves the hostility of the Jesuits, who considered their views supported predestination and other Protestant beliefs; and so began
the struggle of seventy years culminating in the destruction of
Port Royal by the government in 1710 and the condemnation
of Jansenism by the Papacy through the Bull *Unigenitus* in
1713.

This, however, was not the end of the matter. Jansenism itself
deteriorated as a religious movement. Persecution produced
convulsionaires and other extravagant fanatics among its members. In 1732 cures, prophesyings, conversions and scenes of
hysterical frenzy occurred at the tomb in Paris of a young Jansenist deacon until the government closed the cemetery, which produced from a wit the famous epigram:

> *De par le roi, défense à Dieu*
> *De faire miracle en ce lieu.*

Jansenism had now, in fact, become merged as an effective
force with the long-standing Gallican movement, which insisted
upon the existence of special *libertés de l'église gallicane* in opposition to papal prerogatives. Religious affairs were increasingly
tangled with the intricate struggle for power between the court
and the Parlement of Paris, most of whose members were Gallican in attitude and Jansenist in sympathy and found the ecclesiastical situation an excellent opportunity for intervention in politics
and opposition to the crown.[1]

The result was a further struggle which lasted for fifty years.
The Parlement of Paris did not register the Bull *Unigenitus* until
1720 and then with reservations in favour of the Gallican liberties. During the Regency period, the Jansenists received considerable official support, and several bishops were sympathetic;
but Cardinal Fleury wished to minimize the trouble they caused
the government, and when their leader, Cardinal Noailles, Arch-

[1] P. 155.

bishop of Paris, submitted shortly before his death in 1729, the episcopate became the allies of the court and the Jesuits.   At the same time, the lower clergy became largely Jansenist, since for them it meant the defence of their rights against the rule of their superiors.   The efforts of the bishops to enforce discipline on their clergy and to deny the sacraments to suspected Jansenists brought renewed resistance by the *parlements*.   Louis XV showed his fatal lack of resolution in dealing with this problem as with others; when he exiled the Parlement of Paris for its defiance, he soon repented and allowed it to return to the capital.   His vacillations prevented the adoption of any firm official policy. When France suffered the humiliations of the Seven Years' War, he ordered the Bull to be recognized as part of the law of the Church, but when this provoked renewed turmoil, he once again gave way.   The final compromise was the absurd *loi de silence* of 1754, decreeing that no one should publicly mention the Bull, and this was naturally not obeyed.

By now the Jansenist controversy, even in its attenuated eighteenth-century form, was expiring of inanition; but the *parlementaires*, reinforced by the *philosophes*, were as bitterly hostile as ever to the Jesuits.   The Society had already been ejected from Portugal when the successful attack upon it was mounted in France.   The pretext for this arose through the bankruptcy of the Society's commercial enterprise in Martinique when the British navy ruined the trade of the French West Indies during the Seven Years' War.   By foolishly appealing to the Parlement of Paris against their creditors, the Jesuits played into the hands of their opponents.   In 1762 the Parlement condemned their moral and political teachings, confiscated their property and closed their schools.   The King, as well as the Queen and the Dauphin, supported the Jesuits, but otherwise they had few friends.   The universities and the secular clergy regarded them as rivals; some of the royal ministers were hostile to them, and so was Madame de Pompadour.   Choiseul, the most powerful minister, was not prepared to risk a domestic conflict over them.   Two years later Louis XV was forced to issue an edict ending the existence of the Society in France.   It was the greatest blow struck at the Church before 1789.

The first events of the Revolution brought no direct attack upon Christianity or the Church, but the Constituent Assembly, to meet pressing financial needs, confiscated ecclesiastical property and substituted a state grant to the Church in 1789.[1] The next year the monasteries were dissolved. In 1790 also the Civil Constitution of the Clergy was imposed on the Church. This measure did not make any change in doctrine or ritual, but the power of the Pope was abolished and the clergy were to swear allegiance to the Constitution; the number and boundaries of the bishoprics were made identical with the eighty-three new departments in France; all ecclesiastical offices became elective and stipends were fixed and paid by the government.

These innovations aroused more opposition than the Voltairian *parlementaires* in the Assembly had expected. When the Constitutional Oath was imposed on the clergy, only seven of the 130 diocesan bishops and about a third of the lower clergy took it. This minority was organized into the Constitutional Church in 1791 under the protection of the Assembly. The others, the *réfractaires*, were immediately deprived of their offices, but many bishops and others among them ignored the new laws and continued to exercise their functions. The majority of the faithful sided with them; and in 1791 Pius VI in the Brief *Caritas* condemned the Constitution formally as heretical, sacrilegious and schismatical.

The triumphs of the Jacobins, which were followed by a campaign of *déchristianisation*, brought persecution to the Constitutional Church itself, and many of its priests apostatized. Churches were closed and services restricted. Notre Dame in Paris became a Temple of Reason. A new republican calendar was drawn up.[2] In the spring of 1794 it was said that mass was still celebrated in only 150 French parishes. After Robespierre's fall in that year, a certain amount of toleration was granted, though the government now refused to pay the Constitutional clergy and virtually brought about a separation of Church and State. Under the Directory from 1795 to 1799, those clergy who would swear hatred of royalty and anarchy were not otherwise molested.

The Concordat of 1801 between Napoleon and Pope Pius VII recognized Roman Catholicism as the religion of the great majority of French citizens. All existing bishops, both those who had been canonically invested (and had mostly emigrated since the Revolution) and those who had been elected in the Constitutional Church, were to tender their resignations to the Pope, so

---

[1] P. 319.   [2] P. 329.

that hostile royalists and discredited Constitutionalists were eliminated. The dioceses were further reduced in number. Henceforward there were to be ten metropolitans and fifty suffragan bishops nominated by the government for appointment by the Papacy. Alienated ecclesiastical property was not to be restored, but the government agreed to maintain the bishops and the parish priests. The religious orders were tolerated, and some monasteries were re-established. These terms, however, were considerably modified through the publication by Napoleon in 1802 of the Organic Articles, which imposed governmental control over papal decrees and officials, provincial councils and synods, seminaries and parish boundaries, and even compelled those preparing for ordination to accept the declaration of Gallican liberties formulated in 1682.

Nevertheless, the result of the Concordat was to promote within the French Church the growth of Ultramontanism or support for papal authority over the whole Church. Gallicanism was compromised by the reproach of having allied itself with the liberal and anti-Christian movements of the Revolution, and Napoleon's brutal treatment of two popes deprived it of popular support for the future. Moreover, the Concordat gave the Papacy greater authority over the French Church than it had possessed in the eighteenth century. Papal authority was required for the resignation of the existing bishops, the fresh distribution of sees and the investiture of all new bishops. The failure to restore their former lands to the bishops made them more dependent on the Papacy, while the parochial clergy were now brought under full ecclesiastical control. When, therefore, at the Bourbon restoration a strong body of opinion in France was pro-papal in its sympathies, the new centralization of the French Church was to make possible that growth of Ultramontanism which was to be so marked in the nineteenth century.

Portugal and Spain: the Jesuits

The first country from which the Jesuits were expelled was Portugal, where they came into conflict with the sustained effort to increase the power of the crown by the Marquis de Pombal, who was chief minister during the reign of the inactive Joseph (1750–77). Pombal has been called by Professor Gershoy 'the most spectacular and dynamic ruler of the eighteenth century', which is very great praise considering the other claimants for this title. Behind his policy was a determination to rescue the country from its backwardness and bring it into line with the development of the age. He believed that the monarchy was the only possible means of reform and that he must strike severely at the Church, as also at the nobility, to remove opposition to his actions.

The Jesuits were the richest and strongest community in the Portuguese Church and had long exercised a powerful influence upon education and governmental policy. When Spain agreed by treaty in 1751 to cede to Portugal most of Paraguay, where the Jesuits had their most famous mission, they organized resistance to the change; and provocatively they ascribed the terrible Lisbon earthquake of 1755 to divine retribution for the sins of the government. Pombal's answer was to expel the Jesuits in 1757 from the court, where they had acted as royal confessors; and two years later, he issued a decree condemning the Society as 'corrupt, deplorably alienated from its divine institution, rebellious and perfidious', imprisoned two hundred of its members and expelled the remaining six thousand to the Papal States. When Pope Clement XIII retaliated by expelling all Portuguese from his territory, Pombal confiscated Jesuit property in Portugal.

Pombal's overthrow of the Jesuits enabled him to create grammar schools and a secular College of Nobles and to introduce scientific studies into the universities. He also allowed considerable freedom of the press and between 1751 and 1769 deprived the Inquisition of most of its authority. Moreover, he reduced the influence of the Papacy so much that for the rest of the century the Portuguese Church was practically immune from its jurisdiction.

Much the same motives were behind the ecclesiastical policy of Charles III in Spain.[1] He was himself sincerely religious, but determined to increase the crown's power and initiate a policy of reform, and he believed that the Church was a major obstacle to his policy. The Spanish Church, which possessed 160 bishoprics and at least 400,000 clergy, was larger than the French Church, though Spain's population and wealth were smaller. It was still the centre of the people's life. There was a parish church in the smallest village, thousands of religious associations promoted devotion and charity throughout the country, and magnificent cathedrals and abbeys were still built. It was also, however, a

[1] P. 179.

reactionary Church; the Inquisition in particular had long restricted intellectual freedom and isolated Spain from outside influences. Charles set out to diminish its influence. He claimed the right to appoint to ecclesiastical posts and prohibited the publication of papal bulls without his permission; and from 1767 he progressively reduced the powers of the Spanish Inquisition.

Such a policy inevitably led to an attack on the Jesuits, especially as Charles III's chief minister, the Count de Aranda, was their enemy. Riots in Madrid, Barcelona and other cities in 1766 were officially attributed to the Society's intrigues, and the next year, after careful preparation, though without warning even the Pope, Charles ordered the expulsion of its members from Spain and all her possessions. He gave no reasons for his action and forbade public comment – 'I impose silence regarding this matter on all my vassals, it not being incumbent on them to judge or interpret the commands of their sovereign'; but most of the Spanish bishops supported the drastic step. Some 10,000 Jesuits from Spain and the Indies were shipped to the Papal States, but the Pope refused to accept them. After months on shipboard in the Mediterranean, they found shelter in Corsica, then possessed by Genoa, but upon French acquisition of the island in 1768, their further expulsion forced the Pope to admit them to his territory.

As in Portugal, the ecclesiastical policy of the government did much to reduce the age-long hold of the Church over Spanish society, especially in the field of education. The 120 colleges and seminaries of the Jesuits and twenty-four universities were now reformed by the crown. Textbooks and curricula were revised in accordance with the new ideas of the time, the experimental method in science and medicine was introduced, and the study of the writings of the *philosophes* was encouraged. These developments met with opposition, and their progress was slow, but the beliefs of the Enlightenment had at least been introduced into educated circles in the Iberian peninsula.

The example of the Bourbons in France and Spain was followed by the smaller Bourbon governments in Italy. The reforming minister of the Kingdom of the Two Sicilies, the Marquis di Tanucci, reduced the number of ecclesiastics, diminished their privileges and expelled the Jesuits. When the Duke of Parma, Ferdinand VI, demanded the same power over the Church as the Spanish crown possessed, Pope Clement XIII refused and in

1768 threatened to excommunicate the Duke, who defied him by expelling the Jesuits.   All the Bourbon states united in demanding that the Pope should withdraw, and when he refused, France occupied Avignon, and the Two Sicilies seized Benevento and Pontecorvo, papal possessions in Naples.   This was followed, not only by the expulsion of the Jesuits by Modena, Venice, Bavaria and even the Order of St. John in Malta, but also by a Bourbon demand for the abolition of the Society, the attainment of which was only delayed by the Pope's death in 1769.

Germany: Protestantism and Febronianism

In Germany, the political theory of Protestantism was strongly influenced by the Lutheran conception of princely rule by divine right and the part it had played in the German Reformation. This applied equally to states which had adopted the religion of either of the two great Protestant confessions – Lutheranism and Calvinism.   In every Protestant state in Germany, the prince was able to control the Church in his territory through his possession of the administrative authority of a *summus episcopus*.   German Protestantism was, therefore, a collection of separate Churches, each in spiritual communion with the others of its own confession, but each also a *Landeskirch*, governed by the State and coterminous with its territorial boundaries. Churches divided and managed in this way were not in a position to enjoy much independence from the State, and the age of Enlightened Despotism saw Protestant princes exercising a rigid control over the Churches.

This was especially true of Frederick the Great of Prussia, though he did not accept the traditional Lutheran conception to justify his own position as ruler.   His policy of religious toleration was accompanied by an insistence upon his supreme ecclesiastical powers over both Protestantism and Roman Catholicism in his dominions.   He thus reserved to himself the right to appoint all Roman Catholic ecclesiastics under his rule – from parish priests to bishops.

There was, indeed, a similar trend towards state Churches in Germany under the control of the great prince-bishops who united civil and ecclesiastical functions in their rule.   Such bishops were especially forward in insisting that they received their powers directly from Christ and not from the Pope.   Their outlook found expression in the movement known as Febronianism, which may be regarded in some respects as the German equivalent of Gallicanism. In 1742 the three Archbishop-Electors (of Mainz, Cologne and Treves) asked Nikolaus von Hontheim, Bishop suffragan of Treves, to investigate their existing grievances against the Papacy. He embodied the results of his studies in a work, *De statu ecclesiae et legitima potestate Romani pontificis*, published in 1763 under the pseudonym of Justinius Febronius. Its conclusions supported the Gallican appeal to Christian antiquity. It acknowledged the Pope as head of the Church and supervisor of ecclesiastical administration with the right to pronounce judgement on matters of faith and morals, though this might be subject to a decision of the Universal Church or a General Council; but it urged the annulment of all papal claims to temporal power which had become accepted in the Middle Ages and especially those based upon the False Decretals, a collection of documents claiming early authority for papal supremacy, which had been disproved by Renaissance historians. It held that the authority of the Church in every country should be exercised by national or provincial synods of bishops, who would merely accord the Pope a primacy among themselves.

The book was put on the Index in 1764, but its influence was considerable. It suited both the outlook of the age and the growing spirit of national independence in many European countries. It had a large circulation and was translated into German, French, Italian and Portuguese. The Febronians gave valuable support to the measures by which Joseph II of Austria secured control of the Church in his dominions.[1] In Germany the book was supported by the Archbishop-Electors, who in 1785 joined with the Archbishop of Salzburg in demanding that no papal bull should be published in a German diocese without the permission of its bishop, that appeals to Rome should be limited and that papal nuncios should no longer be appointed to German states. They failed, however, to obtain support from other German bishops, and the outbreak of the French Revolution submerged their plans for constitutional reform in the Church.

The Papacy and the Jesuits

Frederick the Great of Prussia in his confidential *Political Testament* of 1752 dismissed the Pope as 'an old neglected idol in his niche. . . . His thunderbolts are extinguished. His policy is

[1] P. 100.

known.   Instead of laying people under interdict and deposing
sovereigns as of yore, he is satisfied if no one deposes him and lets
him say mass peacefully in St. Peter's'.   When Frederick wrote
these words, the occupant of the Papacy, Benedict XIV (1740–
58), was of unusual intellectual distinction among eighteenth-
century popes.   He was a historical scholar and an exemplary
administrator, who wished to strengthen the Papacy's moral influence; but he himself was well aware that the weakness of his
position in contemporary Europe made a conciliatory attitude
towards secular rulers inevitable.   In his own description of his
policy he said, 'I prefer to let the thunders of the Vatican rest.
Christ would not call down fire from heaven . . . Let us take care
not to mistake passion for zeal, for this mistake has caused the
greatest evils to religion'.

By the eighteenth century, the political influence of the
Papacy, which had been declining since the early fourteenth
century, had almost vanished.   The situation of the Papal States
in the centre of the still divided Italian peninsula had preserved
the sovereign independence of the popes, but little deference was
paid to their claims by national rulers.   From 1648 onwards,
every territorial settlement in Europe was made without consulting the Papacy.   The papal legate was excluded from the
negotiations which preceded the Treaty of Utrecht, and the
traditional claims of the popes to suzerainty over Sicily were
ignored when the future of the island was decided.   Moreover,
even Roman Catholic monarchs treated the international position
of the Papacy with practical contempt.   The consistent anti-
papal policy of the Bourbon powers – France, Spain, Parma and
Naples – marked this period which culminated with the violent
actions of Napoleon.

In addition, the position of the popes within the Church was
not definitely established.   The Council of Trent in the sixteenth
century had increased papal ecclesiastical authority, but only
Italian theologians were Ultramontane in their views.   The ideas
of Gallicanism and Febronianism found widespread acceptance,
not least among bishops who wished to assert their authority.
Many bishops, indeed, such as those in France, were able to make
themselves in practice almost independent of the Papacy, and the
aristocratic character of the episcopate in some countries encouraged this.   'The Pope has his rights,' said the Bishop of
Lombez near the end of the century, 'and we have ours.'   This

viewpoint was increasingly held during this period; and it is not surprising, therefore, that secular rulers should have considered themselves justified in circumscribing papal authority within their realms.

The position of the popes was further weakened by their financial difficulties. The Reformation and Counter-Reformation had considerably reduced papal income from a number of sources, and past popes had raised large loans for the purpose of erecting buildings in Rome and endowing their families. The popes of the eighteenth century had to struggle with an inheritance of debt which crippled their administrative and ecclesiastical activities. Their efforts at financial reform were not ineffective, but on the outbreak of the French Revolution the Papacy was still close to bankruptcy.

While the popes of this period were without the vices of their Renaissance predecessors, they did not belong to the great reforming popes of the Counter-Reformation. The excesses of nepotism and favouritism had been curbed, and they generally ruled through cardinal-secretaries. They were worthy, pious, respectable men, all members of the Italian aristocracy, but mostly without ability, zeal or moral force. The austere but ineffective Clement XI (1700–21) was not untypical of the popes of the period, and the well-known remark made about him by Victor Amadeus of Savoy – 'He would always have been esteemed worthy of the Papacy if he had never obtained it' – might equally have been applied to others. At the same time, the decadence of the Church, the political ambitions of national rulers and the secularizing outlook of the age faced them with situations which would have severely tried the resources of men of greater capacities than themselves.

This was shown during the determined and prolonged pressure applied to two successive popes, Clement XIII (1758–69) and Clement XIV (1769–74), chiefly by the Bourbons, to dissolve the Society of Jesus. Clement XIII did his best to defend its members. When Pombal expelled them, all relations between Portugal and the Papacy were severed. To a demand by the Parlement of Paris for drastic alterations in the constitutions of the Society, he refused with the famous words, 'Sint ut sunt aut non sint', and upon the expulsion of its members from France he issued the Bull Apostolicum pascendi munus, which praised the Society and its work. He could not prevent, however, Jesuit expulsions from other countries; and, finally, in 1769 the three ambassadors of France, Spain and Naples demanded the complete and irrevocable dissolution of the Society and the secularization of its members throughout the world.   This is believed to have hastened Clement's death from apoplexy a few days later.

In the ensuing conclave, the Bourbon courts did their best to prevent the election of a *Zelante* (a pro-Jesuit); they made it known to the cardinals that they would recognize only a pope ready to dissolve the Society.   A Franciscan friar, Cardinal Ganganelli, became Pope as Clement XIV, but it is uncertain whether he gave such a pledge.   With some skill he temporized, proposing alternatives and attempting compromises and concessions to placate the Bourbon rulers, but they remained adamant.   The Spanish ambassadors threatened schism and even an invasion of the Papal States if the Society were not suppressed. Clement, unable to delay any longer, issued in 1773 the Brief *Dominus ac Redemptor* – 'For the sake of peace, and because the Society can no longer attain the aims for which it was founded, and on secret grounds which we enclose in our hearts, We suppress the said Society'; but the dogmatic and moral teaching with which the Society had so largely identified itself was not condemned.

The papal suppression was carried out in predominantly Roman Catholic countries, but the Society was not destroyed. In Austria, Switzerland and many of the German states, its members were allowed to perform some of their duties as seculars and in some places were allowed still to live in communities. Frederick the Great of Prussia wished them to continue their educational activities, which they did with tacit papal approval. Catherine the Great of Russia also valued them so much as educators, especially in her newly-acquired Polish territories, that she would not allow publication in her empire of the papal brief of suppression.   The Society, therefore, was able to remain in full existence in Russia.   There it enrolled both old and new members from other countries, elected a new General and even circulated a forged papal brief, dated 1774, expressing the Pope's joy at its continued existence under Catherine's rule.   In 1780 a novitiate was opened in White Russia, and in 1801 Pope Pius VII formally recognized the Society in Russia.   Meanwhile, the Society had gradually been managing to re-establish itself in other countries, and in 1814 Pius VII reconstituted it by the Bull *Sollicitudo omnium ecclesiarum.*

Though Avignon and Benevento and Pontecorvo were returned to the Papacy, the dissolution of the Society of Jesus failed to arrest the attacks of rulers on the Church or to save popes from further humiliations. Clement XIV's successor, Pius VI (1775–99), was faced with the situation created by Josephinism[1] in Austria. He took the exceptional course of going himself to Vienna in 1782. Joseph received him magnificently, but his mission was a fiasco, Josephinism continued until the Emperor's death. The French Revolution brought him still greater troubles. It was followed not only by the persecution of the French Church and the seizure of Avignon, but also the French military triumphs in Italy under Napoleon in 1796 and 1797. Napoleon occupied the Papal States, where in 1798 a republic was proclaimed and the Pope deposed as a temporal ruler. Pius was taken prisoner and, eighty years of age and ill, was removed first to Siena and Florence and then, after several other moves, across the Alps to the citadel of Valence, on the Rhone, where he died.

The next Pope, Pius VII (1800–23), suffered almost as much during the years of the contest between Napoleon and Britain. The ecclesiastical settlement in France, established by the Concordat of 1801, survived the appearance of the Organic Articles, and Pius agreed to come to Paris for Napoleon's coronation as Emperor of the French.[2] It was territorial disputes which brought matters to a head. In 1808 a French army entered Rome, and the next year the Papal States were incorporated into the French Empire. When Pius promptly excommunicated the 'authors of attacks upon the Holy See', he was arrested and taken to Savona, on the Riviera. In 1811 he had to agree that French bishops might be instituted by the metropolitans without papal cognizance; the next year he was moved to Fontainebleau, where he was subjected to further demands. The issue was terminated by the disasters which overtook Napoleon, who signed his abdication while Pius returned to Rome in triumph.[3]

The events of the eighteenth century were followed not only by a general religious revival, but also by new developments in the relations of Church and State. The monarchs who regained their crowns after the defeat of Napoleon believed that the

[1] Pp. 99–100.   [2] P. 356.   [3] P. 381.

Church, which had shared with them the hostility of the Revolution, could be a valuable ally to enable them to maintain themselves in power. The papal envoy was received with respect at the Congress of Vienna, the Papal States were reconstituted, and the Church was accorded privileges in their kingdoms by the newly-restored rulers as part of their desire to 'wrap the tendrils of tradition about their shaken thrones'. Indirectly the Church was able to exercise much influence, but national sovereignty, whether monarchical or republican, was not prepared to allow it any revival of its political power.

Within the Roman Catholic Church, the aftermath was a considerable increase in the ecclesiastical authority of the Pope. His loss of political power was offset by the determination of theologians and administrators to enhance his prerogatives over the Church. This movement was to attain its climax when the Vatican Council of 1870 defined the primacy of the Pope over all other bishops and his infallibility in pronouncing upon matters of faith and morals, so dealing a final disclaimer to the ideas of Gallicanism and Josephinism.

VII · WAR AND DIPLOMACY

The Balance of Power

THE English term, the 'balance of power', together with the French equivalent, *équilibre européen*, came into current use early in the eighteenth century. This also was an idea which owed much in its manner of expression to the teaching of Newtonian physics.[1] The idea of balance was believed to be inherent throughout the operation of the universe – 'The attraction of the glass is balanced . . . by the contrary attraction of the liquor'. So in diplomacy it came to be held that such an adjustment of power among sovereign states as ensured that no single state was in a position to threaten the independence of the rest would best maintain international equilibrium. The *London Gazette* in 1701 spoke of the 'glorious design of re-establishing a just balance of power in Europe', while forty years later Sir Robert Walpole used the term to describe his foreign policy in the House of Commons.

The notion of the balance of power, however, is older than this period which brought about its general acceptance in Europe. It may be traced back to fifteenth-century Italy and was always in the background of the thought of Machiavelli, who asserted, for instance, that the Prince 'should make himself the leader and defender of his less powerful neighbours, and endeavour to weaken the stronger ones, and take care that they are not invaded by some foreigner not less powerful than himself'. The emergence of this notion here may be ascribed to the conditions of the time in Italy. The peninsula was so divided that no single ruler could hope to impose his will on the rest; the most he could hope to achieve was the preservation of his independence by deliberately maintaining the prevailing political equilibrium of the states.

The adoption of this notion in eighteenth-century Europe largely occurred because there developed on a larger scale very much the same conditions as had prevailed in Italy. For the greater part of this period European statesmen regarded the preservation of a balance of power as the best policy for their own

[1] Pp. 19–20.

countries. In 1717 the British envoy in Paris, Lord Stair, told the Regent that the foreign policy of Lord Stanhope (1673–1721) was founded on the principle of a balance of forces, which aimed at making Austria as near as possible in strength to France and ensuring that neither state grew more powerful and influential than the other; he frankly added that should France try to make herself stronger than the Emperor, she would be deserted by her allies. And in Spain, Alberoni, throughout his period of office, wished to revoke the settlement established by the Treaty of Utrecht as contrary to the balance of power and inimical to Spain and Italy.[1]

The adoption of the idea of the balance of power in European diplomacy was accompanied by a limitation in the nature of warfare which lasted until the Revolutionary and Napoleonic Wars at the end of this period. Until then, no war in Europe, except those bringing about the partition of Poland, was fought to the point at which the power of one side to resist had been completely destroyed. The peace treaties at the end of these wars were negotiated and not dictated by the victors to the vanquished under conditions of unconditional surrender. Modern writers have sometimes praised the limited diplomatic aims and restricted warfare of the eighteenth century and suggested that the states and statesmen of this time had attained a commendable degree of restraint, prudence and humanity in war and peace. It may be that the absolute rulers of this period were likely to be able to limit their objectives and make concessions to their opponents more easily than the modern representatives of demagogic governments; but fundamentally the conditions of diplomacy and warfare were related to the scientific and material progress of the time.

The well-known definition of war by Karl von Clausewitz (1780–1831) has won general acceptance – 'War is not merely a political act, but also a political instrument, a continuation of political relations, a carrying out of the same by other means'. The effectiveness of war, however, depends finally upon successful tactics, and these in their turn are closely related to the weapons available to the combatants. Quick, decisive victory can only be gained by a material and moral preponderance such as no eighteenth-century state could command. The diplomatic balance of power was, therefore, bound up with the prevailing

[1] Pp. 171–2.

military balance of power. Armaments developed only slowly during the century. Armies and navies were limited in size, expensive to maintain and difficult to expand. The loss of a regiment or a ship could not easily be made good. This meant that wars were fought as economically as possible, and every effort was made to preserve forces intact; the emphasis was upon defence and not attack; sieges prevailed over battles and single combats between ships over general naval engagements.

It meant also that war was generally only the last resort as a political instrument, to be used when other means of securing a balance of power seemed to have failed. Royal marriages were still common means of effecting the transference of territories. The three main conflicts of the first half of the century – the Wars of Spanish, Polish and Austrian Succession – were dynastic wars, fought through the failure of matrimonial arrangements to solve the European problems involved.

Moreover, when wars broke out, they were lengthy but not intensive. They were not necessarily humane as evidenced by Marlborough's fiercely contested victory at Malplaquet in 1709, the brutal treatment of the Loyalists by the victorious colonists after the American War of Independence and the terrible losses through neglect suffered by the British expeditions to the West Indies; but they were generally fought for limited objectives. Wars of position were more common than wars of movement. Small successive advantages were the most that commanders could hope to achieve. Complete defeat of the enemy was beyond the means of any state. The aim was a war of attrition, coupled with the seizure of fortresses and other key-points by land or sea, to place one side in a stronger position to bargain at the peace conference. Wars so often ended in political compromise because of the prevailing military deadlock in Europe. The War of the Spanish Succession, the War of the Austrian Succession, the Seven Years' War (in Europe) and the American War of Independence finished without a definite victory because one side considered it undesirable or impossible to attempt such a conclusion. The idea of a balance of power, therefore, so attractive in many ways to the thought of the age of Enlightenment, rested strongly upon military considerations.

Military Warfare

For the greater part of the eighteenth century, an evident feature of military warfare was the part assigned to the infantry. Its supreme importance in battle was unchallenged. Cavalry might sometimes deliver a charge, which succeeded as shock tactics, but horsemen alone could not hold off counter-attacks or retain what they had won. It is true that during the middle years of the century the use of artillery increased, in proportion to other arms, more rapidly than at any other time from the sixteenth to the twentieth centuries; but until the French improvements later in the century, it continued to be regarded mainly as a siege-weapon. Cannon still fired balls of iron, lead or stone. The largest were forty-eight pounders, some twelve feet long, weighing 8,000 pounds and requiring twenty-four pounds of powder each time one was fired; it was commonly accepted that they could not be fired accurately. Field guns were lighter, but still difficult to handle, and few armies had more than a dozen, each of which might fire half-a-dozen rounds during an engagement.

The importance of the infantry dated from the last years of the previous century when the flintlock musket and bayonet replaced in one weapon the older firelock and pike. Technical improvements further increased the infantryman's effectiveness. At the beginning of the eighteenth century, the average well-trained soldier could fire about a round a minute. By the middle years, the use of cartridges and iron ramrods had enabled this rate of fire to be trebled in the most efficient European armies.

Throughout the century, however, all infantry continued to use the smooth-bore musket, which was usually a short, thick weapon, charged with 5 ounces of iron or $7\frac{1}{2}$ of lead and an equal amount of powder. One reason for the success of the colonists in the American War of Independence was that they had the 'Kentucky rifle', which had four times the range of 'Brown Bess', the Redcoat's musket. Rifling had, indeed, been devised in the sixteenth century, but rifled firearms were harder to load than smooth-bores and thought to be unsuitable for infantrymen. Some cavalry were armed with rifled carbines from the time of Frederick the Great, but rifles were still confined mainly to European sportsmen and American pioneers. Despite the lesson of the American War of Independence, military caution did not permit the replacement of muskets by rifles until some time after the Napoleonic War.

Tactics in the eighteenth century, therefore, were dominated by the use of the musket and bayonet. Though the musket was only effective at close quarters, it could be decisive in battle if fired in unison and concentration. To do this, the infantrymen had to stand closely in line, but as the weapon could not be loaded quickly, the normal order of battle was three or four rows of musketeers, covered on the flanks by cavalry. When one row of men was firing, the others were reloading, and so continuous, massed volleys could be maintained. To get troops into such an order of battle was a slow and complicated process. The rows had to be formed at a safe distance from the enemy, and then the army had to march in rigid formation until the enemy were well within musket-shot, a manoeuvre which required well-drilled troops.

Equal discipline was required when fighting began because of the low standards of markmanship. British military manuals barely allude to aiming, and there was a saying in the army that it 'took a man's weight in bullets to kill one'. Even by the year of Waterloo a musketeer standing at the foot of Ludgate Hill could not have been sure that his weapon would enable him to hit the dome of St. Paul's. Such inaccurate shooting meant that advancing troops had to get very close to the enemy, and that both attackers and defenders had to reserve their fire until they could deliver their first concentrated volley with effect. That is why Lord Charles Hay was determined that his First Foot Guards should not fire first at Fontenoy in 1745.

Infantrymen capable of marching and firing under these conditions were only produced as the result of lengthy, intensive training and drilling. Such men were valuable and not to be lightly squandered in battle. Prudent generals were wary, therefore, of taking unnecessary risks. They did not wish to divide their forces or face an encounter with an army larger than their own. Austrian generals in particular were inclined to believe that it was better to preserve their own troops than to destroy those of the enemy. An army might manoeuvre, therefore, with the deliberate intention of avoiding the enemy and yet at the same time win a victory by compelling him to retreat or cut off his communications or leave the protection of his fortresses. Such tactics meant that defence predominated over offence in the eighteenth century, and except for the campaigns of Marshal de Saxe and Frederick the Great, battles were infrequent and campaigns unproductive.

Physical conditions also told against the decisiveness of military operations. The absence of metalled roads afforded armies little mobility, which was further reduced in the much-fought-over Low Countries, where invading armies had to transport heavy siege-guns to breach the fortresses which blocked the main routes by land and water. Moreover, military operations in Europe were generally confined to little more than half of the calendar year, since it was almost impossible to conduct a winter campaign. Frost-bound or swamped roads prevented the movement of guns or supplies. As soon as bad weather came, both sides sought the security of their winter quarters and could renew their organization and restore their equipment for the next season's campaign.

Again, the nature of eighteenth-century warfare was strongly shaped by the social composition and military structure of the participating armies. National armies raised by conscription began with the *levée en masse* of revolutionary France. Until then, as Professor Dorn has said, 'such mass participation presupposed an entirely different social system no less than political objectives far different from those which the War of the Austrian Succession could provide'. Conscription was made impossible by the existence of privileged social classes and by the demands made on the labouring classes through mercantilist attempts to raise the level of agricultural and industrial production. Rulers wanted their armies to correspond to the social system of their state and not weaken its productive elements. Accordingly the officers came from the nobility and the soldiers from the unemployed, beggars, vagabonds and even criminals.

The requirements of even the limited wars of the eighteenth century, however, made moves towards compulsory service necessary. Prussia, Russia and France early attempted a rudimentary form of conscription, and so did Austria and Spain after the Seven Years' War; but in all these countries men were levied only from certain peasant and artizan classes. It was calculated that in Prussia at the end of the century 1,700,000 of a total population of some 6,700,000 were entirely exempt from military service. As in previous centuries, no country, except Russia, could dispense with foreign troops, who formed between a quarter and a third of all armies. Swiss and Irish volunteers formed a high proportion of such troops, as in the previous century, but many were now also obtained by treaties with the smaller German states.

In 1740 the approximate numbers of men in the forces of the chief belligerents were – France 190,000, Austria 108,000, Spain 67,000, Prussia 80,000, Russia 130,000, Bavaria 40,000, Saxony 34,000, Holland 30,000, Hanover 20,000 and Britain 18,000. Though countries naturally increased their military strength in wartime, most soldiers enlisted for long terms of service. Whether they were natives or mercenaries, they did not fight for a cause, but to make a living. Eighteenth-century armies, therefore, were without the unifying force of national homogeneity and the fervour of patriotism. All armies lost men by desertion. After the Seven Years' War it was said that the Austrian army had lost over 62,000 men in this way, the French army about 70,000 and the Prussian army about 80,000.

These circumstances were largely responsible for the strict discipline and severe punishments which characterized armies of the time. There was thought to be no other way of preventing desertion and maintaining obedience among regiments composed of social outcasts and hired foreigners. Often soldiers were brutalized by constant flogging, which was the common penalty for many offences against order and discipline. Major-General William Howe, who commanded the British troops in Massachusetts at the outbreak of the American War of Independence, was considered a humane officer and was popular with his men, but his orderly book lists case after case in which offenders tried by court martial were sentenced to be publicly flogged with 800 or 1000 lashes of the cat-o'-nine-tails. Nor were camp-followers exempt. In the summer of 1745, when the Duke of Cumberland's forces were stationed north of Brussels, three disorderly women each received 200 lashes of the cat and were drummed from guard to guard out of the camp.

It was also mainly in the interests of military discipline that devastation, atrocities and plundering by troops were discouraged. Frederick the Great said in his *Political Testament* that when he was engaged in war the civilian population should not be aware that a state of hostilities existed. This was not due to humanitarianism, but because it was feared that if soldiers were allowed to loot or forage in the countryside, they would disappear among the civilian population. Consequently, all military powers organized a system of state magazines to be used to supply their armies in war and regulate the price of grain in peace. On the eve of a campaign, ample stores were collected at frontier-points for provisioning armies in the field. Two or three days' march from the magazines, ovens were built and flour was brought by mule-trains to be baked into loaves for the troops. Each man could carry rations for four to six days, but the magazines were still the main source of supply, and generally an army could not march safely for more than five days from a supply base or over fifteen miles from a navigable river. Consequently, the mobility of armies was further limited. The failure of Frederick the Great to capture Olmütz in 1758 was an illustration of the way in which the vulnerability of an army's baggage-train prevented it from operating far from its magazines in a hostile country.[1]

At the opening of the eighteenth century, the French army of Louis XIV was generally agreed to be the best in Europe, and it was to excel itself still more under Napoleon's command at the end of the century; but Louis XV's army was mediocre. It was deficient in competent generals, a military spirit among its officers and unity and discipline in its regiments. It acquitted itself creditably during the War of the Austrian Succession under the brilliant leadership of Maurice de Saxe, but by the Seven Years' War it could never, despite numerical superiority, defeat decisively the armies of three small German states – Hanover, Hesse and Brunswick – supported by a small number of British and Prussian troops.

This decline was partly due to its inadequate financial resources, its neglect by Fleury and later the King, its respect for obsolete past traditions and its control by the court and bureaucratic *gens de plume*, who paralysed initiative and checked innovation; but, above all, the French army suffered through the deficiencies of its social composition, which made it weakest where the Prussian army was strongest – among its officers. Commissions were obtained by birth and money and not by merit, a system which brought about the appointment of many officers with little ability or military training. So strong was the dependence of many French noblemen on military pay or pensions for their livelihood that the number of officers increased astonishingly.

'*J'ai des officiers dont je n'ai pas besoin*,' said Louis XV, '*mais je sais qu'ils ont grand besoin de moi.*'

The Prussian army had an average of one officer to thirty-seven men, but the French army had one to fifteen, while in modern armies the proportion is usually one to fifty. Commissions were now created for the nobility instead of nobles for commissions. Many senior officers lived luxuriously at Versailles or Paris and rarely joined their troops. Regiments had no confidence in commanders whom they only saw in camp or battle. When they were with the army, their numerous staff, servants and baggage further reduced its mobility in the field. Sometimes, when commanding officers were especially numerous, they acted in rotation, each one exercising authority '*de jour*'. Yet only a small proportion of officers were ever engaged on active service. In 1775, when the total strength of the army was 170,000, there were 60,000 officers, whose pay and pensions accounted for over half the military budget, and only a sixth were with their regiments.

Even worse, the purchase of military commissions introduced into the army with particular bitterness the social struggle between the nobility and the bourgeoisie which was becoming acute throughout the nation. The outburst of speculation under Law did not reduce the price of commissions, though the army increased in size, and because the impoverished lower nobility could not afford to buy them, the government, despite aristocratic protests, made them available to the sons of wealthy merchants. In 1750, when almost a third of the infantry officers were of middle-class origin, a royal edict created a new military nobility by allowing a *roturier* to be ennobled simply by the purchase of a commission. Some 275 officers were ennobled in this way up to 1789.

Though few in number, these bourgeois intruders often held high rank, and the hostility of the older noble officers towards them was unconcealed; often jealousy and quarrels between them destroyed unity, subordination and discipline. Repeated legislative attempts to abolish the distinction between noble and bourgeois officers failed, and the social cleavage persisted. Moreover, the addition of these bourgeois officers to the French army made no difference to its efficiency, since money was no better substitute than noble blood for ability and experience. The Seven Years' War showed only too clearly that both noble and bourgeois officers possessed little professional competence.

The rising standard of living in France made recruits for the army particularly hard to obtain. The captains, who were responsible for enrolling their company, found it increasingly difficult to find sufficient recruits from the poorer classes even in peacetime. Accordingly, the French army always relied considerably upon foreign mercenaries. It had over 150,000 of them in the middle of the century and still more than 40,000 on the eve of the Revolution; but even such numbers, especially in wartime when the army was on the Rhine or Weser, did not meet its deficiencies, and so a provincial militia was organized, for which peasants were conscripted by lot from each parish. First intended for garrison duty, it was soon used abroad, and in the War of the Austrian Succession militiamen were retained permanently in the regular army. Yet even more serious than the shortage of numbers was the poor fighting quality of many French troops. This was largely due to their lack of training through the ignorance and incompetence of their officers, and was made worse by an absence of uniform drill and manoeuvring regulations, which could create confusion on the field.

While these circumstances were contributing to the defeats suffered on the European battlefields by France, the wealthiest and most populated state of the continent, her army, despite its greater numbers, was being outmatched by the Prussian army, which substantially owed its superiority to Frederick the Great. In building up and perfecting Prussia's military strength, Frederick was following the Hohenzollern tradition laid down during the reign of Frederick William, the Great Elector (1640–88), and this was, indeed, a policy imposed upon the country's rulers by its geographical circumstances. Its territories were scattered, its economic resources weak, and in 1740 it was probably twelfth in population among the states of Europe. A national entity like France could suffer military defeat without eclipse as a great power, but any reverse was critical for Prussia because she was simply an artificial state and not a nation. Prussian rulers before Frederick had, therefore, seen the need for a policy which gave their state a large, efficient standing army, and they had concentrated all their resources upon its execution with surprising singleness of purpose. Frederick consummated their efforts. As Professor Dorn has stated, 'It is no exaggeration to say that it was not Prussia that made the army, but the army that made modern Prussia.'

Frederick's achievements were possible because he inherited from his predecessors, not only a considerable standing army, but also the corresponding political machinery which made him both an autocrat in the state and supreme commander of his army. Such a concentration of political and military power enabled him to unite all policy under his direction. He enjoyed a position comparable to that of Alexander the Great or Napoleon, and it accounted in a large measure for his success in organizing his army and directing it in wartime.

The Prussian army was founded by the Great Elector, who before the end of the Thirty Years' War decided that the interests of his dynasty demanded an army under his control. A *miles perpetuus*, a standing army, was first set up in 1644 and retained, at reduced strength, in peacetime. Frederick William I (1713–40) inherited an army of 40,000 from his father, Frederick I. By his death he had doubled it. France and Austria, with ten times greater populations, had armies which were in no way comparatively greater;[1] but Frederick the Great was determined to make his army still larger, and in eleven years he raised its peacetime numbers to 135,000 with a capacity of expansion up to 200,000.

Frederick was regarded by Napoleon as the greatest soldier of the past; he certainly was, after the passing of Maurice de Saxe, the greatest soldier of his time. His military achievements were the utmost possible in Europe until the French Revolution brought in national, conscript armies and aggressive, mobile, combative strategy. His strategic methods remained those of his age, confined within the limits of the war of position with its complex manoeuvres and small gains; but his tactics were original. He sought to break through the defensive technique of the century by aggressiveness, discipline and surprise. When opposed by a force occupying a fixed position which was strong against frontal attack, his plan was to assail swiftly one flank with part of his troops, while employing the rest to give the impression that he intended to attack elsewhere, and so break through the enemy line before reinforcements could be brought up. Of his ten great battles in the Seven Years' War, he won six by the use of this oblique battle-order, his victory at Leuthen in 1757 being his tactical masterpiece. He lost three by unwise departures from this plan, while at Zorndorf in 1760 the tenacity of the Russian

[1] P. 131.

troops and their formation in a square discounted his tactics and qualified his victory.

Frederick's tactics demanded strict discipline throughout his army. The Prussian infantry continued to be drilled with the thoroughness initiated by his father, the 'Sergeant-King', which gave its movements in battle a mobility and uniformity unknown in other armies. A similar discipline was maintained among the officers, drawn almost exclusively from the territorial nobility, the Junkers, whose chief duty was held to be military service. Frederick William had emphasized this in 1722 by founding the *Cadettenhaus* in Berlin, where young officers were trained as a prelude to years of military service, constant drill and exacting reviews. Negligent officers sometimes committed suicide before a review rather than face Frederick the Great, who rarely forgot failure in battle and punished it by years of cancellation of leave and lack of promotion. Such rigorous duties had their compensations for the Prussian nobility. Their financial status was enhanced, for they were not a wealthy class, and they were recognized as the first estate of the realm; they had supreme power over their troops, whom they could flog or even execute at will. Their social uniformity, privileged position and extensive authority combined to make them a unique military class in Europe.

Recruiting presented Frederick with a constant problem in his determination to provide Prussia with an increasingly large army. In his *Political Testament* of 1752 he insisted that Prussia could not sustain a national army recruited from her people alone. Even after the conquest of Silesia made her population 4,500,000, Prussia was a thinly-populated country; her industries and agriculture both suffered from insufficient labour. Yet in 1761 the army in Prussia amounted to $4\frac{2}{5}$ per cent of the population compared with $1\frac{1}{5}$ per cent in France. This would have been impossible without the employment of a high proportion of foreign troops; but Frederick could not afford to pay the price for troops that the Bourbons and Habsburgs did. Consequently, Prussian recruiting officers raided weaker German states, depriving villages of their whole male population, and in wartime deserters were accepted and even prisoners of war pressed into service; there were entire battalions of Austrian deserters in the Prussian army. These were supplemented by native troops, raised by a system of conscription which excepted 'useful hardworking people' in

town and country.   In 1742 a third of the Prussian army was
native, in 1750 a half and in 1753 two-thirds, these figures reflec-
ting Frederick's growing difficulties in obtaining foreign recruits.

An army, which contained even later in the century a large
foreign element, was difficult to maintain intact.   There was more
desertion from the Prussian army than from any other in Europe.
To prevent this was a serious problem in peace, but much worse
in war. A long campaign demoralized the army, and it did not
always recover while in winter quarters; at the end of the Seven
Years' War its cohesion had almost disappeared.   Such a situation led Frederick to adopt very severe military discipline.[1]   It
also seriously affected his methods of fighting.   Fear of desertion
made him seek to avoid rapid marches, night attacks, hand-to-
hand fighting and the thorough pursuit of an enemy.   Despite
his army's superiority over other contemporary armies, its composition prevented him dealing such devastating blows with it as
Napoleon could with the French armies of the Revolution.

The tactics of Frederick the Great and the organization of the
Prussian army exercised a dominant influence in Europe between
the Treaty of Paris in 1763 and the defeat of the Prussians at
Valmy in 1792, while the Prussian army itself used them until
it met disaster in 1806.   Meanwhile, remarkable improvements
had been taking place in the French army.   These had begun
with the military changes introduced by Choiseul, who established
a school for the training of officers with scholarships for the sons
of poor noblemen, brought armaments factories under royal control and reorganized the artillery into a corps of six regiments;[2]
and his successors introduced other similar reforms.   Such
measures made it possible for a remarkable group of French
military reformers to achieve results.   Among them was Jean-
Baptiste de Gribeauval (1715-89), an officer in the army of
Louis XVI, who resumed, after a century and a half, the work of
Gustavus Adolphus in developing artillery.   He invented in the
1770's light, mobile field-guns – a twelve-pounder gun drawn by
only six horses and an eight-pounder by only four, instead of the
eighteen and twelve horses previously needed.   France now
gained a supremacy in artillery which she kept until 1870.   The
new importance thus given to artillery enabled armies to be
broken up into smaller units; a move was made towards divisional
organization, and war began to lose its inflexibility.   Another

[1] P. 194.   [2] Pp. 297-8.

officer, Hippolyte de Guibert (1743–90), saw the implications of this for fighting and wrote books in which he urged the importance of speed and offensive action whenever possible.

These technical reforms and the new spirit which accompanied them had already made the French army, despite all its imperfections, probably the best in Europe by 1789, but a much greater change was produced by the country's political convulsions. It retained its technical standards, for most of the artillerymen and engineers of the royal army continued to serve under the tricolor, but it lost its incompetent officers, and promotion by ability became the rule. Moreover, circumstances combined to give the French army a new emphasis on mobility and attack. The events of the Revolution initially disrupted the army and caused it to suffer defeats in 1792, but the artillery halted the Prussians at Valmy, and after the deposition of the King in August 1792, the country had a government determined to secure survival at any cost. The *levée en masse* produced thousands of raw recruits, who could not be drilled in the precise movements demanded by the line of battle, so the republicans developed a column charge with fixed bayonets to overwhelm the enemy's musketeers. Such attacks brought heavy losses, but men were plentiful and held cheap; bravery in action gained promotion, while fear of the guillotine forced commanders to be energetic. In addition, since the government could not afford to provide its armies with baggage-trains, the soldiers had to live off the countryside through which they moved and so could only feed themselves by continually advancing. The capability of the French army to advance was further increased by the permanent organization of the larger numbers brought in by conscripts into smaller units. The war ministry established them in divisions of between ten and twenty thousand men, and under the Directory there appeared the army corps composed of two or three divisions with its own reserves of artillery and cavalry. Such developments gave the French army a mobility denied to its opponents.

By 1794, when the great crisis had ended, France had a unique army and from his first campaign in Italy Napoleon made few changes in it.[1] He brought no innovations in armaments or methods of fighting; he used what he had received from the military reformers and the revolutionary politicians. The Grand Army gained repeated victories under him mainly because, until

[1] P. 340.

1809 at least, it was undoubtedly the most formidable fighting force in Europe. Not only was it ahead of other armies in its organization, its armament and its offensive spirit, but also it had very many excellent officers from its marshals downwards. These qualities did much to instil in the Grand Army its pride and self-confidence which enabled it to perform feats so bewildering to its enemies.

To this army Napoleon contributed the devotion which his personality and career inspired. He once estimated his own worth on the battlefield at 40,000 men. Moreover, the army was solely under his command; he enjoyed a political and military supremacy which none of his opponents possessed. As a soldier, his greatness lay in his strategy. He attacked as rapidly as possible and marched his troops with amazing speed. 'They little know,' he once said, 'how quickly I can make 200,000 men pirouette into Germany.' In 1805, when an Austrian army waited in Bavaria for the Russians to arrive in southern Germany, Napoleon marched the Grand Army from Boulogne to the Danube, covering 600 miles in eight weeks, and took the Austrians in the rear and forced them to surrender. He also persisted in attack until the enemy was completely defeated. This quality was revealed in his exploitation of the victories of Jena and Auerstädt, which brought him into Berlin as a conqueror. It was also revealed in 1809 when, after sustaining the shock of the offensive of the Archduke Charles, he threw the Austrians back towards Vienna; Napoleon himself regarded this as his best campaign.[1]

Napoleon's warfare reversed the eighteenth-century reluctance to suffer casualties. 'What do the lives of half a million men matter to a man like me?' he once remarked. He lost more men in his marches than in all his battles, but at the height of his career his army could endure losses as the price of victory. France and her vassal states afforded him great reserves of manpower. From 1809, however, his army inexorably lost its advantage. France exhausted and dissipated her strength while her enemies learnt Napoleon's methods and created new armies. After 1812, when Napoleon had lost possibly more than 400,000 men in Russia and had another 290,000 immobilized in Spain, the tide of military power turned against him.[2] His army was defeated because it could not, in the end, increase its numbers, and French

[1] P. 375.   [2] P. 380.

industry could not equip it sufficiently to maintain its preponderance against the rest of Europe.

Naval Warfare

The seventeenth century had seen the specialization of the fighting ship and the creation of navies themselves.   Before about the middle of that century no European state had a navy in the modern sense – a fleet of ships maintained and organized by a government solely for warfare.   Thus, in 1587 England had twenty-five royal warships, and half the ships which fought the Armada were hired or commandeered merchantmen, while the forays into the New World were made by privately-owned ships seeking gain and supplemented by a royal ship or two in return for a share in the profits of these ventures.

The change from such a confused and haphazard situation was initiated by the demands of the three Anglo-Dutch wars in the second half of the seventeenth century.   The large-scale actions of these wars made increasing demands upon the firepower of a fleet and showed that no merchant ship, however large, could any longer hold its place in the line of battle.   By the end of the seventeenth century, the leading European states had to rely upon a regular, organized naval force instead of a nucleus of warships to be supplemented when needed by hastily-secured merchantmen.   From this development there was no return in the eighteenth century, for the scale of naval-gunnery in sea fights continued to grow.   In 1794, for instance, the *Queen Charlotte* on the Glorious First of June fired 130 broadsides with no less than 60 tons of shot.

Nevertheless, in the eighteenth century national navies were closely and inevitably related to merchant fleets and seaborne trade.   The leading European sea-powers at the opening of the century were Britain, France, Spain and Holland because they were countries with a large overseas commerce.   Navies rested upon mercantile marines, which supplied the wealth for constructing ships, the sailors to man them and transports to carry troops.   Large merchant ships and warships were still built in much the same way, needed similar repairs and followed the same rules of navigation; the same shipyards and docks could, therefore, serve both.

As long as each colonial power endeavoured to enforce the principle of a national monopoly in commerce within its empire, trade relied on naval protection, and naval strength depended on trade. Spain, despite her large empire, suffered a permanent disadvantage because she was unable to develop commercial shipping and manufactures to sustain her overseas trade. This was reflected in Spanish naval weakness. During the War of the Spanish Succession, the Spanish navy hardly fought at sea and by its close had practically ceased to exist. In the following two decades there was a rapid revival under such able ministers as Alberoni and Patiño.[1] By 1735 the Spanish navy had 34 line-of-battle ships of 60 to 114 guns. Its losses in the great wars in the middle of the century were not heavy, and another Spanish statesman, Ensenada, promoted another increase in naval strength. By 1774 Spain had 58 ships of the line, and by 1789 she had 72; but she never ranked among the most formidable naval powers during this period.

Holland was still a great naval power at the end of the seventeenth century, but she declined rapidly in the early years of this period. The reason for her weakness was not the same as that of Spain. Her geographical position compelled her to attempt the task of both naval and military defence. She had to maintain an army of 30,000 men to garrison the barrier fortresses in the Austrian Netherlands, which the Treaty of Utrecht had granted her, to defend her territory against the ever-present fear of invasion. At a time when the Dutch were losing their leading position in the commerce of Europe, this imposed a burden which made it impossible for them to maintain a great navy as well. During the War of the Spanish Succession they had seldom been able to keep more than 50 warships of all sizes at sea simultaneously through their concentration on military operations, and they never recovered their naval strength. By 1745 Lord Chesterfield wrote that Holland had no more than a courtesy title to the name of a maritime power.

France had also had to sacrifice naval to military needs during Louis XIV's later wars, so that in 1719 she possessed only 49 ships of all rates. Twenty years later, however, largely through the efforts of Maurepas, she had 50 ships of the line. The war of 1744–48 against Britain brought her quite heavy losses, but by 1754 she had 57 ships of the line and 24 frigates. Her losses in the Seven Years' War were much more disastrous. By its end she had only 35 ships of the line and 10 frigates, mostly in bad

[1] Pp. 171, 174.

condition.   Choiseul set out to rebuild French naval strength yet
again;[1] and the efforts continued after his fall from office.   By
1770 she had 64 ships of the line and 45 frigates, and ten years
later 86 ships of the line and 78 frigates.   She had been able to
challenge British naval power in the American War of Independence, but the financial strain had been serious, and on the eve of
the Revolutionary War less than a third of her ships could put
immediately to sea.

Britain maintained the largest fleet in the world throughout the
eighteenth century.   Her island position relieved her of the need
to have a strong army as well.   The end of the War of the League
of Augsburg in 1697 left her the greatest European naval power,
a position she never lost.   In 1721 she possessed 124 ships of the
line and 105 smaller vessels, about a quarter of them having been
built since 1714.   Her naval strength was about the same when
war with Spain began in 1739, though, through lack of maintenance under Walpole, only 35 ships of the line were ready for
immediate use.   By 1762, however, her numbers were 141 ships
of the line and 224 smaller vessels, and by 1783 these had become
174 and 294, easily the most powerful navy yet seen.   When war
broke out with revolutionary France, her ships of the line had
been reduced to 141 in number, but 115 of them were ready for
action, as were most of her 157 frigates.

In 1715 Britain had about a third of the world's warships,
France and Holland together about another third, and Spain,
Portugal, Denmark, Sweden and Russia the remaining third.
Succeeding years saw, besides the Dutch decline, a marked growth
of Russian naval strength.   Through the efforts of Peter the
Great, Russia, by his death in 1725 had become one of the leading European naval powers.   Under his successors, naval policy
was neglected, but it was revived during the reign of Catherine the
Great with such effect that by the last decade of the century
Russia had 37 ships of the line in her Baltic fleet and 22 in her
Black Sea fleet.   Her naval strength was thus about equal to
that of Spain and not very far short of that of France.

Nevertheless, the main contestants for the possession of a maritime empire and commercial and naval supremacy were still
Britain and France.   In 1715 these two powers alone possessed
the three factors necessary for an attempt to secure naval
supremacy – an effective battle-fleet, a flourishing mercantile

[1] P. 297.

marine to provide seamen in wartime and overseas bases for the conduct of military operations. Despite Britain's gains through the Treaty of Utrecht, the world-wide Anglo-French struggle for commercial and colonial supremacy – in the Mediterranean and the Levant, India and the African coastal slave-trading stations, North America and the West Indies – was not yet over, and after a period of peaceful rivalry, it broke out again in 1744 into a renewed universal struggle.

Even before the beginning of hostilities, Britain was already the superior naval power in almost every way. The British navy, despite neglect by Walpole, was more than twice that of France. Half the world's trade was carried in British merchant ships, and this, as even Adam Smith admitted when he criticized the mono-polistic Navigation Acts, provided the navy with an incomparable source of trained sailors. None of the efforts of her statesmen enabled France to secure naval parity with Britain. Out of her limited financial resources she had to maintain the largest army in Europe for her commitments on the Continent; and in war-time it was common French policy to concentrate on privateering, the *guerre de course,* so that the British navy remained intact, and despite the depredations of privateering, her commerce was strong and active, while French commerce was almost com-pletely swept from the seas. And during the Seven Years' War Britain developed to perfection the strategy of maritime war by using her naval power for the conquest of colonial territories by combined operations from overseas bases.

One undoubted superiority possessed by the French and Spanish navies over the British was in naval architecture. British men-of-war, ship for ship, were not as good in several ways as the best produced in the French and Spanish dockyards. They were not as heavily armed, for though Britain built a greater number of ships, she did not produce greater-gunned ships. On the outbreak of the Revolutionary War, while the largest British ships, those of the *Victory* class, were nominally of 100 guns, France had eight sail of the line which mounted from 110 to 120 guns, the largest of which, the *Vengeur* (later *L'Impérial*) of 3,000 tons, could mount 130 guns and was incontrovertibly described as '*le plus fort et le plus beau vaisseau qui eut jamais été cónstruit dans aucun pays du monde*'. Nor were British ships as effective in gun-fire. A British ship of 70 guns could not engage a French or Spanish ship of its own class, while a French ship of 52 guns could hold its own against a British ship of 72 guns. Finally, British ships were not as seaworthy or as stiff in a breeze. A light squall might make British ships heel enough to prevent the opening of the ports of the lower deck, where the heaviest guns were mounted, so that the enemy's 32- and 40-pounders could only be fought with 12- and 18-pounders.

Indeed, the best ships in a British fleet were often French men-of-war which had been captured. The British government paid handsome sums to captains who took enemy ships. Captured ships were also studied by British shipbuilders. Thus, when the British captured at the end of the century the French frigate, *La Pomone*, reputed to be the fastest warship afloat, they used her lines in the construction of new vessels.

Nevertheless, the British pioneered the two inventions which were responsible for the greatest increase of efficiency in eighteenth-century warships. One was copper-sheathing, generally adopted by the 1770's to reduce fouling of ships' bottoms by weeds and consequent reduction of speed. The other, introduced about the same time, was the carronade, a short-barrelled, large-calibre gun, which was mounted on the upper deck. With a low muzzle-velocity and easily handled, it made an important contribution to the victories of Nelson's time.

It was the superiority of its officers which mainly enabled the British navy, like the Prussian army, to triumph over the French. The outbreak of war in 1739 encouraged a band of younger men who were to make this century outstanding in naval successes. Prominent among them was Lord Anson (1697–1762), who sailed round the world between 1740 and 1744 and won the first Battle of Cape Finisterre in 1747. By the close of the Seven Years' War the officers of the British navy were without rival in Europe. Though most of them belonged to the nobility and gentry, there were always exceptions. Their training was thorough. They normally first went to sea between the ages of thirteen and sixteen as captain's servants, and their promotion to the rank of midshipman rested entirely with the captain. They could not be commissioned until they had served six years as a midshipman or mate and passed the lieutenant's examination, which was not usually before they were twenty-one years old. It was a system that ensured that officers had gained experience, training and self-reliance by the time they were commissioned.

By contrast, French naval officers displayed much the same weaknesses as their military counterparts. They were as aristocratic and, since naval commissions were not sold, even more exclusive. They despised the bourgeois merchant marine officers who were commissioned only for the duration of war, and the bad relations between these two classes of officers often demoralized French naval tactics. Their theoretical training was good, but they lacked practical experience in navigation, and naval administration was dominated by men with little knowledge of active service at sea. Nor did the Revolution revitalize the French navy as it did the army, but rather civilian interference and the replacement of royalist officers by even less experienced men reduced its efficiency.

During the frequent wars of the eighteenth century, the British navy's need for seamen was insatiable, for its strength steadily rose from 35,000 in 1740 to 70,000 in 1760, to 85,000 in 1780 and to 129,000 in 1802. It was a problem to raise these numbers because no one below the rank of an officer was in regular service. When a warship was paid off at the end of a commission, its company was discharged from the service as well as from the ship in the same way as merchant seamen were freed at the end of a voyage for which they had signed articles. In peacetime, therefore, Britain maintained only about a fifth of the men in the navy that were needed in war. This system existed because of the general economy of the country and also because it was reckoned that the navy could always obtain men in wartime from the mercantile marine. Few, however, were secured voluntarily. Many more were orphan and pauper boys, prisoners of war and other foreigners, debtors, rogues and vagabonds and impressed men.

Dr. Johnson said, 'No man will be a sailor who has contrivance enough to get himself into a gaol; for being in a ship is being in a gaol, with the chance of being drowned.' Men did not want to serve in the navy because of the system of pay, the harsh discipline and the life itself. A seaman's wages were the same as during the Commonwealth, although the cost of living had risen 30 per cent, and were often not paid to him until six months after his arrival in a home port. In a ship at sea for long periods there was little to restrain tyrannical officers, and flogging was no less severe than in the army. The Articles of War clearly laid it down that no captain of a ship was to inflict more than twelve lashes upon the bare back with a cat-o'-nine-tails without a court martial, but this was generally disregarded. Two or three dozen lashes were normal, a hundred was by no means uncommon and two or three hundred not unknown. The men were crowded together, living and sleeping amid the guns; food was bad, and many died of the scurvy through lack of vegetables. The *Annual Register* for 1763 recorded that in the Seven Years' War 1,512 seamen were killed in battle and 133,708 died of disease or were missing.

It is not surprising, therefore, that navies suffered from the same crippling rates of desertion as eighteenth-century armies. Between 1776 and 1780 over 42,000 men deserted from the British navy, and there is nothing to suggest that this was an unusual figure for any contemporary navy. The complacency of the age towards conditions in the navy was increased by the social gulf between officers and men. The mutinies of 1797 in the British navy consequently took everyone by surprise.[1] Afterwards the care taken of their men by such officers as Howe and Nelson became more common.

France had possessed a system of naval conscription since 1689, *inscription maritime*, which was applied to the whole seafaring population. All the sailors of the maritime provinces were divided into three, four and five classes, each class serving one year out of four, five or ten, according to the number of seamen in the province. When one class was drafted for the navy, the others were free to serve in the mercantile marine; they were called up in rotation and received half pay when not needed, but remained at the navy's disposal all their lives. This plan did not, however, produce enough men in wartime, when there had to be, as in Britain, a system of impressment, and to prevent men deserting, *garnissaires* – troops who had to be fed by their families – were sometimes quartered in their homes. On the whole, this French attempt at conscription failed to solve the problem of naval recruiting, which was fundamentally the same as that of the British navy.

The use of naval power as an offensive weapon was limited by several considerations in the eighteenth century. One was that it was believed that the defence of trade was a primary function of naval strategy, so that combatants in every war devoted much of their fleet to this purpose before giving any consideration to offensive action against the hostile navy. To protect the movements of merchant ships to and from their colonies, all naval

[1] P. 341.

powers resorted to the convoy system. Commanders of war-ships escorting convoys were instructed to make the safety of the merchant ships their first consideration and not pursue even a defeated attacking force. In the later years of the War of the Austrian Succession so many squadrons of French ships of the line were engaged in protecting convoys that any other naval operations were rendered practically impossible; and in the Revolutionary War, when the French fleet of Villaret-Joyeuse in 1794 was covering a grain convoy to America, he suffered the capture of six and the sinking of one of his 26 ships of the line on the Glorious First of June to enable it to reach harbour in safety.

Again, as with armies, navies could not undertake campaigns in the winter. As soon as the autumn threatened bad weather, warships went back to port and were refitted for the next fighting season. In November 1703 the English fleet, while anchored in the Downs on its way back from the Mediterranean, was struck by a violent storm which sank twelve vessels and showed only too clearly the danger of keeping the great ships at sea after September. In West Indian waters, where there was much naval fighting during this period, climatic conditions also forced a respite. From November to April the trade wind blew down on the Windward Islands from a little to the north of east, but then it veered round almost to the east, and the last three months of the following period were made impossible for naval operations by hurricanes. The main fleets then sailed northwards up the eastern coast of the American continent, a factor which was of decisive significance during the American War of Independence.

Above all, these years belonged to that period of British history, which extended from the early eighteenth century to the end of the First World War, when the outcome of a major war depended upon the professional competence of the admiral commanding the main fleet, for its destruction would have meant his country's total defeat. A severe naval loss would have immediately given control of the vital sea-lanes of communication to the enemy, and a vanquished navy would take years to replace. Sir Winston Churchill's comment on the Battle of Jutland, that the Commander-in-Chief of the British Grand Fleet 'was the only man on either side who could lose the war in an afternoon', might be applied at any time during this period of two hundred years.

This factor resulted in changes in naval tactics, which made sea battles as indecisive as those on land. Until the middle of the seventeenth century, fleets had hardly manoeuvred during an engagement. The admiral exercised control of his fleet while it approached the enemy, but after the first broadside each captain sought an opponent, and the battle became a series of individual combats between ships, most of which were well under 1,000 tons. By 1685, however, the evolution of the valuable capital ship of 1,400 tons, which carried a hundred or more guns, led to the conception of squadron formation and line of battle. Admirals were expected to follow carefully the *Fighting Instructions* of Sir George Rooke of 1703, which were based upon those issued by Admiral Edward Russell in 1691. Their underlying idea was to keep the fleet together in the fighting line when opposed to an enemy of approximately equal strength and deliver only a general massed attack.

Moreover, battle was rarely joined unless the fleet could oppose an enemy with an equal number of ships of the same class. Until the Battle of the Nile in 1798, where all thirteen British ships of the line took a fairly uniform part, naval clashes had always been marked by a number of unengaged vessels firing only passing shots and suffering no casualties. Generally a battle was a gun-duel between two rival fleets, drawn up in two parallel lines, which produced no important result. Between Barfleur in 1692 and The Saints in 1782 no decisive victory was achieved in a naval battle fought under approximately equal conditions. The only battles which produced some effective result, such as Lagos and Quiberon Bay in 1759, were mostly those where there was a marked superiority of power on one side. On other occasions, fleets were robbed of victory through conformity to the *Fighting Instructions*. Admiral Mathews abstained from vigorous pursuit of the Franco-Spanish fleet at the Battle of Toulon in 1744; and Admiral Byng, though personally brave, was deprived of individual initiative in his action off Minorca in 1756 by his conviction that he must maintain the close-hauled line of battle under all circumstances.

The more adventurous spirit produced in British officers by the wars of the century led to a gradual ignoring of the *Fighting Instructions*. Anson, while waiting for a month in 1747 in the Bay of Biscay for the French fleet, constantly exercised his fleet in battle formations and manoeuvres, and when the enemy appeared, changed the correctly formal line into a general chase

which led to the capture of all the French warships by nightfall.[1]
Above all, Rodney won the Battle of the Saints in 1782 by con-
founding the enemy with an original plan of attack. The two
opposing fleets were passing on opposite course when Rodney
ordered the captain of his flagship, the *Formidable,* to put over the
helm and led his squadron through the French line; Admiral
Hood, bringing up the British rear, did the same lower down the
enemy's line. The French fleet was thrown into confusion and
lost five of its ships, including the great flagship, the *Ville de Paris,*
with Admiral de Grasse on board. The rest sailed away, leaving
both the West Indies and the Atlantic in undisputed British control. This was the first battle of the century in which a contest
between two fleets of about the same size resulted in a definite
triumph for one of them.

Henceforward, British admirals could depend upon their own
tactical genius, and it was possible for the most brilliant naval
strategist among them to indulge in that 'Nelson touch', which he
displayed so audaciously at the Battle of Trafalgar, his last and
greatest victory. Here the thirty-three Franco-Spanish ships
were extended in a half-moon five miles long. Nelson with his
twenty-seven ships drove at their centre in two columns. Not a
single British ship was lost, but the enemy lost twenty-two of their
heaviest vessels, and none of the rest ever fought again. The
battle was won by superior seamanship, gunnery and initiative in
command; it epitomized the qualities that secured for Britain the
command of the sea which went unchallenged for the remainder
of the war.

[1] P. 213.

VIII · FRANCE
THE REGENCY AND FLEURY

The End of Louis XIV's Reign

LOUIS XIV died in the early morning of Sunday, 1st September
1715, after an illness of three weeks and within three days of his
seventy-seventh birthday, so bringing to an end a reign which had
lasted over seventy-two years. He died in his great gilded bedchamber, overlooking the *cour de marbre*, in the middle of the
vast palace he had erected at Versailles – 'the place', in the words
of Mme. de Motteville, 'he designed for his magnificence in order
to show by its adornment what a great king can do when he spares
nothing to satisfy his wishes'.

Here were scenes and memories recalling the brilliant earlier
years of his reign. Next to the King's bedchamber was the *Cabinet
du Conseil*, in which Louis had spent many hours with his ministers and administrators to direct policy and control government
by the efficient middle-class bureaucracy with which he had
equipped the country. Within the palace also were the Chapel,
in which he had worshipped regularly; the Dining-Hall, in which
he had taken his meals in public, attended by the members of the
once-factious nobility whom he had reduced to glittering, sub-
servient courtiers; and the *Galerie des Glaces*, where he had presided over dancing and music amid the sparkling mirrors and the
large pictures depicting the victories of his armies in Holland,
Germany and Spain. Outside was the magnificent park with
vast flowered *parterres,* a cross-shaped sheet of water, parallel and
radiating tree-lined avenues and walks flanked by tall, clipped
hedges. Here there had been masquerades and feasting, when
thousands of lights among the trees sparkled on the waters, and
pageants and fireworks to celebrate royal births and marriages,
victories and peace treaties.

There were, however, other memories recalled by Versailles.
'Behind and beyond the radiance of Louis and his courtiers',
wrote Lytton Strachey, 'lay the dark abyss of an impoverished
France, a ruined peasantry, a whole system of intolerance and
privilege and maladministration'; and in the last years of the

King's reign, sombre forebodings penetrated even the splendour of Versailles. In a marshy valley not far away the ruins of the Cistercian convent of Port Royal des Champs were a reminder that, though this centre of Jansenism had been destroyed by royal order, the controversy still disturbed France and the Church, while reports from *intendants* indicated that the Revocation of the Edict of Nantes and the savage penal laws had not destroyed the Huguenots. During the black years of 1708 and 1709 reports told also of bad harvests and peasant revolts, and these were followed by bread-riots in Paris and even demonstrations outside the Palace of Versailles. And, finally, as the Duc de Saint-Simon (1675–1755) has recounted in his *Mémoires*, there were the dark winter nights during the War of the Spanish Succession when the courtiers pressed their faces against the window-panes of the palace to see the messengers ride in from the battlefields with despatches that told the King that for the first time his armies had been overwhelmed, his kingdom had been invaded and he would have to sue for peace.

The failures and disappointments at the end of Louis XIV's reign, which replaced its earlier achievements and triumphs, seemed to be accompanied by signs of disintegration in the court itself. Etiquette was breaking down, and the King's hold on the nobility was weakening. The younger nobles, tired of the boredom and constraint at Versailles, deserted its cramped and crowded discomfort for the freer life of Paris and the ease of the smart *hôtels* they built or bought themselves there. Moreover, the religion which had inspired French life during the seventeenth century appeared to be losing its power. Noblemen openly professed unbelief and scepticism; they mockingly nicknamed the Duc de Bourgogne's friends the *cabale des saints*. Irreligious compositions circulated in manuscript. Unpleasant tales of poisoning and witchcraft, involving the court and even the King's mistress, were told in Parisian society. The strength of the beliefs and observances, which Louis had held so important, was waning.

Personal losses added to the sorrows of the last years. In April 1711 his only son, the Dauphin, died. In February and March the next year, there died in rapid succession his eldest grandson, the Duc de Bourgogne, of whom he had expected great things, the Duchesse de Bourgogne, his favourite, and their eldest son, next in the line of succession. Since Philip of Anjou had renounced the throne, the only direct male heir was another son of the Duc de Bourgogne, then a weak, two-year-old baby. Now, three years later, this young prince succeeded his grandfather as Louis XV.

The new King was to have a reign of fifty-nine years, but his period of personal rule was to be much shorter. Since he was only five years old, a regent had to manage the affairs of state until he reached his legal majority in 1723, and thereafter he was content to have policy controlled by Cardinal Fleury, his former tutor. Only when Fleury died in 1743 did Louis XV assume – or claim to assume – authority for himself. During nearly the whole of the first half of his reign, therefore, he exercised practically no influence in the political sphere.

The Regent's Failure

Louis XV's legal heir, according to the terms of the Treaty of Utrecht, was Philippe, Duc d'Orléans, a nephew of the late king and the first *prince du sang*. Louis XIV inevitably nominated him as Regent in his will, but he mistrusted him so much that he bequeathed real power to the royal bastards and set up a *Conseil de Régence* which was to exercise effective authority '*sans que le Duc d'Orléans, chef du conseil, puisse seul et par son auctorité particulière rien déterminer*'. The two preceding reigns had each opened with regencies, and both times the previous king had made arrangements which had been ignored after his death. Having won over to his side the officers of the household troops, the *princes du sang* and the councillors, Orléans acted as had Marie de Medici in 1610 and Anne of Austria in 1643. He successfully requested the Parlement of Paris to annul the will and so secured completely the authority enjoyed by the *grand monarque*, though his purpose was to use it to destroy the system of monarchical despotism.

As Orléans came to power, a violent and sweeping reaction against the previous reign set in. Whether he himself led or followed this, he certainly typified much of it. Paris, where he had long lived, was again to be the centre of France. The young King was brought to the Tuileries, and Versailles was closed and placed under caretakers. Operas, concerts, balls and parties marked the social life of the capital. Among innovations in feminine dress were the *panier* and the *négligé*, while patches, rouge and powder were applied without restraint; and Orléans himself made embroidered waistcoats, diamond rosettes and cascades of Brussels lace popular as masculine fashions.

The Regent, who was now nearing his forties, was a man of considerable ability and culture, wit and charm, but he was completely lacking in moral sense. Indulged from his youth in all his desires, he grew up to exhibit the worst consequences of Louis XIV's policy of allowing the *noblesse d'épée* merely to embellish his court. Throughout the Regency he led a wild life among depraved noblemen and loose women. Nearly every night his Paris home, the Palais Royal, was the scene of scandalous, drunken parties, and he gave a new word to the language by mockingly calling his dissolute companions '*ses roués*', fit only to be broken on the wheel. Such habitual debauchery weakened his ability to follow a consistent policy in the face of France's numerous problems in the years after 1715 and brought on his early death at the age of forty-nine.

Nevertheless, when he became Regent, Orléans did realize the need to remedy the weaknesses in Louis XIV's system of rule which had become increasingly apparent during the later years of his reign, and produced widespread resentment and criticism among the powerful classes excluded from a share in the government of the country. Previous French regencies had seen aristocratic attempts to seize power and consequent governmental chaos. In 1715 there seemed to be a real danger of a repetition of the Fronde, the princely and noble revolt which had torn France during Louis XIV's minority. By gaining exclusive power, Orléans placed himself in a position to permit a reversal of the policy of the previous reign and avert such a situation.

In return for the annulment of Louis XIV's will, Orléans had promised to restore to the Parlement of Paris the *droit de remonstrance*.[1] He had also agreed to introduce an important reform, known as the *Polysynodie*, in the system of government. Louis XIV had purposely excluded the *princes du sang* and great noblemen from any participation in the administration. Each government department had been in the charge of bourgeois Secretaries of State, such as Colbert and Louvois, who reported directly to the King and received their instructions from him, though they might also serve as Ministers of State in the *Conseil du Roi*, the select, powerful royal council over which the King presided. The great nobles hated this '*régne de vile bourgeoisie*',

[1] P. 42.

and the changes made by Orléans were intended to appeal to them by circumscribing the power of the Secretaries of State, whom Saint-Simon described as '*les monstres qui avaient dévorés la noblesse*'.

Orléans placed at the head of each department a council instead of a single man.   There were altogether six councils, dealing with internal affairs, religion, war, navy, finance and foreign affairs.   A great nobleman presided over every council, but only about half of the ten members of each council were from the *noblesse d'épée*.   The rest were experienced officials of the *noblesse de robe*, who had little patience with the manifest failings of their new colleagues.   The incapability of one set of members and the hostility of the others soon reduced the councils to impotence.   By 1718 the failure of the *Polysynodie* had to be admitted.   The councils were dissolved, and the Secretaries of State resumed their former functions.   The end of this aspect of the aristocratic reaction in eighteenth-century France deprived the great nobility of their last chance under the *ancien régime* to partake in the government of the country.

Meanwhile, the *noblesse de robe* had been seeking to increase their political power through the use of the *droit de remonstrance* recently regained by the Parlement of Paris.   Within two years of the beginning of the new reign, the Parlement voted to reject a financial edict and successfully demanded that it should be given an account of the national income, expenditure and debts since the start of the Regency.   It seemed as if the Parlement would manage to re-assert its power as it had traditionally done during regencies.   In 1718 it not only used the *remonstrance* against financial edicts of the government, but also forbade the manufacture and issue of the coinage.   The royal mint, however, continued to work under military guard; and the Regent resorted to the recognized way of overcoming a recalcitrant Parlement by holding a *lit de justice*, a special meeting of the body at which it was forced to register the edicts.   The Parlement was then deprived of the *droit de remonstrance*, and three of the most troublesome councillors were exiled.   Two years later, when the Parlement repeatedly refused to register a financial edict, the Regent exiled the whole body to Pontoise for some six months. This was the first time such an event had occurred in French history, but it was not to be the last.

Relations between the Regent and the Parlement were made

still more difficult by the Jansenist controversy inherited from the last reign.[1]   Louis XIV had died before the Bull *Unigenitus,* condemning the doctrines of the Jansenists, had been registered by the Parlement.   The Regent freed those who had been imprisoned for opposition to the Bull, but at the same time hoped to solve the problem by securing its acceptance.   Not until 1720, however, did he induce the Parlement by threats to register the Bull with reservations, and, in fact, political developments made the Regent's efforts to settle this religious dispute no more successful than his plans to meet the other difficulties inherited from Louis XIV.   It was yet to bring Louis XV and the Parlement into violent opposition.

The most pressing problem facing the Regent, and the one which initiated his difficulties with the Parlement of Paris, was the condition of the royal finances.   By the end of Louis XIV's reign, the national debt was 3,000 million livres, estimated annual expenditure was 148 million livres and income about the same, while much revenue was pledged for two years ahead.   The aristocratic reaction was strong enough to prevent the new *Conseil des Finances* adopting the proposal of Louis XIV's last *Contrôleur Général* to levy taxes from which the clergy and nobility should enjoy no exemption.   It set up a *Chambre de Justice* to investigate the huge profits made by the *financiers,* but this achieved little and was suppressed after a year.   Efforts were made to reduce the national debt by partially repudiating government bills issued by Louis XIV, reducing the interest on *rentes* or loans from five to four per cent and sometimes the capital as well, and calling in the coinage in circulation and reissuing it at the rate of 120 for 100.   The *rentiers* were not yet powerful enough, as they were by 1789, to prevent these measures, but their effect was to lower the government's credit for little financial gain.   Nor did limited reforms in the financial administration and a few economies in public expenditure effect much improvement in the financial situation.

The need for more drastic financial changes led the Regent to listen to the proposals of John Law (1671–1729), who was already well known to him.   Law was the son of an Edinburgh goldsmith and banker, from whom he inherited a considerable fortune. As a young man he went south to London, where he led a gay life until he had to flee abroad because he killed a man in a duel.

[1] Pp. 111–3.

His travels on the Continent brought him to the gaming-dens of Paris, where he won and lost vast sums and attracted the attention of Orléans. He had also, however, studied the monetary operations of the financial capitals of Europe and evolved his famous *Système*, which he now put before the Regent.

Law's ideas were the bold systemization of notions of banking, trade and credit commonly held in western Europe at the end of the seventeenth century. Opinion in many countries had been impressed by the way in which two small states like England and Holland had been able to resist and humble France, raise and sustain heavy national debts and engage in flourishing, world-wide commerce. All this, it was commonly believed, was to be explained by their financial institutions and practice. Law expounded the *Système* in his *Money and Trade Considered*. He said that national power and wealth depended on trade and that trade depended on money and on the easy, rapid circulation of money, but that credit, if in circulation, had all the beneficial effects of money. He urged, therefore, the establishment of a national bank to create and increase instruments of credit. This should issue paper money, which was most likely to circulate rapidly and could be backed by land or other property equally as well as gold and silver. Law strongly believed in the omnipotence of governments: he saw the evils of minor monopolies and the private farming of taxes. Large monopolies, notably the Dutch and English national banks and chartered trading companies, appealed to him. He suggested that, besides a bank to control national finance, there should be a state company to engage in commerce to the ultimate exclusion of all private ventures. Bank and company together would form a huge monopoly of finance and trade managed by the State for the people, from the profits of which the national debt might be extinguished and even revenue raised without resort to taxation.

The *Conseil des Finances*, the merchants and *financiers*, were hostile to Law's ideas, but the Regent was always prepared to try experiments and take risks, and in 1716 he allowed Law to set up a *Banque Générale*, a joint-stock bank modelled on the Bank of Amsterdam, with powers to receive deposits, issue notes (which should be payable in the currency of the date of issue) and discount bills. It was a private bank, but three-quarters of its capital consisted of government bills, and the government accepted its notes in payment of taxes. It was, therefore, from the start closely connected with the finances of the State and the national debt.

Law's bank was immediately successful, which enabled him to proceed with the second part of his *Système*. In 1717 he floated a joint-stock trading-company, the *Compagnie d'Occident*, which was granted a monopoly of trade with North America and was to exploit the new French possessions at the mouth of the Mississippi. This was linked with both his bank and the treasury since government bills were accepted for the purchase of its shares. Law gradually extended the Company's operations. In 1719 it absorbed the existing largely moribund *Compagnie des Indes Orientales*, *Compagnie de Chine* and other rival trading companies to become the *Compagnie perpetuelle des Indes*, which controlled the whole of France's foreign trade. The *financiers*, and especially the *fermiers-généraux* with their profitable right of collecting the indirect taxes, opposed Law so violently that he had to outbid them and take over for his Company the tax-farm. He followed this by taking over the royal debt; holders of *rentes* were given shares in the company which received from the State only three per cent interest.

The *Système* attained its greatest prosperity and power in the years immediately before 1720. The Bank became the *Banque Royale* in 1718; its notes now no longer had to be convertible into currency, but were guaranteed by the King. Early in 1720 the Bank and the Company were united, and Law, now naturalized and hastily converted to Roman Catholicism, was appointed to the revised post of *Contrôleur Général*, the most important in the government of the country under the *ancien régime*. He was now, therefore, officially able to direct the finances, currency and most of the overseas commerce of France. This stupendous power, attained by such incredible success, he proposed to use to make widespread reforms, such as a tax to be levied on all classes in the country, the suppression of many unnecessary administrative posts and the initiation of schemes of public works.

All this depended, however, on the prosperity of his company. To attract capital for it, Law represented in glowing terms the potential wealth of Louisiana; and the government transported criminals, vagabonds, foundlings and prostitutes there to provide it with settlers. His efforts created a wild outburst of speculation, for this was the age of the Darien Company in Scotland and the South Sea Bubble in England, when it was believed that fortunes were readily to be made from joint-stock trading-companies. People from all classes hastened to invest money in his company. Its shares rose from their par value of 500 livres to 15,000.

By the summer of 1720, however, a decline in confidence had set in, perhaps engineered originally by rival bankers like the Pâris brothers. Speculators now hurried to realize their gains by selling their shares; many people also began to present their notes at the Bank and demanded currency. Soon there was a catastrophic panic. In a few days the value of the Company's shares fell by 50 per cent. Before the end of the year, the Regent was forced to dismiss Law, who fled abroad penniless.

The results of the 'Mississippi Bubble' were mixed. The encouragement which had been given to trade and industry was not completely lost. The seaports especially continued to benefit from the development of colonial trade, which still grew, though not as spectacularly as Law had hoped. Many had done well out of the speculation in the Company's shares. Landowners, noblemen and even some of the *princes du sang* like the Duc de Bourbon, who was to succeed Philippe d'Orléans as chief minister, had taken advantage of their position to sell out before the crash came and made enough money to pay their debts. There were also *nouveaux riches*, who had risen socially through the fortunes they had made, while the *financiers* emerged stronger than ever after the fall of their upstart rival. On the other hand, thousands of families had been ruined, and the increase in prices, brought about by the sharp inflation, caused distress, particularly to the urban lower class.

The immediate consequences of the *Système* for the treasury were beneficial. The acceptance of government bills in payment for shares in the Bank and the Company did much to reduce the national debt, which, in fact, by 1720 was only half what it had been at the beginning of the Regency. Nevertheless the long-term results of the crash were less beneficial. All the reforms proposed by Law came to nothing; the hopelessly inefficient and unfair French financial system remained unchanged. This was not only in itself disastrous for the country, but any future financial reforms were impeded. While in England the South Sea Bubble produced bitterness and cynicism, public confidence in the government remained strong enough for it to borrow the money needed to win the country's political and military victories of the eighteenth century; but in France the situation was different.

There the distrust of the government's financial capability and intentions was so general that throughout the *ancien régime* there was a strong prejudice against paper money and large centralized financial institutions. Not until Napoleon was Consul did France possess a state bank with the foundation of the *Banque de France* in 1800, a century after the establishment of the Bank of England.[1]

In foreign affairs also, the Regent inherited difficulties from the events of the previous reign. The Treaty of Utrecht had forced the King of Spain, Philip V, who was a grandson of Louis XIV, to renounce his claim to the French crown, but his ambitions, supported by his domineering wife, Elizabeth Farnese, and his minister, Cardinal Alberoni, led him still to regard himself as the rightful heir. The young Louis XV was not a healthy child, and should he die Philip would certainly try to gain the succession to the throne from Orléans. During these years of uncertainty Philip remained, therefore, constantly hostile to the Regent and a potential supporter of the Bastard Princes (the illegitimate sons of Louis XIV), the leading courtiers and ministers of the previous reign and others opposed to the Regent's rule in France. Orléans saw the need for a foreign alliance to meet this threat.

The country to whom he turned was Britain, the most resolute enemy of France in recent years. Nor was it in vain, for the new regime there seemed equally as precarious and in need of an ally as the Regency in France. Though the 'Fifteen, the Jacobite rising which followed George I's accession, had failed, the position of the ruling Whigs remained weak, for they were only a minority of about seventy great landed families supported by the London merchants, and the more numerous rural population was mainly Tory in sympathy. Accordingly, an alliance was concluded in 1716 between Britain and France, which became first the Triple Alliance when Holland joined it the next year, and then the Quadruple Alliance when the Emperor Charles VI joined it in 1718.

The successful conclusion of this alliance was due largely to the able diplomacy of the Abbé Dubois (1656–1723), formerly tutor to the Duc d'Orléans and his secretary since he had become Regent. It led to the appointment of Dubois as Secretary of State for Foreign Affairs in 1718. It also led in 1718 to a plot against Orléans in France, involving the Spanish ambassador, the Prince of Cellamare, and this produced a declaration of war by

[1] P. 352.

France and Britain upon Spain, which had already embarked upon an Italian adventure in furtherance of Elizabeth Farnese's ambitions.[1]

French troops started to invade Spain, and the British fleet attacked Spanish ships and ports, but Philip sought peace. In 1719 Dubois obtained Philip's accession to the Quadruple Alliance, recognition of the Regent's right to the French succession and agreement to the betrothal of the Spanish Infanta (aged five) to Louis XV (now eleven years old). For himself Dubois secured the aristocratic archbishopric of Cambrai in 1720, though he was of modest bourgeois beginnings and was not ordained until then. He became a cardinal the next year, while in 1722 he was granted the title of *Principal Ministre*, which had been in abeyance in France for many years.

Louis XV achieved his legal majority at the age of thirteen in February 1723, and the Regency came nominally to an end. Dubois retained his position of *Principal Ministre*, but died in August. He was succeeded by Orléans, who himself died of apoplexy in December during a conversation with his mistress. So the first period in Louis XV's earlier years came to an end. It had been marked by undoubted success in foreign affairs, for the policy of Orléans and Dubois brought France, after nearly a quarter of a century of hostilities, a period of relative tranquillity which was to last until the outbreak of the War of the Austrian Succession in 1740 and the resumption of colonial and commercial conflict with Britain. France's ability to benefit from those peaceful years, was, however, greatly minimized by the failure of the Regent's domestic policy. Orléans was able to prevent a repetition of the unrest and administrative disorder of previous French regencies, but his plans for a fundamental solution of the country's governmental problems came to nothing. This cannot be attributed mainly to the Regent's defects of character and Law's misjudgements and misfortunes. Rather, failure lay in the inherent contradictions in the system of government inherited from the past, which were to become increasingly obvious as the country progressed.

Prosperity under Fleury

The attainment by Louis XV of his legal majority saw the re-establishment of the royal court at Versailles, but the King's youth made it inevitable that a regency would continue in everything except name. Orléans was succeeded by the next *prince du sang*, the Duc de Bourbon, who was bleary-eyed, knock-kneed and stupid, but had a pretty, ambitious and intelligent mistress, Mme. de Prie, the daughter of a *financier*. She shared with Bourbon a desire to enjoy power as long as possible. Since the death of the young Louis would bring the son of the late Duc d'Orléans to the throne, they resolved to arrange a marriage for him which might safeguard the succession sooner than the projected Spanish match. The Infanta was, therefore, sent back to her parents, and from a list of eighty-nine possible princesses, they chose Marie Leszczynski, daughter of Stanislas, ex-King of Poland.[1] The marriage took place in 1725 when she was twenty-two and Louis fifteen. The indignation it aroused in Spain gave new life to the Franco-British alliance. To Mme. de Prie its great advantage was that, since the new Queen was poor and did not belong to an important ruling family, she would not become a rival for political influence.

The promoters of the marriage did not, however, long enjoy their triumph. They got the inexperienced Queen to urge her husband to exile from the court his old tutor, Cardinal Fleury, who exerted a strong influence over him and had already become a member of the *Conseil du Roi*. The attempt was disastrous for them. Louis would not be parted from Fleury. Bourbon was suddenly dismissed from his post, and Mme. de Prie was exiled with her husband to their château in Normandy. Fleury now gained power at the age of seventy-three and retained it until he died in 1743 in his ninetieth year. To flatter Louis that he was now old enough to rule himself, Fleury did not take the title of *Principal Ministre;* he remained only a Minister of State, but he was the real ruler of France.

Through his continued retention of the young King's confidence and his own administrative ability and assiduous devotion to duty, Fleury was able to maintain himself above the rival noble factions of the court. His domestic policy was conservative. There were no further attempts to reform the system of government while he was in office. He did not have to contend with the same opposition as did the two great cardinal-ministers of the previous century, Richelieu and Mazarin, but like them he sought to give France competent, orderly government. By a

[1] P. 279.

combination of tact and firmness he even succeeded in damping down the new Jansenist controversy and securing a temporary lull in the running fight between the *parlements* and the Church.[1]

Though he had known poverty in his younger years, his frugal and unostentatious life in office showed that he had no wish to enrich himself now. He carried these qualities into his administration, and as the son of a tax-collector, he was not unaware of the importance of finance. In 1726 he fixed the standard of the currency and fortified the credit of the government by initiating the regular payment of the interest on the national debt. Four years later he appointed Philibert Orry, a former *intendant*, as *Contrôleur Général*, who held the post for fifteen years and by 1738–9 had secured a surplus of 15,000,000 livres in the treasury instead of the customary deficit. Orry also began a plan to provide France with a system of state roads by procuring in 1738 a *corvée royale* which exacted forced labour from the peasants and materials and equipment from prosperous farmers. This was to give France, as Arthur Young had later to admit, better roads than the English turnpikes, but the discontent it aroused from both peasants and farmers added yet further to the grievances under the *ancien régime*.

Fleury's government enabled this period to be one of moderate prosperity for France. His stabilization of the currency was followed by a gradual rise in prices which extended over the middle of the century. The French economy reacted to the increased stimulation. Overseas trade developed rapidly, and many fine buildings were erected in Bordeaux, Marseilles, Lyons and other large towns. The great *financiers,* headed by the able Pâris brothers, whose position had been threatened by Law's schemes, resumed their profitable activities. In particular, the *fermiers généraux*, whose functions Law had suppressed, resumed their contract on advantageous terms. It is true that this prosperity did not touch many classes, and in parts of the country the famines of 1739 and 1740 brought considerable suffering. Fleury's carriage was held up in 1740 in Paris by a mob of starving women who shouted, '*Du pain! Du pain! Nous mourrons de faim!*' Nevertheless, the years of Fleury's rule were, as Professor Cobban has said, 'the most prosperous and successful period in the history of eighteenth-century France'.

If Fleury's domestic achievements were ensured by the success

[1] Pp. 112–3.

of his financial policy, this in its turn was made possible by his pacific foreign policy. He saw that war would bring financial disaster upon the country, and to bring her peace and security he persistently endeavoured to prevent the revival of such a strong European alliance against France as had defeated Louis XIV. Here he was assisted by Sir Robert Walpole, who controlled British policy from 1721 to 1742 and was equally anxious that Britain should not be involved in any Continental war. The Franco-British alliance, created by Dubois, was therefore maintained, and the peaceful lull in the rivalry between the two powers continued.

By negotiating the Treaty of Seville in 1729, Fleury was able to avert the threat of a general war contained in Elizabeth Farnese's alliance with the Emperor.[1] Nevertheless, the aggressive spirit and traditional anti-Austrian feeling still had its supporters in France, notable among whom was Germain-Louis de Chauvelin, who had become Secretary of State for Foreign Affairs in 1727. Their opportunity came with the events which followed the death of Augustus, Elector of Saxony and elective King of Poland, in 1733, His heir was Augustus III of Saxony, who had married the eldest daughter of the Emperor Joseph I; but Stanislas, Louis XV's father-in-law, resolved to make a bid to regain the Polish throne. He went to Warsaw, where the Diet proclaimed him King. Austria and Russia, however, feared this might be followed by French interference in Poland and decided to support Augustus III. An invading Russian army compelled Stanislas to flee the country and secured the enthronement of his rival. These events made it impossible for Fleury to prevent Chauvelin and the war party procuring the entry of France into the War of the Polish Succession, and in the same year the signing of the First Family Compact with Spain brought that country into war with Austria also.[2] Since Walpole was very ready to keep Britain neutral, Fleury was, however, able to limit the scope of the War. He refrained from large-scale military operations and would not allow an invasion of the Austrian Netherlands.

In fact, Fleury made no serious effort to restore Stanislas to his throne. The fighting actually came to an end in 1735, and in 1738 Fleury won an important diplomatic victory by the third Treaty of Vienna. The Duke of Lorraine, Francis Stephen, who had married Maria Theresa in 1736, gave up

[1] P. 173.   [2] P. 174.

his duchy to Stanislas as compensation for the loss of his Polish throne. In return Francis Stephen was given Tuscany, its last Medici ruler having died in 1737, while Lorraine was to revert upon the death of Stanislas (which occurred in 1766) to his daughter, the Queen of France, and her children. Meanwhile, Chauvelin had been intriguing with the Duc de Bourbon against Fleury, but the Cardinal was not to be intimidated. In 1737 he dismissed Chauvelin and exiled him first to Bourges and then among the mountains of Auvergne. Chauvelin never returned to Paris, and his friends were eliminated from power.

These achievements, however, marked the culmination of Fleury's successes. Before the end of his career, France was in a European conflict, and war with Britain was at hand. In 1739 English mercantile interests forced Walpole to enter upon the War of Jenkins's Ear with Spain. Fleury's advancing age increasingly weakened his influence upon affairs. The next year came the crisis brought about by the death of the Emperor Charles VI. Fleury was no longer in control of the situation. France had accepted in the Third Treaty of Vienna of 1738 the Pragmatic Sanction in which Charles VI had asserted the right of his daughter to succeed to the whole of the Habsburg dominions; but the anti-Austrian war party, now led by the Maréchal de Belleisle, was strong enough at court to compel Fleury against his better judgement to take France into the War of the Austrian Succession, in the cause of the Elector of Bavaria and on the side of Frederick II of Prussia against Maria Theresa. When Fleury died in 1743, the French had suffered a bad reverse in Bohemia, and the replacement of Walpole by Carteret foreshadowed active British participation in the War, which was to continue for five more years.

The long years during which Fleury clung to power, despite his increasing infirmities, formed a period of unspectacular but sound progress for France. By giving the country stable government, financial confidence and almost unbroken peace, he enabled her to recover from the effects of Louis XIV's wars and resume the place in Europe to which national resources and population entitled her. To some this period was the golden age of the *ancien régime*. It had, at any rate, much to commend it in comparison with the later part of Louis XV's reign.

IX · THE SPANISH BOURBONS

The Condition of Spain

By the beginning of the eighteenth century Spain was in a condition of economic collapse. The crown had declared itself bankrupt in 1692 for the third time, despite the heavy increase in taxation throughout the seventeenth century. The ubiquitous sales tax, the *alcabala*, had been raised to eleven per cent in 1639 and fourteen per cent in 1663; and fresh taxes had been placed on a variety of commodities which included stamped paper, oil, wine, vinegar, soap and even ice. Yet all these impositions had merely worsened the country's condition without satisfying the crown's needs. The signs of the fundamental and almost continuous national decline were by now many and unmistakable. Toledo, Granada, Seville and other once-flourishing cities could not even raise funds to maintain roads, bridges and drains. Manufacture of the fine wools of Andalusia and silks of Valencia had almost ceased. The diminishing population of the countryside had resulted in the disappearance of villages and the abandonment of fertile land. The towns had also declined in population, Burgos and other provincial capitals even more than Madrid. The volume of Spanish shipping plying between Spain and the Indies had fallen by three-quarters during the seventeenth century, while the Spanish navy had never recovered from the disasters it had undergone during Philip II's later years.

The basic cause of Spain's decline lay in the circumstances of her rise to power. During the sixteenth century she had experienced both the sudden discovery and conquest of an empire overseas and the simultaneous and equally sudden inheritance of another at home. These two events determined the fate of the small but energetic middle-class Spain possessed at the beginning of the sixteenth century. Without the New World colonies and European family lands, this class might gradually have obtained a secure and important place in the old Spanish feudal society and brought growing wealth to the country through trade and industry. Instead, that wealth came suddenly and rapidly as bullion from overseas. As much as possible was brought into the country and little exported.   The Spanish military aristocracy and clergy, whose national supremacy had been established during the long medieval crusades against the invading Moors, received new strength and prestige.   Enriched by American silver, they pursued their traditional occupation in the wars of empire, and throughout the Spanish dominions their ruling position was strengthened.

Inevitably, Spanish economic policy was based on the interests of this aristocracy; it favoured consumers rather than producers. The government sought to keep prices down by forbidding the export of corn, cattle, cloth and other commodities, and food-production was sacrificed to the *Mesta*, the aristocratic sheep-farming corporation.   Under such a policy, the clerical, aristocratic society flourished, but the middle-classes weakened and failed, while the working population was reduced by overseas emigration induced by the attraction of the bullion of the New World.   Spain had to rely increasingly, not only upon foreign experts, such as Italian financiers, Flemish industrialists and Jewish merchants, but also upon foreign sailors and labourers.

Such a situation could endure in the sixteenth century because of the steadily mounting flow of bullion from overseas, but in the seventeenth century the exhaustion of the mines and other causes made bullion imports fall as rapidly as they had previously risen. Prices fell and the revenue of the government declined.   There followed the trade depression, heavy taxation, unemployment, de-population and other features of Spanish ruin which had become so serious by the end of the seventeenth century.

The greatest obstacle to restoring Spanish prosperity in the eighteenth century was still that same social structure of the country which had contributed so much to its decline.   The Church retained its importance in Spanish society, and about two per cent of the Spanish population relied upon it for a profession. The large religious orders were unproductive; clerical celibacy assisted the decline of the population; mortmain hindered agriculture; indiscriminate monastic and parochial relief fostered rather than cured unemployment; tithes and other ecclesiastical exactions contributed to the impoverishment of the husbandmen; and the clergy encouraged the laity in conservatism and superstition.   Indeed, the eighteenth century was to show that the Spanish Church gave the reforming policy of the new dynasty very little assistance and was rather an impediment.   Equally general was the indifference presented by the nobility, who comprised about five per cent of the population. For them the ownership of land was still the only acceptable form of wealth, and office in one of the military orders or at court the only occupation. Consequently, to quote Penfield Roberts: 'While Adam Smith was meditating his *Wealth of Nations*, Spaniards were still discussing whether a commercial career could be honourable.' The middle-class, whether merchants or professional men, remained few in number and displayed an apathy towards reform which was only exceeded by that of the country people.

Philip V and Elizabeth Farnese

Despite such opposition to reform, many hoped that the accession of Philip V (1700–46) would bring better times for Spain in the new century. Philip, Duke of Anjou, had been born at Versailles as the younger son of the Dauphin and named King of Spain in the will of the weak, childless Charles II. He came to Madrid at the age of seventeen. Physically he was courageous; he acquitted himself well in battle, both in Italy and Spain, during the War of the Spanish Succession and was flattered by his courtiers with the title of *El Animoso*, the spirited one. He was, however, morally weak, though he had shared the careful education given to his brother, the Duc de Bourgogne, by Archbishop Fénélon, and throughout his life he suffered from fits of melancholy, which became worse in his later years and were sometimes so bad that he would not even speak. He was also easily led by women and during the early years of his reign was ruled by his first wife, Marie Louise of Savoy, who was herself under the domination of the Princesse des Ursins (1642–1722), the twice-widowed French lady who acted as her maid of honour. She had been sent to Spain by Louis XIV as confidante to the Queen to ensure the promotion of French influence, desired both by Louis and also by the Spanish reformers who believed it would promote the changes needed in the country.

Not until 1714, however, was Philip really King of Spain and at peace with the world. Only after a long-drawn-out struggle of eleven years, in which all Europe participated, was it recognized that the obstinate adherence of the Spanish people to Philip made it impossible for the Archduke Charles of Austria, the Habsburg claimant to the throne, to conquer and hold the kingdom by force; and the final will of Charles II was allowed to prevail.   Moreover, this was obtained at the cost of the partition of the Spanish Empire.   Philip was recognized as King of Spain and her colonies on condition that the French and Spanish crowns were never united; and Britain insisted that those territories which she did not want France or Spain to have should be assigned to her allies.   Spain, therefore, had to yield the Netherlands, Naples, Sardinia and Milan to Austria, while Savoy received Sicily.   Britain also shared in the partition, retaining Gibraltar and Minorca, besides making valuable commercial gains.[1]

These British gains and the loss by Spain of all her European possessions were greatly resented by Spaniards, but were both probably inevitable.   Her European losses, indeed, were in many ways advantageous to the country.   Spain no longer had to accept the defence of distant and dangerously-situated territories, which she had not been strong enough to undertake successfully in the later years of the seventeenth century.   The reforms, which were carried through in eighteenth-century Spain despite obstacles, would have been much harder to achieve if her responsibilities in Europe had still been so extensive and costly.

The long years of fighting during the War of the Spanish Succession were also important in their effect upon Spain's internal affairs.   The result of the War was to reveal once more the latent disunity in this, the newest of the important powers of Europe.   It re-opened the fissure, which had always undermined Spanish unity, between the kingdom of Aragon and the kingdom of Castile, joined only in the person of the monarch.   Aragon again took the lead in resisting the traditional royal policy of Castilianization, the strengthening of centralized monarchical government and the elimination of the frontiers and institutions of the different provincial regions.   So the separatist tendencies of the eastern part of the Peninsula found expression in revolt and support of the Archduke Charles.   Philip had to reduce Aragon Catalonia and Valencia by arms; Barcelona withstood a long siege until 1714, after the signing of the Treaty of Utrecht, and Majorca did not submit until the next year.

That Spain could wage a war, expel a foreign invader and subdue rebellious provinces was due very largely to the French officials and experts who came to the country with Philip.   Led by Jean Orry (1652–1719), they did much to overhaul the country's inadequate financial system, though it was never possible to

[1] P. 65.

embark upon a comprehensive scheme of reform. Among the first steps they took was to abolish the lavish offices, pensions, grants and concessions which had been made to favourites in past reigns and to prevent any such wasteful use of national resources in the future. Considerable success was also achieved in ensuring the more efficient and honest collection of taxes and keeping of accounts. The result was that, while in the previous century Spain had seemed unable to meet the financial requirements of warfare, Philip could maintain his forces until his possession of the country was decided and internal resistance overcome.

The Frenchmen were also amazed at the number of councils and boards and the complexities of *gueros* or local liberties through which provincial particularism challenged the centralization of Spanish government. They, therefore, began a movement, which continued throughout the reigns of Philip V, Ferdinand VI and Charles III, to approximate the Spanish crown more closely to the French type of monarchy by the encouragement of centralization and the restriction of local privileges. After the reduction of Aragon, Catalonia and Valencia, the *cortes* of these once-independent kingdoms were abolished, while the Castilian *cortes*, which had not met under Charles II, was very infrequently summoned. The Spanish *covachuela* or bureaucracy was also reformed. The favourites of previous reigns were replaced by regular ministers, and the *juntas* or administrative councils – with the exception of the Council of Castile – gave way to six departmental ministries of foreign affairs, justice, navies, the Indies, war and finance on French lines. Other characteristic French institutions introduced included the office of superintendent of finance (corresponding to the French *Contrôleur Général*) and provincial agents like the *intendants*.

The greater power enjoyed by the Bourbon kings made possible the triumph of the party, known as the *Regalistas* and composed of lawyers and public officials, who wished to uphold the regalities or rights of the crown against the encroachments of Pope and Inquisition. Even during the golden age of Spanish religion in the sixteenth century, the crown had always insisted upon its considerable ecclesiastical rights, and now these were greatly increased. Philip V actually broke off relations with the Papacy because it supported his rival for the throne during the War.

Negotiations for a new agreement were begun in 1714, but did not achieve success until the signing of the concordat of 1754, which virtually placed the Spanish Church under the authority of the crown.

The reign of Philip V also saw the beginnings of the influence of French culture in Spain, which was to be continued under his successors. Landmarks in this development are the creation of the National Library in 1711, the Royal Spanish Academy in 1714, the Academy of History in 1738 and the Academy of Fine Arts in 1752, as well as the publication of the great Academy dictionary between 1726 and 1739. Together with French literature, which included encyclopaedic literature, came in French amusements and fashions, buildings and roads. Despite royal encouragement, these foreign influences did not result in a period of intellectual and artistic greatness comparable with that displayed in the days of Spanish political power. Rather they tended to destroy the moral and intellectual unity, which had produced that greatness, and prepared the way for the political ferment and revolutions which were to distract the Peninsula in the future.

Indeed, the extent to which Spain had become exposed to foreign interests was shown immediately Philip had established his authority in his kingdom. In 1714, the same year as the fighting finally ended, his first wife died. The early attacks of his incapacitating melancholia had made Philip rely increasingly upon her, and he now transferred his dependence to the Princesse des Ursins, who set about arranging a suitable second marriage for him. In this she was assisted by Giulio Alberoni (1664–1752), the Italian who was soon to assume an important part in Spain's political affairs. The son of a poor vine-dresser, Alberoni had taken holy orders and originally come to Spain as the secretary of a French commander, the Duc de Vendôme, in 1711; after his patron's death he remained as diplomatic agent of the Duke of Parma, a position which made him intimate with the court. He suggested to the Princesse des Ursins that Philip might marry Elizabeth Farnese, the Duke of Parma's niece and step-daughter. The Princesse des Ursins agreed; she hoped it would secure the restoration of Spanish influence in Italy, and she believed that the young princess would submit to the rule of herself and her ally, Alberoni.

In this belief she was, however, quite mistaken. Her first

meeting with the new Queen at a wayside inn produced a deliberately-fomented quarrel which resulted in her being hustled into a coach, dressed only in her court dress, and taken shivering over the bleak Pyrenees during a snowy winter's night back to France. Her exile was followed by that of Orry. Elizabeth relied upon Alberoni as her adviser and had him made a cardinal in 1717. Though he never held any recognized Spanish administrative office or title, his influence with the Queen enabled him to dominate administration and policy between 1715 and 1719.

Alberoni was to prove himself one of the greatest names in Spanish history. Despite his short tenure of power, he was able to effect several valuable internal reforms. He continued the reduction of the powers of the councils in the government of the country and also Orry's policy of cutting down pensions and eliminating abuses in the collection of taxes. He endeavoured to encourage trade by paying bounties to certain industries, imposing protective tariffs, attracting the immigration of foreign craftsmen and abolishing internal customs duties. The result of these reforms was to increase the revenue of the treasury, which rose from 142,000,000 reals in 1700 to 211,000,000 reals in 1737, and to assist industrial production; the number of looms in Valencia, for instance, increased from 300 in 1717 to 2,000 in 1722. Above all, Alberoni began to build up a new Spanish navy, which had sunk to as low as twenty ships in 1700.[1]

Alberoni showed himself greatest, however, in foreign affairs. The Treaty of Utrecht was not followed by a period of peace for Spain, but by fifteen years of international intrigues and tension, alliances and war, brought about by the ambition of Elizabeth Farnese, who soon acquired the nickname of 'The Termagant'. Philip had two sons by his first wife. When his marriage with Elizabeth produced two more sons, Don Carlos and Don Philip, their mother, since they could not aspire to the Spanish throne, wished to secure their succession to her family principalities in Italy. 'Her passionate maternal love', as Salvador de Madariaga has said, 'proved nearly as devastating for Spain as Philip II's religious dreams', for Louis XIV's death in 1715 and Philip V's continued aspirations to the French succession and consequent hostility to Orléans provided her with an opportunity to exploit her aims. French political influence in Spain was now, therefore, at an end, and the country embarked upon a policy of Italian

[1] P. 141.

adventure which threatened to plunge Europe into a renewal of general war.

Alberoni, who was himself ready to renew Spanish influence in Italy, sought to prevent the Empire receiving the assistance of allies while Spain overran its Italian provinces.   So James Stuart, the Old Pretender, was invited to Spain with the promise of an expedition to place him on the English throne, and intrigues were encouraged in France against Orléans.   By 1717, despite the formation of the Triple Alliance of Britain, France and Holland, Alberoni thought it now safe to act.   In that year he sent an expedition which occupied Sardinia without difficulty, and the next year sent another expedition against Sicily; but when this was followed by war with France and Britain, Spain was in no condition to resist.[1]   Philip dismissed Alberoni, acceded to the Quadruple Alliance and renounced his claims to the French throne.   By the Treaty of London in 1720, the Emperor obtained Sicily from Piedmont in return for the much less valuable Sardinia, but Spain also benefited from Alberoni's policy, for Don Carlos, Elizabeth Farnese's elder son, was recognized as heir to the Duchies of Tuscany, Parma and Piacenza.

The immediate effect of this episode was a revival of good relations between Spain and France.   Elizabeth Farnese was not content with what Alberoni had done for her.   She wanted immediate territorial gains in Italy and now decided that any attempt to alter the Utrecht settlement would be more likely to succeed with the support rather than the opposition of France. Since the betrothal of the Spanish Infanta to Louis XV seemed to promise a long period of Franco-Spanish accord, Philip put into effect an earlier resolve and in 1724 abdicated in favour of his eldest son, Louis.   He retired to the Palace of St. Ildelfonso de la Granja, which he had built to remind himself of the Versailles of his youth; but after only seven months the death of Louis from smallpox brought him back to the throne for another twenty-two years.   His second reign proved to be no more peaceful for Spain than his first and for the same reason.   Philip still nursed designs upon the French succession, and his wife still wanted to obtain Italian thrones for her sons.

This made a long-lived Franco-Spanish friendship impossible. Elizabeth was already impatient at the lack of French support for her ambitions when Bourbon annulled the proposed marriage of

[1] Pp. 159–60.

Philip's daughter to the French king in 1724. Elizabeth's thoughts were now directly turned towards the idea, which she had entertained for some time, of an alliance with the Emperor. Charles VI was also ready to consider this. In order to develop the trade of the Austrian Netherlands with the East Indies, he had founded the Ostend Company to which the maritime powers were violently opposed. He also wanted to secure general European support for his Pragmatic Sanction. A Spanish alliance might gain him useful support for both these schemes.

In 1724, therefore, Elizabeth sent Baron Ripperdá as her envoy to Vienna. Ripperdá was a Dutch adventurer, a nobleman of some wealth who had originally represented his country after the Treaty of Utrecht at the Spanish court, where he announced his conversion to Roman Catholicism and gained such influence over the Queen that he decided to settle in the country. He succeeded in arranging the First Treaty of Vienna between Spain and Austria in 1725 by which the Emperor renounced his claim to the Spanish throne, recognized Don Carlos as heir to Tuscany, Parma and Piacenza and promised to help Spain recover Gibraltar and Minorca from Britain, while Philip recognized the Pragmatic Sanction and granted trading concessions to the Ostend Company.[1]

The Treaty was supposed to be secret, but news of it became public and resulted in the signing in 1726 of the Treaty of Hanover between Britain, France and Prussia, who were later joined by Holland, Sweden and Denmark. The news had become known through Ripperdá's boastful garrulity, and Elizabeth discovered that the Emperor had no intention of agreeing to marriages between his two daughters and her two sons, as Ripperdá had asserted. Ripperdá was arrested, but escaped to Morocco to become a Moslem and Grand Vizier to the Sultan.

When Spain besieged Gibraltar, the Emperor gave her no assistance, Walpole did not want a general war to develop, and Fleury exerted his influence towards the restoration of peace. Elizabeth, therefore, was ready to relinquish her alliance with the Emperor, and in 1729 Spain signed the Treaty of Seville with Britain and France. By this Spain tacitly relinquished her claim to Gibraltar and Minorca and revoked the Ostend Company's privileges, while the two other powers agreed to support the claims of Don Carlos to the Italian duchies. Since the Emperor

[1] P. 200.

was anxious to obtain further guarantees for his Pragmatic Sanction, he signed the Second Treaty of Vienna in 1731 with Britain, Holland and Spain in which he recognized the Italian claims of Don Carlos and dissolved the Ostend Company in return for the acknowledgement of the Pragmatic Sanction by Britain and Holland. In the same year the Duke of Parma died, and Don Carlos sailed with a Spanish force and escorted by a British fleet to take possession of Parma and Piacenza.

By now, therefore, Spain had regained a foothold in Italy and reasserted herself in European diplomacy. This was due not only to Alberoni and Elizabeth Farnese, but also to Don José de Patiño, the first really capable native Spanish statesman of the century. Originally a Jesuit novice, he played an important part in the organization of the army during the War of the Spanish Succession and was brought to Madrid by Alberoni. On the fall of Ripperdá, he became Minister for Marine and the Indies and shortly afterwards Minister of Finance. During his tenure of office, he continued the restoration of the navy and was able to send in 1732 a fleet of 600 ships with an army of 30,000 men to recapture Oran, which the Moors had taken twenty-four years previously. Through a system of bounties he encouraged Spanish trade with the Americas and the Philippines, and he continued the financial reforms of Orry and Alberoni. Like them, he was able to ensure, without remodelling the system of taxation itself, that Philip V and Elizabeth Farnese never lacked the resources to support their political ambitions, and by the time of his death in 1736 Spain had recovered much of her lost prestige and power.

The tranquillity secured in Europe in 1731 did not last long. Elizabeth Farnese's success in Parma had intensified the struggle of Spain and Austria for Italian predominance, and friction between Spain and Britain over South American trade was steadily becoming more acute. In such a situation, Spanish and French interests seemed to have much in common, and this was emphasized by the events which led up to the War of the Polish Succession. Elizabeth at first thought of trying to secure the Polish crown for Don Carlos, but when France firmly supported Louis XV's father-in-law, she agreed with the suggestion of Patiño that, while the Emperor was occupied in Poland, Don Carlos should take Naples and Sicily. France also was agreeable to this, since it would divert the Emperor from Central Europe, while

Philip V, since the birth of a son to Louis XV in 1729 had considerably diminished his chances of succeeding to the French throne, was ready for more cordial relations with France.

By the First Family Compact of 1733 the two powers mutually guaranteed their possessions against attack by either Britain or Austria. The next year Don Carlos conquered Naples and then Sicily. He was confirmed in his possession of these, with the traditional title of King of the Two Sicilies, by the Third Treaty of Vienna in 1738, but the Emperor obtained Parma and Piacenza, and Tuscany was granted to the Duke of Lorraine as compensation for the cession of his duchy to Stanislas. This aroused the resentment of Elizabeth Farnese, who now wished her second son, Philip, to have territories and was to continue her policy of intriguing in European affairs to secure her object.

It was not, however, the royal policy which soon involved Spain in war again. This time she drifted into hostilities with Britain over the South American trade, where the *Assiento* and the right to send one ship each year to Porto Bello, granted to Britain by the Treaty of Utrecht, had been producing constant friction. Both sides practised fraud and violence. The British abused the 'annual ship' by refilling it from so-called supply vessels, and numerous smugglers carried on a contraband trade with the Spanish West Indies; the Spanish *guarda-costas* arrested many traders, both innocent and guilty, confiscating ships and cargoes. This situation produced the notorious case of Captain Jenkins.[1] Both sides made an effort to settle peacefully the dispute, which the incident raised, by the Convention of Pardo early in 1739, but the trading community in England wanted to fight, and in the same year the War of Jenkins's Ear began. The War proved that Patiño had made Spain strong enough to withstand even British sea-power. Admiral Vernon sacked and destroyed Porto Bello, but similar attacks by him on Cartagena and Santiago de Cuba were repulsed.

The death of the Emperor Charles VI and the seizure of Silesia by Frederick II of Prussia widened hostilities into the War of the Austrian Succession in 1740 and brought about the Second Family Compact between France and Spain in 1743. Elizabeth induced Philip to claim the whole Habsburg inheritance through his descent from the great Emperor Charles V who had separated Spain and the Empire upon his abdication in 1555. Her

[1] P. 76.

intention, however, was to use this claim as a means of obtaining the Austrian dominions in Italy – Milan, Lombardy, Parma and Piacenza – to be united with Tuscany (whose ruler, the former Duke of Lorraine, was Maria Theresa's husband) to form a kingdom for her second son. With this object Spanish troops fought a series of campaigns in northern Italy which were marked by many vicissitudes and reverses, and at the Treaty of Aix-la-Chapelle in 1748 Philip received only Parma and Piacenza, which he had to promise to renounce if he should ever succeed to the throne of Spain or the Two Sicilies.

Before the end of the War, while peace negotiations were in progress, Philip V died of apoplexy in 1746. In itself his death meant nothing to the country, for the last years of his life had been passed in long periods of almost complete derangement; but it did mean that Elizabeth Farnese no longer controlled Spanish foreign policy, which ceased to aim at gaining Italian territories. This change in foreign policy brought hopes that Spain might now be allowed a period of peace to enjoy the remarkable material progress which she had made during the reign of the first of her Bourbon kings.

Ferdinand VI and Charles III

The new king, Ferdinand VI (1746–59), was the survivor of Philip's two sons by his first wife and had married a Portuguese princess, Barbara of Braganza. He was almost as dominated by his wife as his father had been, but neither he nor she was much interested in foreign affairs. Both wished Spain to follow a policy of peace and neutrality. Though Ferdinand's reign saw the growing hostility of France and Britain, which culminated in the Seven Years' War, this policy prevailed until his death. Ferdinand's two chief ministers, José de Carvajal and the Marquis de la Ensenada, sympathized respectively with Britain and France, and their conflicting inclinations did much to nullify the continual attempts of each power to persuade Spain into a definite alliance. The peaceful years of Ferdinand's reign, in fact, allowed both of these statesmen to devote themselves to internal reforms.

Carvajal's efforts were largely confined to attempts to revive Spanish industry by encouraging the immigration of skilled foreign workmen, but Ensenada's reforms were more extensive and important. A banker and merchant by origin, Ensenada was a naval administrator until he became Minister of Finance,

War, Marine and the Indies in 1743. He made his mark on many aspects of Spanish life and continued Patiño's economic and financial policy. He was the first minister to give Spain some modern roads and canals, which brought great advantages to industry. Mining was encouraged by removing the ban on the export of metals, so that long-abandoned mines were re-opened. His greatest financial reform was the abolition of tax-farming and the raising of the revenue of the treasury by five million ducats a year. He also encouraged the Spanish intellectual revival; the foundation of academies continued, scholarships were founded to promote research both at home and abroad, and foreign scholars were attracted to Spain.

Nor did Ensenada lose his interest in the navy and defence. He believed that Spain could not hope to have an army to rival that of France nor a navy to rival that of Britain, but should try to attain sufficient naval, military and financial power to enable her to secure her neutrality and exercise some influence in international affairs. He improved the arsenals at Cartagena and Caracca, made Cadiz an effective naval base, fortified the Portuguese frontier, raised new regiments and laid down a number of new capital ships. Such naval activity increased British hostility towards Ensenada, thus making him still more strongly French in his sympathies. When Carvajal died in 1754, Ensenada began secret negotiations with France, which were discovered, however, and led to his dismissal from office. He had given Spain a valuable short breathing-time of peace and reform, and when Ferdinand died in 1759 the country was comparatively prosperous, with a powerful fleet and a substantial reserve in the treasury.

Ferdinand was childless and in his will acknowledged the right to the Spanish throne of his elder half-brother, Don Carlos, who renounced the Neapolitan throne in favour of his third son, the eldest being insane, and was crowned king as Charles III (1759-88). With his accession began the development of a new phase in the rule of the Spanish Bourbons. Under the two previous monarchs, reforms had been directed by ministers and put into effect largely through the influence of diplomatic and naval needs. Neither ruler had given any leadership himself in this direction. Charles, however, was an example of an Enlightened Despot of the later eighteenth century and the best and most capable of the Spanish Bourbons. He had a genuine concern for reform and, at the age of forty-three, the advantage of twenty years' experience as a ruler in the Two Sicilies. His appearance and tastes did not seem consistent with his abilities. He had always a somewhat rustic air and was remarkable for his sharp, long nose, cold, blue eyes and strange, mask-like face so reminiscent of Louis XI of France. The years he had spent in Italy had given him an appreciation of the arts and made him something of a dilettante. Nevertheless, the achievements of himself and his ministers effected a great advance in the progress of Spain during the century. It was his misfortune that events and circumstances after his reign prevented the continuance of this advance.

Like many progressive Spaniards of the period, Charles was much under the influence of French ideas. While in Naples he had openly opposed the policy of neutrality followed by Spain during Ferdinand's reign, and now he wished to pursue an actively pro-French policy. The Seven Years' War was at its height when he became king, and in 1761 he made the Third Family Compact, which brought Spain into the war.[1] Had France received Spanish support from the first, the alliance might have produced effective results, but at this stage of the War it came too late. It only postponed the conclusion of peace and involved Spain in the misfortunes suffered by France through the successes of the British navy. The Treaty of Paris in 1763 forced Spain to cede Florida to Britain. Though France transferred Louisiana to her as compensation, this vast territory was as yet of little value.

Charles III's reign had as unpropitious a beginning at home as abroad. He appointed as Minister of Finance his Italian favourite, the Marquis of Squillaci, whom the Spaniards called Esquilache. King and minister were both shocked by the backwardness and squalor of Madrid and its inhabitants. At once arrangements were made for the streets to be paved and drained, swept and lit at night. Such reforms, for which Squillaci was believed to be responsible, alarmed the conservative Spaniards, and when sumptuary laws followed, the 'Esquilache Revolt' of 1766 broke out. Charles wished to make the Spaniards wear cocked hats, bag-wigs and short coats instead of their wide-brimmed hats, side-locks and long cloaks (useful for concealing a dagger). Officials were posted in the streets with shears to trim offending garments to the right length. Rioting broke out in

[1] P. 227.

Madrid and other cities against Squillaci, who fled to Naples. Charles had to give way and withdraw the unpopular measures, though he secured his end by making the traditional costume the official attire of the public executioner.

Squillaci was replaced by the Count de Aranda, who was able and vain, liberal and anti-clerical. He and Charles regarded the clergy and especially the Jesuits as responsible for the troubles, and their determination to end clerical opposition to their reforms led to an attack on ecclesiastical privilege and the sudden expulsion of the members of the Society in 1767.[1] In domestic affairs Charles and Aranda mainly continued Ensenada's aims. The *alcabala*, which had remained so long at fourteen per cent, was halved, the loss of revenue being partly made up by a tax of five per cent on land and property rents and by a state lottery, which soon became popular. An attempt was made to arrest rural depopulation by attracting immigrants, notably 6,000 Bavarians who were dissuaded from going to the Indies and settled in thirteen new villages in the Sierra Morena, the broad mountain ridge in the south of Spain. Industry was stimulated by a combination of the removal of restrictions on imported raw materials and the establishment of a high tariff on foreign manufactured goods. Glass, porcelain, cotton, velvet, fine leather and fancy goods flourished especially. The increased prosperity of the country raised the national revenue during Charles III's last years to more than three times what it had been a century earlier, despite lower taxation. It also enabled the government to embark on schemes for irrigating the land and building hospitals, asylums and almshouses. Finally, the population of the country rose notably in this period.[2]

After his unfruitful intervention in the Seven Years' War, Charles doubted the value of an active French alliance, and his mistrust was increased in 1770 when Choiseul persuaded Spain to eject Britain from the Falkland Islands, only to have to withdraw through lack of support from Louis XV, an episode which brought about the fall of both Choiseul and Aranda. Nevertheless, when France supported the insurgent American colonies against Britain, Charles allowed himself to be tempted by the possible prizes. He made ready after the news of the defeat of the British at Saratoga and then entered the War in 1779. Spain was better prepared for war than she had been for a long time; in particular, Ensenada's

[1] Pp. 116–7.   [2] P. 11.

naval policy had given her a large number of ships of the line.[1] Though her attack on Gibraltar failed, Minorca and Florida were taken and retained at the Treaty of Versailles.   This was the first time Spain had made gains in war for many years, and her empire in the New World was now at its height, comprising all South and Central America, except Brazil and Guiana, and Mexico, California, Louisiana and Florida in North America; but the foundation of the United States, which she had supported, was to encourage her colonies to seek their independence.

With the death of Charles III in 1788, as has been truly said, 'an epoch in Spanish history ended'.   He was succeeded by his second son, Charles IV (1788–1808), who at the age of forty was amiable and well intentioned, but lacking in both statecraft and fortitude and dominated by his wife, Marie Luisa of Parma, grand-daughter of the Farnese, who herself was influenced by a succession of favourites.   His accession was soon followed by the French Revolution.   Spain was engulfed in war, losing her navy to Britain and her independence to France.   It was an end to her return to the position of a great power under her Bourbon kings, and in the nineteenth century her lack of industrial resources was to place this aspiration beyond the possibility of attainment.

[1] P. 141.

X · THE RISE OF PRUSSIA

Prussian Origins

THE foundations of the Kingdom of Prussia were laid in the seventeenth century when the careful plans of the Hohenzollern rulers of the Electorate of Brandenburg bore fruit. Since the early fifteenth century, when these military adventurers from Swabia in south-western Germany had acquired Brandenburg and the electoral dignity from the Emperor Sigismund in return for helping him to win the Imperial crown, few of the Hohenzollerns had been outstanding. They had, however, sought territorial gains by numerous matrimonial and hereditary alliances with other German princely houses, and even renounced Lutheranism in favour of Calvinism in order to sustain their claim to the Duchies of Cleves and Jülich. This policy achieved its successes in the first half of the seventeenth century. The Hohenzollerns in rapid succession acquired Cleves, Mark and Ravensburg in western Germany in 1614, the Duchy of Prussia in eastern Germany in 1618, the province of East Pomerania, the secularized bishoprics of Cammin and (as compensation for Sweden's retention of Western Pomerania) Minden, Halberstadt and the reversion of the Archbishopric of Magdeburg in 1648. These scattered territories, comprising 44,000 square miles as against the 14,000 square miles of Brandenburg alone, did not form a single state, but provided the possible framework of one.

The newly-enlarged Brandenburg-Prussia was unfortunate in being ruled by one of the least capable of the Hohenzollerns, George William (1619–40), during the greater part of the Thirty Years' War. He was unable to maintain the neutrality which he desired for his territories, and they were devastated by Imperial and Swedish forces in turn. The Elector's own troops, being too weak to withstand the invaders, became utterly demoralized and often themselves joined in the violence and pillage. The War also had important political consequences for Brandenburg-Prussia. It reduced the power of the Estates, since the Elector's first minister, Count Adam zu Schwarzenberg, governed in Berlin without consulting them, and it also increased the power of the army and the bureaucracy.

It was these two political developments which were, in fact, to raise Prussia above the other German states in the years after the Treaty of Westphalia. The wide dispersal of Hohenzollern territory and the critical position of Prussia in Central Europe, which laid her open to threats from such great powers as Sweden, Austria and Russia, were a strong incentive for her rulers to follow a policy based upon these twin aims of eliminating the importance of the Estates and strengthening the functions of the army and bureaucracy. So, during the second half of the seventeenth century, Prussia became a bureaucratic-military state in which the obligation of all its inhabitants to serve the ruler found its greatest expression in a strong standing army with its accompanying administrative organization.

Prussia was initiated upon this course during the strenuous reign of Frederick William, the Great Elector (1640–88). Electoral absolutism was established. The Diet of Brandenburg ceased to meet, the Diet of Cleves was overawed by Brandenburg troops, and the Diet of Prussia was subdued after Frederick William had imprisoned one of its leaders for sixteen years until he died: another, who fled to Poland, was kidnapped by his orders in Warsaw and taken to Königsberg, where he was tortured, tried and beheaded. Gradually governors, tax-commissioners and other electoral officials gained control of the central administration of the territories. In particular, the revenue required for the upkeep of the army was placed under the management of the *Kriegskommissariat*, the newly-founded military supply organization, and the raising of it made wholly independent of the Estates by the substitution of an urban excise for the occasional subsidies granted by the Diets. By such means Frederick William was able to equip Prussia with a highly-trained standing army, which, with the assistance of Dutch and French subsidies, had been raised to about 30,000 men during the last years of his reign and was further increased by his successors.[1]

In addition, Frederick William endeavoured to improve the internal economic strength of his state. In this he was assisted by his adoption of the principle of religious toleration. A devout Calvinist himself, ruling over Lutherans in Brandenburg and Prussia, he saw that this was the only possible policy in his scattered and diverse dominions and appreciated the economic advantages it had brought to Britain and Holland. Jews were

[1] P. 135.

allowed to settle in Berlin, and even Roman Catholics were tolerated, while industrious Huguenots from France were welcomed. This enabled him to initiate plans for colonizing the land and establishing new industries, both of which were needed by his backward and war-devastated state. And the practice of religious toleration proved to be an important addition to the military means by which Prussia was to achieve greatness.

Frederick William's son, Frederick III (1688–1713), is best remembered as Frederick I, the first Prussian king, who delighted in pomp and ceremony and built stately palaces in Charlottenburg and Berlin, where he attempted to hold a court based upon Versailles under Louis XIV. He did, however, make not unimportant contributions to the advance of Prussia. He increased his army to 40,000 men, and his troops fought in the great battles of the War of the Spanish Succession at the end of which Prussia gained Spanish Guelderland, and he advanced Prussia's lead in the promotion of German culture by founding the University of Halle and the Berlin Academies of Arts and Sciences.

Above all, Frederick secured for his dynasty the coveted royal title which embodied and stimulated its ambitions. After lengthy negotiations, the Emperor Leopold, anxious to obtain Prussian help in the approaching war with France, agreed that the Elector of Brandenburg might become a monarch. The Emperor did not, however, bestow the title himself; Frederick assumed the position of King of Prussia, which was outside the Empire. Thus the ruler of Prussia became a king a century before the rulers of Saxony, Bavaria and Württemberg were made monarchs by Napoleon. The new monarchy inevitably assumed the leadership of the Protestant interest in Germany, held since the Reformation by the Electors of Saxony, but recently lost when Augustus the Strong announced his conversion to Roman Catholicism to make possible his election to the Polish throne. The potentialities for Prussia of her new position were to be realized fully by the first king's grandson a generation after his death.

Frederick William I (1713–40)

Frederick I's son, who succeeded him on the throne in 1713, was cast in a sterner mould; his contribution to the development of Prussia was less spectacular but far more solid. Indeed, his character and his aims were largely based upon opposition to his father, whose extravagance, fondness of court etiquette and dependence upon foreign allies he resented and despised. This reaction did much to form both his virtues and his defects. His daughter Wilhelmina, whose memoirs – though exaggerated – show clearly why she disliked the unbelievable tyranny which he exercised as unrestrainedly over his family as over his state, said he 'possessed all the qualities for a great man, with an elevation of the spirit capable of the greatest deeds'.

Frederick William was pious and moral; he possessed a high sense of duty, unwearying industry and constant concern for detail. He rose at dawn or soon afterwards and busied himself with parading his troops, meticulously supervising state affairs, ensuring economy in the court and vigorously managing his family. Particularly he spent many hours at his desk, wearing canvas half-sleeves to protect his uniform, as he read and composed official documents. Nevertheless, as Dr. Eyck has observed, 'as a human being he was merely a grotesque sergeant-major, constantly laying about him with his cane, a man whose ideal even in non-military matters was the regular beat of the parade ground'. He ruled as an absolute monarch whose will was to be obeyed instantly. If he decreed the death of any one of his subjects or vented his displeasure on passers-by in the street by ordering them lashes, the sentence was carried out. He made his daughters engage in house and farm work like any serving-maids and was dissuaded with difficulty from putting his own son to death in defiance of a recommendation of his own court. His officials were expected to use the same methods in their own families. A high administrator received a royal order to box his wife's ears soundly in the presence of several officers whom she had not treated with sufficient respect. He found relaxation in his *Tabaks Kollegium,* informal gatherings of his closest advisers for smoking, drinking and barrack-room talk. And he lost no opportunity to express his contempt for art and poetry, philosophy and letters.

Frederick William ascended the Prussian throne in the same year as the signing of the Treaty of Utrecht, but he wished to increase his army rather than reduce it and to make its existence independent of foreign subsidies. By an amazing concentration of effort, which was assisted by the general peacefulness of Europe, he was able to achieve both his aims by the end of his reign. He is popularly remembered for his regiment of tall grenadiers, his 'blue boys', whom he secured by recruiting or kidnapping from all parts of Europe and took pleasure in drilling at Potsdam. His care for his army, however, extended beyond these ornamental guards. By his death he had doubled the Prussian army to 80,000 men; it was one in twenty-five of the population when the French army was about one in a hundred and fifty.

This expansion was only made possible by the enrolment of a considerable proportion of the army from the Prussian population. Foreign mercenaries were still employed in large numbers, but the high cost of recruiting abroad led Frederick William to devise means of obtaining native conscripts, who eventually provided him with about half of his troops. The recruiting officers were given definite districts from which they had to obtain a fixed quota of men from the sons of peasants and craftsmen, who served for a year or two in the ranks and were then followed by replacements from the same district. In this way there gradually developed a kind of conscription among the lower classes.

All the German states at this time maintained standing armies. None was as large or efficient as Prussia's, but an even more important distinction was that her army was maintained from her own national resources, while the others relied to some extent upon subsidies from France, Spain, Holland or the Empire. Frederick William was determined not to follow the example of his grandfather and father in seeking foreign subsidies. Military finance had, therefore, to be raised entirely at home.

This was not an easy task. His father's attempts to imitate Louis XIV left Frederick William an almost empty treasury at the beginning of his reign, but he soon reduced expenditure and increased income. Economies were enforced upon everything except the army. The feudal tenure, upon which the nobles had hitherto held their lands, was replaced by a single uniform land tax. The royal domains, especially extensive in Prussia, where they accounted for about a third of the land and a quarter of the peasants, were carefully administered, and a system of shorter, more profitable leases was introduced for the farming out of estates, with the result that the income derived from these lands approximated to the total yield of taxation. The excise was continued and an extensive tariff imposed on foreign imports (for mercantilist as well as financial reasons). The Prussian historian, Professor Droysen, has estimated that by such measures Frederick William raised his revenue from 3,655,000 thalers in 1714 to

5,483,000 in 1730 and to almost 7,000,000 in 1740. Although by the end of his reign annual military expenditure consumed some 5,000,000 thalers of this enlarged revenue, Frederick William was able to leave at his death a war treasure of 6,000,000 thalers.

Not only did Frederick William give Prussia a large army and ample financial resources. He also gave the Prussian officers' corps, intitiated by the Great Elector, a definite and permanent position. The establishment of the *Cadettenhaus* in Berlin put into practice his conception that service in the army was the chief duty of the Junkers, who henceforward became a nobility of military service, rewarded by a political and social status which made them a privileged caste in the State.[1]

In his administrative reforms, Frederick William was less successful. The dispersed and varied nature of the territories under his rule had enabled them to retain into the beginning of the eighteenth century a political structure weakened by disunity and medieval survivals. The King directly managed his domain-lands in Prussia very much in the manner of a private estate; elsewhere administration was shared among provincial departments and chambers, towns and country officials. Frederick William secured unification through his ordinance of 1723, a code of civil administration and administrative law which combined and centralized the system of government. He did very little, however, to achieve specialization. The General Directory, which he formed at the same time to act as the supreme authority in his new system, was hardly a ministry. It was really an administrative board, whose five members dealt with all sorts of business except foreign affairs and justice with an inevitable lack of efficiency and promptitude. The Prussian central administration was to remain unsatisfactory for the rest of the century and to contribute towards the downfall of the State during the Napoleonic War. In Frederick William's reign it nevertheless functioned adequately through the unifying ability and industry of this royal autocrat, who once said, 'You can tell the Prince of Anhalt that I am the Field Marshal and the Finance Minister of Prussia'.

Frederick William also continued Hohenzollern policy in promoting immigration into his territory by active encouragement and religious toleration. People from other countries and par-

[1] P. 136.

ticularly from other German states were attracted by promises of exemption, for a period of years, from taxation and military service; the largest group were about 20,000 Lutheran peasants, evicted from the Archbishopric of Salzburg in 1728, who were settled in East Prussia. The expanding Prussian army itself increased the population of the country, for it is estimated that between 300,000 and 400,000 foreign mercenaries entered its ranks during the eighteenth century, the majority of whom married and settled in Prussia. Skilled craftsmen from abroad were highly desired, for Frederick William endeavoured through administrative controls to encourage the development of manufactures, especially the clothweaving industry at Brandenburg which exported much of its products to Russia.

The army, which Frederick William built up at such great cost, hardly went into action during his reign. At the conclusion of the two wars with which his reign opened, he followed a policy of peace and non-aggression. In the west, the War of the Spanish Succession, in which he himself fought at Malplaquet, had really ended when he came to the throne, and he joined Britain and Holland in making a separate peace with France that brought Spanish Guelderland to Prussia. In the east, the Great Northern War (1700–21) was remorselessly exhausting Sweden. Frederick William entered the War on Russia's side in 1715. After his troops had besieged and occupied Stralsund, he deserted Russia – Peter the Great jibed that he wished to fish without wetting his feet – and bought from Sweden in 1720 part of West Pomerania, including Stettin on the Oder.

For the rest of his reign, Frederick William nursed the ambition of securing Jülich-Berg, the half of the original Rhineland Duchy of Cleves which Brandenburg had failed to obtain a century earlier and which now had a childless ruler; but he did not intend to go to war for it and was unable to induce by diplomatic means the Emperor Charles VI to promise him the succession to it, despite Prussian recognition of the Pragmatic Sanction in 1726. He made no permanent alliances and got no further provinces for Prussia. Albert Waddington has said that Frederick William had no head for foreign policy. He mistrusted allies and did not care to risk his army in uncertain campaigns; he was always conscious of the strategic weaknesses of his territory and the smallness of its population. Consequently his reputation never achieved the brilliance of his son's, but, had he not been content to husband his potential power, that son might never have been able to follow such a successful foreign policy.

Indeed, the extent to which he has been overshadowed by his famous son has largely obscured recognition of the value of Frederick William's contribution to the future greatness of Prussia. Besides providing the army which his son used to such effective purpose, he also laid down a tradition of devotion to the State, strict financial economy and emphasis upon military efficiency which his son also followed. Above all, his insistence upon the personal absolutism of the ruler and upon the military duty of the nobility towards the State was to be of lasting and far-reaching consequence in Prussia and, in fact, later in Germany as a whole.

The Early Years of Frederick the Great

Frederick II, commonly known as Frederick the Great, succeeded his father as King of Prussia in 1740 and ruled until his death in 1786. He was born in 1712, his mother being Queen Sophia Dorothea, sister of George II of Britain. An appreciation of his character must begin with his boyhood experiences. Until the age of seven he was brought up by nurses and governesses; then his father put him under tutors who were to give him a rigorous education in which the emphasis should be upon military training with a company of cadets formed for this purpose from the sons of noble families. His father wished to mould him according to his own outlook and tastes, but Frederick was a boy with a quick intelligence and a constant thirst for knowledge and interest in languages, letters and the arts. The growing divergence between father and son produced angry scenes which sometimes ended in the infliction of physical violence and brutal floggings upon Frederick. When his only playmate, his sister Wilhelmina, three years his senior and the only woman he ever loved, took his part, she was subjected to the same treatment as himself.

At the age of eighteen, while travelling with his father in western Germany, Frederick tried to escape to France, but was stopped and brought back. He was kept in solitary confinement for six weeks at Küstrin, and then he and Lieutenant von Katte, his friend and accomplice, were sentenced to death, though the court martial recommended that both should be pardoned. Katte was beheaded in the yard of Frederick's prison, and he was forced to stand at a window to witness it. Frederick's life was probably only saved by the intervention of several foreign courts.

His father commuted the sentence to one of imprisonment and deprivation of his rank as crown prince. He was soon released, but ordered to reside at Küstrin and take part in the management of provincial administration and finance.

After fifteen months of this exile, Frederick resolved to submit to his father and obtained his pardon. He was restored to his rank in the army and in 1732 was given command of a regiment at Ruppin, a small town some forty miles north-east of Berlin. He now acted as an obedient son and avoided opposition to his father. Though he had wanted to marry his first cousin Amelia, daughter of George II, he unwillingly accepted at the age of twenty-one his father's choice, Elizabeth Christina, daughter of the Duke of Brunswick-Bevern and niece of the Empress. The marriage was childless, and Frederick left her as soon as he came to the throne.

Though Frederick had thus subjected himself to his father's will, the next seven years were the happiest of his life. His submission had brought him freedom at last to do much as he chose with his life. His father presented him with the pleasant estate of Rheinsberg not far from Ruppin. Here he could play his flute and read his books without being knocked down. He read widely in literature and history and studied philosophy in the writings of Locke and, above all, the French *philosophes*, whose outlook appealed to him and influenced him strongly. In 1736 he wrote to Voltaire, and the ensuing correspondence flattered both men. It also gained Frederick the approbation of the *salons* of Paris – which he did not lose even when he fought France during the Seven Years' War – and so of the intelligentsia throughout Europe. Frederick also wrote in French, imitating the works of the *philosophes*, especially in *L'Antimachiavel*, revised by Voltaire and published anonymously in 1740, in which he proclaimed that the ruler must be the first servant of the State and that war was only allowable if required by its interests.

When Frederick ascended the Prussian throne in 1740, however, the policies upon which he embarked were hardly in complete accordance with the long-continued esteem he enjoyed from the *philosophes*. He had his limitations as an Enlightened Despot.[1] His internal policy was conditioned also by the policies of his predecessors and the needs of his kingdom, which were never

[1] P. 198.

allowed to be sacrificed to the ideas of the Enlightenment; and his foreign policy revealed an uninhibited adoption of all the unscrupulous political arts commonly associated with the great sixteenth-century Florentine against whom he had written.   Above all, his character was not that of one destined to lead mankind into the age of progress and humanity imagined by the *philosophes*.   The British ambassador, Lord Malmesbury, said of him, 'Although as an individual he often appears and really is humane, benevolent and friendly, yet the instant he acts in his royal capacity . . . he carries with him desolation, misery and persecution.'   This may seem excessive, but in weighing up his achievements, the inhuman treatment of his soldiers in peace and war may be set, for instance, against his humanization of the penal code.[1]   Still more, his whole policy scarcely seems to have been motivated by a benign purpose.   Despite his appellation of 'great', his industry and courage, he became as a writer has said, 'that most formidable of political beings, a logical autocrat' in circumstances which enabled him to act in this way to the full.   For this the embittering circumstances of his terrible youth, so different from the usual circumscribed, uneventful upbringing of most princes, must bear much responsibility.

The Wars of the Austrian Succession and Seven Years

The first half of Frederick the Great's reign was occupied by wars in which Prussia fought against Austria.   His original declaration of war on Austria precipitated the military and diplomatic events of the period from 1740 to 1763 in which occurred the War of the Austrian Succession, the Diplomatic Revolution and the Seven Years' War.[2]   For Prussia his actions made this the period when her power gained her such influence and prestige that her position in the Empire was established as equal if not superior to that of Austria.

The death of Frederick William I in May 1740 was followed by the death of the Emperor Charles VI in October of the same year.   This event, Frederick wrote to Voltaire, 'destroyed all my peaceful thoughts'.   Before the end of the year his troops invaded the Habsburg province of Silesia.   His action seems to have been suddenly decided upon rather than long premeditated.   He had, however, thought for some time that a state such as Prussia could only hope to make territorial gains if she seized a favourable

---

[1] P. 194.   [2] P. 202.

opportunity to act promptly with a definite object in view. The Emperor's death seemed to provide him with this opportunity, and the fact that Prussia had signed the Pragmatic Sanction did not deter him. To the rule of the Habsburg lands had now come an inexperienced girl whose position was insecure, whose provinces were disunited and badly governed, whose ministers were incompetent, whose revenue was small and whose army was weak. It seemed quite likely that France would make use of this opportunity to strengthen her influence in Germany. An attack by Frederick on Austria now would probably make France sooner or later desire him as an ally. In the unlikely event of France not doing so, Britain might be ready, as France's opponent, to co-operate with him. He put forward legal claims for Prussian possession of Silesia, but these were feeble and probably not taken seriously even by himself. He believed that 'negotiations without arms are music without instruments' and in 1737 had suggested the forcible seizure of Jülich-Berg by Prussia immediately its ruler died. His real reason for the attack on Austria he gave later in his life when he wrote in his *History of My Time*: 'An army ready for action, a well-filled war-chest and perhaps also the urge to make a name for oneself.'

Moreover, Silesia was a rich prize for Prussia. The province was then one of the most prosperous territories in Central Europe. Its agricultural resources were sufficient to support a population of about a million and also to provide raw materials for industry. The wool from its two million sheep was of excellent quality, much of it being exported to Austria, Bohemia, Saxony, Holland and Britain, though some of it was made into cloth in Silesia itself, and there was also an important linen industry as well. The vast coal reserves of Upper Silesia were as yet hardly known, but several metals, such as iron, silver, zinc and lead, were already being worked. Valuable trade routes also passed through the province. Many goods traversed the Oder valley on their way between the Baltic and a large part of Central and East Europe; and trade between Warsaw and Prague commonly went through Silesia, crossing the Oder at the important trading-centre of Breslau. Possession of Silesia would, therefore, give Frederick a considerably richer province than any he already had. It is true that it would lengthen the already very long frontiers which the Prussian army had to protect, but at the same time one of Frederick's potential enemies, the Elector of Saxony, would be weakened by the way this new wedge of Prussian territory would separate his German land from his Polish kingdom.

Events were to demonstrate the value of Silesia to Prussia. When the War of the Austrian Succession was ended by the Treaty of Aix-la-Chapelle in 1748, Austria had recovered the Imperial crown, but had irrecoverably lost both territory and prestige to Prussia.[1] Frederick gained the greatest advantages from the Treaty, though he was not a party to it. The rivalry between Britain and France at Berlin to secure credit for promoting the article which gave a European guarantee to his possession of Silesia indicated international recognition of the strength of Prussia's new position. The Holy Roman Empire was fatally shaken. Austrian dominance in Germany was now out of the question. The Habsburg monarchy no longer ruled over a predominantly German state.

Maria Theresa's attempt to reverse the course of events failed. The Seven Years' War, which was largely the result of her policy, merely showed that Prussia was now able to withstand a coalition of three great powers and must therefore be regarded as a great power herself. The Treaty of Hubertusburg in 1763 definitely proved that the Empire no longer contained only one great power but two; and of these two powers Prussia was essentially the German state able to exert her influence over Germany. The Union of Frankfort of 1744, the first alliance of German princes under the leadership of Prussia, was a portent for the future.[2] The transference of Silesia from Austria to Prussia was sufficient to change the relative strength of the two powers to the extent of making them rivals for leadership in Germany. The enterprise upon which Frederick embarked in the first months of his reign and sustained through the years of fighting was of outstanding importance in the development of Prussian power.

Frederick's success in war owed much to his genius, energy and perseverance.[3] Though the splendid victories he gained were matched by some shattering defeats, which were often the consequence of his own mistakes, his reputation for military prowess was not undeserved. He had to move his troops continually between the Elbe and the Oder; his vital need was to prevent a union of the Austrian and Russian forces. This forced him to take speedy, decisive action, designed to defeat each opponent in turn, even if it meant forcing one or the other to fight. To resist

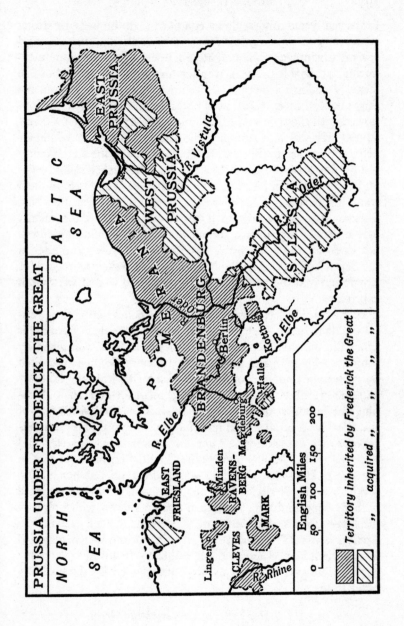

PRUSSIA UNDER FREDERICK THE GREAT

NORTH SEA

BALTIC SEA

EAST PRUSSIA

WEST PRUSSIA

R. Vistula

POMERANIA

SILESIA

R. Oder

BRANDENBURG

Berlin

Kottbus

R. Elbe

R. Elbe

Halle

Magdeburg

EAST FRIESLAND

Minden

RAVENS-BERG

MARK

Lingen

CLEVES

R. Rhine

English Miles

0   50   100   150   200

Territory inherited by Frederick the Great

" " acquired " " " "

" " " " " "

for seven years under these conditions an immensely strong coalition was an amazing feat. It is true that he possessed several advantages. He fought with interior lines of communication which enabled him to transfer his troops speedily from one scene of action to another as circumstances demanded, and the single control he exercised over his army and his campaigns contrasted with the failure of his enemies to co-operate among themselves. He was also sustained by British financial and military help, and in the end his preservation was due to the fortunate results of the death of Elizabeth of Russia. Nevertheless, his tactics and organization of his army were unsurpassed; and behind them were his devotion and courage. Even as early as the First Silesian War, he stated that if he were captured by the enemy, 'My orders in my absence are not to be followed, and the state is not to do anything unworthy to obtain my release', and later in the Seven Years' War he similarly forbade 'the slightest regard for my person and the paying of any attention to what I write from captivity'.

At the same time, Frederick's military policy brought out another side to his character. The strict discipline demanded in his army through his tactics and fear of desertion was imposed by subjecting his troops to inhuman treatment. Soldiers, recruited by subterfuge and compulsion, were retained within the ranks by extreme brutality, the common punishment for deserters of 'running the gauntlet' often resulting in death. Frederick's fear of desertion from his army led him, indeed, to commit his most outrageous act of tyranny. After an apprehended deserter had declared that a Jesuit priest, Father Faulhaber, had told him in the confessional that desertion was a great sin but not an unforgivable one, Frederick had the priest hanged without trial and without opportunity for confession upon a gallows which already displayed the rotting body of a deserter. Such actions by Frederick were performed, however, in an age which regarded severe discipline as essential for military effectiveness, and the accomplishments of his army were unequalled by those of any other state.

The Later Years of Frederick the Great

The year 1763 marked an important stage in Frederick's reign. Under his leadership Prussia had withstood successfully the vigorous attacks of an alliance of great powers and come out of the struggle without loss of territory at the Treaty of Hubertus-burg; but his kingdom had suffered severely. Parts of it had been devastated in a manner reminiscent of the Thirty Years' War. Berlin had three times endured hostile assaults; East Prussia had twice been invaded by Russia, who remained in occu-pation of the province from 1758 until the conclusion of the peace treaty; and Silesia had been the scene of five military campaigns. The financial condition of the State was weak, and the coinage had been debased. The army had suffered such heavy casualties that even Frederick's brutal methods had only preserved discipline in the ranks with difficulty during the last year or two of the War.

These circumstances had their effect upon Frederick's military policy in the later years of his reign. Except during the times of manoeuvres, he retained hardly half of his soldiers in their regi-ments. Most of the conscript sons of peasants were allowed to return home on indefinite leave when they had completed their first year of training, while many of the foreign mercenaries were given permission to live with their families and engage in civilian occupations for a part of each year. During such periods these soldiers received no pay, though the commanding officers of the regiments continued to receive capital payments in recognition of their responsibility to maintain the arms and equipment of all the troops on their rolls. This system inevitably brought about a decline in the effectiveness of the Prussian army during Frederick's later years, and it did not acquit itself well in the War of the Bavarian Succession in 1778–9.[1]

Consequently, Frederick did not want to be involved in an-other great European war, and he followed a peaceful policy in this second half of his reign. Not that he ever relinquished the idea of securing further territory for his kingdom. This he was able to do through the First Partition of Poland, which was made possible by the alliance he skilfully engineered with Catherine of Russia.[2] His share, Polish Prussia, was smaller in territory and population than the gains made by either Austria or Russia, but it was of great strategic and political importance for Prussia. It established a territorial connexion between East Prussia and Brandenburg, delivering Prussia from the fear of Russian aggres-sion and gave her effective control of the basin of the Lower Vistula with its valuable grain trade.

[1] P. 196.   [2] Pp. 268–9, 283.

Frederick also did not relinquish his determination to oppose Habsburg power in Germany, and this, despite his reluctance to fight, brought about his intervention in the question of the Bavarian Succession. In 1777 the Elector of Bavaria died childless and was succeeded by the Elector Palatine, who had only illegitimate children and wished to provide for them. To secure Imperial support for his purpose, he agreed to allow the ambitious Emperor Joseph II to seize over a third of Bavaria. This would have strengthened considerably the Habsburg position in Germany, and Austrian troops entered Bavaria in 1778. Frederick considered that such Austrian expansion would become a dangerous threat to Prussia. He supported the claim to Bavaria of the Duke of Zweibrücken, the next heir to the Elector Palatine, and sent Prussian troops into Bohemia, where they failed even to bring the Austrians to battle. Russia and France joined to compel a peaceful settlement which was embodied in the Treaty of Teschen in 1779. The Elector Palatine was recognized as Elector of Bavaria, while Austria secured only a small part of southeastern Bavaria. Frederick's gain from the settlement was Austrian recognition of the reversion of the duchies of Bayreuth and Ansbach to Prussia. A second attempt by Austria to obtain Bavaria was frustrated by Frederick in 1785 through the formation of the League of Princes, which aimed at retaining the constitution of the Empire as it had been settled by the Treaty of Westphalia.[1]

During these peaceful years in the later part of his reign, Frederick devoted himself to repairing the devastation of war and making Prussia strong and prosperous. Towns and villages were rebuilt, farms were restocked, cavalry horses were turned over to agricultural work, woods were planted, waste land was drained and brought into cultivation, rivers were dredged, and roads were built. The debased coinage was called in, and a national Bank of Berlin was founded in 1765 to finance commercial and industrial enterprises. The encouragement of immigrants as settlers of the land was continued, and foreign artisans were enrolled to develop new industries.[2] Holdings of land were also distributed to ex-soldiers. During the twenty-three years in which Frederick strenuously supervised these undertakings, the only extravagance he allowed himself was the building of a third palace, the Neues Palais near Potsdam, but this was not accompanied by any

---

[1] Pp. 244-5.   [2] P. 60.

increase in the size or ceremonial of his simple, small court.

This period was also occupied by a number of internal reforms undertaken by Frederick. The administration of justice was improved. The collection of taxes was made more efficient by the appointment of French tax-farmers.[1] A beginning was made in the establishment of specialized ministries by the creation of those for military affairs, trade, and Silesia, though the General Directory continued to act as the main central authority in the administration. Generally, indeed, Frederick failed to initiate much in the way of administrative reform, and he reversed one development which his father had instituted. Frederick William I had employed many men of common birth in administrative posts, but his son's outlook on this matter was conservative, and during his reign there was a large increase in the number of noblemen holding governmental and military positions.[2]

Frederick, however, shared completely his father's determination to supervise personally the whole of Prussian administration. He bombarded officials with written instructions, read numerous reports and wrote comments on them, carefully checked government expenditure and income and every summer made tours of inspection examining officials and investigating complaints. Few administrators were not familiar with '*der alte Fritz*' in his old blue coat with frayed red collar and cuffs, with his glaring blue eyes, sneering left nostril and thin, compressed lips. In the last years of his reign, indeed, the arbitrary nature of his rule grew. He interfered in cases and trials, punished judges whose verdicts he considered perverse, dismissed able officials and officers and persisted in unpopular governmental measures which yet brought him little gain, such as the state monopoly in tobacco, coffee and salt, instituted in 1766 and enforced by the hated French officials. He would trust no one and became steadily more of a misanthrope, still inspiring fear but no longer enjoying the popularity he had once possessed. Mirabeau has recorded the relief of the people of Berlin when Frederick died.

The Aftermath

The rise of Prussia in the first half of the eighteenth century was a very important European development, comparable with the emergence of Russia. Building upon the foundations laid by

[1] P. 97.　　　　　　　　　[2] P. 98.

their predecessors, the Prussian rulers of these years had asserted the superiority of their state in Germany and her claim to be regarded as a great power.   Frederick II left Prussia with a strong army, which had already played a powerful part in international politics, and with an administration centred firmly upon the personal will and supervision of the monarch.

Nevertheless, the years had not brought a development in Prussian administrative institutions and methods such as the larger, stronger, richer state demanded if it were to face the future with confidence.   The weaknesses of the unspecialized Prussian central administration became more and more apparent in the second half of Frederick's reign and were made worse by his growing arbitrariness.   It was not really possible for him to exercise an effective, rational personal control over the whole range of administration, but he was not prepared to admit it and resented violently any suggestion from an official that this might be the case.   Many of his orders were so unrealistic and confused that officials resorted to elaborate subterfuges to enable them to carry on with their work without disastrous interference by him.

The decline of Prussia in the later eighteenth century was not primarily due, as has frequently been suggested, to the weaknesses of Frederick's successors – Frederick William II (1786–97) and Frederick William III (1797–1840) – but rather to the rigid maintenance of the antiquated system of administration.   For the rest of the century, no important reforms were undertaken.   The government of the country was continued essentially along the lines developed by Frederick William I, but its efficiency and incorruptibility largely disappeared.

At the same time, nothing was done to improve the condition of the Prussian peasants.   Serfdom and manorial power still provided the basis of the State and its army.   And this army, once so invincible under Frederick the Great, was to prove no match for the new forces of the French Revolution and Napoleon.

XI · THE AUSTRIAN SUCCESSION

The Accession of Maria Theresa

IN the history of eighteenth-century Europe, the year 1740 may be held to mark a turning-point in the development of international relations. Within a short period of the opening of this year, the rulers and statesmen of the leading countries of Europe, who had directed affairs during the generation after the Treaty of Utrecht, were replaced by others with new policies and new issues to consider. Three European monarchs died in 1740 and were succeeded by their heirs. The Emperor Charles VI was followed by his daughter Maria Theresa, Frederick William I of Prussia by Frederick II and Anne of Russia by Ivan VI. In Britain, Sir Robert Walpole, after steadily losing his political influence, was forced in 1742 to yield place to an administration whose real head was his chief opponent, Lord Carteret; and in France the next year the aged Cardinal Fleury died, to make way for the accession to power of the faction led by the warlike Maréchal de Belleisle. Finally, the death of Philip V of Spain brought Ferdinand VI to the throne in 1746 and an end to the influence of Elizabeth Farnese.

Moreover, these new figures came to power at a time when the European situation was changing. For over a quarter of a century after the end of the War of the Spanish Succession, the outbreak of another general war had been avoided. Now events were occurring which were to tell against the continuance of peace in the future. Britain and Spain had already gone to war in 1739 over trade in Central America; and Britain and France had begun an increasingly intense unofficial commercial and colonial contest in North America and India. The younger Whigs, led by William Pitt, were denouncing the Bourbons as the enemies of Britain; the fresh generation of French soldiers longed to avenge Marlborough's victories over Louis XIV. France was also still mindful of her long-standing desire to destroy the power of the Habsburgs in Germany, while Spain could still hope to recover her supremacy in Italy. To these rivalries between the established states of Europe was now added the determination of the newly-powerful Prussia to secure her dominance over Germany, a determination which did more than anything else to shatter permanently and irrecoverably the continental balance established by the Treaty of Utrecht. Soon from this discordant situation came a general war between the powers.

The event which produced this was the death of the Emperor Charles VI and the accession of Maria Theresa. Charles VI had succeeded his brother, Joseph I, as Holy Roman Emperor in 1711. He had a daughter, Maria Theresa, who was born in 1717, but no son to carry on his line. Shortly after her birth, therefore, he drafted a document called the Pragmatic Sanction, which appointed her as his successor in all his family territory. Between 1720 and 1723 he secured acceptance of this by the diets of Austria, Hungary and the Austrian Netherlands within this territory. Then, as his hopes of a son disappeared, he devoted much diplomatic effort in the later years of his reign towards securing guarantees of his daughter's succession from the major powers of Europe. Spain promised to uphold it in the First Treaty of Vienna in 1725. The next year brought recognition from both Russia (through her alliance with the Empire) and Prussia. Britain's guarantee was included in the Second Treaty of Vienna in 1731, and the Imperial Diet accepted the Pragmatic Sanction in 1732. The Elector of Saxony relinquished his wife's claim to the Habsburg lands and recognized the Pragmatic Sanction in 1733 in order to obtain the Emperor's support for his candidature for the Polish throne. The Third Treaty of Vienna in 1738 secured its recognition from France and later from Piedmont also.

Such a dynastic provision, which had long been usual practice in the German states, could not apply constitutionally to the Imperial throne. This was an elective position, and the question of a successor to Charles was solely a matter for the Electors, despite the long tradition of Habsburg Emperors. No woman had ever been elected to this throne, but in 1736 Maria Theresa married Francis Stephen, Duke of Lorraine, who relinquished his duchy to Stanislas Leszczynski at the close of the War of the Polish Succession.[1] Charles hoped that when he himself died the Electors would appoint Maria Theresa's husband as Holy Roman Emperor, so retaining possession of the Imperial crown for the house of Habsburg, though in the female line.

[1] P. 161.

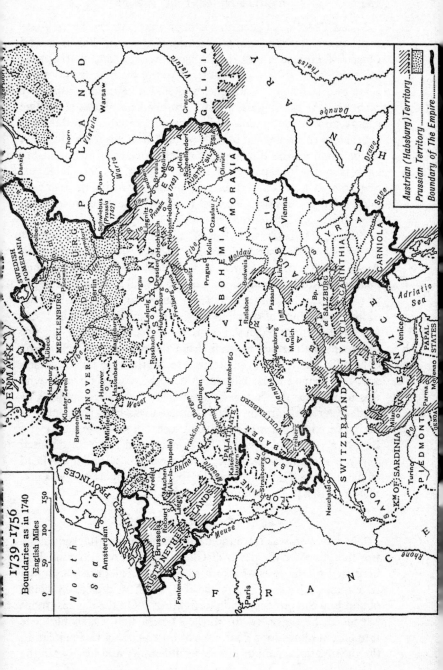

1739-1756
Boundaries as in 1740

English Miles
0   50   100   150

Austrian (Habsburg) Territory
Prussian Territory
Boundary of The Empire

When Charles VI died in October 1740, Maria Theresa was proclaimed Archduchess of Austria, Queen of Bohemia and Queen of Hungary, and she declared her husband co-regent in her territories. She was an untried young woman, twenty-three years old, strikingly handsome, and had a charming, attractive manner. At the same time, she possessed an almost masculine energy and determination which was supported by an unfailing courage, firm religious principles and a high sense of duty. These qualities she displayed as much in state affairs as in her later favourite occupation of match-making for her daughters. She was to guide the Habsburg monarchy through a critical period in its history, saving it from dismemberment and strengthening it by internal reforms.[1]

Britain, Holland and Russia recognized Maria Theresa's accession. Other states delayed. Fleury, pressed by the anti-Austrian party of the Maréchal de Belleisle, said that the French guarantee had been only in support of 'lawful possession' and not of a mere claim; Elizabeth Farnese hoped to use Spanish recognition as a means of obtaining the Austrian dominions in Italy; and the Elector of Saxony, now King of Poland, and the King of Piedmont both hoped to profit from the occasion as well. The only ruler likely, however, to dispute Maria Theresa's accession seriously seemed to be Charles Albert, Elector of Bavaria, who was married to the younger daughter of Joseph I, Charles VI's predecessor as Emperor. He claimed the whole Habsburg inheritance on the basis of a sixteenth-century marriage between a Bavarian ruler and a Habsburg princess and also of a disputed document which, he held, prevented a woman becoming the head of the house of Habsburg; but he found no support and was not, therefore, in a position to press his cause.

The War in Central Europe

The situation was revolutionized when Prussia attacked Silesia two months after the death of Charles VI. Frederick, much as he prized Silesia, was as aware as his father of Prussia's limited resources, and was ready to see if a resort to diplomacy could obtain him the province without fighting. On the day his troops advanced, he suggested to Maria Theresa that she should cede it to him in return for a guarantee of the rest of her German lands, the payment of a sum of money as indemnity and his vote in the

[1] Pp. 237 ff.

Electoral College in favour of her husband's candidature for the Imperial throne. Soon afterwards he even indicated that he might be satisfied with only part of Silesia if she would make a 'reasonable and sincere agreement' with him. Although her ministers were ready to come to such a compromise with Prussia, Maria Theresa refused even to discuss it. She sent an army of 20,000 men to oppose Frederick, but it was defeated (though Frederick himself fled) by an equal number of Prussians at the Battle of Mollwitz in April 1741. Frederick now possessed practically all of Lower Silesia.

More important, this battle encouraged the war-party in France to press for intervention. As early as January 1741 the Maréchal de Belleisle had prepared plans for a large-scale French campaign in Germany. Now he was able to overrule the aged Fleury and made a notable tour through Germany, seeking alliances with France from various princes of the Empire. In May France made the Treaty of Nymphenburg with Charles Albert of Bavaria, supporting his candidature for the Empire, and the next month the Treaty of Breslau with Frederick, recognizing his possession of Lower Silesia.

The prospect of a revival of French aggression alarmed Walpole into granting Maria Theresa a British subsidy, but in August George II, fearful at the possibility of a French or Prussian attack on Hanover, declared his Electorate neutral, so making it almost impossible for Austria to receive military help from her ally. And in October a French army entered the Empire to join with Bavarian forces in an invasion of Upper Austria. Saxony now entered the anti-Austrian coalition, and Spanish troops landed in Italy, prepared to attack Milan.

The coalition, however, was not to prove as formidable as it at first appeared. Maria Theresa was able to avert the complete collapse of her dominions largely through the disunity of her enemies. By January the French and Bavarian troops had advanced down the Danube as far as Linz and were only three days' march from Vienna. Frederick wished them to advance on the capital, but France feared this would lead Austria to make terms with Prussia, and so the forces were turned northwards into Bohemia, where they captured Prague. They were followed by Charles Albert, who was proclaimed King of Bohemia before an assembly of 400 noblemen in the Cathedral of St. Vitus.

The capture of Prague, however, produced just the result

which France wished to avoid.   Maria Theresa, who had now strengthened her position by gaining the support of the Magyar nobles at the Diet of Hungary, decided that it gave her an opportunity to conciliate Frederick so that she might concentrate against the French and Bavarian invaders.   In October 1741, therefore, she made with him the secret Convention of Klein-Schnellendorf, which acknowledged his occupation of Lower Silesia, though without definitely recognizing his claim to it, in return for a suspension by him of hostilities against Austria.

Maria Theresa was now able to check the advance of her enemies in Bohemia and even to threaten Bavaria, but Frederick did not wish to see Austria gain the initiative.   He decided that 'the true principles of the policy of my House' required the renewal of his alliance with France in the hope of gaining Upper Silesia also.   He broke the Convention of Klein-Schnellendorf, invaded Moravia and captured the important town of Olmütz, menacing the two Austrian armies in Bohemia and Bavaria. Though he had a chance of taking Vienna, neither the French nor the Bavarian forces occupying Prague would leave Bohemia. Frederick had to retreat through Bohemia and in May 1742 defeated an Austrian army which sought to oppose him at the Battle of Chotusitz, the first of his great victories.

Meanwhile, the Austrians had driven the French and Bavarians first from Upper Austria and then from Bohemia and had begun to invade Bavaria.   French influence secured the election of Charles Albert as Emperor in January 1742, but on the day he was crowned at Frankfort-on-Main, the Austrians captured Munich, the capital of his state.   Yet Maria Theresa agreed to come to terms again with Frederick.   This was partly because of the Prussian victory at Chotusitz, but still more because of British pressure upon her.   Carteret wished hostilities to be concentrated against France.   Maria Theresa's reliance upon British subsidies and her hope that a strong attack upon France would be made by Britain, Holland and Austria from the Austrian Netherlands led her to agree.   Accordingly she signed the Treaty of Berlin with Frederick in July 1742 and ceded, though she believed only temporarily, the whole of Silesia to him in return for a promise of Prussian neutrality.   Soon afterwards Saxony, who had joined the anti-Austrian coalition after the French invasion of Bohemia and sent a contingent of troops to share in the occupation of Prague, also withdrew from the War.

The Treaty of Berlin ended the first part of the War of the Austrian Succession known as the First Silesian War. By now the position in Central Europe had really been stabilized. Events had shown that Frederick's seizure of Silesia was not to be reversed and also that Austria was not to be defeated by the coalition formed against her. The War was to last for a further six years, but this was to remain the fundamental position. That the War continued and was extended on a vaster scale was due to Maria Theresa's determination to obtain Bavaria from the Emperor and Alsace and Lorraine from France as territorial compensation for the loss of Silesia. It was due also to the active intervention of Britain in the War through a desire to strike at French power on the Continent and overseas.

Austrian prospects improved during 1743. Bavaria was occupied and was to remain in Austrian possession until the end of the War. In June the 'Pragmatic Army' of British, Hanoverian and Austrian troops, recently formed in the Austrian Netherlands, won an important victory over the French at the Battle of Dettingen under George II's leadership, which drew off a part of the French forces from the east. Still anxious to concentrate hostilities against France, Carteret sought to induce Maria Theresa to effect a reconciliation with the Emperor and relinquish Bavaria. She refused, but Carteret did succeed in persuading her to make the Treaty of Worms in September with the King of Piedmont, promising him part of Milan in return for his support against the Spanish in Italy.

This treaty, however, stimulated Frederick into active hostility again. The fact that the Pragmatic Sanction was upheld in the Treaty of Worms without any mention of Silesia aroused his suspicions, and he rightly suspected Maria Theresa of designs upon Bavarian territory. He could not feel safe while Austria strengthened herself. And so in May 1744 he joined with the Emperor, the Elector Palatine and the Landgrave of Hesse-Cassel to form the Union of Frankfort, nominally to uphold the authority of the Imperial throne, but really to partition the Habsburg lands. This union of German princes marked the resolve of Frederick to prevent any consolidation of Habsburg power in Germany, a resolve which was to be the mainspring of his foreign policy for the rest of his reign and also that of his successor in Prussia.

The Treaty of Worms similarly provoked a closer union

between France and Spain against Austria and her allies.   In
October 1743 the two countries initiated the Second Family Compact by the Treaty of Fontainebleau.   Britain had been at war
with Spain since 1739, but only indirectly with France since 1741
as an ally of Austria.   Early in 1744 France declared war on
Britain and made ready to support the Young Pretender in his
projected attempt upon the throne.   Frederick was now able to
make a treaty of mutual assistance with France, and she joined
the newly-formed Union of Frankfort in June of that year.   So
began the Second Silesian War.

In the summer of 1744 the Austrians crossed into Alsace,
paralysed the French army in Flanders and threatened France
herself.   Frederick signified his renewal of hostilities by an invasion of Bohemia.   By September he had captured Prague.
This destroyed Maria Theresa's hopes of conquering Alsace from
France for the Austrian troops now had to be brought back from
across the Rhine.   She was, however, in a strong position to meet
Frederick.   When his forces advanced southwards towards
Vienna, since France gave him no support the Austrian troops
were able to check him, and lack of provisions for the troops compelled him to make a humiliating retreat back to Silesia with
heavy losses by death and desertion.

Other events improved Maria Theresa's circumstances.   At
the beginning of 1745 the Emperor Charles VII died, so depriving the Union of Frankfort of its ostensible purpose and
bringing it to an end.   His successor as Elector of Bavaria, Maxi-
milian Joseph, was a young man of eighteen, who wanted peace
and did not wish to be a candidate for the Imperial throne.
When he hesitated about making terms with Austria, Maria
Theresa sent troops into Bavaria and threatened Munich.   The
young Elector fled to Augsburg and was obliged to submit.   By
the Treaty of Füssen in April 1745 Austria recognized his
possession of Bavaria in return for his acceptance of the Pragmatic Sanction and promise to vote for Francis Stephen at the
forthcoming Imperial election.   The next month the Elector of
Saxony, by the Treaty of Warsaw, agreed also to support the candidature of Francis Stephen and to send troops to help Austria on
condition that he was given a share of Prussian territory.

Frederick was now practically isolated in Germany.   His only
allies were France and Spain.   He could not expect Spanish help,
while French efforts were concentrated upon the invasion of the

Austrian Netherlands which they had launched in the spring of 1745. The defence of the Netherlands devolved largely upon Britain, who did not receive much assistance from Holland. When the Duke of Cumberland tried with a British and Hanoverian army to relieve Tournai, he was defeated by a French force under Maurice de Saxe, mainly through Dutch inaction. Frederick said sarcastically that this victory would be as useful to him as the capture of Babylon by Tamas-Chouli-Khan; but he hoped that it might induce the British government to press for peace, especially as Carteret had been replaced by the cautious Henry Pelham, and Cumberland and his forces were now withdrawn to England because of the 'Forty-Five. Maria Theresa, however, immediately sent a combined Austrian and Saxon force into Silesia. Frederick inflicted a crushing defeat upon it at the Battle of Hohenfriedberg in June and followed the fleeing troops into Bohemia as far as Königgrätz; but this success still left him in a weak condition. His resources were exhausted. France would not grant him an adequate subsidy and withdrew her forces from Germany.

Maria Theresa succeeded in obtaining the election of her husband as Emperor in September. Her defeat at Hohenfriedberg had not diminished her belief in the strength of her position. Habsburg possession of the Imperial office had now been reestablished. Saxony was freed from the threat of French invasion; Austria had been well supplied with British subsidies. Although George II had signed the Convention of Hanover with Frederick, which recognized Prussian possession of Silesia in return for an acknowledgement of the neutrality of Hanover, and although the British government wanted the War to end, she remained adamant, saying that she would 'as soon part with her petticoat as with Silesia'. She threatened to make peace with France rather than come to terms with Prussia and planned to make yet another attempt to regain Silesia.

Frederick, having exhausted the supplies of north-eastern Bohemia, fell back into Silesia, after inflicting another defeat on the Austrians at the Battle of Sohr in September. Then he heard that the Austrians intended to make an attack on Berlin itself and decided to anticipate them; he invaded Saxony and won a victory at Gross Hennersdorf in November. The next month another Prussian army, led by the Prince of Dessau, defeated a force of Austrians and Saxons at Kesseldorf, and Frederick entered

Dresden. These defeats, combined with her failure to make a separate peace with France and a threat by the British government to withdraw its subsidies, at last compelled Maria Theresa to end hostilities against Prussia.

The Second Silesian War was brought to a conclusion by the Treaty of Dresden in December 1745. It confirmed the Treaty of Berlin and the Convention of Hanover. Frederick acknowledged Francis Stephen as Emperor and guaranteed Maria Theresa her German territories, but not those elsewhere. Maria Theresa agreed with great reluctance to recognize Frederick's possession of Silesia. Prussia had thus been saved from disaster by Frederick's audacity. He kept Silesia and so secured a paramount position for his kingdom in Germany.

The War in Italy and the Netherlands

With the Treaty of Dresden Prussia withdrew from the contest, and Central Europe ceased to be the main theatre of fighting. Efforts made by the French government to induce Frederick to take the offensive against Austria for yet a third time met with no success. For the remaining years of the War of the Austrian Succession, the combatants were Britain, Holland and Piedmont against France and Spain; and the hostilities were practically confined to a struggle of Austria against France and Spain in Italy and the Netherlands, and of Britain against France in North America and India.

Throughout the first part of the War of the Austrian Succession – the period covered by the First and Second Silesian Wars – Italy had provided a secondary, yet important, scene of hostilities. With the exception of Prussia, all the chief belligerents were prepared to devote much of their energies to a contest for influence and territory in the peninsula. The war-party in France saw it as an obvious field for attacking Austria. Spain hoped that the Habsburg plight would enable her to regain completely her previous position in Italy, and so joined the coalition against Austria as early as the spring of 1741. The desire of Charles Emmanuel III of Piedmont to obtain the Duchy of Milan and secure an outlet to the Mediterranean by seizing Genoese territory made him ready to support any power which might promise him these gains. Finally, Britain's determination to uphold her position in the Mediterranean led to her increasing intervention in Italian affairs.

During the vicissitudes of the fighting in Italy the prospect of Spain being able to re-establish her supremacy over the peninsula seemed more than once to be favourable. The British fleet did not prevent two Spanish expeditions landing in Italy in 1741 and 1742; and later in 1742, when Charles IV of the Kingdom of the Two Sicilies planned to attack with the aid of Spanish troops the Austrian territories in North Italy, he was only induced to desist by the threat of a British naval bombardment of Naples. At the beginning of the following year a Spanish army, which had been established in southern France, occupied Chambéry, the capital of the old Duchy of Savoy, and remained there until the end of the War. It was this threat from Spain which at last made Maria Theresa, in September of the year, act upon British advice and obtain the support of the King of Piedmont through the Treaty of Worms. Charles Emmanuel was not dependable as an ally, but even his half-hearted help was valuable to her at this stage of the War. The conclusion of the Second Family Compact between France and Spain the next month was directed against Austria and Britain and prepared the way for the resumption of fighting in Italy.

The British fleet had now established control of the Mediterranean and was able to prevent Spain landing any more troops in Italy.[1] Nevertheless, the Franco-Spanish forces won considerable successes in the peninsula in 1745, which culminated in the capture of Milan. This disastrous news, which threatened the loss of Austria's Italian provinces, helped to bring about Maria Theresa's acquiescence in the Treaty of Dresden, since peace with Prussia would enable her to strengthen the Austrian forces in Italy.

Charles Emmanuel also found himself faced with the prospect of military disaster and was ready, therefore, to listen to the overtures of the Marquis d'Argenson, who had become French Foreign Minister in November 1744. D'Argenson, a visionary and an idealist, had drawn up an ingenious scheme for Italy, no less than a 'project for forming a republic and a lasting association of Italian powers' on the lines of political arrangements in Germany, Holland and Switzerland, which involved driving back 'beyond the Alps all foreign rule in order to establish a federal bond among the sovereigns of Italian nationality'. If France were to settle Italian affairs in this way, both Austria and Spain

[1] P. 212.

would have to be expelled from the peninsula, and a French alliance with Piedmont might be a useful first step in this direction. It soon became clear to Charles Emmanuel, however, that this plan would inevitably mean the establishment of French domination in Italy, and after the Treaty of Dresden he merely prolonged negotiations with France in order to gain time until Austria should be ready to take the offensive in Italy.

When this offensive was mounted in March 1746, it gained immediate successes. The ill-feeling and suspicion left by D'Argenson's ideas made united action between the French and Spanish forces impossible. Then Philip V of Spain died in July, bringing to an end the influence of Elizabeth Farnese upon Spanish policy. Though the new Spanish king, Ferdinand VI, also depended much on his wife, she was a Portuguese princess, favourable to Britain and little interested in Italy. Accordingly, Austria and Piedmont found it comparatively easy to drive both the French and Spanish forces out of Italy and even attacked Provence. Here, however, they were repulsed by Belleisle in February 1747. And so the war in Italy ended in a deadlock.

For the French, however, the main theatre of hostilities was the Netherlands. As long as Prussia was a belligerent, Frederick had tried to insist that France should support his efforts in Bohemia, since Austria could be defeated decisively only in Germany. The French government would not agree to engage in major operations here because for it the chief enemy was Britain, who could be attacked effectively only in Flanders. After the Treaty of Dresden, France was quite free to concentrate all her military resources here. To this attempt to drive British forces from the Continent, she was prepared to subordinate her activities in all other spheres of fighting – military and maritime, European and overseas – and gained victory after victory.

The successful French campaign in Flanders was led by the brilliant Maurice de Saxe (1696–1750), one of about thirty illegitimate children of Augustus II, Elector of Saxony and King of Poland, and now a marshal of France. In 1741 he had led the army which invaded Bohemia and took Prague by storm, and in the spring of 1745 he had conducted the French advance into the Austrian Netherlands and defeated the Duke of Cumberland at Fontenoy. Now he profited by Cumberland's recall to England to meet the Jacobite rising. During 1746 he won a series of victories unequalled in French history. He took Brussels in

February and Antwerp in June, while Mons and Charleroi fell shortly afterwards to him. Then he met the allied army, commanded by the incapable Charles of Lorraine, and won the Battle of Raucoux in October. By the end of the campaigning season of that year, the French were in occupation of the whole of the Austrian Netherlands with the exception of Limburg and Luxemburg.

The next year opened with the dismissal of D'Argenson by Louis XV in January. D'Argenson had opposed a French attack on Holland because he hoped, despite the unwillingness of Britain and Austria to enter into negotiations, to arrange a general peace and bring the War to an end; but his failure to achieve this, and the French reverse in Italy, had discredited him. The triumph of his opponents at the French court prepared the way for an invasion of Dutch territory. The allies made a determined effort to raise an army to check the French advance, the command being given to Cumberland, who had increased his prestige by defeating the Young Pretender at Culloden the previous April; and a popular revolution in Holland overthrew the ruling aristocratic party and made William IV of Orange Captain-General and Stadholder. Saxe, however, continued to advance. He defeated Cumberland at the Battle of Lawfeldt in July. By the spring of 1748 the great fortresses of Bergen-op-Zoom and Maastricht were in his possession, and the conquest of the whole of Holland appeared possible. The French victories in the Netherlands had more than offset her defeats elsewhere.

The Maritime War

Meanwhile, outside of Europe a conflict of a very different sort had been proceeding, a conflict between warships and privateers, colonists and overseas troops. Britain's growing commercial and industrial interests made this struggle of more concern for her than it was for France, but the governments of both countries regarded the maritime war as of secondary importance compared with the military campaigns in Europe. This was to be expected of France with her land-frontiers to defend and position to maintain on the Continent, but British statesmen of the time also were surprisingly persistent in regarding the European war as the primary field of operations for their forces. The result was that so many British troops were sent to fight in Flanders that none were available for colonial campaigns. Not until the last year of the War did Britain despatch a single military contingent to the colonies. Similarly, the British navy was largely used in the Continental conflict. The part it played here, however, was an earnest of the future importance of sea-power to Britain, and so also, despite the few squadrons that could be spared for oceanic warfare, were the naval actions fought in other waters.

On the outbreak of the War of Jenkins's Ear in 1739, the capture of ports in Spanish America was planned, but the ventures failed;[1] and when France became the more formidable enemy in the War of the Austrian Succession, the Mediterranean was the main scene of naval activity. Britain's object was to prevent the Bourbon powers using the Mediterranean for the passage of troops. By 1742 Spain and France had 20,000 men in Italy, but their commanders wanted another 50,000, and the sea-passage was the only practicable route to take them there. In that year Admiral Thomas Mathews (1676–1751) was appointed Commander-in-Chief in the Mediterranean and Plenipotentiary to the King of Piedmont and the States of Italy and was instructed to prevent the passage of further Bourbon troops to the peninsula. Opposed to him were the French and Spanish fleets, now united in the deep, unassailable double bay of Toulon. He himself had the advantages of a good base at Port Mahon, but he held command after a long period of naval inactivity, and the British navy had yet to be restored to efficiency by the reforms initiated by Lord Anson after his return in 1744 from his long voyage round the world.[2]

Mathews needed a squadron of small, fast vessels to keep watch for troop-ships, besides ships of the line to cover the enemy's battle-fleet in Toulon; but he never received the frigates or cruisers which he continually requested. He was left, therefore, without a flotilla and attempted to meet all eventualities by a blockade of the enemy's base. This plan succeeded until 1744, when the Franco-Spanish fleet was ordered to sail from Toulon and clear the route to Italy. It was attacked by Mathews and fled to Spanish ports, though without suffering much damage.[3] Mathews was dismissed from the service for conducting the battle half-heartedly. Nevertheless, he had prevented a single troop-ship emerging, and the Bourbons had lost all hope of restoring their sea-communication with Italy for the rest of the War.

¹ P. 175.   ² P. 148.   ³ P. 148.

The British navy was also needed to protect England from threats of French invasion. Less than a fortnight after Mathews had fought the Battle of Toulon, a French fleet sailed from Brest under the command of Admiral Roquefeuil and appeared off Dungeness. Saxe had been preparing secretly for some months at Dunkirk for a Jacobite invasion which was to be covered by this fleet. Fortunately the British government had heard of these plans, and a superior fleet commanded by Admiral Norris was on the watch. This would probably have overwhelmed Roquefeuil had not strong easterly gales, which crippled the troop-ships at Dunkirk, also driven the French fleet out of the Channel before Norris could encounter it. The next year the effectiveness of Britain's naval power around her coasts was indicated when the Young Pretender slipped out of Nantes in the *Doutelle*, escorted by the *Elizabeth*, a well-armed privateer carrying his arms and ammunition. They were intercepted by a British warship, and after a running fight lasting six hours, the badly disabled *Elizabeth* had to put back to France with her vital cargo. The *Doutelle* escaped to land the Prince in Scotland with only seven companions.

There were four oceanic actions during this war which emphasized the growing importance of naval power in deciding the issue of a conflict. The first was the capture of the great French fortress of Louisbourg on Cape Breton Island in June 1745 by a British squadron under Commodore Warren with the help of colonial troops from Massachusetts. Louisbourg stood at the entrance of the St. Lawrence. Its capture made it possible for military expeditions to pass along the waterway into the French settlements of Canada. The French sent two convoys of troops and supplies, both heavily protected by warships, in their efforts to recapture Louisbourg. The first was decisively defeated in May 1747 by Anson in the first Battle of Finisterre, a naval fight which foreshadowed a change in the pattern of maritime warfare.[1] Five months later the second convoy was almost as thoroughly overwhelmed in the second Battle of Finisterre by Hawke. These two victories of Finisterre broke French naval power in the Atlantic and were to initiate a new period in British oceanic fighting.

The fourth engagement to illustrate the value of sea-power in this war was fought in Indian waters and was not favourable to

---

[1] P. 148.

Britain. The energetic Dupleix induced Mahé de la Bourdon-nais, Governor of the French island of Mauritius, to send into these waters a fleet which wrested the local command of the sea from the British, who were also handicapped by the lack of a well-equipped base. This enabled the French to capture Madras in September 1746. Admiral Boscawen was sent out with a superior British fleet to recapture it. His first attempt failed, and the War ended before he could make another attack. British naval victories elsewhere had, however, prevented the French sending further troops to India and strengthening their position; and so Madras could be exchanged for Louisbourg when peace was made.

These naval actions of the War of Jenkins's Ear and the War of the Austrian Succession had brought home clearly to British public opinion the importance of having command of the sea. The ease with which Porto Bello had been taken by Vernon entirely from the sea aroused, indeed, enthusiasm altogether out of proportion to the importance of the operation. Imagination was also stirred by Warren's capture of Louisbourg by a squadron of warships and its retention throughout the War despite French efforts to retake it. The implications of the twin battles of Finis-terre could clearly be understood, and it was also understood that Madras had been lost because of the eclipse of British sea-power in that part of the world. Such examples prepared the way for a greater emphasis by Britain upon naval strength in future wars.

The Treaty of Aix-la-Chapelle (1748)

EVER since the last days of 1744, when D'Argenson had become Foreign Minister in France, there had been a possibility of con-cluding the War. The French and Spanish victories of 1745 in the Netherlands, at Fontenoy and in northern Italy over the Austrians and Piedmontese produced a readiness for peace in both Holland and Piedmont. Maria Theresa continued to trust that she might yet reconquer Silesia, but Frederick's victories over her forces compelled her to make the Treaty of Dresden in December 1745, so ending the war with Prussia. The war in the west, how-ever, was prolonged by British hopes which endured until France declared war on Holland and inflicted a decisive defeat upon British troops in the Austrian Netherlands. Then, early in 1748, William of Orange told the British government that Holland could not con-tinue to fight without a large loan. This made peace inevitable.

Britain could not herself continue to fight on the Continent without the Dutch, but Parliament would not have agreed to make them a loan. The decisive negotiations for peace were between Britain and France, and their success was assisted by the moderation of Louis XV, who refused to countenance French annexation of a large part of the Netherlands lest Britain should be provoked into continuing to wage a purely naval war. When these two countries had reached agreement, the other belligerents had to accept the terms presented to them.

The Treaty of Aix-la-Chapelle was almost a revival of the *status quo ante bellum*. The important modifications were few. The acquisition of Silesia by Prussia was recognized and guaranteed. Parma and Piacenza were ceded to Elizabeth Farnese's younger son, Don Philip, who had married Louis XV's favourite daughter, Marie Louise. Charles Emmanuel of Piedmont was given the part of the Milanese promised him in 1743, after which the map of Italy was to remain unchanged until Napoleon's campaign of 1796-7. Otherwise the Treaty arranged a mutual restitution of conquests. The French withdrew from the Austrian Netherlands and restored the barrier fortresses to Holland, though they had signally failed in their intended purpose of checking a French invasion. Madras was restored to the English East India Company and Louisbourg to the French. Spain renewed the *Assiento*. France promised to expel the Young Pretender from her territory and dismantle the fortifications of Dunkirk. All the signatory powers confirmed the Pragmatic Sanction and recognized the election of Francis Stephen as Holy Roman Emperor.

The results of the War brought considerable disappointment in France. '*Bête comme la Paix*' was a common saying in Paris after the signing of the Treaty of Aix-la-Chapelle in which the sweeping French victories in Europe reaped no reward beyond the fact that the Habsburg power in Germany had been weakened. Nor was disappointment confined to France. Frederick of Prussia and Charles Emmanuel of Piedmont both benefited from the Treaty, Prussia especially so.[1] The other powers were not as fortunate and were bound to regard the settlement as unsatisfactory. Austrian policy under Maria Theresa still would not accept the permanent loss of Silesia and continued to seek its recovery from Prussia. Britain and France, the main

[1] P. 192.

combatants, had, in the words of an English writer, 'gained nothing but the experience of each other's strength and power' in both the European and colonial fighting.

Ostensibly the War of the Austrian Succession had settled the question which had caused its outbreak, but no one regarded the confirmation of the Pragmatic Sanction as an important part of the Treaty of Aix-la-Chapelle. Behind the dynastic issue which gave the War its name were the national policies which had really brought about the participation of the great powers in it. Moreover, the War itself had further aroused resentments and inspired aspirations among both foes and allies. None of these were resolved by the peace settlement; and hence the transitory and inconclusive nature of the Treaty which was followed by a resumption of hostilities in less than ten years. 'The Seven Years' War', it has been truly said, 'was the logical outcome of the rivalries engendered in the course of the War of the Austrian Succession.'

XII · THE DIPLOMATIC REVOLUTION
AND THE SEVEN YEARS' WAR

The Reversal of Alliances

THE Treaty of Aix-la-Chapelle proved to be not only a temporary truce, but also a badly-kept agreement between the two chief signatories, Britain and France. Both continued to fight each other overseas and to prepare for decisive resumption of the struggle. Maria Theresa similarly persisted in refusing to accept as final the severance of Silesia from the Habsburg territories and was determined to try to regain the province by risking once more the chances of war. Moreover, the years between 1748 and 1756 were a period of transition in European international relations, which culminated in the *renversement des alliances* of the Diplomatic Revolution, the result of deep-seated changes and developments affecting the relationships and policies of the leading powers.

The Austrian government prepared for the recovery of Silesia by a series of internal reforms in the Habsburg dominions.[1] It also engaged in a programme of intense diplomatic activity directed towards the same objective. This was largely under the control of Prince von Kaunitz-Rietberg (1711–94), who had represented Austria at the peace conference at Aix-la-Chapelle, where he became convinced that Britain, owing to her increasing overseas interests, would make no attempt to help his country in the recovery of Silesia. After the signing of the Treaty, Maria Theresa asked her secret conference of ministers for advice on future Austrian foreign policy. All its members, with the exception of Kaunitz, then the junior member, said that the alliance with Britain and Holland should be maintained as the most likely means of regaining Silesia. In a paper as long as those of the other ministers combined, he asserted that the recovery of Silesia, so essential to Austria's position as a great power, meant that Prussia, and no longer France, was her chief enemy, and that, indeed, efforts should be made to replace the British alliance by a French alliance, which was likely to be more effective.

[1] Pp. 237 ff.

Maria Theresa was convinced by Kaunitz's ideas. He became for many years her most faithful and trusted adviser. Though he dressed like a dandy and often behaved in a frivolous way, he was an acute and resourceful diplomat. In 1750 Maria Theresa sent him as Austrian ambassador to the French court at Versailles. He spent three years there trying to win over the French government to his plan, but to no avail. Louis XV and his ministers did not wish to acquire fresh Continental entanglements. Kaunitz made friendships in French official and court circles, which were to prove useful to him later, but when he returned to Vienna in 1753 to become Chancellor, there was nothing to suggest that he would ever achieve an alliance with France.

The situation, however, was rapidly changed by events in North America – the establishment of Fort Duquesne by the French in the valley of the Ohio the year after the Treaty of Aix-la-Chapelle, and the failure of George Washington in 1754 and General Braddock in 1755 to drive them out of the region.[1] The British government retaliated by ordering Admiral Boscawen to attack a French convoy bound for Canada and by seizing over three hundred French merchant ships.[2] Open war with France was now inevitable. George II expected his British ministers to provide for the defence of Hanover. The Duke of Newcastle asked Austria to send troops to defend Hanover and to strengthen her garrisons in the Netherlands in order to meet the possibility of a French invasion. To both of these requests Kaunitz gave an evasive reply. Since it was now clear that Austria no longer valued her alliance with Britain, the British government approached Russia and succeeded in making an agreement by which the Czarina Elizabeth undertook to protect Hanover with 50,000 Russian troops in return for a subsidy.

This agreement alarmed Frederick the Great. From April 1753 he knew, through a number of documents which were regularly stolen for him from the foreign offices at Dresden and Warsaw and the Austrian embassy in Berlin, that a new war was approaching. Moreover, he 'feared Russia more than he feared God'; and the presence of Russian troops in Germany would add greatly to his danger. He also knew that France mistrusted him as an ally after his actions in the previous war. Prussia was obviously the country best fitted to safeguard Hanover. Hitherto Frederick had rebuffed British approaches to him, but now he was ready to make an alliance with her. Accordingly the Convention of Westminster was signed in January 1756, by which Prussia agreed to protect Hanover, provided that Britain did not call upon Russian troops, and both countries promised jointly to resist the entry of foreign troops into Germany.

Frederick had wanted the Convention primarily to ensure the neutrality of Germany, but the reactions it produced on the Continent were warlike. Prussia would now obviously be useless to France as an ally in the event of a war with Britain. Kaunitz turned again to Louis XV with a renewal of his plan for an alliance, this time choosing his confidante, the Marquise de Pompadour, as an intermediary. It was not easy to persuade Louis, despite his indignation at Frederick's treachery, to jeopardize French chances of a maritime victory over Britain by entering into a new Continental commitment. The action of Elizabeth of Russia, however, did much to overrule his hesitations. In April she announced that she considered her agreement with Britain now at an end and made Maria Theresa the offer of an attack on Prussia with 80,000 Russian troops and a promise not to make peace until Silesia had been recovered.[1] France, without an ally in Europe, might have to face Austria, Russia, Britain and perhaps even Prussia as well. The next month the First Treaty of Versailles was signed between France and Austria. Each country agreed to defend the territory of the other in Europe if attacked, though France did not promise to assist in the recovery of Silesia. Austria engaged herself to aid France if she were attacked by an ally of Britain on the Continent, but declared that she would take no part in the overseas hostilities between Britain and France.

In this way the British agreement of 1755 with Russia, which never came into effect, had set off the Diplomatic Revolution. The British approach to Prussia was destined to bring her a powerful new ally on the Continent. The alliance of France with Austria, which was to dominate her foreign policy up to 1789, was a reversal of her traditional aims. Not only was her long-standing enmity with the Habsburgs relinquished, but she also abandoned her old, and declining allies, Sweden, Poland, Turkey and the German Protestant states, in favour of new links with Austria and Russia.

The result was to bring about the merging into a general war

[1] P. 259.

of the two contests – the rivalry between Austria and Prussia for hegemony in Central Europe, centred in the dispute for the possession of Silesia, and the struggle between Britain and France for naval supremacy and overseas empire.   Yet, in reality, the exchange of allies among the powers of Central and East Europe by the two contestants in the colonial issue indicated that the interests of the two groups of powers were entirely different.

The War in Europe

The Continental conflict from 1756 to 1763 has been called by Thomas Carlyle the Third Silesian War.   Though it became a general war in 1757, involving all the European powers except Spain, Holland and Piedmont, military action was confined to the east of the Rhine and centred upon Frederick the Great.   Like the previous struggles for the possession of Silesia, the great issue that depended upon it was whether Austria or Prussia was to be dominant in Germany; and this time it was a fight for the survival of Prussia against a powerful coalition intent upon reducing her territory to the extent of dismemberment.   It proved to be a desperate and dramatic contest, marked during its course by extraordinary fluctuations of fortune in the positions of the belligerents.

The War was not actually begun by the signing of the First Treaty of Versailles, for this was defensive in form and intended by France to be so.   As with the fighting between 1740 and 1742 and between 1744 and 1745, it was the result of an attack by Frederick the Great.   His fear, which was not without justification, was that Austria, Russia and Saxony, supported by France, would launch an attack upon Prussia in 1757, if not earlier.   He therefore began to mobilize his troops.   When Austria did the same, he asked her in July 1756 for a promise that no attack would be made upon him within the next eighteen months, but only received an evasive reply.   It now seemed to him that his only chance of safety lay in resorting to aggression himself in order to forestall his enemies before their warlike preparations were complete.   He resolved to attack Austria, his most formidable adversary.   'If Austria,' he said, 'is pregnant with war, I shall offer the service of a midwife.'   To defeat Austria in a single campaign required the elimination of the risk of a hostile Saxony in his rear, and so in September he suddenly, and without consulting Britain, began the Seven Years' War by invading the territory of the Electorate without any declaration of hostilities.

Events, however, did not go as Frederick had planned. Although Augustus III, Elector of Saxony, had only an army of 17,000 to oppose 65,000 Prussians who were advancing southwards, he put up an unexpected resistance, entrenching his forces on the rocky hills a few miles above Dresden, so blocking the route of the Elbe. This deprived Frederick of the advantage of his sudden attack and gave Austria time to complete the mobilization of her troops. An Austrian army was sent northwards through Bohemia to relieve the Saxons. Frederick left half his forces to invest the Saxons and marched southwards into Bohemia with the rest to meet the Austrians, whom he fought at the Battle of Lobositz in October. This engagement was inconclusive, for the Prussians suffered the heavier losses, but the Austrians were compelled to retire. The starving Saxon troops now had to capitulate. The Elector retired to Warsaw, his Polish capital. Frederick occupied the whole of Saxony and forced her army to serve under him.

Frederick had won the opening campaign of the War, but the Saxon resistance had thwarted his hopes of striking swiftly and saved Austria from likely catastrophe. Now the coalition against him was strengthened. In January 1757 the Imperial Diet declared war on Prussia and put Frederick to the ban; but this was no great danger to him for the Protestant princes favoured him and the Imperial army was practically useless. Much more important was the Convention of St. Petersburg, made the same year between Austria and Russia, in which Austria agreed to pay Russia about £100,000 a year in return for her help in conquering Silesia and partitioning Prussia. The following May, France and Austria signed the Second Treaty of Versailles. France promised to continue to fight until Silesia was conquered and Prussia partitioned, during which time she would pay Austria a subsidy of £1,000,000 a year and raise an army of 100,000 men. When Silesia had been regained by Austria, France was to obtain Mons, Ostend, Nieuport, Ypres and other districts in the Austrian Netherlands, the remainder going to Don Philip, Louis XV's son-in-law. In return, Parma and Piacenza were to go to Austria, while if Don Philip had no children, the Netherlands were to revert to Austria. France also succeeded in this year in bringing Sweden into the War on her side.

These developments made Frederick resolve to renew his tactics of the previous year and take the offensive. He invaded Bohemia, where he defeated an Austrian army before Prague in May 1757; but the next month a relieving force defeated him with heavy losses at the Battle of Kolin on the Upper Elbe. He had to raise the siege of Prague and retreat from Bohemia. This defeat immediately brought serious consequences for Prussia. Britain and France had been openly at war since the French capture of Minorca in June of the previous year.[1] Now the French were encouraged to send a force into northern Germany which defeated the greatly inferior force of Hanoverian and Hessian troops under the Duke of Cumberland at the Battle of Hastenbeck in July 1757, and forced him to sign the Convention of Klosterzeven by which he was to disband his army and Hanover was to remain in French occupation for the duration of hostilities. Soon afterwards a Russian army entered East Prussia and defeated the Prussians at the Battle of Gross-Jägerndorf, while the Swedes invaded Prussian Pomerania. This was followed in October by an Austrian advance into Silesia and a raid on Berlin by Austrian cavalry, who captured and occupied the city for a few days.

Frederick's opponents seemed now to be advancing upon him from all sides, and he had only one army in the field to oppose them. That he survived was due partly to a lack of co-operaion among the forces of the powers in the coalition against him. The rivalry of court factions at home prevented the French force in Hanover from taking advantage of its victory at Hastenbeck; the victorious Austrian army at Kolin also failed to exploit its success; and the Russians, alarmed by a false rumour that the Czarina Elizabeth was dead, withdrew from East Prussia. Still more, Frederick's survival at this juncture of the War was due to the superiority of the Prussian army and his own tactical ability; both of these were to be shown fully in the two battles he fought at the end of 1757 which were the greatest of his victories.

By the late autumn of 1757, the retirement of the Russian army to its winter quarters had left Frederick safe from any threat from the east and able to exploit his interior position. He advanced against a combined French and Austrian force, which he overwhelmed in the Battle of Rossbach in November. This was the most decisive battle of the War and the first great victory won by

[1] P. 229.

the Prussians over the French, who were compelled to retire across the Rhine, while the Austrian army dispersed. Frederick then turned back eastward and attacked the Austrian force which had just taken Breslau and gained temporary possession of Silesia. This force was nearly twice as large as his own, but he defeated it in the Battle of Leuthen in December and conquered almost all of Silesia. Though next in importance to Rossbach, Leuthen was the supreme example of the success against a numerically superior enemy of the oblique battle-order which he developed during this war.[1]

These two victories enabled Frederick to expel the Swedes from Prussian Pomerania in the winter of 1757–8 and even to advance deeply into Swedish Pomerania. More important was their effect upon British policy. The outbreak of the Seven Years' War had broken up the government of the Duke of Newcastle, whom the Elder Pitt compared to 'a child driving a go-cart on the edge of a precipice'. Now Pitt himself became Secretary of State, determined to employ the main British war-effort on the sea and in the colonies, to make Hanover a base of operations for a military diversion on the Continent, which should be fought largely by subsidized allies, and so to contain France in Europe while the maritime war was fought overseas. This is what he meant when he spoke later, with characteristic exaggeration, of 'conquering America in Germany'. Frederick's victory at Rossbach enabled Pitt to repudiate the Convention of Klosterseven and appoint to the command of the British and Hanoverian forces the able Prince Ferdinand of Brunswick, who by the end of March 1758 had driven the French out of Hanover and across the Rhine. The next month Pitt made a treaty with Frederick in which he promised him a subsidy of £67,000 a year.

For the rest of the War, Prussia was protected from French attack on the west by Ferdinand's army in Westphalia. Austria and Russia were now the two enemies Frederick had to fight and seek to contain with his dwindling forces. Despite the grievous losses his army had suffered in the fighting of the previous year, he managed to raise 150,000 troops for active service in the spring of 1758, the same number he had possessed twelve months earlier. Yet again he decided to attack Austria, still his chief opponent. He advanced into Moravia and besieged the fortress of Olmütz, the capture of which would enable him to threaten Vienna, but

[1] P. 135.

he failed owing to lack of mobility through difficulties of supply.[1] The Austrians captured on the road a convoy of 4,000 waggons despite the determined resistance of the 13,000 Prussian troops escorting it. Since Frederick depended upon the supplies and ammunition it carried, he had to raise the siege and retreat through Bohemia into Silesia, which he did with great skill in the presence of superior forces.

Meanwhile, the Russians had again invaded East Prussia and were about to join with the Swedes in Pomerania in an attack on Brandenburg. Frederick advanced rapidly and in August fought the Russians at the Battle of Zorndorf, near Cüstrin on the Oder, which was one of the bloodiest struggles of the century. After a confused and desperate conflict lasting some ten hours, the Russians were defeated and forced to withdraw into Poland.

In the autumn, however, the Austrians sent two armies against Frederick. One entered Saxony and the other Silesia. Frederick moved against the first of these armies and met it in October at Hochkirch, near Bautzen. Here Frederick acted rashly, exposing his flank to the enemy, and lost the day, but the failure of the Austrians to follow up their victory both saved him from the consequences of defeat and enabled him by a series of forced marches to drive the armies in turn out of each of the invaded provinces. During this year Ferdinand of Brunswick had been able to hold Hanover and Westphalia and in June defeated the French at the Battle of Crefeld.

So Frederick survived the year 1758. He had beaten off the attacks of his enemies and seemed to possess telling advantages over them. His own territory was intact, and he still occupied most of Saxony. The French had been driven back across the Rhine, while overseas they had suffered defeat at Plassey in India and the loss of Louisbourg and Fort Duquesne in North America.[2] Yet time was not on Frederick's side. Prussia's small population inevitably told against her. The War had now become, as one German historian has described it, 'a struggle of five million against ninety million'. The strain was beginning to tell seriously on the country, and her military resources were dwindling to the point of exhaustion. When the spring of 1759 came, Frederick could only put 100,000 men into the field, many of whom were untried recruits. This time he could not take the initiative by launching an offensive; and the newly-appointed

[1] P. 132.   [2] Pp. 78–9.

French Minister of Foreign Affairs, the Duc de Choiseul, was determined to continue the prosecution of the War on the Continent with vigour, and even to attempt an invasion of England.[1]

In 1759, therefore, it was the Russians who made the first move. By the summer they had advanced as far as the Oder and captured Frankfort, where they were reinforced by a small Austrian force. Frederick met them in August at Kunersdorf, a village four miles east of Frankfort, and here one of the most remarkable battles of the War was fought. At first the Prussians were successful, but then Frederick made several errors which precipitated his complete defeat by the Russians and Austrians whose numbers were nearly twice his own. It was the most disastrous set-back of Frederick's career. An advance upon Berlin, which Frederick would be unable to oppose, seemed likely; but the Russian commanders, aware that the Czarina's health was precarious, were unwilling to press their advantage against a man who was so admired by the heir to the throne, the Grand Duke Peter, and refused to join with the Austrians in any further offensive. Frederick, who had talked of suicide immediately after the battle, was allowed to rally his broken army and resume the struggle. The Austrians were able, however, to occupy Saxony and take Dresden and Torgau on the Elbe.

Once again, Frederick had escaped complete defeat, and this year also brought further French defeats. Choiseul tried to reconquer Hanover, but was beaten in August at the Battle of Minden by Ferdinand of Brunswick, among whose troops was a British contingent which took an important part in the fighting. There followed further French disasters overseas – the fall of Quebec and naval defeats at Lagos and Quiberon Bay which ended Choiseul's plan to invade Britain. Even before these events, Choiseul had decided that France must concentrate her war effort against Britain, her most dangerous enemy, and reduce her commitments in Germany. In March 1759 he had by the Third Treaty of Versailles reduced French subsidies to Maria Theresa by a half, limited French military support for her to 100,000 troops to serve in Germany, refused to guarantee the return of Silesia to Austria and renounced on behalf of Don Philip, Duke of Parma, the Austrian Netherlands, which the Second Treaty of Versailles had arranged were to be exchanged for the restoration of Parma and Piacenza to Austria.

[1] P. 297.

The year 1759, therefore, ended badly for both Prussia and France. Prussia had been brought to the verge of destruction, and France was being ruined in the maritime and colonial contest without being able to achieve success on the Continent. Yet the difference in the positions of the two countries was shown by the attitude of each ruler. Frederick had saved Prussia by his fortitude and military ability in which he had been assisted by the mistakes and disunity of his enemies; Louis XV through his weakness and incapacity had prevented France making a concerted, sustained effort in the War and continued to disregard the lesson of events by refusing to consider a realistic approach which would compel his allies to accept a peace settlement.[1]

The next year was to be the last great year of the War. By strenuous efforts of organization, Frederick was able to raise a force of about 100,000 men, but there were 223,000 opposed to him. His enemies still held the initiative, and he had again to defend himself against Austrian and Russian attacks. Clearly his position was becoming steadily more critical. He himself had grave doubts about the number of troops he would be able to raise should there be yet another year's fighting.

This time the Austrians were the first to take the offensive. They sent an army into Silesia, but Frederick was able to defeat it at the Battle of Liegnitz in August 1760. Meanwhile, a Russian force entered Brandenburg and occupied Berlin in the early days of October, but on the approach of Frederick, it retired across the Oder. Frederick then turned on another Austrian army which had invaded Saxony. He defeated it in November at the Battle of Torgau, which enabled him to regain the greater part of Saxony, though the Austrians retained Dresden. Frederick described Torgau as the severest battle in the War. It was also the last pitched battle which he ever fought. It upheld his tactical supremacy, but confirmed the exhaustion of both sides and the condition of strategic stalemate now so evident throughout the military contest.

Indeed, the strain and losses of the War were beginning to tell upon the coalition almost as much as upon Prussia. Kaunitz warned Maria Theresa in December 1760 that Austria now possessed the resources for only one more campaign, and in the spring of 1761 financial weakness compelled the reduction of the strength of her army by 20,000 men. The remaining military

[1] P. 298.

operations of the War were, as Carlyle said, 'like a race between spent horses', and no important engagement was fought in Germany during 1761. Two political events, the making of an alliance between France and Spain and the rupture of the alliance between Britain and Prussia, occurred elsewhere, however, with serious consequences for these closing months of the struggle. Each was connected with the accession of a new monarch – Charles III of Spain in August 1759 and George III of Britain in October 1760.

Charles III was ready to intervene in the War with the hope that it would restore Spain to her former greatness in Europe. He was willing, therefore, to listen to Choiseul who wished to revive the former alliance of France and Spain against the naval and colonial power of Britain. The result was the signing of the Third Family Compact between the two countries in August 1761.[1] This stated France would not make peace until Spain's numerous grievances against Britain had been remedied, while in a secret article Spain promised to declare war on Britain if peace had not been made by 1762. This treaty had no decisive effect upon the outcome of the War; it had come too late for that. It merely delayed the making of peace and led to the loss of some Spanish colonies to Britain.

The Treaty did, however, indirectly affect the war in Germany for it was the occasion of Pitt's resignation from office. Pitt soon received information from intercepted despatches about the secret article and wished to declare war immediately upon Spain. He was opposed by the cabinet, who shared the growing view in the country that the War should be ended rather than extended now that the British maritime and colonial interests had been secured. George III supported the opposition, and Pitt handed in his seals of office in October 1761. The Earl of Bute, who succeeded him, was the King's favourite and agreed with the peace-party. It was unlikely now that Britain would continue her subsidies to Prussia, and they were, in fact, discontinued within a year. Moreover, the fact that Bute was compelled to declare war on Spain in January 1762 increased his opposition to British participation in the Continental fighting and his desire to open peace negotiations.

Frederick was now at his lowest ebb of fortune. Silesia and much of Saxony were occupied by the Austrians, and Prussian

[1] Pp. 178, 297.

Pomerania by the Russians.   Prussia remained unconquered, but in a parlous condition.   Frederick had only 60,000 men left, and recruits, money and provisions were now growing less and less. Should his enemies make one more move against him, it seemed as if his kingdom would inevitably be destroyed.   He believed that his only chance of salvation lay in the entry of Turkey into the War, which he had long tried in vain to bring about.   'If fortune continues to treat me so pitilessly,' he wrote to his friend, the Marquis d'Argenson, at the close of 1761, 'no doubt I shall succumb; she alone can deliver me from my present position.'

Fortune did, in fact, relent and deliver Frederick very soon after he had written these words.   Early in January 1762 the Czarina Elizabeth of Russia died.   Since 1759 she had been the mainspring of the alliance against Frederick, refusing to consider peace negotiations and determined to partition Prussia.   Her successor, the unstable Peter III, mistrusted Austria, disliked France and had long been a fervent admirer of Frederick.   Early in May Peter not only made peace with Frederick, but also withdrew his troops from all conquered Prussian territory and the next month signed an alliance with Prussia, which was directed not only against Austria, but also against Denmark, to uphold the Czar's dynastic claims in Schleswig-Holstein.

This action compelled Sweden to withdraw from the War and conclude peace with Prussia.   Peter sent 20,000 Russian troops to support the Prussian army.   Frederick might now hope to expel the Austrians from Silesia.   The alliance was, however, destroyed by the murder of Peter and the accession of his German wife as Catherine II in July.[1]   Catherine confirmed the peace, but withdrew the Russian troops.

Nevertheless, Frederick was able in July and October to inflict two defeats upon the Austrians which secured Silesia for him; and Ferdinand of Brunswick conducted a successful campaign during the autumn against the French in western Germany.   Meanwhile, throughout 1762, Britain had been winning signal successes against the French and Spanish and rapidly reducing their West Indian islands.[2]   There was nothing now for France to do but to end hostilities without further damage to herself.   The Continental war had now developed wholly into a dynastic struggle between two German rulers in which France had no further interest, particularly since the impossibility of wresting Silesia

<hr>

[1] P. 259.   [2] P. 230.

from Prussia deprived her of any hope of securing compensation in the Austrian Netherlands for herself. Maria Theresa, now virtually isolated, had to recognize that she could not recover Silesia. So Choiseul renewed his negotiations with Bute for peace, while the Austrian and Prussian envoys met to discuss terms for a treaty in a Saxon hunting-lodge at Hubertusburg.

The Maritime and Colonial War

Naval warfare between Britain and France began before the actual declaration of war between the two countries. In June 1755 Admiral Boscawen, acting on the orders of his government, attacked, off Newfoundland, a large French convoy taking re-inforcements to Canada. The British government had hoped he would destroy it, but the fog, which is so common in those waters, saved the situation. Boscawen captured two French warships, but the others escaped to the protection of Louisbourg. During the following months the British navy seized more than 300 French merchant ships on the high seas. These actions made inevitable a French declaration of war upon Britain, which was only delayed until May 1756 by the weakness of Louis XV and his ministers.

The contest thus precipitated by Britain began badly for her. Foreign governments were well aware that the British navy had been neglected since the Treaty of Aix-la-Chapelle, and France thought she might assert her power in the Mediterranean. In April 1756 she attacked Minorca, which Admiral Byng failed to save. Whatever his own faults in battle, the ministry was much to blame. It sent him out to the Mediterranean too late and had long neglected the defence of both Minorca and Gibraltar. Byng considered that he must sacrifice the one to save the other. He was court martialled and shot on his own quarter-deck at Portsmouth – '*pour encourager les autres*', in Voltaire's phrase.

The loss of Minorca, the largest British overseas base, discredited the government and made certain the replacement of Newcastle by Pitt, who conducted the War upon a scale hitherto unknown in Britain. The size of the army was increased to nearly 150,000 men and the navy to over 400 ships. Parliament voted £10,000,000 in 1758 and £15,000,000 in 1760, while over £1,000,000 was paid to the American colonies.

Pitt's plan of war made full use of sea-power, and he took much of the conduct of hostilities upon himself, often issuing fleet orders without consulting the Admiralty. He was among those who had been impressed by Warren's capture of Louisbourg during the previous war and decided that a second assault should be made upon Cape Breton Island. He sent a strong fleet into North American waters commanded by Admiral Boscawen, whom he especially trusted, saying to him: 'Others make difficulties; you find expedients'. At the same time, Pitt also sent a fleet under Admiral Hawke to Brest and another under Admiral Saunders into the Mediterranean to prevent French reinforcements being sent to Canada. So effectively did these fleets perform their mission that not a single French ship was able to cross the Atlantic to the assistance of Louisbourg, which Wolfe succeeded in capturing with the support of Boscawen's fleet in 1758.

The year 1759, which ended so disastrously for both France and Prussia, was the 'year of victories' for Britain. A number of telling successes in different parts of the world were the result of the aggressive use Pitt was able to make of British sea-power. Quebec was captured, and so also were the valuable sugar island of Guadeloupe in the West Indies and the French slaving-posts of Senegal and Gorée in West Africa. Choiseul hoped to stop these successes by an invasion of England, but he could not even break the blockade to unite his fleets. The French Mediterranean fleet ran out of Toulon in July and tried to escape into the Atlantic, only to be pursued by Boscawen and destroyed off Lagos Bay on the coast of Portugal. When the Brest fleet came out in November, it was boldly attacked and destroyed by Hawke in the rocky and shallow Quiberon Bay, despite a rising storm and the closing darkness of a winter night. And this was also the year in which British infantry won the Battle of Minden. People had become used by that time to hearing of victories and seeing the church-bells of Cherbourg and colours from Louisbourg in Hyde Park.

A year later the fall of Montreal completed the destruction of French power in North America. The French had perhaps displayed superior military skill in Canada, but naval supremacy had enabled Britain to establish an advantage in men and material and threaten the French settlements with a shortage of food. British sea-power gained further successes in North American waters towards the end of the War with the capture of French and Spanish West Indian islands. Martinique, Grenada, St. Lucia and St. Vincent were all taken early in 1762, while Havana, the capital of the Spanish island of Cuba, was captured, together with twelve ships of the line and some £3,000,000 in gold and silver.

Meanwhile, the events of the contest in India had been subjected to the same controlling influence of sea-power.[1] The Anglo-French struggle here also was largely determined by naval operations. The French were defeated though they possessed more than twice as many troops, held more territory and exercised a wider political influence among the native princes than did the British. In 1756, when the news of the Black Hole of Calcutta reached Madras, the British fleet on that station was under orders to return to England. Admiral Watson's decision to ignore the instructions of the Admiralty certainly saved the situation in India. Clive would have been practically powerless without the help of his fleet, which conveyed his punitive expedition to Bengal and enabled him to win the victory at Plassey. Similarly in the Carnatic, Lally was forced to raise the siege of Madras by the arrival of British sea-borne reinforcements from Bombay and was defeated at the Battle of Wandewash in 1760 by Sir Eyre Coote, whose advent from England with a battalion of regular troops was made possible by growing British naval power and command of the long sea-route to India. Finally, Pondicherry was captured early the next year by a combined sea and land assault.

When Spain entered the War, British naval strength struck at her in the East Indies. Manila, the capital of the Philippine Islands, was taken, together with all the islands; and in these same waters a British warship captured the annual Spanish treasure-fleet, which sailed from the East Indies to Panama, with a cargo worth over £3,000,000. The British navy even struck at France herself, when Belle Isle in the Bay of Biscay was occupied in 1762 as a useful bargaining point in peace negotiations.

These successes were the result of the use of the British naval supremacy devised by Pitt. Both the French and Spanish navies had been beaten and driven off the seas. The British navy had been able, therefore, to co-operate with the army in conquering the colonial possessions of these powers. Despite Pitt's well-known phrase, America was not really 'conquered in Germany'. Both it and India were conquered by naval blockade and overseas military operations. Even if Frederick II had been completely defeated on the Continent, France would hardly have been able to retain her power in these other parts of the world.

[1] P. 78.

The issue had been decided upon the high seas months before the end of the War and could not be reversed.

The Treaties of Paris and Hubertusburg (1763)

The Treaty of Paris between Britain, France and Spain was signed in February 1763. The French surrendered Canada and the right to fortify their factories in India; most of the West Indian islands were returned to them.[1] Minorca was recovered in exchange for Belle Isle. Havana was exchanged for Florida and Manila given back to Spain in exchange for a ransom. Pitt came to Parliament from a sick-bed to denounce these terms as ruinous. He especially criticized the return of 'all the valuable West India Islands' to France, because it had 'given her the means of recovering her prodigious losses and of becoming once more formidable to us at sea.' Probably the British peace-makers assumed that British naval supremacy would always secure the Caribbean without the retention of the French and Spanish bases. In fact, Pitt's forebodings were to be realized within his own lifetime. The French were able in the 1770's and 1780's to take many islands in the Leeward and Windward groups and threaten the safety of the whole of the British West Indies.

Yet, although Pitt was shown to have a clearer understanding of the problems of imperial defence than his contemporaries, he was still primarily, as Burke sarcastically complained, the spokesman of the London merchants, 'a parcel of low toad-eaters', and knew very little of the 'great extensive public'. Though France wanted an end to the War, it was believed that she would not make a peace which involved any settled colony. There was some debate in Britain about keeping Guadeloupe in preference to Canada, but a prime motive of the British war-effort had been to deprive the French of any chance of superiority in North America and India, and if this were achieved, public opinion on the whole saw no reason to risk prolonging a 'bloody and expensive war'. The Treaty of Paris, therefore, secured for Britain the original objectives of her participation in the War and satisfied the ambitions of most of the British people. It also placed before the nation an immense commercial and colonial future.[2]

Five days after the Treaty of Paris, the Treaty of Hubertusburg was signed between Austria and Prussia, for Frederick refused to accept the mediation of Britain and France and made his

[1] P. 79.   [2] Pp. 67-70, 79-82.

own settlement with Maria Theresa. Moreover, he compelled Kaunitz to accept the restoration of the *status quo*. Prussia retained Silesia, and by a secret article Frederick promised to give the electoral vote of Brandenburg to the Archduke Joseph, the son of Francis I and Maria Theresa, for election as King of the Romans, the recognized prelude to gaining the office of Emperor. Frederick agreed to evacuate Saxony, but refused to allow the Electorate any compensation for the contribution she had been forced to make to his cause throughout the War – 'Not a foot of land and no compensation to Saxony', he said contemptuously, 'not a village, not a penny.' In Europe, therefore, the peace brought no changes in the boundaries of the states. 'A million of men had perished,' a writer commented, 'and yet not a hamlet had changed its ruler.'

At the same time, the political consequences of the Seven Years' War were considerable. Prussia and Austria, though both exhausted by the years of fighting, had shown themselves formidable military powers, while Russia's intervention in the War, despite the inconsistencies imposed upon it by internal dynastic considerations, had established her claim to be a leading European state. Consequently, in the years after the War, the balance of power on the Continent moved eastwards. Austria, Prussia and Russia dominated its affairs, and this development was accentuated by the resolve of France to husband her strength and avoid European distractions in preparation for a renewal of the colonial contest with Britain. In particular, France was now prepared not to take up arms to forward her interests in eastern Europe, and so important events, such as the partition of Poland in 1772 and the losses suffered by Turkey in 1774, were accomplished without French intervention.

France, indeed, regarded the settlement made at Paris and Hubertusburg as '*la paix déshonorante*', and public opinion looked for its reversal as speedily as possible. Moreover, the disastrous outcome of the War was commonly identified with the new policy of alliance with Austria, and the traditional hostility to the Habsburgs was still strong. Not that the alliance of France and Austria came to an end after the War. Just as the French alliance with Spain continued because of the common interests in the colonial field, so did this alliance because of similar interests in Italy. Yet, though cemented by the marriage in 1770 between the future Louis XVI and Princess Marie

Antoinette, the daughter of Maria Theresa, it was never popular in France; and Girondins were to have the support of public opinion in 1792 when they hurriedly reverted to the former policy of enmity towards Austria.

The alliance between Britain and Prussia, on the other hand, did not survive the War. It ended amid mutual recriminations. Historians have usually placed the blame upon Britain. It is true that Bute was anxious to withdraw from the contest in Germany, particularly after the British declaration of war on Spain early in 1762, but Frederick had never hesitated to break alliances in his own interests, and what really led the British government to refuse further subsidies to him was the fear that he would use the money, after his agreement with Russia, to continue the war against Austria and even start a new one with Denmark. Moreover, the British national debt had been more than doubled during the War, and popular opposition to the payment of subsidies to Prussia was steadily growing now that France was clearly defeated.

Nor is there truth in the suggestion as expressed, for instance, by Basil Williams, that the ending of the alliance between Britain and Prussia created 'a distrust of us which . . . left us friendless when, barely more than ten years later, we had to fight for our empire'. This situation came about rather because the colonial contest became divorced from Continental issues, and so there were no mutual interests to provide Britain with allies. On the one hand, French abstention enabled Prussia, Russia and Austria to pursue their separate eastern European interests, while the Polish question, in bringing Frederick an alliance with Russia, gave him adequate security against Austria. On the other hand, Britain was to be without allies in the American War of Independence, not because the rest of Europe believed Frederick's imputations against her of treachery and instability of policy through her parliamentary system of government, but because France no longer seemed likely to seek European dominance and because the Continental states were not interested in events in North America. Moreover, by the time France intervened to help the American colonists, they were probably already within sight of victory.

XIII · THE HABSBURG DOMINIONS

The Emperor Charles VI (1711–40)

WHEN the Archduke Charles succeeded his brother, the Emperor Joseph I (1705–11), as Holy Roman Emperor and ruler of his family lands, the Habsburgs had passed through a critical period in the history of their dynasty. The Thirty Years' War (1618–48) had frustrated their final attempt to assert their Imperial claims over Germany; and the War of the Spanish Succession (1701–13) brought Habsburg rule in Spain to an end. Nevertheless, the Habsburgs in Austria not only managed to survive these crises, but also established themselves successfully as rulers of their own territories. None of these were lost at the Treaty of Westphalia (1648), and the Emperor Leopold I (1658–1705) incorporated Hungary, Croatia and Transylvania with his other lands, a step which was essential if the dynasty, having been repulsed in Germany, was to establish for itself a new, powerful dominion on the Danube.

At the same time, a beginning had been made in a policy of centralization which was designed to form the Habsburg lands into a single, unified state. This ideal may be said to have begun with the Emperor Ferdinand I (1556–64), who made the central departments of state in Vienna – composed of his Austrian ministers and officials – deliberative and policy-forming bodies for all his territories, the most important being the privy council, which advised him on general matters of policy and prepared business for the Bohemian, Hungarian and other diets. The next stage in the attempt to reform the Habsburg dominions came with Leopold I. Under him the privy council increased its control over the many subordinate provincial bodies, and an administrative bureaucracy was built up, staffed by middle-class men dependent upon the Emperor's favour for advancement. The Habsburg chancellors became trained administrators and were able to exert a growing influence throughout the family lands in the ruler's name; 'the chancellors', Oscar Hintze has said, 'from the Thirty Years' War onward, became the tools of monarchical centralization.' By the opening of the eighteenth century, therefore, the

235

Habsburgs had survived the critical external and internal problems facing them since the Treaty of Westphalia and made considerable advances in improving the administration of their family lands.

Yet the Habsburg monarchy was still essentially decentralized. Besides holding the elective office of Holy Roman Emperor, Charles VI ruled over each of the hereditary possessions of his family by a separate title; he was Archduke of Austria, King of Bohemia and Apostolic King of Hungary. In each of the two medieval kingdoms, Bohemia and Hungary, the great noble families had retained extensive autonomous right and privileges, and their influence was strong throughout the century; the administrative reforms of Charles VI's daughter, Maria Theresa, and her son, Joseph II, were significantly to be carried out by ministers who came mainly from the nobility. The two kingdoms had each also their own independent diet, and Charles VI, like every Habsburg heir, was crowned separately in the capitals of Prague and Buda. Above all, nearly every important division of the Habsburg lands, such as Upper and Lower Austria, Bohemia, Milan and the Netherlands, preserved its own political traditions expressed through powerful, conservative local institutions. In particular, Hungary during the eighteenth century kept its own system of administration, dominated by the nobility who enjoyed considerable exemption from taxation. Finally, the Habsburg monarchy lacked in many of its territories, and especially in Hungary, the support of a strong middle-class such as in other European countries provided the main foundation for centralized absolutism.

These factors combined to make Habsburg authority weak in comparison with that of other contemporary rulers. Charles VI never enjoyed more than half the revenue of the British government, though the population of his territories, including the wealthy Austrian Netherlands, was at least two-and-a-half times that of the United Kingdom. Charles was at no time able to raise an army of as many as 100,000 men, and many of his troops were of doubtful military value, while Frederick William, King of Prussia, had by the end of his reign 80,000 fully-trained, well-equipped soldiers, though the population of the Habsburg lands was ten times that of Prussia.[1] It was these weaknesses which Frederick the Great was able to exploit so well.

[1] P. 131.

Despite the fact that the obsolete, semi-feudal system of government in the Habsburg dominions was proving increasingly inadequate, no significant administrative or political change was made in its structure during Charles VI's reign, because of his preoccupation with securing acceptance of his Pragmatic Sanction.[1] This was, however, in itself a constitutional achievement of considerable importance. It secured its internal purpose satisfactorily, for when Maria Theresa succeeded to the Habsburg lands on her father's death, she met with no serious domestic opposition; even the Hungarian nobility recognized her as their ruler after she had reaffirmed their privileges.[2] Had this not been so, it must have meant the end of Habsburg rule, which could hardly have survived both an internal and international crisis at this juncture. The Pragmatic Sanction, therefore, although designed by Charles merely to preserve intact the Habsburg dynastic inheritance of semi-feudal possessions, proved to be in fact an important contribution towards the development of the Austro-Hungarian Empire of the nineteenth century.

The Empress Maria Theresa (1740–80)

Another decisive contribution towards the growth of the later Austria–Hungary were the administrative reforms of the eighteenth century. The first impulse to these came as a result of the failure of the Pragmatic Sanction to secure its international purpose owing to Frederick the Great's aggression. Maria Theresa was determined to resist the Prussian attack, but lacked the means to do so. The War of the Austrian Succession made the Empress and her advisers realize that improved administration of her hereditary lands, and particularly greater governmental uniformity and unity, was essential for the recovery of Silesia and perhaps even for the survival of the Habsburg monarchy.

The early stages of the War showed the disruptive possibilities of aristocratic opposition in the two Habsburg kingdoms. In Bohemia, Charles Albert, Elector of Bavaria and claimant to the Imperial office, was recognized by many of the nobility as their king in 1741.[3] Two years later, after the Austrians had driven their enemies from Bohemia, Maria Theresa removed the Bohemian royal regalia from Prague to Vienna to signify her resolve to ensure the permanent incorporation of the Czech crown in the Habsburg dynasty. This was enforced by a series of

[1] P. 200.   [2] P. 238.   [3] P. 203.

administrative orders which considerably increased the power of
the central government over the kingdom.   Early in 1749 the
Bohemian court chancery, which had exercised both judicial and
administrative functions, was abolished and replaced by new
government offices with authority over Austria and Bohemia together.   Bohemia was eventually placed under an Austrian code
of law, and judicial appeals had to go to a supreme court in
Vienna.   The teaching of the German language was made compulsory in schools and its use enforced in all government offices.
Such measures involved abrogation of autonomous rights,
guaranteed since the seventeenth century to Bohemia, and were
an intensification of the Habsburg attempts to weaken Czech
nationalism, language and separatism.

In the other Habsburg kingdom, Hungary, the Magyar nobility
did not welcome an invader as had numbers of the Bohemian
nobility, but they were prepared to take advantage of Maria
Theresa's military weakness to gain concessions from her.   When
the Diet met in 1741, after an interval of twelve years, to consider
the formalities of her coronation, they were able to insist upon
the reaffirmation of their privileges, notably exemption from
taxation, immunity from Habsburg administrative control and
the reservation of the higher offices in Hungary, lay and
ecclesiastical, for themselves.   After Maria Theresa had been
crowned, her worsening military situation required large reinforcements of troops which only Hungary could provide.   Her
requests to the Diet were accompanied by a long series of concessions, including a promise that she would build a palace and
reside in Buda; but each concession brought a fresh demand.
Eventually she summoned the Diet and made a dignified speech
to its members in which she declared with tears that she entrusted
the fate of herself, her infant son and her crown to their bravery
and devotion.   Her appeal was not without its effect upon the
Magyar nobility.   In return for the ratification of their privileges,
she was promised 100,000 troops.   She never received this full
number, but such Hungarian contingents as did join her forces
fought well.   Still more important was the political effect of the
Diet's action, which strengthened her position considerably and
influenced the course of the War at a critical juncture.

Maria Theresa made no attempt to deprive the Magyar
nobility of the privileges which she had recognized in 1741, but to
prevent them making fresh demands, the Diet, which according

to the Golden Bull of 1222 should have been convoked annually, met only three times during her long reign. At the same time she gradually established a party favourable to herself among the nobility. Magyar noblemen were encouraged to come to her court at Vienna, where they learned to speak German, abandoned their distinctive national costumes and accepted the titles of prince, count and baron of the Empire. She even met some of their wishes. Hungary was excluded from the measures initiated by Haugwitz during her reign to secure bureaucratic centralization, owing to, as she said, 'the special conditions there'; and several Magyar noblemen were appointed to foreign embassies and other high offices. This policy towards Hungary was part of the price which had to be paid to secure the survival of the Habsburg territories, and it marks a move in the direction of the dualism of the monarchy which was to be established in 1867.

The Reforms of Haugwitz

Maria Theresa entrusted the general administrative reforms throughout her territories to Count Wilhelm von Haugwitz (1702–65). Though less well known than his successor in the chancery, Kaunitz, who was concerned chiefly with foreign affairs, Haugwitz did much to strengthen the power of the central authority through the determination with which he carried out his measures. His actions, Maria Theresa wrote after his death to his widow, 'brought the government from confusion into order'. A Silesian nobleman and the son of a Saxon general, Haugwitz had been employed during the War of the Austrian Succession to reorganize the administration of the part of Silesia retained by Austria. The ability he displayed in this task secured him an invitation to express to the government his ideas on the general situation facing Austria through the loss of her wealthiest province. He at once evolved a comprehensive plan which further secured him the chancellorship. Having been strongly impressed during the War by the efficiency of Frederick the Great's civil administration, he wished to reorganize the entire Habsburg system of government, outside Hungary, Milan and the Austrian Netherlands, to bring it closer to that of the Prussian state.

Such a reform necessitated the establishment of an adequate standing army and the raising of sufficient money to maintain it. Haugwitz estimated that the Habsburg monarchy needed for its

security an army of at least 108,000 men, the upkeep of which
would require an annual sum nearly a third greater than the
contribution usually voted by the territorial estates. To obtain
this additional sum, he introduced a series of measures which
gradually abolished the exemptions of the Church and the
nobility and introduced a universal income-tax and a graduated
poll tax. The estates were deprived of the revenue from indirect
levies on tobacco and salt and from the stamp duty, and they were
made to present their accounts of income and expenditure for
approval by a Chamber of Accounts in Vienna. Moreover, in
1748 Haugwitz persuaded all the estates of the lands of the
Bohemian and Austrian crown to sign contracts for increased
taxation for a period of ten years, so practically destroying their
historic right to grant taxes. As a result of these financial reforms by Haugwitz the annual revenue of the Habsburg
dominions was trebled during Maria Theresa's reign.

These financial measures inevitably weakened the powers of
the provincial estates and the local nobility. Although the estates
continued to meet almost annually, their legislative activity soon
fell into abeyance. The crown adopted the practice of promul-
gating important laws without the participation of the estates,
who were unable to resist this development, so clearly had the
military disasters of the War of the Austrian Succession shown the
urgent need for administrative centralization. At the same time,
an attempt was made to weaken the social dominance and so the
political influence of the nobility by legislation limiting the almost
absolute control they enjoyed over their serfs.[1] Only a very small
beginning was made, and the legal position of the serfs remained
fundamentally the same, but at least more was done to improve
their position than in Prussia under Frederick the Great. In
particular, royal commissions were established in both Austria and
Bohemia which drew up a written register of the manorial dues
owed by serfs to protect them from capricious exactions by their
lords.

As the power of the nobility and the estates was weakened, so
the authority of the central government was increased by Haugwitz through the evolution of a system of administrative councils.
The way for this was prepared by the abolition of the Bohemian
court chancery in 1749.[2] Then judicial work was definitely
separated from financial and administrative affairs and made the

function of a Supreme Court. The financial and administrative business was given to a Directory, which was, however, later divided into a Central Chamber for finance and a Supreme Chancery for executive purposes. Finally, the secret conference of ministers was replaced by a Council of State, which exercised supreme control over all the other bodies.

This reorganization of internal administration was accompanied by the establishment of royal commissions at various times to consider a number of social and political questions. Some results were achieved from these, such as the abolition of the more cruel forms of punishment and the elimination of sorcery as a crime, the result of a report of a judicial commission. Generally, however, these commissions, since most of them were efforts to change manners and morals by law, were not very successful. This was particularly true of a chastity commission, which was set up at Maria Theresa's insistence to consider the possibility of preventing improper love-making.

The new administrative system established at Vienna required a reorganization of local government to ensure that its decrees were obeyed in the provincial territories. Hitherto permanent committees of the local diets had acted as executive bodies between sessions, but gradually administrative powers were withdrawn from them and given to ten colleges, each of which managed the affairs of a district under the control of the Directory. The nobility, now that the diets were little more than formal assemblies which generally voted the crown's demands, were given places in these colleges, but the real work was done by the professional, middle-class officials among their members. One important consequence of these changes was the end of Bohemia as a separate state, for it was now amalgamated administratively with the other Habsburg dominions. And, indeed, throughout the territories to which these reforms were applied, the agents of the crown could now move freely and enforce their orders, often in areas where they had not before been able to penetrate.

Reforms were also introduced which affected education and religion. Early in 1746 the nomination of the professors of the University of Vienna was placed in the hands of the crown. This was the first of a series of measures designed to bring all universities and secondary schools under the authority of the State and to control their entrance requirements and syllabuses. At the same time, the powers of the Church over elementary education

were restricted.   Maria Theresa was a sincere Roman Catholic,
and Frederick the Great called her an 'apostolic hag', but she was
determined not to permit papal interference in ecclesiastical
affairs within her domains.   Bishops were forbidden to correspond directly with the Papacy, and in 1773 she joined with other
Roman Catholic countries in enforcing the suppression of the
Jesuits, though in Austria some of the members of the Society
were allowed to continue to take a part in education.[1]

Finally, Maria Theresa and Haugwitz, like Joseph II afterwards, made considerable efforts to industrialize the western part
of the Habsburg lands, but the encouragement given to Austria
and Bohemia was not extended to Hungary.   On the contrary, a
system of differential tariffs was deliberately employed to keep
this kingdom as an agricultural country and a source of raw
materials for the Austrian industries.   This measure was justified
on the grounds that tariffs were the only way of obtaining from
Hungary any considerable revenue, since the Magyar nobility
refused to renounce its traditional privilege of freedom from
taxation.   Maria Theresa and Haugwitz also created a large
internal market by uniting all the Danubian dominions, except
Hungary, the Tyrol and the free cities of Cracow, Brody and
Trieste, into a single customs unit.   This considerably benefited
Austrian industry, which shared with Hungarian agriculture a
further stimulus under the Continental System during the
Napoleonic War.[2]

The effect of the reforms of Maria Theresa and Haugwitz was
uneven.   It was particularly limited geographically.   The administrative measures had little effect in the Austrian Netherlands
and Italy and, above all, in the kingdom of Hungary.   As late as
1764, the other Habsburg provinces, excluding Milan and the
Netherlands, paid over four times as much in taxation towards
the maintenance of the Habsburg army as did Hungary.   Nevertheless, these reforms did improve the government and increase
the strength of the Habsburg monarchy.   A single indication of
this was the greater effectiveness of the Austrian military effort in
the Seven Years' War as compared with its weakness in the War
of the Austrian Succession.   Moreover, the way had been prepared for Joseph II's more rapid and thorough reforms long
before he gained sole power in 1780 or even before he became
co-regent with his mother in 1765.

[1] P. 122.   [2] P. 371.

The Emperor Joseph II (1780–90)

'Since I mounted the throne,' wrote Joseph in 1781, 'I have made Philosophy the legislator of my empire. Her logical principles shall transform Austria.' Such was the resolve which he continued to hold and strive to put into effect throughout his reign, never losing his determination even amid the many signs of failure which marked his last days. He took the reforms of Maria Theresa and Haugwitz to a radical conclusion and was in many ways the most perfect example of contemporary Enlightened Despotism, being nicknamed the 'people's emperor'.[1] Unfortunately, Joseph was not entirely well suited by character and upbringing to carry out his self-appointed task with success. His mother had ordered that he was to be educated only by means that attracted and amused him and not by the old-fashioned ways of compulsion and punishment. In this way the young Joseph acquired many and keen interests and was able to develop his considerable ability. He was early inspired by the spirit of the Enlightenment and impressed by the new ideas of the Encyclopaedists. At the same time, however, his natural self-confidence received no check, and his impatience with opposing views became boundless. He displayed his mother's enthusiasm for reform, untempered by her common sense.

Moreover, the medieval imperialism of Joseph's foreign policy contrasted curiously with his revolutionary modernism at home. He sought to carry out an ambitious foreign policy at the same time as he promoted his drastic internal reforms; and his foreign policy was his greatest failure. It was no expression of Enlightenment, but merely a desire for territorial expansion. He had been born as Frederick the Great was taking Silesia, and in his foreign policy he continued, with the support of the still-powerful Kaunitz, Maria Theresa's constant aim to recover Silesia or obtain compensation for it in order to restore Habsburg supremacy in Germany.

Prussia would certainly oppose such a policy, but so also probably would Russia, and fear of Catherine the Great led Joseph to meet Frederick at Neisse in Prussian Silesia in 1769. They met again the next year because Joseph wanted to secure a share of Polish territory before Prussia and Russia divided up the country between themselves. Maria Theresa had been firmly

[1] P. 98.

opposed to participation in the partition of Poland, describing it as an 'immoral game', but Joseph did not share her scruples and obtained Galicia in 1772. Joseph's journeying took him in 1777 on a visit to his sister, Marie Antoinette, in France, where he predicted the approaching downfall of the French monarchy.

The gains of Austria in Poland had been small compared with those of Russia and Prussia. Joseph, therefore, despite Maria Theresa's protests, intervened in 1778 in the question of the Bavarian Succession.[1] He plunged his country into war with Prussia, which threatened to develop into a general European conflict, but French and Russian mediation compelled him to accept a treaty which granted him only a fragment of what he desired. When his mother's death in 1780 freed him from all restraints, Joseph was now ready to seek success in the East. Maria Theresa had declared that if Austria were to extend her frontiers to the very walls of Constantinople, she would gain nothing except 'unhealthy, barbaric provinces, uninhabited or populated by unreliable Greeks, who would exhaust, not add to, the forces of the Monarchy'; but Joseph agreed to co-operate with Catherine the Great at the expense of Turkey. He went to Russia and made a treaty with her in 1781, but the only result was that she was able to annex the Crimea without a war in 1784, while he got nothing.[2]

Joseph, meanwhile, had turned to the west again. He realized that if he were to strengthen his dominions, the distant Netherlands must be made more defensible. Britain was at this time occupied by the revolt of her American colonies and at war with Holland, which had joined the League of Armed Neutrality formed in 1780 by the northern powers, Denmark, Russia and Sweden, to protest against British interference with neutral shipping. So Joseph believed he could safely take action against Holland. Late in 1781, he insisted that the barrier fortresses must be abandoned. When the Dutch complied, he demanded in 1784 the cession of Maestricht and the freeing of navigation on the Scheldt; but Britain had now made peace with her colonies and with Holland and France. The Dutch resisted, and Joseph had again to accept French mediation, being advised by Catherine 'de ne pas aller trop loin et d'accepter la conciliation'. By the Treaty of Fontainebleau in 1785 he withdrew his demands in re-

---

[1] P. 196.   [2] P. 271.

turn for an indemnity which France, anxious for a settlement, paid.

Joseph now revived the old idea of exchanging the Netherlands for Bavaria, which would be easier to defend and would greatly promote Habsburg influence in Germany. The Elector of Bavaria was again ready to agree with his ideas, but Frederick the Great thwarted him this time also by forming the League of Princes against him in 1785. Since neither France nor Russia was ready to help him with arms, Joseph had to relinquish this second attempt to obtain Bavaria.[1]

Consequently he was ready to fall in with the plans of Catherine the Great for a renewed campaign against Turkey. Ceaseless work and travel had aged Joseph beyond his years, but he went in 1787 to the Crimea, when Catherine made her famous last journey there and agreed to join her as an ally when war broke out with Turkey that summer.[2] While the two monarchs were discussing the division of the Turkish Empire, Joseph learnt that the Netherlands were in revolt and hastened back to Vienna, but by now illness and exhaustion had impaired his participation in events. The seizure of power in Brussels by the rebels encouraged the Turks to attack the Russians on whose side Joseph had just committed himself. Finally, revolt broke out in Hungary, forcing him to revoke many of his reforms there.

During the whole of his reign, Joseph had been faced by an undeveloped administrative system, widely scattered territories and no strong middle-class or public-spirited aristocracy such as existed in England. He did not recognize this as a great handicap because of his own authoritarian views. He was prepared to act as a comprehensive autocrat. At the age of nineteen he wrote, 'A single head, however mediocre, is better fitted to run a political organization than ten far more competent who have to act as a body.' He maintained this principle in all the actions of his reign, but the result was that when things began to go wrong, they went wrong completely, and the entire blame rested upon him. On his deathbed in 1790 Joseph believed, therefore, that he was an utter failure and chose as an epitaph for himself, 'Here lies Joseph who was unfortunate in all his enterprises.'

Yet even amid such complete, final despair, he wrote more hopefully to the aged Kaunitz, who corresponded with him, but could not overcome his horror of physical suffering to visit his dying master. To him Joseph expressed an undaunted confidence that posterity would judge him more favourably than his contemporaries. Success, he believed, would come to his policy after his own time. And this was to be so, though not always in ways intended or foreseen by himself. He died amid manifestations of widespread criticism and violent opposition in his dominions, and few of his internal reforms survived him, yet the consequences of some of them, as A. J. P. Taylor has suggested, were strangely considerable and long-lasting.

In his religious policy, for instance, though Josephinism played an important part in Austrian history for more than a generation after his reign, it encountered early resistance in the Austrian Netherlands, where religion and national feeling were so closely bound up together, and its effect in Europe was later lost in the general reaction against the French Revolution. More important was the effect of Joseph's establishment of religious toleration, which meant that secular thought could at last begin to take an increasingly important part in the intellectual and cultural life of the Habsburg lands. Protestantism also revived, notably in Bohemia. Above all, toleration gave opportunities to the Jews which they were quick to seize. Until Joseph's reign, the Jews (of whom Maria Theresa had written, 'I know of no worse plague for the State than this race') had formed an inconsiderable minority in the Habsburg lands, but the acquisition of Galicia brought the monarchy part of the large Jewish population of Poland. Freed by Joseph from civil disabilities, they took a leading part in Austrian industry which was to make them, by the opening years of the twentieth century, easily the most influential and richest people of the Habsburg Empire. By tolerating them, Joseph also brought into being a group who, alone among the peoples under Austrian rule, were untroubled by the conflict between dynastic and nationalistic claims, which became increasingly tense in the nineteenth century, and who became, therefore, loyal supporters of the Habsburg dynasty.

Most far-reaching in their results were Joseph's most spectacular measures – his agrarian reforms.[1] The abolition of serfdom was a common aim of eighteenth-century Enlightened Despots, but none brought about the same decisive consequences as Joseph did. This was not because he himself intended to do so. There seems no doubt that the principal motives of his policy were to

[1] P. 101.

continue the diminution of the power of the nobility, which had been begun by his mother and Haugwitz, and to prevent an increase in noble land-holdings, which paid less taxes in Austria and Bohemia and none in Hungary. Yet its effect was to preserve the peasantry of the Habsburg dominions, because Joseph almost alone emancipated the serfs without weakening their connexion with the land they tilled.

When the German princes abolished serfdom in their states, they did not give the peasants security of tenure; generally only the wealthier peasants retained their holdings, and the poorer ones became landless labourers. Joseph's measures gave his peasants a security which elsewhere in Europe was gained only through the French Revolution, and this ensured that when serfdom was finally abolished in the Habsburg territories in 1848, they did not lose their land. Moreover, the poorer peasants could still sell their holdings and leave the countryside, but when they did so, they could only sell them to richer peasants and not to any noble landowner, large or small. There could be no transference of land from the peasantry to the nobility.

In this way, the peasant communities survived in the Habsburg dominions. Politically the monarchy remained an absolutism. Socially, however, the continued existence of the peasantry made it more like revolutionary France than was Prussia or even western Germany, and consequently it was to be more susceptible to the penetration of French political ideas in the nineteenth century.

At the same time, the Habsburg monarchy in its upper social structure remained obviously very different from the France of the Jacobins. Joseph's agrarian policy was largely responsible for this also. The great nobility was destined to flourish and become the class which imparted distinctive features to the empire of the Habsburgs because Joseph's measures were strangely to its advantage. The granting of security of tenure to the peasantry was disadvantageous to the lesser nobility, since it was now unable to create large estates and so rise in the social scale; but the great nobility already had ample estates and increased them at the expense of the lesser nobility.

Again, the development of a money economy with the growth of trade and industry and the commutation of serf-obligations into money-payments harmed the lesser nobility, who usually dissipated the small sums they received in more ostentatious living than they could afford, while the great nobility received sums large enough for them to invest and become capitalists. The Habsburg nobility, therefore, became like the English gentry, who lived on rents and dividends. Only in Hungary were there noblemen who worked the land themselves, like the Junkers of Prussia, and after 1848 they did not lead the same sort of lives as the Junkers.

Through Joseph's measures, therefore, the Habsburg monarchy retained in a flourishing condition a great nobility and a land-holding peasantry, two classes which were declining in numbers and importance elsewhere in Europe. The nobility made Austria more conservative than the rest of Central Europe, while at the same time the peasantry made it more radical. Both acted as a check to the rise of an urban capitalist class, which in other countries was the main upholder of the aspirations of nine-teenth-century liberalism. Joseph had wanted to form his dominions into a German state, but paradoxically his agrarian policy delayed the triumph of that social class and the economic system which was to promote German nationalism. Among Austrian peasants there was no desertion of the land on a scale comparable to that which took place in England or Germany, with the result that industry in the Habsburg empire was long without the cheap labour provided by a landless working-class. Its backward manufactures required the continuance of the pro-tection of high tariffs which Joseph himself initiated. This kept Austria out of the Zollverein, the customs union formed among the German states by Prussia in the first half of the nineteenth century, so that German trade inevitably turned from the Danube valley to the ports of the North Sea and further excluded Austria from Germany.

The Austrian Empire

Joseph was succeeded by his younger brother, Leopold II (1790–2), who had been assigned, on the death of his father, the Emperor Francis I, in 1765, the Grand Duchy of Tuscany, where he had introduced a number of enlightened administrative and judicial reforms. His short reign was spent in retreating from his brother's ambitious schemes, making peace with Turkey, seeking friendly relations with Prussia and avoiding war with revolutionary France. He revoked most of Joseph's reforms, though the essentials of the new agrarian system remained. He also set about restoring the shattered authority of the Habsburg monarchy over its dominions.

In doing this, Leopold's attitude towards his two kingdoms was fundamentally the same as that of past Habsburg rulers. He was prepared to be crowned as King of Bohemia, but he would not agree either to change the Revised Ordinance of 1627, which had established Habsburg supremacy over the country, or to revive the Bohemian Chancery. As with Maria Theresa, his concessions were only of real consequence in Hungary. The Diet of Hungary was summoned, and at an especially solemn session the separate privileges of the kingdom were re-asserted with fresh formality. In particular, the counties fully regained their powers of autonomous administration, which had been abolished by Joseph, and this ensured the maintenance of the political power of the Magyar nobility. Thus, in this crisis the same essential pattern of events was followed as in the earlier crisis of 1741. A compromise was again reached between the claims of the Habsburg dynasty and the liberties of Hungary. A further step was taken towards the establishment of the Dual Monarchy.

This was itself preceded by the establishment in 1804 of a separate Habsburg empire (as distinct from the shadowy Holy Roman Empire).[1] It is hardly likely that this would have been possible without the administrative reforms of the eighteenth century, which gave the Habsburg lands a relatively effective government and enabled them to survive the defeats, indemnities and mutilations inflicted upon them by France between 1796 and 1810. Still more, these reforms, in the words of the American historian, Dr. Padover, had the effect of 'galvanizing the monarchy and giving it a new lease of life for a century and a half'.

The Habsburg dominions entered the nineteenth century with their unity upheld in several ways. Though in Hungary Protestantism was influential and tolerated, the monarchy remained essentially Roman Catholic and had not been deprived of the support of the clergy by the policy of Josephinism, which had increased the power of the State over the Church. Vienna, rather than Rome, was the ecclesiastical centre of the dominions, and loyalty to their ruler was taught to the peoples as a religious duty. Again, the nobility dominated both the social life of the towns and the economics of the countryside, and with the

[1] Pp. 4, 367.

exception of the Hungarians and Poles, were a cultured, international class, who spoke French, Italian or their own type of Latinized German. They were aloof from the Slav and German populations and did not share their national aspirations. The nobility monopolized the higher command of the army, which was a loyal agent of the monarchy and itself promoted unity. Finally, the reforms of Maria Theresa and Joseph II had supplemented and given increased vitality to the unifying influence of these other forces.

Both Maria Theresa and Joseph II had tried to amalgamate the diverse territories of their dynasty in Central Europe into a Danubian kingdom. They did not succeed in establishing a genuine national unity such as existed in the compact, consanguinous kingdoms of Britain and France, but the administrative, judicial and social reforms of these two monarchs did manage to check the disruptive forces apparent in the constituent states of their empire. Their centralization of government and uniformity of law was sufficient to enable the new Austrian Empire to act as a leading power in Europe and survive into the twentieth century the stresses and strains which an age of growing nationalism inevitably brought it.

XIV · THE EMERGENCE OF RUSSIA

Peter the Great (1694–1725)

DURING the first quarter of the eighteenth century Russia was under the rule of the dynamic, forceful Czar Peter I. As a boy, he had received very little formal education, but through realistic war-games with his friends developed a taste for military matters. Later, sailing boats led him to acquire an equal interest in ship-building and naval warfare. Indeed, he had a passion for things practical all his life. He boasted in later years that he was proficient in fourteen trades, which included stone-masonry, carpentry, joinery, cobbling and printing. He acted as court dentist, keeping in a little bag the teeth he extracted, and courtiers were terrified of falling ill lest he should want to use forceps or knife on them. He enjoyed beheading criminals and soundly birching disobedient servant-girls. Seven feet tall with an amazingly powerful frame, Peter combined a violent and unstable temperament with an active and shrewd intelligence. Above all, he was devoted to what he conceived to be the good of Russia and gave himself to the service of the State with all his strength.

From the beginning of his reign, Peter devoted himself to the continuance of the policy, already initiated by his predecessors, which sought to make Russia a great western power. In 1697 he himself went with fifty Russian noblemen to study and gain experience in western Europe. What he saw there of the way in which wealth, trade, manufactures and knowledge could bring power and prosperity to a nation convinced him that Russia urgently needed to learn from the west so as to match it in these things and be strong enough to survive as a great power. He came back with at least 750 technicians of various nationalities to work in Russia and purchased quantities of military and naval material.

Upon his return, he was able to reorganize his army. He raised new guards regiments to form an up-to-date professional force, effectively trained on European lines by foreign officers. Other regiments followed, based on a system of conscript levies, and when Peter died Russia had a standing army of 210,000 men, including a field army of perhaps 100,000, which was smaller than the French army, but about the same as the Austrian and far greater than that of Sweden or Prussia. Peter realized that Russian expansion westwards also needed a sea-going navy. His own experience of shipbuilding in Amsterdam and Deptford enabled him, with foreign assistance, to construct and handle a powerful fleet which before his death gave him, with nearly 50 ships of the line, 800 smaller vessels and 20,000 sailors, the mastery of the Baltic and the strongest naval force in that sea.

Peter saw that Russian development first needed a Baltic foothold to be, in his well-known phrase, 'a window through which his people might look into Europe'. To secure this object, Peter was at war almost all his reign; only one of its thirty-one years was entirely peaceful. Fortunately for him Sweden, which had dominated the Baltic since the Treaty of Westphalia, was now past her prime. After suffering a serious initial defeat, Peter persevered to win a decisive victory over the Swedes at the Battle of Poltava in 1709 and by the Treaty of Nystadt in 1721 gained all the Baltic coastline from Riga to the Gulf of Finland. At his triumph in Moscow he was proclaimed as 'Father of the Fatherland, Peter the Great, Emperor of all the Russias'.

Most strikingly symbolical of Russia's new position on the Baltic was Peter's city of St. Petersburg, the outlet to the western seas for which the Great Northern War had been fought. He began its construction as early as 1703 on the delta of the River Neva, which was a waste of swamps and islands. Here for ten years massed labour forces, under terrible conditions, built dykes and canals and drove in thousands of piles on which buildings were erected. By 1714 Peter could proclaim it the new capital of Russia and move his court and government departments there. This in itself provided a further reason for defeating Sweden. 'The ladies of St. Petersburg,' Peter said, 'could not sleep peacefully so long as the Swedish frontier ran so close to our capital.' By the time of his death, with its 75,000 inhabitants, it was the largest city in northern Europe.

It was in his new capital that Peter persisted in his efforts to compel the Russian nobility to imitate the externals of western civilization. He forced (and assisted) them to shave off their beards and abandon their oriental dress; he ordered clothes to be cut in the German style and women to abandon their traditional seclusion and to participate in society. He directed the production of the first Russian guide to etiquette, which condemned dancing in boots, spitting on the floor, gnawing bones at meals and talking with one's mouth full. These well-known actions of Peter must not, however, be over-emphasized. His encouragement of European dress and manners symbolized his western policy, but his fundamental aim was not to impose a western culture on Russia; it was to give her western knowledge and skill which would bring her power and prosperity.

Peter deliberately, therefore, set out to imitate western economic practices and achievements. He sent hundreds of students to Europe to learn arts and skills and examined them rigorously himself when they returned. He also had agents in several countries to recruit foreign workmen for Russian industry. Among the most important of the new industrial undertakings started by him was the introduction of blast furnaces in the Urals, the strategic value of which to Russia in both peace and war was well understood by Peter. Many of the new enterprises were founded and run by the State; others were managed by companies under the encouragement of subsidies and exemption from taxation. In 1721 Peter placed industrialists upon much of an equality with land-owners by allowing them to purchase serfs for permanent attachment to their factories and mines.

Peter also initiated a policy of administrative reform, designed to make the Czardom's absolutism more thorough and effective. The country was divided into twelve provinces, over each of which was a governor responsible to the Czar. In 1711 Peter followed this by setting up a small Senate, an advisory board of state officials to administer justice and control finance, and four years later created a system of nine Colleges or ministerial departments, each with a clearly defined administrative task, which was modelled upon the collegial board system obtaining in Sweden and other northern European states. Peter's chief financial reform was the introduction in 1718 of a uniform poll-tax on all males, except the nobility, gentry and clergy; this became the main source of direct taxation and accounted for over half the national revenue. For the nobility, Peter wished to establish a system like that of Prussia, which should make them serve the State, but within fifty years of his death they had secured the abolition of all compulsory official service.[1]

Finally, Peter placed the Russian Church under the control of

[1] P. 44.

the State. When the Patriarch of Moscow died in 1700, he refused to allow the election of a successor and in 1721 replaced the patriarchate by a Holy Synod of bishops. Attached to it was a lay secretary, the Upper Procurator, who was appointed by the Czar. Peter called him the 'Czar's eye', and his function was to ensure that the Church was bound closely to the government. This system of ecclesiastical administration was to remain in force as long as the existence of the Czardom.

A Russian historian has summarized Peter's main achievements for his country as 'the adoption of European techniques and technical instruction, the encouragement of essential industries, the creation of a modern army and navy, the transformation of the theocratic monarchy into a secular absolutism'. Westernization had begun in Russia before Peter's reign. Seventeenth-century technical advances had already reached the country and done something to increase its wealth. Peter, in B. H. Sumner's phrase, 'opened wider with sledge-hammer blows fissures which had already been spreading in the half-century before 1700'. His policies were original and brilliant, but at the same time they were along the lines of his country's development, and despite the series of mediocre rulers between himself and Catherine the Great, they were largely continued, and most of his work remained undestroyed.

The Supremacy of the Guards (1725–62)

The greatest misfortune of Peter's reign was that his eldest and only surviving son, Alexis, was a weakling and out of sympathy with his father's radical policy, especially as it affected the Church. He increasingly became the centre of the hopes of the reactionary elements in Russian society until in 1718 he was arrested, knouted and died soon afterwards. Three years later Peter issued a ukase declaring that in future the reigning Czar should nominate his successor on the throne, but he himself left it too late. As he was dying in 1725, he tried unavailingly to tell his womenfolk his choice of an heir.

The succession was now left to be disputed by force, and it was determined by the decision of the imperial guards, the privileged regiments of the army created by Peter. They were the only body sufficiently united to be able to take political action. Between the death of Peter in 1725 and the accession of Catherine II in 1762, ultimate power in Russia resided in their barracks in St.

Petersburg. Six times during the years the throne changed hands, and each time the succession was resolved by a palace revolution dominated by the guards. This internal instability naturally made an unfavourable impression on western observers. 'The Russian throne,' said a contemporary diplomat, 'is neither hereditary nor elective; it is seized.'

The obvious heir to the throne in 1725 was Peter, the ten-year-old son of Alexis and the sole surviving male of the Romanov line, but this would have meant that power would have fallen into the hands of the old nobility. Alexander Menshikov and other ministers of humble origin, whom Peter the Great had promoted, desired, therefore, the accession of Catherine, Peter the Great's widow. She was a Lithuanian peasant servant-girl, taken by the Russians at the capture of a Swedish fortress, whom Peter married in 1711. Since she was popular with the guards, having accompanied them on several campaigns, she received their support and was proclaimed as Catherine I.

Very quickly an attempt was made to limit the autocracy established during the previous reign. In 1726 a Supreme Secret Council was set up. It consisted of six members, drawn from the old and new nobility, and presided over by the Czarina. Its powers included complete control of legislation, but it aroused such strong opposition from the nobility that these had to be restricted. Nevertheless, this permanent council was an important stage in the movement towards a Russian constitution which was a feature of these years.

Catherine reigned for only two years. On her death, the claims of her step-grandson, Peter, were now too strong to be resisted. Menshikov tried to protect his position by betrothing his daughter to Peter; but no sooner did Peter succeed to the throne than he broke off his betrothal and exiled Menshikov to Siberia, where he died two years later. The reign of this boy-czar was a triumph for the conservative nobility. Foreign experts and administrators were discharged, and the Russian capital was moved from St. Petersburg back to Moscow. The reign, however, was to last only three years. Early in January 1730 Peter II died of smallpox at the age of fifteen, and the male line of the Romanov family became extinct.

By Catherine I's will, her daughter, Elizabeth, should now have ruled Russia, but Prince Dimitri Golitsyn, who belonged to one of the oldest Russian families, persuaded his fellow-members of the Supreme Council to offer the throne on strict conditions to Anne, the widowed, childless Duchess of Courland, who was the daughter of Ivan, Peter the Great's half-brother and joint-czar with him in the early years of his reign. The conditions imposed on her were that she must obtain the consent of the Supreme Council when she wished to marry, name her heir, declare war or peace, raise new taxes, create new noblemen or make military appointments above the rank of colonel. If put into effect, these proposals would have replaced the Russian autocracy by an oligarchy; but the nobility were not prepared to accept this, and neither were the guards. Immediately Anne arrived in Moscow she, therefore, renounced her acceptance of these conditions and disbanded the Supreme Council. She also moved the court back to St. Petersburg.

Anne's reign of ten years was despotic and demoralizing. She was coarse and cruel, harsh and tyrannical, with an insatiable lust for pleasure; court expenditure under her was five times as much as it had been previously. Through her Secret Chancellery, she had innumerable secret spies and informers to discover any criticism of her rule, which she met with torture, exile and execution. Although she sought the support of the nobility by granting certain of their claims to relief from service to the State,[1] she ruled with German favourites, ministers and agents. She brought her lover, Count Biron, from Courland and made him Grand Chamberlain. The Chancellor and the Commander-in-Chief of the army were Germans, as also were many important executive officials. This was contrary to Peter the Great's strict rule of employing foreigners always as expert advisers and allowing only Russians to hold the commanding posts in the State. Consequently Anne's reign increased, even among the nobility, the traditional Russian dislike and suspicion of foreigners.

During these years, however, Russian participation in European affairs continued. Peter I had valued the friendship of Austria and, therefore, of her ally France, to strengthen Russia against Turkey, and in 1726 Catherine I had made a treaty with Austria, which involved Russia in the War of the Polish Succession in 1733.[2] After the Third Treaty of Vienna in 1738, Austria and Russia were ready to attempt a partition of Turkey. Russia's objective was the Crimea, which her troops thrice invaded and devastated, being each time forced to withdraw by

[1] P. 44. [2] P. 163.

unexpectedly strong Turkish resistance. Another Russian army gained a victory in Moldavia, but Austria was less successful and insisted upon peace being made by the Treaty of Belgrade in 1739. Russia kept Azov, which she had captured, but on condition that its fortifications should be destroyed and a stretch of surrounding territory devastated to hinder a future Russian attack on the Crimea.

Anne died in 1740. She had not married and in her will appointed as her successor the newly born son of her niece, Anna, who was the daughter of her sister, Catherine of Mecklenburg, and the wife of Prince Anton Ulrich of Brunswick-Lüneburg. He was to reign in his cradle as Ivan VI for only a year. Anne had also appointed Biron as Regent, but after three weeks the guards arrested him and sent him to Siberia. Ivan's mother now became Regent. She was a debauched and stupid woman, who continued to rely upon the German favourites. Public opinion now looked to Elizabeth, the daughter of Peter the Great and Catherine. She also realized that the time had come when she must either seek the throne or face banishment to a convent, the time-honoured expedient for disposing of unwanted women in Russia. She went to the barracks of the guards, who enthusiastically declared their loyalty to her. The infant Ivan was imprisoned in a fortress, his mother and family were sent to the provinces, the German ministers were removed, and Elizabeth was proclaimed Czarina.

Elizabeth resembled her parents in both appearance and character. She was her father's daughter in Russian sentiment and a desire to pursue policies which she believed were in the country's interest. One of her principal advisers was Count Ivan Shuvalov, who did more than any other man since Peter the Great himself to advance education in Russia. He considered that the country needed education in the arts and humanities as well as technical instruction. With Elizabeth's support, he was largely responsible for the foundation of the first Russian university, the University of Moscow, in 1755 and of the Academy of Arts in St. Petersburg two years later. It was also through his encouragement that Russia exchanged the influence of the petty German courts for the study of French literature and thought as representing the best of contemporary western culture. At the same time, the nobility began to speak the French language instead of their own, and the ladies of the court adopted the latest

French fashions; and the admiration which Russian society conceived for France was to last until the Revolution of 1917 severed the connexion.

From her mother, Elizabeth inherited her beauty and sensuality, her pleasure-loving and easy-going nature. She delighted in her favourites and her entertainments, yet was devoted to the Orthodox Church. Her extravagance was prodigal. She dressed magnificently, piling up debts with her Paris milliners until they stopped the imperial credit, and at her death she left a wardrobe of fifteen thousand gowns. In addition, she indulged in expensive building operations, notably the Winter Palace at St. Petersburg, which cost ten million roubles. Yet despite her lavish expenditure, her able Treasurer, who was another Shuvalov – Count Peter Shuvalov – was able to strengthen the country's finances by means of several economic reforms, and to lessen slightly the burdens of the people.

Indeed, historians have tended to diminish the importance of Elizabeth's reign, usually in order to magnify the achievements of her successor. In doing this, they have relied upon the dispatches of French, German and British diplomats, who were unable to prevent her persisting in a foreign policy objectionable to them and so were very ready to retail malicious gossip about her. In fact, her extravagances were slight compared with those of Catherine II, and though she was indolent by nature and often preferred her pleasures to the affairs of State, she was far from being insensitive to national interests and made sure that her ministers were men of ability. Moreover, she lived in an age when rule by women was still alien to the patriarchical outlook of the Muscovites. Despite Peter the Great's reforms, women were still treated as social inferiors, and the continued prevalence of wife-beating, sister-beating and daughter-beating in Russian households expressed the common belief in the need for their subjection to male authority. The reigns of Catherine I and Anne had done little to make a female monarch more acceptable, but by the end of Elizabeth's reign the Russians were more reconciled to the idea.

Probably what did most to earn Elizabeth the affection of her people, and especially of the army, was the way in which she restored to Russians their self-confidence and national pride. She revived her father's policy of relying exclusively upon her subjects in important positions in the State, yet at the same time employed the services of able foreigners, particularly to revive the army which he had created. The success of this was demonstrated by the part played by Russia in diplomacy and war during the later years of Elizabeth's reign.

It was Russia's accession of military strength which led Britain to approach the imperial government in 1755 to make a treaty for the protection of Hanover, but Elizabeth's purpose in agreeing to this was to provide a convenient opportunity for a combined attack upon Frederick the Great, who seemed to be an increasing threat to Russia. When it was immediately followed, however, by the conclusion of the Convention of Westminster between Britain and Prussia, Elizabeth took the steps which brought Russia into the Seven Years' War on the side of Austria and France.[1] Henceforward her aim was to secure the complete defeat and partition of Prussia. During the fighting, Russian officers were handicapped by lack of experience owing to the promotion of foreigners to high rank during Anne's reign; they were handicapped also in following up victories through uncertainty about Elizabeth's life. Yet the part taken by the Russian army in the War foreshadowed the triumphs it was to win in the next reign. Frederick, in fact, was only saved from disaster at Russian hands by Elizabeth's death early in 1762 and the consequent reversal of Russian policy.[2]

Soon after her accession, Elizabeth had summoned to St. Petersburg her nephew, Peter, the son of her sister, Anne, Duchess of Holstein. He had a dull, narrow mind and an obstinate, deceitful character. While reluctantly accepting conversion to the Orthodox Church, he remained wholly German in outlook, fervently admiring Frederick the Great and Prussia. His great passion was military drill, which he practised first with toy soldiers and then with Russian regiments. In 1745, Elizabeth married him, at the age of seventeen, to Princess Sophia Augusta of Anhalt-Zerbst, who was brought to St. Petersburg for the purpose. Demure and plain, she was his second cousin and a year younger than he. When received into the Orthodox Church, she accepted the name of Catherine, in honour of her husband's grandmother, and set out with ardent calculation to win the favour of Elizabeth and the Russian ruling circle.

Her marriage, however, proved hopelessly unhappy. She soon despised her husband, and he entirely neglected her, living openly

[1] P. 219.   [2] P. 228.

with mistresses.   Elizabeth was anxious for an heir to the throne, but Peter was impotent and unable to consummate the marriage. So Catherine, through no fault of her own, fell into disfavour and was forced to live an unnaturally restricted life in the St. Petersburg suburb of Oranienbaum, during which time she read widely, enlarging her knowledge and training her mind.   At last, in 1754, she bore a son named Paul, whose father may well not have been Peter, but the first of Catherine's many lovers, Sergei Saltykov (which would mean that none of the seven last imperial rulers of Russia was of Romanov blood).   Paul was immediately taken from his mother and brought up by Elizabeth.

These were the formative years of Catherine's life.   Her husband hated her, and she felt contempt for him.   She had been deprived of her son.   As she grew up, she had become a woman of lively attractiveness and ability, adroit and ambitious.   It is not surprising that during this period her powerful personality turned in on itself and the pursuit of power became her predominant aim.

When Peter III, immediately he became Czar, not only made peace with Frederick the Great, but also offered him an alliance, it came as a painful shock to the nation and especially to the army.   Further measures by Peter abolished the Secret Chancellery and formally emancipated the nobility from their obligations to the State, so completing the process which entirely destroyed Peter the Great's conception of compulsory service from them in return for the rank and privileges they enjoyed.[1]   In normal circumstances, these measures would have strengthened Peter's position on the throne, but the sense of national humiliation remained, and he proceeded to take further actions which outraged public opinion.   He ridiculed the Church and wished to secularize its property and reform it on Lutheran lines; he introduced Prussian drill into the army and proposed to disband the guards regiments.   He publicly insulted Catherine at a state dinner and threatened to divorce her and send her to a convent.

During this time, Catherine carefully refrained from taking an active part in any opposition movement.   She let it be known that she disapproved of Peter's domestic and foreign policy, but left it to others to engage in conspiracies, until after six months of mounting discontent, her latest lover, Gregory Orlov, whose son

[1] P. 44.

she had borne two months earlier, summoned her to the guards barracks in St. Petersburg. There she was proclaimed Catherine II, Czarina of Russia. When the troops reached Peter at Oranienbaum, he made a humiliating abdication and was taken by the Orlovs to an estate a few miles from the capital, where a few days later he died in circumstances which have never been established. This was the last palace revolution of the century, and it began the thirty-four years of Catherine the Great's reign.

The Absolutism of Catherine

As Czarina, Catherine displayed considerable personal charm, intelligence and patience, while the long, unhappy years preceding her accession to the throne had taught her prudence and caution. She displayed also a typically German efficiency and thoroughness. She rose regularly at five o'clock, lit her own fire at six and even made her own breakfast and then worked alone at her desk, clad in a long, loose robe with wide sleeves, for several hours until her secretaries joined her. Normally the rest of her day was crowded with state interviews, court functions and entertainments, but some days she worked continuously for fifteen hours, toiling with her four secretaries, each at a little table assigned to different subjects, until she fell exhausted into bed late at night. It was this efficiency, together with her desire to attract service and devotion, which accounted for her success as a ruler. In all official matters Catherine was determined that her efforts should succeed and her will prevail.

She displayed the same attitude in her amorous activities. She had at least twenty lovers altogether, varying in origin and temperament, but all expected to flatter her by their personal adulation. She called them her 'pupils', rewarding them with lavish gifts of money and jewellery, estates and serfs, and frequently retaining their homage by regular payments after she had cast them off. The most celebrated of her favourites was Prince Gregory Potemkin (1739–91), whom she secretly married in 1773. Their affair lasted for only two years, but the bold and astute Potemkin retained her favour until his death. He was given military command and also generally allowed to choose her younger favourites, though before these were accepted they had to undergo a medical examination by her Scots physician and to satisfy a lady-in-waiting, one of whom was subsequently dismissed for showing excessive zeal.

Catherine was also thorough in her patronage of art. The excavation of whole streets and houses in Pompeii in 1748 had strengthened mid-eighteenth-century Europe's devotion to the classical tradition.   Catherine shared the contemporary attachment to ancient Greece and Rome; she had a terrace at Tsarkoe Selo (the palace near St. Petersburg erected for the Czarina Elizabeth) decorated with an avenue of sculptured busts of such heroes and philosophers as Caesar, Achilles, Cicero, Demosthenes and Seneca.   In architecture, she revolted against the baroque style which had appealed to her predecessor and preferred the sterner classical temper, the ordered discipline and grandeur of which assisted her plan to glorify her adopted state and her own personification of it.   She had a passion for building. '*La fureur de bâtir est chose diabolique, elle dévore l'argent, et plus on bâtit, plus on veut bâtir*', she wrote in 1779.   Typical of her patriotic purpose in building was the Tauride Palace in St. Petersburg, raised at Catherine's command for Potemkin to commemorate his conquest of the Crimea, the most magnificent feature of which was the great Catherine Hall with its double row of huge ionic columns.

Catherine was similarly a persistent collector of pictures and works of art.   At least half of the best paintings in the Hermitage Gallery, established by her, are there through her efforts.   Personal agents in Paris, Rome and London secured many masterpieces for her.   She purchased from Houghton Hall in Norfolk the fine collection of pictures gathered by Sir Robert Walpole. Josiah Wedgwood designed for her a sumptuous dinner service of 800 pieces, while she ordered another of 750 pieces in turquoise blue from Sèvres.   Catherine had little taste or understanding of the arts herself, but she did choose men of genius and discernment to carry out her commissions, which enabled her in art and architecture to set the fashions for the nobles to follow and make dominant in Russia.   Her patronage of arts achieved its intention. Combined with magnificent state banquets and ceremonies, it contributed to the splendour of her reign in the eyes of the contemporary civilized world and helped to win her the title of 'Great'.

The same motives inspired her less successful attempt to secure recognition as the patron of advanced political literature and an exponent of the ideas of Enlightened Despotism.[1]   It was

[1] Pp. 93 ff.

ambitious pride which made her correspond unwearyingly with the leading contemporary intellectual figures or to boast of her 38,000 books and her 10,000 pictures. Catherine's enthusiasm for the new ideas of the Enlightenment certainly led Russian noblemen to study them eagerly and to travel to Paris and to other European capitals, but as time passed she became less favourable towards free thought and more nervous of its possible consequences. After the outbreak of the French Revolution, which filled her with dread, she was increasingly reactionary. She regarded the revolutionaries as '*canailles*'. Frenchmen living in Russia were compelled to swear an oath renouncing the '*athées et impies français*', and all French books were banned. Lest the '*frisson nouveau*' should affect her people, she instituted a wholesale suppression of ideas and persecution of writers in Russia.

In fact, Catherine was determined throughout her reign to rule as an absolute monarch and do what she could to strengthen the position of the imperial crown. This was displayed in the *Nakaz* she drew up, in her reform of local government and in her policy towards the nobility and the Church.[1] She was an ardent despot, unwilling to share her power or allow it to be restricted in any way; she was also resolved that there should be no rivals to her power and no pretenders to her throne. As soon as she was strong enough, she set out – in the words of a British envoy – 'to humble the guards, who placed her upon the throne'; and in 1764 Ivan VI, who had remained imprisoned since his deposition in 1741, was put to death by her order. Her absolutism was of a piece with her whole policy. She brought no measure of liberal reform to the government of her empire, except on paper. Rather she resolved to save the Czardom from the weaknesses to which it had succumbed since Peter the Great's death, and she made it strong enough to face the storms which swept Europe at the end of the century.

The Nobility and Serfdom

Nevertheless, Catherine soon found that she could not wield the same autocratic power as Peter the Great and earlier czars had enjoyed. She depended for her throne upon the support of the nobility. This involved restraints such as other Russian rulers

[1] Pp. 94-5.

had never known because she had to take care to ensure that she had the continued support of her nobility and make concessions to it. Catherine's reign has been called the 'golden age of the Russian nobility'; and, indeed, as a class its members obtained from her all that they sought with the promulgation of her charter of the nobility in 1785. In return, she gained from them persistent support for her power.

The nobility secured the extension of its rights and privileges at the expense of the Russian peasantry. The monarchy of the *ancien régime* in France had made certain that its nobility accepted its rule by the multiplication of titles, pensions, court offices and sinecures enjoyed by aristocratic holders, but the Russian Czardom used serfdom to win the loyalty of its nobility, who alone could possess serfs. The burdens of the Russian serfs and the powers enjoyed by the nobility over them were already heavy and considerable when Catherine came to the throne, and she increased them.[1]

In 1736 each nobleman had obtained the right to decide for himself the punishment of fugitive serfs and in 1754 'full power without exception' over his serfs and freedom to move them 'for his own advantage'. Now, as early as 1765 while she was starting work on the drafting of her *Nakaz*, Catherine granted to noblemen the power to sentence their serfs to hard labour for life in Siberia, with the result that in twelve years over 20,000 peasants had been sent to eastern Siberia alone by their masters. Two years later, during the early sessions of the *Zemstvo*, she deprived the serfs of their ancient right to appeal to the imperial authorities against their masters; and there are only twenty recorded instances of intervention by the government to punish illtreatment of serfs by a landowner during the whole of her reign. Generally serfs might undergo the most grave injustice or severe cruelty at the hands of their masters without any hope of relief or redress.

It is not surprising, therefore, that the everyday conditions of existence for the Russian peasantry became increasingly degrading and brutalized during Catherine's reign. Serf girls were offered for sale at ten roubles each in the gazettes of St. Petersburg. Other serfs were sold at public auctions together with horses, cattle and household goods. At the same time, the obligations exacted from serfs were often made heavier. In the

[1] P. 95.

southern, black-soil provinces, under the stimulus of the expanding trade in grain, the average weekly labour required from serfs was increased from three to four or five days, and during the harvest they were commonly made to work every day in their master's field. Money dues were increased from an average of two roubles a year to five.

Many nobles were paternal towards their serfs and treated them with kindness, but the prevailing outlook, which regarded corporal punishment as the usual means of enforcing the discipline of serfdom, encouraged oppression and excesses. There was no control over the chastisements inflicted by serf-owners. Peasants of all ages were commonly birched or beaten for every manner of misdemeanour, and regular penalties might be imposed, such as sixty strokes of the rod for a man and twenty-five of the cane for his wife for absence from church. On some estates, the knout was frequently used, and there were some notorious cases of ill-treatment of serfs. It was said of one landowner that all his serfs, from the labourers in his fields and barns to the youngest maids in his house, bore the scars of the lash, while a noble lady was reported to have consoled herself for her premature widowhood by flogging to death in the course of ten years 140 serfs, mostly women and girls. Nor did most industrial serfs and serfs taken for recruits in the army fare any better than those in agricultural or domestic service. Archdeacon Coxe concluded that the Russian serfs in general were 'cruelly oppressed'.

Moreover, Catherine's reign saw a vast increase in the number of serfs under her rule. The secularization of the lands of the Russian Church transferred about two million former ecclesiastical serfs to the crown. Serfs on the crown lands were comparatively unburdened, but Catherine also delivered some 800,000 crown serfs to the harsher conditions of proprietary bondage through the frequent and enormous grants of estates which she made to her favourites. Indeed, the reign was noted for its wealthy serf-owners. On most estates the serfs might number from a hundred to a thousand, but several noblemen possessed as many as 80,000, while one had 300,000. At the same time, the system of serfdom was extended to regions more recently included within the frontiers of Russia. Between 1763 and 1783 Catherine established serfdom in the great area of the Ukraine; and in 1797 Paul I was to do the same in the Crimea and the Caucasus. The estimated figures suggest that by the end of the century all but two million of the population were serfs, mostly on private estates.[1]

Such conditions produced almost continuous discontent and disorder, both agrarian and industrial, in Russia during the second half of the eighteenth century. At the time of Catherine's accession, no fewer than 49,000 industrial serfs were said to be in revolt, while in the first seven years of her reign seventy-three peasant risings are known to have taken place in different parts of the empire. At the same time thousands of peasants fled to foreign countries to escape servitude. Many others sought refuge in the steppe-lands and similarly thinly-populated areas where they were hunted down by troops.

This widespread social disorder culminated in the uprising led by Emelian Pugachev (1741 ?–75), which broke out in 1771 and was not completely suppressed until 1775. The disturbance started in the Urals and along the Volga, where Don Cossack tribesmen, resentful at the incursions of the government from Moscow into territory to which they had migrated, made cause with the industrial serfs in the iron and copper undertakings established by Peter the Great and with the peasants on the great estates to the south and south-east. Pugachev was a Cossack who had served in the Russian army, fought in the Seven Years' War and been knouted several times for desertion. Now he appeared in this region, claiming to be the Czar Peter III, and soon had an immense following. Industrial serfs brought him guns from the imperial cannon works, while the capture of the fortified posts along the Yaik swelled his army with deserters. He married a Cossack girl and set up his court in a farmhouse, surrounding himself with his henchmen, to whom he gave the names of Catherine's favourite courtiers, and village girls, whom he beat until they learned to drop curtseys and behave as maids of honour. Over a large area landowners and their families were slaughtered, mansions plundered and burned down, officials, merchants and priests shot or hanged. Moscow itself was threatened, and Pugachev said he would shut up Catherine in a convent. The first imperial forces sent against the insurgents were routed in pitched battles. It required determined efforts by Catherine's leading generals before the peasant war was finally crushed with ferocious reprisals. Pugachev was taken to Moscow in an iron cage and beheaded early in 1775.

After the rebellion had been put down, the noblemen emerged

[1] P. 48.

from their hiding-places or refuges in the towns and returned to their country estates. Few granted their serfs reforms. Most treated them even more harshly than before and suppressed with severity any sign of unrest on their estates. Such behaviour did nothing to diminish peasant hatreds, which had been enflamed by the rising. There remained a burning desire for revenge which nothing could eradicate in future years.

Catherine herself was well aware of the social dangers of serfdom. Shortly after Pugachev's execution, in writing to her Minister of Justice about the peasants, she said: 'If we do not consent to reduce cruelty and to moderate a situation which is intolerable to the human race, then sooner or later they will take this step themselves.' Had she sincerely believed the enlightened principles which she publicized abroad, she must have taken action, and she was in a position to do so after Pugachev's rebellion, for it had made the nobility realize that they depended upon the throne for protection rather than for furthering their own power. For Catherine to apply these principles in Russia, however, might have given rise to circumstances and movements dangerous to her throne. Therefore, she made no attempt to reform serfdom or even check its spread, but on the contrary increased and intensified the conditions of the system. By the end of her reign, indeed, the situation of the Russian peasantry had probably gone beyond reform, and eventual revolution had become almost inevitable.

Foreign Policy

From the beginning of her reign, Catherine applied herself closely to foreign affairs; in fact, she always gave more attention and energy to the external than to the internal problems of Russia and made her greatest reputation through her foreign policy. Diplomacy attracted Catherine. It enabled her to exercise her boundless ambition in the sight of both Russia and western Europe. It also meant that she could become the victorious leader of the Russian people, so securing their loyalty to her person and even distracting their attention from their hardships and relieving their disappointment at her failure to implement her promised reforms. Moreover, compared with the innumerable and insoluble domestic questions which faced her, Russian foreign policy was relatively simple and likely now to produce successful results.

Many circumstances favoured Catherine in the international sphere. Peter the Great had made Russia an important power, not only in the north, but in western Europe as well. He had made the czardom strong and extended the frontiers of the empire to the shores of the Black Sea. He had also built up powerful armed forces, which though neglected and mishandled by his immediate successors, had shown their capabilities under the Czarina Elizabeth during the Seven Years' War. In addition, Russia's previous enemies were now no longer dangerous. Sweden had been brought down by the Great Northern War, Poland was weak and disunited, and the Turkish Empire, though still capable of offering serious resistance to Russia, was becoming increasingly decadent. So Catherine was placed in the position of being able to resume the foreign policy, laid down for Russia's rulers by Ivan the Great (1462–1505), which sought to increase the imperial territory to the west and the south in the cause of national survival and power.

The first and immediate decision which Catherine had to make in foreign affairs concerned her relations with Prussia. Her open disapproval of Peter III's pro-Prussian attitude had helped to gain the support of the guards in putting her on the throne, and Maria Theresa and Kaunitz now hoped she would reverse his policy and renew the Russian alliance with Austria. Catherine, however, did not want to continue to fight Prussia. She believed that Russia needed peace. The Seven Years' War had placed a heavy strain upon the resources of the imperial treasury, which had been unable to pay the Russian troops for the last eighteen months. There was much, therefore, to justify Catherine's decision to make peace with Frederick the Great in 1762, but Elizabeth had been right in regarding the militant Prussian state as inevitably Russia's enemy. Catherine made a mistake in accepting Frederick's proposal for an alliance between their two countries in 1764. Exhausted and without allies after the Seven Years' War, Frederick needed this alliance, which he used skilfully, but it cost Catherine the friendship of Austria and France, so valuable in strengthening Russia against Turkey, and it was of no real value to her.

Catherine had agreed to the alliance with Prussia in order to carry out her Polish policy, but she probably did not really need it for this.[1] It meant that she became to some extent the agent of

[1] P. 195.

Frederick, who was as unprincipled as herself, but far more astute. All three partitions of Poland took place during Catherine's reign.[1] She engaged in the First Partition on Frederick's initiative, but she herself inspired and dominated both the later ones.   Her annexations under the first two partitions were not without justification. The lands she seized on these occasions had originally been Russian, and their population still remained largely Russian in character.[2]   It was in supporting Prussian and to a lesser extent Austrian demands that Catherine was at fault, while in the Third Partition she showed a serious lack of statesmanship, acting to further her own glory and immediate gain rather than Russia's national interests.   Peter the Great had desired to regain the Russian lands within the Polish frontiers and then to try to make an ally of Poland.   Catherine not only strengthened Prussia, but also aroused among the Poles an undying hatred of the Russians for which they were to pay dearly in the future.

More than Poland, the territory of the Turkish Empire in the area of the Balkans and the Black Sea attracted Catherine. Early in his reign, Peter the Great had opened a campaign against Turkey and captured Azov, but he relinquished this policy in favour of expansion to the Baltic, enabling the Turks later to recapture Azov; and the war fought against Turkey during Anne's reign, though securing Azov, had not realized Russian hopes of large conquests.[3]   The idea of taking Constantinople, long the summit of Russian ambition, appealed strongly to Catherine, but when war came with Turkey it was unexpected and unwelcome.   Russian designs upon Poland alarmed the Turks, and French diplomacy successfully induced the Sultan to declare war in 1768.[4]   Catherine was not yet ready to challenge the Turks, and since Austria was no longer her ally, she had to face them alone.

Yet this war was immediately marked by spectacular Russian victories.   By 1770 most of the Danubian provinces of Moldavia and Wallachia had been overrun, and the next year the Crimea was occupied.   Most remarkable, a Russian fleet – partly officered and manned by British naval volunteers – sailed from the Baltic in 1769 through the English Channel and the Bay of Biscay to the eastern Mediterranean and in 1770 destroyed a Turkish fleet at Chesmé on the coast of Asia Minor.   This was

[1] Pp. 281 ff.   [2] Pp. 284, 287.
[3] P. 257.   [4] P. 283.

the first time Russian warships had appeared in the Mediterranean. It startled western Europe.

Each new Russian success, in fact, made a general European war more likely. Austria, being particularly alarmed at the prospect of Russian domination of the Lower Danube, made a treaty with Turkey in 1771; and France, dismayed at the Russian entry into the Mediterranean, would certainly support Austria. A conflict now seemed imminent. Frederick of Prussia was dismayed. He had no wish to be drawn into fighting as Russia's ally. To prevent a crisis arising over the situation in eastern Europe, he suggested that the powers should join in a partition of Poland. Austria would not agree to Russian retention of Moldavia and Wallachia, but if Catherine would accept territorial compensation in Poland instead, war might be averted, and Austria and Prussia would also obtain equivalent shares of Polish land. As Catherine did not want war with Austria and mistrusted Prussia as an ally, she agreed. The result was the First Partition of Poland in 1772.[1]

Negotiations were now opened for peace between Russia and Turkey, but they made slow progress. Catherine, though faced by the crisis of Pugachev's rebellion, was determined to secure control of the Crimea, the home of the Sultan's Tartars who for generations had ravaged southern Russia, burning and plundering villages, killing settlers and capturing young men and women to sell in the slave-markets of the Mediterranean. The Turks, however, maintained a stubborn resistance, and not until a Russian army had crossed the Danube and inflicted a heavy defeat upon them were they ready to make peace.

The war ended with the signing of the famous Treaty of Kuchuk Kainarji in 1774. Russia returned to Turkey most of her conquests, which included Georgia, Moldavia, Wallachia and Bessarabia, but she was confirmed in the possession of Azov and gained the Kerch straits and the mouths of the Dnieper and the Bug, so obtaining access to the Black Sea. This not only gave Russian ships a share of the Black Sea, but also passage through the Bosporus and the Dardanelles into the Mediterranean. The Crimea was declared to be independent, but since it was now enveloped by Russian territory, the way was prepared for its eventual annexation. Russia also obtained the right to make representations on behalf of 'the church to be built in Con-

stantinople and those who serve it'. This vague clause, giving
Russia the right to a place of worship in the Turkish capital, was
to be made the basis in the next century of far-reaching claims
by her to act as the protector of all the Orthodox subjects of the
Sultan.

The Treaty of Kuchuk Kainarji was to be of great importance
in the history of eastern Europe. Turkey was now shown to be
in a moribund condition, unable to uphold the frontiers of her
extended empire by her own strength. Russia, having secured
her position in the west and fastened her grasp upon Poland,
could take advantage of Turkish weakness and strive to establish
her predominance in eastern Europe. Already she had revealed
the way she would do this – by military action combined with
intervention in Turkish affairs on behalf of the Orthodox
Christians. The Treaty of Kuchuk Kainarji, therefore, may well
be regarded as marking the beginning of the Eastern Question –
the problem of the decline of the Turkish Empire and the
expansionist policy of Russia – which was to trouble Europe for
more than a century and contribute much to the situation leading
to the outbreak of war in 1914.

After the Treaty of Kuchuk Kainarji, dreams of empire-
building in the Balkans increasingly possessed Catherine, who
sought to exploit her triumph to the full. Russian possession of
Constantinople at last seemed possible. For a grandson born in
1779, the younger son of the Czarevich Paul, she chose the name
of Constantine, since she planned he should reign over a Byzan-
tine Empire revived under Russian protection. Her schemes
required a change from Prussia to Austria as an ally, and the
death of Maria Theresa in 1780 enabled her to make a treaty
with Joseph II the next year. She was now strong enough to
annex the Crimea, which she did in 1784 and made Potemkin
governor of the new province. This gave Russia a greatly-
extended coastline on the Black Sea and new bases for the powerful fleet she was now establishing there.

Three years after its annexation, Catherine paid a triumphal
visit to the Crimea, taking with her a brilliant retinue, the
ambassadors of the leading European states and the Emperor
Joseph to see what she called 'mon petit ménage'. She was
enthusiastically received by her new subjects, and Potemkin made
elaborate preparations to impress her guests still further.
Regular post-stations with fresh horses were set up along their

route, and at night huge bonfires were lit at short intervals at the roadside.   Houses were freshly painted, though often only the walls that faced the street; only well-dressed people were to come outdoors; and the best places in the crowds were assigned to girls who were told to comb their hair, wear new dresses and strew flowers in the roadway.   The climax of the tour came at Sebastopol, where a fine harbour sheltered newly-built warships.   The whole expedition was intended to show the rest of Europe, and especially the Emperor Joseph, the development of Russian power towards the south.   It was also designed as a deliberate provocation to Turkey, and here it achieved its intended purpose.

Later that year, the Sultan declared war, bringing the Crimean tour to an interrupted end.   Joseph remained true to his engagement of 1781.   His troops immediately attacked Belgrade, though he did not declare war until the spring of 1788.   The Turks fought unexpectedly well.   The attempt on Belgrade failed, and the Turks invaded and ravaged Hungarian territory. They also more than held their own against the Russian forces commanded by Potemkin, who was without military habits, experience or ability; but the effectual conduct of the main episodes in the War passed to Alexander Suvorov (1729–1800), the greatest of all Russian generals.   The tide of hostilities turned in favour of the Russian troops, who captured two great Turkish fortresses – Ochakov on the Black Sea in 1788 and Izmail on the Danube in 1790.

Austria also won victories, but when the less ambitious Leopold II succeeded his brother on the throne, he made peace with Turkey in 1791.   Catherine continued the War and gained further successes.   Since events in France had now deprived Turkey of any hope of help from her traditional and most powerful ally, she had to sue for peace.   By the Treaty of Jassy, at the beginning of 1792, Turkey recognized the Russian annexation of the Crimea and ceded the district of Ochakov, so advancing the Russian frontier to the Dniester.   The War had ended without an outstanding triumph for Russia, but Catherine was ready for peace.   Typically she hoped to profit from the French situation. The Second and Third Partitions of Poland were the result.[1]

To the end Catherine acted as an adventuress.   Her methods remained very much the same as those which had brought her, an unimportant princess, to the imperial throne.   During her reign

[1] Pp. 284 ff.

Russia won great victories and gained considerable territory. The emergence of Russia as a leading European power, which had begun under Peter the Great, was decisively continued. Catherine, however, was not genuinely concerned for the advancement of the nation as he had been. She wished primarily to gain renown for herself and, despite her protestations, really cared little for the welfare of the Russian people. The domestic splendour and foreign triumphs of her rule were accompanied by an irremediable deterioration in the condition of the peasantry, which was to have grave consequences in the future.

XV · THE PARTITION OF POLAND

The Decay of the Kingdom

THE origins of the Polish people go back to the Polanes, a tribe that became dominant early in the tenth century among the Slavonic peoples who lived in eastern and northern Europe. Later in that century, they received Christianity from Moravia, when their ruler was baptized, and under German pressure consolidated themselves into an organized kingdom. The territory of the Polish kingdom was extended during the next century beyond the Oder, the Carpathians and the Dniester. The twelfth century brought a contested succession which led to dissensions and the loss of Pomerania. Though the thirteenth century saw warfare with the Teutonic Knights and devastation by the Mongol invasion, the next century saw, in 1386, the marriage of a Polish princess to Jagiello, Grand-Duke of Lithuania. This personal union between Poland and Lithuania (which was made permanent by the Union of Lublin in 1569) was followed by the rule of the Jagiellonian kings who made Poland a strong state in the fifteenth and sixteenth centuries. At its greatest extent the kingdom was subdivided into about forty palatinates, mostly ruled by hereditary magnates of considerable power.

Yet, at the very time when Poland was a great power, she remained a markedly ill-compacted society and state in which the seeds of decay were being widely sown. During the seventeenth century, she lost territory steadily. Livonia was conquered by Sweden in 1605 and ceded in 1660. The Cossacks of the Ukraine went over to Russia in 1654, and the consequent loss of territory was recognized by the Treaty of Andrusovo in 1667. And, finally, the Duchy of Prussia was freed from Polish suzerainty in 1657. The eighteenth century saw her political collapse and disappearance as an independent state with the division of her territory among her stronger neighbours.

Among the causes of Polish failure, the geographical factor is commonly given importance. It is true that Poland, situated in the great European central plain, consisted almost entirely of flat land and was a state with few natural boundaries, which made national defence more difficult; but this need not in itself have been a determining source of weakness. Prussia's frontiers were less favourable, and her territory was not even compact, but this stimulated her rulers into building up her military strength so that she was able to become one of the powers which partitioned Poland.

Failure by Poland to make herself strong and her consequent loss of territory to Russia had made her territory less easily defensible by the beginning of the eighteenth century. As a consequence of the Treaty of Andrusovo, the length of her frontiers lying beyond main rivers, and so strategically advantageous, declined from 70 to 37 per cent, while the length of her frontiers lying on the near side of main rivers, which were a strategic liability, increased from 30 to 63 per cent, and only the length of her boundary actually running along main rivers remained the same. Yet even then, the geographical factor, though it made its contribution, was not a major cause of Poland's political collapse.

Poland was, in fact, partitioned because the Polish state and government was itself backward and weak in several telling ways. The political system of Poland in the eighteenth century was the exact opposite of the prevailing Enlightened Despotism of Russia, Prussia and Austria. The Polish monarchy had not shared in the general development experienced by the system elsewhere. In Europe all monarchies had been, within certain limits, originally elective and became hereditary at a comparatively late date. During the Jagiellonian dynasty, the Polish throne remained elective in law, but was always occupied by a member of that dynasty. The death of the last of the Jagiellos in 1572, however, enabled the nobility, whose power and prestige had been firmly established since the early wars of the kingdom, to assert in practice the elective character of the monarchy, with themselves as electors.

At the same time, the nobility introduced the *pacta conventa* by which each new king had to agree to limitations imposed by them on his authority. The result was that each successive royal election brought intrigues and struggles between noble factions, which led sometimes to civil war, foreign intervention and the election of foreign candidates. The monarch had little more power than dispensing patronage to self-seeking and often traitorous noblemen. He was indeed a King of Kings and Lord of

Lords, a witty Irishman declared, as he had no better than companions and equals for his subjects.

As a privileged class, the Polish nobility in the eighteenth century numbered perhaps nearly as many as a million and a half. Most of this enormous group were poor, and many owned little or no land; some two dozen were really great magnates, possessing large estates and by 1715 enjoying a practical monopoly of political power. Each powerful nobleman had his dependants among the numerous lesser noblemen, over whom he exercised a more than semi-feudal authority. These lesser noblemen met in the local diets and dietines, which they dominated. The dietines sent 400 representatives to the national Diet, all of whom were noblemen and so equal in status. To emphasize this, the Diet in the middle of the seventeenth century adopted the principle of the *liberum veto*, which meant that an opposing vote by even a single member not only defeated a measure but ended the session as well. This was used in the eighteenth century with such frequency and recklessness that the work of the Diet was at times paralysed. 'The people behaved so wildly that one might have been in Poland', reported a German who witnessed a London election in 1710.

Another custom introduced into the Polish constitution was the right of confederation, which made it legal for noblemen to unite in arms against measures they wished to defeat. Early in the seventeenth century a King of Poland wished to establish the principle of majority rule in the Diet, only to be compelled to abandon his purpose, which had widespread popular support, by a confederation organized by malcontent noblemen whose rebellion went unpunished. In the last years of Polish independence, the Diet sometimes formed itself into a confederation to defeat the use by a minority of the *liberum veto*. The actual reform of the constitution was finally accomplished in this way, though on that occasion a small minority immediately formed a counter-confederation to uphold their support of the old constitution.[1]

The Polish system of administration by the eighteenth century was equally disorderly and inefficient. It had undergone no change since the late Middle Ages, and following the Union of Lublin each Polish official had his counterpart in Lithuania. The public revenue, it has been estimated, amounted in the middle of the century to about a thirteenth of that of Russia and

[1] P. 286.

a seventy-fifth of that of France. There was neither a permanent central council nor a professional civil service. Similarly there was no corporate body of judges or qualified pleaders in the law-courts; neither was there a uniform system of law for the whole kingdom nor even a complete code of Polish law. Both administration and justice were largely in the hands of the nobility in their capacity of manorial lords. To this was added military weakness, for the army numbered only between 12,000 and 16,000 officers and men and was never granted sufficient money to enable it to be equipped adequately. An observer, commenting on the government of Poland before the disaster of the partitions had revealed its thorough weakness, described it as 'confused and tumultuous' and a 'perpetual anarchy'.

The anachronistic condition of Poland's institutions was equalled by the backwardness of her economy which, at any rate until the middle of the eighteenth century, was stationary, if not actually contracting. Agricultural production never recovered from the wars of the previous century, although the landowners were able to charge high prices for their grain. Lack of capital forbade technical improvements for which the imposition of heavier exactions upon the serfs failed to compensate. Even worse was the position of the towns, the total population of which was only about 500,000. Manufactures were almost completely lacking, imports exceeded exports, the volume of internal trade was small, and capital was short.

Such economic weaknesses were largely due to the stranglehold exercised over the national economy by the privileged nobility. Though trade and manufacture were not fit occupations for their class, they often allowed the establishment on lease of industrial enterprises in the countryside which, by making use of the raw material produced on their estates and the compulsory labour of their serfs, undercut urban factories and workshops. Moreover, the nobility, besides paying virtually no taxes, were exempt from import and export duties; and the government assisted them by imposing economic controls which kept the prices of home-manu-factured goods low in relation to agricultural prices. Thus Poland's economy, like her government, was made unsound because of the top-heavy domination of her social structure by her upper class.

In these circumstances, such traders or craftsmen as existed in Poland were mainly foreigners, notably Germans and Jews, who were forbidden by the law of the land to engage in farming. Consequently, there existed no Polish middle-class of any size or wealth to fill the void between the nobility and the peasantry, who were treated virtually as slaves by their masters.[1] That these seven or eight million serfs should entertain any greater feeling of patriotism towards their country than the nobility was hardly to be expected. 'To the peasant, who had nothing to lose,' Count von Moltke commented, 'it was a matter of indifference whether he was subject to his territorial lord or a foreign foe.'

Further dissension and disunity were produced by the Polish religious situation. The Reformation had brought to Poland the ideas of Lutheranism, Calvinism and Socinianism, which were at first welcomed by the lower classes who sought social and economic justice, and the nobility who wanted to control the Church. The very political weakness and absence of constraining laws, however, which had at first made possible the growth of Protestantism and brought the country the name of '*paradisus haereticorum*', soon encouraged fatal divisions among its adherents. When, therefore, the Jesuits began work in the country and secured through monarchical favour control of its higher education, they succeeded during the seventeenth century in making it almost uniformly Roman Catholic. By the eighteenth century, the Protestants formed a minority of about 200,000 Dissidents, as Christians other than Roman Catholics were called; they were mostly German Lutheran towns-men and colonists, but included also about a thousand well-born Polish families. Another group of Dissidents belonged to the Eastern Orthodox Church; they numbered at least 600,000, mostly in Lithuania. The Union of Lublin promised complete religious toleration in the enlarged kingdom. All Dissidents, whether Protestant or Orthodox, were to have freedom of faith and worship, representation in and membership of the Diet and all other privileges enjoyed by Roman Catholics.

Just as, however, the great noble families of Poland were in correspondence with foreign powers, so her powerful Roman Catholic hierarchy was Ultramontane and intolerant in its outlook, and in the early eighteenth century its members began an agitation against the indulgence granted to Dissidents. Their churches, monasteries and schools were destroyed or handed over to the Roman Catholic Church, and persecution produced inci-

[1] P. 49.

dents such as the 'blood-bath of Thorn'.[1] Gradually the
privileges of the Dissidents were withdrawn until in 1733 they
were excluded from the Diet. The religious question provided
yet another opportunity for intervention by Poland's neighbours
and, indeed, was the immediate cause of the series of events which
led to the First Partition of Poland.[2]

It was a further misfortune for Poland that she had three
neighbouring states which were as strong as she was weak. Of
these, Russia and Prussia were the most aggressive; Austria had
no designs on Poland until the second half of the eighteenth
century. Nevertheless, as long as Russia and Prussia were potential or actual enemies – as they were throughout the first half of
the eighteenth century – Poland was able to retain, however
precariously, a quasi-independence. Both the Great Elector and
Peter the Great considered the preservation of a weak yet in-
violable Poland to be in their national interests, and their
immediate successors followed the same policy. It was the agreement between Frederick the Great of Prussia and Catherine the
Great of Russia, coupled with the wish of Joseph II of Austria to
obtain his share of Polish territory, which made the progressive
dimemberment of the country practically inevitable.

The Saxon Kings (1697–1763)

The eighteenth century opened on the reign of Augustus II,
Elector of Saxony and King of Poland, who had become a Roman
Catholic and been elected to the Polish throne in 1697 through
the support of the powers which were eventually to partition the
country. Augustus was nicknamed 'the Strong'; he had fought
the Turks with credit and now, in the hope of regaining Livonia
for his new kingdom, he made a pact with Peter the Great to
attack Charles XII of Sweden. After routing the Russians at
the Battle of Narva in 1700, Charles overran Poland and held a
Diet in Warsaw at which Augustus was deposed and Stanislas
Leszczynski, Palatine of Posen, elected in his place. The reign of
Stanislas, however, lasted only as long as he had Swedish protection. When Charles was defeated by Peter at the Battle of
Poltava in 1709, Stanislas was forced to flee. Augustus marched
into Poland and regained the throne.

Though Augustus had triumphed, Peter was the real victor.
Poland was now little more than a Russian protectorate. Only

[1] P. 17.　　　　　　　　　　　[2] P. 283.

Russian help had enabled Augustus to come back to Poland, and it was through Russian help again that he survived, in 1717, a confederation formed against him by the majority of the Polish nobility. The price exacted by Russia was high. The so-called Treaty of Warsaw, negotiated by the Russian ambassador, signed by Augustus and the confederation's leaders and ratified by the Diet, not only limited the Polish army to 24,000 men, but also made financial arrangements which were inadequate for the maintenance of even this small number. In addition, Russia occupied the Duchy of Courland, still nominally a fief of the Polish crown, in 1718 and refused to return Livonia when signing the Treaty of Nystadt with Sweden in 1721.

Augustus tried to escape from his dependence on Russia. As early as 1719 he even made a treaty with the Emperor to force the Czar to evacuate his troops from Poland, but the Polish nobility would not support him in a policy which might involve them in a war against Russia. The Russian government persisted in keeping Poland in a condition of anarchy. In 1720 Russia and Prussia secretly agreed to safeguard Poland's political institutions, which meant opposing all internal reforms which might enable the country to recover its stability and strength. This agreement was renewed in 1726, 1729, 1730, 1732, 1740, 1743 and 1762. Russia also made an alliance with the Emperor to prevent the establishment of a permanent Saxon dynasty on the Polish throne.

Nevertheless, when the death of Augustus II in 1733 resulted in French support for the candidature of Stanislas Leszczynski, Russia reverted to her policy of 1709 and 1717 by enforcing the succession of Augustus II's only legitimate son as Augustus III. Indolent and pleasure-loving, Augustus III spent the thirty years of his reign almost entirely in Saxony. Power in Poland fell into the hands of a wealthy, noble family, the Czartoryskis. Aiming at constitutional reform and permanent supremacy for themselves, they wished to abolish the *liberum veto*, make the crown hereditary, increase its powers and secure it for a member of their family. Opposed to them was another great noble family, the Potockis, who had taken the French side and supported the candidature of Stanislas. Neither family was strong enough to overpower the other. The Potockis defeated the constitutional schemes of the Czartoryskis by using the *liberum veto*; and during Augustus III's reign only one Diet out of fifteen was not disrupted. Poland's helplessness was shown only too clearly in the Seven Years' War when Russian troops, on their way to the battle-fields of East Prussia, occupied and plundered much of the king-dom and so provoked retaliatory raids by Frederick II's armies.

By 1762 Augustus III was ailing and not expected to live much longer. The Czartoryskis now believed that they could secure their ends only with foreign assistance. They decided to come to terms with Catherine II of Russia, who was ready to consider their designs. In the midst of negotiations, Augustus died in 1763. The Saxon period of Polish history was at an end, and dismemberment was at hand.

The First Partition (1772)

The Czartoryskis had established contact with the Russian government by sending to St. Petersburg as a Polish envoy Stanislas Poniatowski (1732–98), who was related through his mother to their family. He had previously been in St. Peters-burg in 1755, when he came as secretary to the British ambassa-dor, Sir Charles Hanbury-Williams, who had got to know him during visits to Warsaw. There the distinction of appearance and intellect displayed by this young Polish count won him the attention of the Grand Duchess Catherine, who made him the second of her numerous lovers; but the Czarina Elizabeth sus-pected him of intriguing against her and had him recalled by his own government two years later.

Now that Catherine was herself Czarina and the Polish throne was vacant, she believed that Poniatowski would fill it admirably. His devotion to her and his gentle, indecisive nature would mean that he was certain to obey Russian directives and do nothing to rid his kingdom of its 'fortunate anarchy', as she termed it. The support of the Czartoryskis would probably have been enough to ensure the success of her candidate, but she was so anxious to accomplish this, her first important venture in foreign policy, that she sought Frederick the Great's co-operation. Frederick, need-ing allies and equally anxious to keep Poland weak, readily agreed. He suggested an alliance between Prussia and Russia. This was signed in 1764 as well as a secret convention in which the two monarchs resolved to uphold the elective character of the Polish monarchy and the continuance of the *liberum veto*. Then Russian troops moved into Poland, and in that same year the Diet elected Poniatowski to the throne.

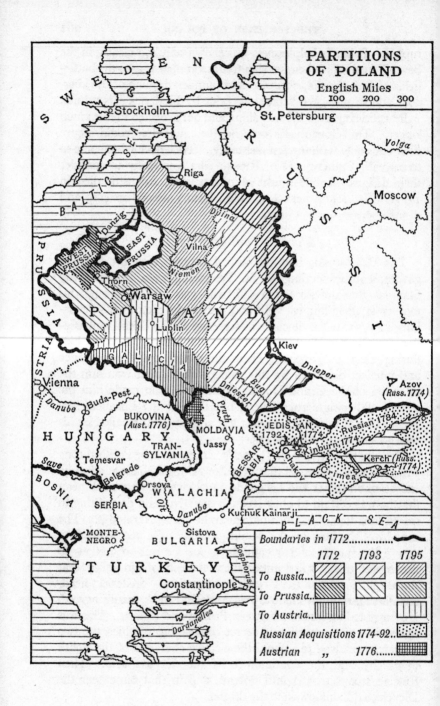

PARTITIONS
OF POLAND

English Miles

0   100   200   300

SWEDEN

Stockholm

St. Petersburg

RUSSIA

BALTIC SEA

Riga

Moscow

Volga

Danzig

WEST PRUSSIA   EAST PRUSSIA

Dūna

Vilna

Niemen

Thorn

Warsaw

POLAND

Lublin

GALICIA

Kiev

Dniester

Bug

Dnieper

PRUSSIA

AUSTRIA

Vienna

Danube

Buda-Pest

HUNGARY

BUKOVINA
(Aust. 1776)

MOLDAVIA

BESSAR-ABIA

JEDISAN
1792   1774

Russian 1784

Azov
(Russ. 1774)

Temesvar

TRAN-SYLVANIA

Jassy

Ochakov

Kinburn, 1774

Kerch (Russ.
1774)

Save

Belgrade

Orsova

WALACHIA

Crimea

BOSNIA

SERBIA

Danube

Kuchuk Kainarji

BLACK   SEA

MONTE-NEGRO

Sistova

BULGARIA

Boundaries in 1772 ....

TURKEY

Constantinople

Dardanelles

Bosphorus

	1772	1793	1795
To Russia...			
To Prussia...			
To Austria...			
Russian Acquisitions 1774-92...			
Austrian „ 1776......			

Catherine's first open intervention to assert Russian power in Poland, after the election of Stanislas, was on behalf of the members of the Orthodox Church. This community had originally been some four million strong in Poland, but in 1596 the Jesuits had won a considerable victory through the creation of the Uniat Church, which combined the retention of Orthodox rites with the acceptance of Roman doctrine and papal authority. The new Church won over the majority of the Orthodox in Poland and supported the persecution of the Dissidents. Public opinion in Russia resented the way in which the Orthodox in Poland had been deprived of their rights, and Frederick the Great was ready to support the cause of the Protestants.

Accordingly, Catherine issued a demand that the Dissidents should have equality of rights and freedom of worship, but this was refused by the Diet in 1766. Thereupon the Dissidents the next year formed the Confederation of Radom, and Catherine sent troops into Poland to support it. Under such pressure the Diet granted the Dissidents toleration and equality and early the following year signed an alliance with Russia which recognized Catherine as 'protector of their laws and liberties' without whose consent no change was to be made in the country's constitution. Such complete domination over Poland served, however, to unite many of the noblemen in hostility to Russia. They formed the Confederation of Bar in 1768 and appealed to France for help.

France took the opportunity to incite Turkey, already alarmed by Catherine's actions in Poland, to declare war on Russia. Catherine's successes in this war threatened to bring about a major conflict involving both Austria and France, but this was in the end avoided by the First Partition of Poland.[1] Continued resistance to her will by the Poles when she was fighting Turkey had angered Catherine, and in 1772 she turned on them. Russian troops at last suppressed the Confederation of Bar, and under the threat of a conquest of the whole country, the Diet consented to a partition according to the terms of a treaty which had been signed between Russia, Prussia and Austria earlier that year.

In the First Partition, Russia secured White Russia, with all that part of Poland which lay between the Dvina, the Dnieper and the Drusch; Austria received almost all Red Russia and Galicia, with part of Podolia, Sandomir and Cracow; and Prussia took West Prussia, Ermeland and Kulmerland, with the exception of

[1] P. 270.

Danzig and Thorn. The territories obtained by each of the powers varied greatly in area, but in population they were approximately equal. Catherine gained more in prestige than in territory, though consolidating her position in Poland. Frederick failed to secure Danzig, for which he had hoped, and obtained less territory than the other partitioning powers; yet his gains strengthened him the most, for the annexation of West Prussia achieved his great object of joining Pomerania to East Prussia. Maria Theresa obtained a large triangle of territory beyond the Carpathians, which was so drawn as to include the valuable salt mines of Wieliczka.

For Poland, the First Partition involved the loss of about a half of her inhabitants and a third of her territory, including the most important section of her seaboard and direct access to the port of Danzig. Most of the people of White Russia were Russian-speaking and members of the Orthodox Church, so that Catherine had this justification in taking the territory. Neither Prussia nor Austria could claim such justification for their annexations, but neither was concerned with the principles of justification. The three powers eventually guaranteed Poland's constitution, but not her territory; she had not even nominal safeguards to protect her against further partition. Her chances of survival, even as a semi-independent state, seemed very uncertain. Most experienced observers after the First Partition shared the view of the much-travelled Archdeacon Coxe, who predicted in 1778 that Poland would be 'totally swallowed up by the neighbouring powers'.

The Second Partition (1793)

Nevertheless, Stanislas and his adherents made a determined effort to secure the survival of the kingdom. The shock of the First Partition aroused many more Poles to a realization of the need for reform. Far-reaching changes took place in Poland during the years after 1772. After the act of partition, Russia had tried to limit still more strictly the royal power by establishing a permanent council, of which the King was only president, with five departments and five ministers; but Stanislas and his supporters succeeded in making this council into an efficient institution for the furtherance of their own aims. The whole administration of the State was concentrated in its five departments, over which ministers were appointed who accepted the leadership of

Stanislas. This gave the country a stable and increasingly effective system of government. Many official measures of reorganization were undertaken by the administration in the course of a dozen years, while reforms were also instituted by private individuals.

Royal commissions assisted the introduction of urgently-needed agrarian improvements. The condition of the peasantry was bettered, agricultural production grew, and the birth-rate rose steadily. Other royal commissions concerned themselves with the revival of the life of the towns, the total population of which now rose to 1,200,000. Some three hundred industrial undertakings were established and several banking houses founded. The volume of imports was reduced, and exports increased as never before, so that the country achieved a favourable balance of trade. The revenue of the treasury from taxation, which had never previously been more than 13,000,000 zlotys, soon rose to 24,500,000 and finally to 40,000,000 in the reduced territory of the partitioned country.

These changes were accomplished against the background of the intellectual developments brought about by the spread of the Enlightenment to Poland. Greater contact with western Europe introduced new and controversial ideas into the country, which now began to have their effect. In 1776, for instance, torture together with the death penalty for witchcraft was abolished. Religious scepticism became fashionable. The secularization of life and thought proceeded, being hastened by the National Education Commission set up in 1773 to administer the property and funds of the Society of Jesus following its dissolution by the Pope. A university was established at Vilna, and a start was made in the organization of a system of secular state schools, in which practical and modern subjects were taught.

Economic and social changes also followed. The growing power of the central government diminished the political importance and social status of the nobility. They were compelled to alleviate the lot of the serfs and to adopt a different attitude towards the townspeople and their occupations. As the early capitalists acquired wealth, industry and commerce became attractive and even respectable. Warsaw became a thriving, fashionable city, its way of life modelled upon that of Paris.

Some fifteen years after the First Partition, conditions in eastern Europe seemed to change sufficiently to make the reform of the

Polish constitution possible. Russia and Austria became allies and involved in war against Turkey.[1] Frederick William II, who had become King of Prussia on the death of Frederick the Great in 1786, was alarmed at the alliance of these two powers, particularly as they both might emerge much stronger from their war with Turkey. He made friendly approaches, therefore, to Stanislas, which encouraged the Polish government to seize its opportunity. In 1789 it rescinded the Russian-imposed constitution and the next year made a defensive alliance with Prussia.

The death of the Emperor Joseph II, however, early in 1790 had the effect of seriously weakening the Polish alliance with Prussia. His successor, Leopold II, immediately withdrew from the Turkish war and then sought friendly relations with Frederick William, so reducing Prussia's need for Polish support. The Polish reformers were still determined to give their country a new constitution. A diet had been summoned in 1788, which was to be known as the Great Diet as it sat for the unprecedented period of four years. To overcome the opposition of a group of reactionary magnates, it constituted itself into a confederation, which enabled it to abide by a majority decision; and in May 1791 the new constitution was promulgated amid scenes of great rejoicing.

Though certainly inspired by the ideas of the French Revolution, this constitution was by no means revolutionary. It did not emancipate the serfs nor did it deprive the nobility of their estates. At the same time, it brought about major reforms. The *liberum veto* and the right of confederation were abolished; the crown was to be hereditary in the family of the Elector of Saxony after the death of Stanislas, who was unmarried; the King was to control the army, approve legislation and appoint his ministers; the Diet was to meet every two years and include deputies from the free towns; the control of the local dietines over the Diet was abolished; and there was to be religious toleration. The constitution was received with enthusiasm in Poland, and the Pope transferred the country's national feast to the day of its promulgation. It was also welcomed by liberal thinkers and statesmen in Europe. Edmund Burke, who hated the violence of the French Revolution, approved this measure – 'Not one man incurred loss or suffered degradation. All, from the king to the day labourer, were improved in their condition.'

[1] P. 272.

Both Frederick William of Prussia and Leopold of Austria recognized Poland's new constitution and agreed to respect her frontiers. Catherine of Russia, however, from the first, made no pretence of welcoming it. She regarded it as a defiance of her power and influence in Poland and was resolved to intervene as soon as her war with Turkey had ended. When a few reactionary Polish noblemen formed the Confederation of Targovitsa against the 'revolutionary, criminal constitution of 1791' and appealed to her for help, she issued a manifesto denouncing the pernicious principles which 'have destroyed Poland after destroying France' and sent 100,000 Russian troops into the country. Although the Great Diet had planned to raise a Polish army of 100,000 men, it so far only amounted to 69,000, and Austria and Prussia were both at war with revolutionary France.[1] The Poles fought well, but were overwhelmed, and Stanislas himself finally joined the pro-Russian confederation. The old constitution was restored and a diet summoned.

Catherine now thought that only another partition of Poland would prevent the repetition of a similar situation in the future. She also thought that the European situation favoured its immediate accomplishment by Russia, though she judged it best to do so in concert with Frederick William, who found the idea acceptable; and the two rulers signed an agreement which decided the terms of the Second Partition. This gave Russia half of Lithuania, the remaining parts of White Russia, most of Black Russia and the whole of the Ukraine west of the Dnieper. As in the First Partition, the lands now taken by Catherine had originally been Russian. Conquered by Lithuania in the twelfth and thirteenth centuries, they had been acquired by Poland through her union with that country in 1386, but they had remained Russian in character and were not an integral part of Poland. Very different were the acquisitions of the other partitioning power. Prussia took the towns of Danzig and Thorn and the whole of Poznania up to a line some twenty-five miles west of Warsaw. This was territory in the heart of Poland, vital to its existence. Danzig had to be bombarded into submission by the occupying troops, and the Diet protested vainly against the Prussian acquisition before accepting the partition.

In the Second Partition, Russia took from Poland territory 90,000 square miles in extent and a population of 3,000,000;

[1] P. 334.

Prussia took 15,000 square miles of territory and a population between 1,000,000 and 1,500,000. Poland was left with 62,000 square miles of territory and a population reduced to four millions. Her new frontiers were purely artificial and almost rectangular, leaving the kingdom no more than a mutilated fragment. As a final humiliation, Poland was forced to make an alliance with Russia by which she accepted the continued presence of Russian troops on her territory and agreed to disband her own army. As L. R. Lewitter has said, 'In 1772 partition had been declared imperative as the only means of saving Poland from anarchy; twenty-one years later, she was punished with partition for having tried to set her house in order. Here was tragic mockery indeed'.

The Third Partition (1795)

The Third Partition followed quickly on the Second. The course of events which brought it about began with a revolt in the Polish army against its disbandment. A cavalry brigade occupied Cracow, the old capital, which was still in the independent kingdom. The movement spread, and the insurgents proclaimed as their leader Thaddeus Kosciuszko (1746–1817), a member of the lesser nobility, who had studied military engineering in France and served on the side of the colonists during the American War of Independence. He had returned in 1785 to Poland and distinguished himself greatly in the hopeless war against Russia in 1792. Now he raised his standard in Cracow, where he was joined by practically all that remained of the Polish army and by crowds of peasants.

Though Kosciuszko had not planned the outbreak of the revolt, he did not accept the leadership of it in a mere spirit of desperation. He and his associates hoped for success as the result of several assumptions. They expected the Polish movement to inspire risings by the oppressed peoples of Hungary, Bohemia and Galicia against the Austrian government, in Silesia against the Prussian government and even in Russia as well; and they hoped that France, finding her enemies thus embarrassed, would be induced to assist Poland fully. They also intended their movement to be completely national, supported by the peasants, to whom they promised personal freedom and a partial remission of their labour obligations. And, finally, they believed they could raise an army 300,000 strong by associating a new volunteer militia with the units of the regular army. Kosciuszko trusted they could do what the American colonists had done and held that, despite her lack of maritime strength, 'Poland would be able to defend herself against the Russian and Prussian powers'.

At first it looked as if these assumptions might be correct. The Poles soon raised an army of about 150,000 men, which acquitted itself well. In the spring of 1794, at Raclawice, a village north of Cracow, it defeated a small Russian force. The people of Warsaw then rose and expelled the Russian garrison; Vilna, the capital of Lithuania, soon afterwards did the same. A provisional Polish government was set up in Warsaw.

The decision of Frederick William, however, to join Russia in crushing the rising made defeat inevitable. It would have needed a country very much wealthier and also enjoying more favourable general circumstances to resist the combined attacks of Russian and Prussian troops, unhindered as they were by natural frontiers. Kosciuszko was defeated at the Battle of Maciejowice and made prisoner by a Russian force. After another force under Suvorov had sacked the suburb of Praga and massacred its inhabitants, Warsaw fell. Stanislas abdicated, and a year later there followed the Third Partition by which Poland disappeared from the map of Europe.

In the negotiations which produced this partition, Frederick William tried to secure as much Polish territory as possible for Prussia, but Catherine was in a powerful enough position to resist him. She resolved to take the greater share for Russia and at the same time prevent too great an accession of strength to Prussia by favouring Austria, which had not received any territory in the previous partition and had not participated in the campaign of 1794. Accordingly, Russia took Courland and the rest of Lithuania and Black Russia; Austria gained territory north of Galicia, including Cracow; and Prussia received the lands between the Niemen and the Vistula, including Warsaw.

In making the Third Partition, the three powers, 'recognizing the necessity of abolishing everything which might recall the memory of a Polish kingdom in face of the performed annihilation of this political body', agreed among themselves 'never to introduce into their titles the name or the joint description "the Kingdom of Poland", which would be abolished since that moment forever'. The total territorial gains of Russia from the three partitions amounted to 181,000 square miles with a population of some 6,000,000; Austria had 45,000 square miles with a population of 3,000,000; and Prussia received 57,000 square miles with a population of 2,500,000.

Poland's own internal weaknesses had rendered her incapable of preserving her national existence as a separate state in the face of the rising strength of the powers on her borders. The trend of events during the eighteenth century, which developed in a manner so dangerous to Poland's independence, overwhelmed her in a space of less than a quarter of a century. Revival and reform, when it was at last attempted, came too late and only hastened the destruction of the kingdom. Circumstances since the period of the partition have been no more favourable to genuine Polish independence, save for a period between the two wars of the first half of the twentieth century. Now, as in the eighteenth century, the struggle for power in eastern Europe still dominates the situation.

XVI · THE FAILURE OF THE FRENCH MONARCHY

Louis the Well-Beloved

WHEN Cardinal Fleury at last died at the beginning of 1743, Louis XV announced – as Louis XIV had done in 1661 after the death of Cardinal Mazarin – that he would in future have no first minister but would himself govern the country. This decision must not be ascribed solely to a personal whim of the King or the prompting of sycophantic courtiers. It was an essential feature of the government of the *ancien régime*, which had been in temporary abeyance through the unusual personal relationship existing between Louis XV and his former tutors. Now that this episode was over, it was generally agreed that the personal monarchy must function again. The kingdom required a sovereign who both reigned and ruled, not a *roi fainéant*.

The year after Louis began his personal rule the Second Silesian War began.[1] In the summer the Austrians invaded Alsace. The King set out to join the French army which was opposing them, but at Metz he fell critically ill. His apparent nearness to death produced a scene of intrigue and passion in which his queen, his heir apparent, the *dévot* party and the clergy participated. His mistress, Mme. de Châteauroux, was driven from his presence, and he himself was induced to make a public confession of his sins and crave pardon for the scandalous example of moral weakness which he had set his people. Louis, however, recovered his health, which was greeted with universal rejoicing throughout France. *Te Deums* were sung, medals were struck and petitions of loyalty were presented by all the provincial *parlements*. The King had reached the heights of popularity and was acclaimed as *Louis le Bien-Aimé*.

Louis did, indeed, begin to govern his kingdom with many apparent advantages. The traditional representation of his reign needs some modification. Historians have relied too much on the intentional belittlement of the King in the memoirs of hostile courtiers and dismissed ministers. His reputation stood high in

---

[1] P. 206.

France in the first years of his personal rule, for he was a popular figure and a monarch upon whom great hopes were placed.   Perhaps his greatest asset was a magnificent presence.   His portraits show that from childhood to premature old age he remained strikingly handsome with a fine, virile though rather sensuous cast of countenance.   Suggestions that he was ignorant are untrue; and his sexual indulgences, given so much prominence by some biographers, were not by themselves especially important or remarkable for a prince of that time.   He was elegant and dignified, intelligent and well intentioned.

The limitations of his character, however, soon began to reveal themselves.   In personality and temperament he was unfitted for the position of a *grand monarque*.   He was naturally irresolute, selfish and lazy, and these defects of character had been intensified by his upbringing amid the elaborate, continuous etiquette of the court of Versailles, which produced in him a sense of boredom with official ceremonial and of inferiority in public affairs.   He conscientiously took his part in the routine established by Louis XIV.   Daily in his great-grandfather's bedchamber he went through the elaborate ceremonial of the *lever* and the *coucher*; every day he took at least one meal in public, alone or with the Queen; and he attended the weekly concerts and balls.

Yet all this he found tedious and wearisome.   Unlike Louis XIV he could not live his life easily in public.   He needed privacy and distraction.   The first he obtained by building the *Petits Appartements*, at the back of the State Apartments in Versailles, to provide himself with a suite of rooms where he could enjoy the comforts of seclusion among his children and friends.   The second he found in hunting and women.   He hunted indefatigably throughout the year, and on the days when he was not out with his hounds, it was said, '*Le roi ne fait rien aujourd'hui*'.   Most of his mistresses enjoyed no more than a fleeting favour, but some exploited his indolence to become politically important, especially the Marquise de Pompadour (1721–64), who was his mistress from 1745 to about 1751 and remained his close and influential friend for the rest of her life.

With such a ruler as Louis XV at its head, the central government of the kingdom could hardly receive careful and effective royal control.   The inauguration of the King's personal rule amounted actually to a triumph for the power of the Secretaries of State.   It was a return in principle to the system under which

Louis XIV had, in conjunction with the *Conseil du Roi*, exercised a central supervision over official policy and seen that each Secretary performed his part in it; but Louis XV was incapable of doing this, for he lacked Louis XIV's devotion to the *métier du roi*. He was unable to decide upon a policy and give it steady and consistent support, while his lack of interest in the business of the Council and inability to take part in its discussions became notorious. Yet throughout his reign he unyieldingly maintained his claim to all the royal prerogatives and privileges as finally established by Louis XIV. After Fleury's death, he confided in no single minister, but adopted a policy of playing off ministers and court factions against each other, which destroyed all unity and stability in the management of public affairs.

Even worse, Louis had a strong predilection for intrigue. After appointing ministers and agreeing with them in council, he did not hesitate to conspire against them in secret. Equally typical of him was the *Secret du Roi* in foreign policy[1] and the *département de l'interception*, a government office established to open letters and make copies of any likely to be of interest to the King.

The inevitable consequence of this situation was that the government of France was largely motivated by court factions. Favourites and mistresses strove to exert their hold over the King. Power depended upon whatever influence was dominant in the court at the time, whether it were that of the Marquise de Pompadour, the Abbé de Bernis, the Duc de Choiseul, the Queen, the Dauphin's coterie or, perhaps most forceful, the Pâris brothers, who after the collapse of Law's *Système* were for a time the leading figures in French financial circles. Struggle and intrigue in the court dominated the political life of the reign and provided the main motive for the appointments and dismissals which marked its story.

This was shown in the first years of Louis XV's personal rule by the fate of Orry, the able *Contrôleur Général* appointed by Fleury.[2] The Pâris brothers disliked his economical financial policy and were able to secure his downfall late in 1745, soon after the rise to royal favour of their protégée, the Marquise de Pompadour. He did, however, have a worthy successor in Jean-Baptiste de Machault d'Arnouville (1701–94). Like Orry Machault had been an *intendant*. He was a careful, honest

---

[1] P. 295.   [2] P. 162.

administrator with a wider outlook than his predecessor. At first he had to devise various expedients to raise money for the War of the Austrian Succession, but the coming of peace enabled him to attempt a measure of basic financial reform. In 1749 he introduced the *vingtième*, a tax of one-twentieth upon all incomes without any exemptions. The nobility refused to pay it, the *parlements* and provincial estates had to be forced to register the edict, but the main opposition came from the clergy, who were supported by the *dévot* party at court, the Jesuits, the Queen, the Dauphin, the King's daughters and the Marquis d'Argenson, the Foreign Minister and a personal enemy of Machault. Since he lacked Louis XV's support, Machault was compelled at the end of 1751 to suspend the levying of the *vingtième* on the property of the clergy; and when he ceased to be *Contrôleur Général* in 1754, all effort to reform the financial system had been abandoned. The episode illustrated both the difficulties of financial reform under the *ancien régime* and Louis XV's readiness to accept any easy solution for a problem, even at the expense of the real interests of the crown, rather than face serious hostility. Nor did the King's complaisance prevent the opposition provoked by Machault's proposals from seriously undermining the authority of the monarchy.

Louis XV remained popular in France until the Treaty of Aix-la-Chapelle, but his reputation steadily declined as the weakness and instability of his government became apparent. The opposition of the *parlements* to the crown, which was to do so much to bring about revolution, rapidly developed.[1] With foreign policy at the mercy of conflicting court factions, French prestige abroad sank low.[2] The effect of this upon Louis XV was to make him embittered and apathetic. As Dr. G. P. Gooch has said, 'His lamentable reputation in history derives less from what he did than from what he never tried to do. For him all evils were incurable.' The last years of his reign saw partly successful efforts to restore the power of France made by Choiseul and then to regain authority for the crown by the triumvirate of D'Aiguillon, Terray and Maupeou,[3] but this was not enough to save Louis from being by then, in the words of M. S. Anderson, 'perhaps more hated and certainly more despised than any king of France for generations'.

[1] Pp. 298 ff.   [2] Pp. 295 ff.   [3] Pp. 299–300.

Foreign Affairs

Serious as the absence of firm control over French policy was at home, its consequences in foreign policy were even more disastrous. When Frederick the Great invaded Silesia at the end of 1740, the failing Fleury and the Maréchal de Belleisle's group, which wanted war with Austria, were at loggerheads.[1] For some months French policy was paralysed, but by June 1741 Belleisle had triumphed, and France, through the Treaty of Breslau with Frederick of Prussia, was committed to war.[2] Belleisle's policy seemed early the next year to have achieved speedy and complete victory. French armies were in Germany, Austria and Bohemia, while Charles Albert, Elector of Bavaria, had been chosen as Holy Roman Emperor.

Yet Belleisle's success was to be short-lived. During 1742 the situation changed, and French prospects of victory were replaced by the threat of defeat. The French army in Bohemia was only saved from surrender by a retreat conducted by Belleisle himself. It was impossible, however, for Belleisle to rescue his own reputation from the reversal of French fortunes. He had seemed destined for power, but when Fleury died in January 1743, he had lost all chance of becoming the old minister's successor.

Foreign affairs now fell into the hands of the Marquis d'Argenson. Despite his visionary outlook and ingenious plans, D'Argenson was incapable of directing an effective policy. His Italian campaign ended in a French reverse which strengthened his opponents at Versailles. Louis XV dismissed him in January 1747. When the War of the Austrian Succession finally ended with the Treaty of Aix-la-Chapelle in 1748, France gained nothing.

Between 1748 and 1756 the control of French foreign policy was very confused. From 1745 onward, Louis XV gave much of his attention to developing a system of secret diplomacy under his personal control, known as the *Secret du Roi*. He established a secret correspondence with French agents at important European courts and also secured the co-operation of several foreign diplomats, who sent him private reports as well as copies of dispatches they had received from his own ministers. This organization functioned alongside the official diplomacy of the French foreign office, sometimes pursuing a directly contrary policy. One of the

[1] P. 164.   [2] P. 203.

main objects of the *Secret du Roi* was to exclude Russian influence from Poland and strengthen and safeguard her independence. The King's diplomatic skill was insufficient to gain any success for his policies, but they did much to distract and weaken French diplomacy, especially in eastern Europe, for the rest of his reign.

The prevailing influence at Versailles was now the Marquise de Pompadour. While the King took his pleasure with a succession of mistresses, she remained his chief *confidante*. Through birth and marriage and her intimacy with the Pâris brothers, she belonged to the circle of the wealthy tax-farmers and not the court aristocracy, who disliked her for occupying an illustrious position hitherto enjoyed by their wives and daughters and called her a *grisette*, a flighty shopgirl. Her direct political power must not be exaggerated. She was not in a position to decide policy herself, but in a government dominated by court factions she was often able to use her personal influence to determine who would be in a position to decide policy.

So when Kaunitz resolved to seek an alliance from France, he chose her as his intermediary.[1] Events in Europe had made Louis XV favourable to the idea; he appointed one of her protégés, the Abbé de Bernis (1715–94), who had recently returned after occupying for several years the sinecure post of French ambassador at Venice, to negotiate with the Austrian government. The result was the signing of the First Treaty of Versailles between the two countries in 1756, and French participation in the Seven Years' War with such disastrous consequences for herself. 'The Peace of Paris', Professor Cobban has said, 'was the price paid for government by weak and wavering ministerial groups and court factions.'

Moreover, the humiliation of this treaty was followed by a further decline of French prestige on the Continent in the course of the remaining years of Louis XV's reign. France was powerless to prevent the First Partition of Poland by Russia, Prussia and Austria, though this was contrary to the aim of the *Secret du Roi*. The alliance with Austria, strengthened in 1770 by the marriage of the Dauphin (afterwards Louis XVI) to the Archduchess Marie Antoinette (1755–93), brought France no gains and remained unpopular. The last part of the reign made Frenchmen ashamed at their country's loss of influence in Europe for which

[1] P. 219.

they blamed the King. '*La faiblesse trompe tous les calculs de la politique*,' wrote the Comte de Ségur in 1802 as he looked back on those years. '*Placez un homme de génie sur le plus petit trône de l'Europe et de princes faibles sur tous les autres, il les dominera et fera une révolution totale.*'

The Attempt at Reform

The Abbé de Bernis, who had become Foreign Minister at the beginning of the Seven Years' War, willingly relinquished office before hostilities came to their disastrous conclusion. In 1758 he became a cardinal and retired into the country. His successor, another protégé of the Marquise de Pompadour, was the Duc de Choiseul (1719–85). He was recalled from the French embassy in Vienna and appointed Foreign Minister late that year. Brilliant, versatile and hard-working, he remained in office until 1770. Though never an all-powerful *Premier Ministre,* he established considerable authority for himself by holding two other ministries – those of Marine and War. He used to say that he was like the coachman in *L'Avare,* putting his hand to every job and doing what he wanted. His main achievements were in foreign policy. His efforts to revive the French cause in the Seven Years' War came too late, though he did something to strengthen her position by making the Third Family Compact with Spain.[1] He could do little more than liquidate the War. The Treaty of Paris cost France much, but it might have been worse.[2] Lorraine passed to the French crown by the death of Stanislas Leszczynski in 1767, and the next year Choiseul was responsible for the purchase of Corsica from the Republic of Genoa. He also negotiated the marriage between the Dauphin and Marie Antoinette in 1770.

Choiseul wished to retain both the Spanish and the Austrian alliances because he wished to restore French power and wage a war of revenge against Britain. Since the Seven Years' War had demonstrated the necessity of naval power in any contest with Britain, he did much to recreate the French navy, encouraging the fisheries as a means of providing men for the fleet and establishing naval bases in both France and the West Indies, besides building capital ships.[3] He also introduced important changes into the army, making possible the work of the military reformers who

[1] P. 227.   [2] P. 232.   [3] P. 142.

brought the French army to such a high degree of effectiveness by the end of the *ancien régime*.[1]

Yet, at the very beginning of his period of office, Choiseul showed that, despite his ability and industry, he was not an outstanding minister. Towards the *parlements* he adopted a fatally yielding policy. Louis XV had already shown his usual lack of resolution in dealing with the Parlement of Paris over the Jansenist dispute. Now Choiseul allowed the suppression of the Jesuits to take place.[2]

More serious, if reform were to be achieved in France, was Choiseul's attitude towards the *parlements* over the financial question. In 1759 and again in 1761 Louis held a *lit de justice* to compel the Parlement of Paris to register edicts creating new taxes for financing the War, and the coming of peace in 1763 immediately produced a fresh conflict over taxation. Overwhelmed with debts, the treasury decided to retain a wartime *vingtième* and aroused the hostility of the privileged orders, including the *parlementaires,* by preparing for a proper land survey which would gradually abolish the grosser inequalities in the assessment of taxes. The King held yet another *lit de justice* to secure the registration of the edict; but then the government gave way. The *Contrôleur Général* was dismissed and replaced by a judge of the Parlement of Paris, who was permitted to insist that *vingtièmes* must be levied on existing assessments. Since this had the twofold effect of perpetuating the existing inequalities and preventing the treasury from profiting from any increase in the national wealth, the problem of reducing the country's deficit was clearly made much more difficult. In fact, Choiseul had relinquished from the start the essential means for securing the restoration of French power and victory over Britain which he desired. Without the recovery of royal authority within the kingdom and the reform of royal finances, any other reforms were bound to be useless.

The weakness of the government during these years was shown by an incident which now brought the provincial *parlements* forward to assert their claims against the royal administration. This was a quarrel between the Parlement of Rennes and the Duc d'Aiguillon, the military commandant of Brittany, who was a protégé of the Marquise de Pompadour and had gained prestige by defeating a powerful British raid at St. Cast, on the Breton coast, in 1758. D'Aiguillon acquired a royal *corvée* to make military roads in the province during the Seven Years' War, but the Parlement supported the contention of the provincial estates that this was an invasion of their rights. The government retaliated by deposing from office a number of its members. This drew indignant protests from both the Parisian and the provincial *parlements*. The Parlement of Paris, claiming that all the *parlements* of France were merely branches of one body, remonstrated against the treatment of the Breton *parlementaires*. The King repudiated this claim at a *lit de justice* in 1766, known as '*la séance de la flagellation*' because of the scathing way in which he spoke at it; he asserted that the monarch was the source of all power, including legislative power. Two years later, D'Aiguillon resigned his post, but the Parlement of Paris attempted to bring him to trial. Such an open challenge, in the face of which Choiseul remained apathetic or even secretly supported the *parlements*, at last roused Louis XV to action.

Since the death of the Marquise de Pompadour in 1764 and the rise of Mme. du Barry (1743–93) to the rank of royal mistress, Choiseul's position at the court had grown weaker. In 1768 Louis appointed René-Nicolas de Maupeou (1714–92) as Chancellor and the next year the Abbé Joseph-Marie Terray (1715– 78) as *Contrôleur Général*; both men were opposed to Choiseul's subservience to the *parlements*. Their chance to secure his removal came in 1770 when Choiseul, by supporting Spain in a dispute with Britain over the Falkland Islands, threatened to involve France in war. Louis had no wish for this to occur. He dismissed Choiseul and exiled him to his country estates. D'Aiguillon took his place as Foreign Minister.

This appointment was a virtual challenge to the *parlements*, and as such was not unwelcome to Terray and Maupeou, both of whom were bold and ruthless. Terray had convinced Maupeou and Louis that drastic measures were needed to solve the financial situation. These could only be affected by destroying the power of the *parlements*. Maupeou was ready to undertake such a course of action, while by now Louis had come to see that he had no choice but to support him. This time the *parlements* found themselves attacked. Late in 1770 Maupeou sent to the Parlement of Paris for registration a royal edict forbidding the *parlements* to act as one body and ordering them to cease exercising their judicial functions. The Parlement was provoked into openly rejecting the King's authority. Maupeou in 1771 exiled its members to the provinces by *lettres de cachet*.

Maupeou then abolished the venal posts of the *parlementaires* without compensation and divided the large area of jurisdiction belonging to the Parlement of Paris into six districts assigned to new courts, called *Conseils Superieurs*, sitting at Arras, Blois, Châlons-sur-Marne, Clermont, Lyons and Poitiers. These courts were nominated by the crown, and in them justice was to be free. He also set up in Paris a new central court of appeal, composed of seventy-five judges also nominated by the crown, which was soon nicknamed the '*Parlement Maupeou*'.

These measures made possible a more extensive attempt at reform than Choiseul had ever considered. Terray now implemented some of the financial reforms which had so long been frustrated. A new assessment of the *capitation* of Paris almost doubled its yield, and a new lease of the indirect taxes to the *fermiers généraux* secured another twenty million livres. He also enforced Machault's edict of 1749, bringing about changes in the *vingtième*, which made it the least defective tax of the *ancien régime*. These expedients, unpopular with the privileged classes and the *financiers*, did something to better the condition of the treasury, but did not bring nearer any solution to the desperate problem of the national finances.

What a few more years of government by the Triumvirate might have brought about in France was to become one of the unanswered questions of history. Louis XV's long reign came to a sudden end in 1774 when he caught smallpox and died at the age of sixty-four. Under the new circumstances of his successor's reign, events were to take a turn which within fifteen years were to bring the *ancien régime* to an end.

Louis XVI and Marie Antoinette

Louis XV's eldest son, the former Dauphin, had died in 1765. It was now, therefore, Louis XV's grandson who came to the throne. Louis XVI was twenty years old at his accession. Heavy and unpleasing in appearance, he was completely without his grandfather's graceful bearing, but he was in many ways a more praiseworthy character. Uniquely among the Bourbon kings of France, he led a strictly moral life; Mme. du Barry and her *protégés* were instantly dismissed from the court and had no successors. The new king was also kindly, honest, pious and almost pathetically well-meaning and full of good intentions.

Yet he was singularly unfitted to rule over France during a period of political agitation and financial confusion. He was thoroughly weak, vacillating and lacking in self-confidence. His brother-in-law, the Emperor Joseph II, wrote of him after a visit to Versailles in 1777, '*Cet homme est un peu faible, mais point imbécile; il a des notions, il a du jugement, mais c'est une apathie de corps comme d'esprit*'. His only vice was over-eating and over-drinking, his hobby was making and mending locks, and his chief pleasure, as with his grandfather, was hunting, the traditional sport of French kings. Sometimes he spent so long in the hunting-field that he fell asleep from fatigue at council meetings during the discussion of business. On any day when there was no hunting, he wrote in his diary, '*rien*', as he did on the day of the tennis-court oath in June 1789 and on other important dates in that year, while on the day in October when the women of Paris marched to Versailles, he wrote: '*Tué à la porte de Châtillon, tué 81 pièces, interrompu par les évenements.*' Indeed, though King of France, he gave the impression of living aloof and uncomprehending amid the critical events which stirred his kingdom.

For very different reasons, the Queen was equally unsuited for her position. The daughter of Francis I and Maria Theresa, Marie Antoinette had been sent from Vienna to become Dauphine at the age of fourteen. Her marriage was disliked in France by a strong party which opposed the Austrian alliance which she represented. To placate them she was made immediately upon her arrival on French territory to strip herself of all her Austrian clothing and re-dress in French silk and lace, but to them she still remained an unwanted Habsburg princess. Nor did she have an easy time at the court of Versailles from her first arrival. Choiseul, who had arranged the marriage, had just been dismissed from office, and she had scarcely a friend and no one to advise her. The old King was well disposed towards her but she was too proud to please him by recognizing Mme. du Barry. Her insensitive and listless husband inspired her with no affection, and for the first seven years their marriage was childless.

The King's three unmarried aunts, who were pious and frigid, sought to impose a monotonous routine on her daily existence. Marie Antoinette was too lively a girl to submit patiently to these

circumstances. She invited criticism by giving herself up to unsuitable companions, nocturnal excursions and childish amusements.

Her accession to the throne at the age of nineteen rescued her
from this humiliating inferiority, and when her children were
born she established an ascendancy over her husband to whom
she was superior in ability. Indeed, she openly despised his
weakness, once referring to him in a letter as '*le pauvre homme*',
to her mother's indignation. So feminine influence continued to
prevail at the court. The old King had been guided by his
mistresses, but Louis XVI was directed by his wife. Her power
over him was generally unfortunate. She had not been well
educated and remained a foreigner who never understood France.
Moreover, she had little taste for politics, allowing herself to be
guided simply by personal likes and dislikes. She tried to get
French support for Austrian policy, which was often contrary to
French interests; she was by no means always able to get what she
wanted here, but her attempts acquired for her the derogatory
nickname of '*l'Autrichienne*'.

Marie Antoinette, indeed, occupied a very different position
from most French queens, except those who had been regents.
They had taken no part in politics, but performed their duties in
the official ceremonies of the court. Marie Antoinette had a
charming manner which would have made her well suited to preside over a brilliant court, but she had a contempt for etiquette
and was not prepared to lead such a public existence, and her
husband disliked such a life as much as his grandfather had done.
She appointed her friend, the Princesse de Lamballe, as *Surin-
tendante de la Maison de la Reine* to enable her to spend most
of her time with a small group of special friends and to indulge
in her favourite amusements. When she was not engaged in
playing for high stakes, dancing, music and amateur theatricals,
she was at the Petit Trianon, the small country-house built in
the grounds of Versailles by Louis XV for Mme. du Barry. This
now became Marie Antoinette's favourite resort, and to it she
added a *jardin anglais* with twisting stream, rustic bridges and
artificial waterfall and a miniature village of mill, kitchen,
boudoir and ballroom by the side of a pond, where she and her
friends dressed themselves as Arcadian shepherds and shep-
herdesses to enjoy the simple delights of country life.

The King and Queen, therefore, lived a life of their own,

isolated from the rest of France. Except for a single visit by Louis to new harbour works at Cherbourg, they never journeyed beyond the royal chateaux around Paris. They even isolated themselves from the nobility of the court, who still counted for much in the *ancien régime*, and to this isolation the Queen contributed. Since she was so seldom among them in the functions of the court, the great noblemen and their ladies seldom came to Versailles from their *hôtels* in Paris. Her frivolity destroyed her prestige, while her love of show and extravagance, which was contrary to the policy of strict economy required by the condition of the royal finances, brought her the further nickname of '*Madame Déficit*'. Her irresponsibility in politics increased the hostility of the court factions which disliked her. From them came the continual malicious rumours and derogatory pamphlets circulating attacks upon her personal character, which have now been completely disproved but seriously marred her reputation within a decade of her accession.

Suspicion and abuse of the Queen's character reached its height in 1785 with the mysterious affair of the diamond necklace, which Napoleon said marked the beginning of the French Revolution. The Cardinal de Rohan, Duke and Peer, Archbishop of Strasbourg and Grand Almoner of France, who sought the Queen's favour, was induced by the Comtesse de la Motte, a pauperized illegitimate descendant of Henry II, to purchase for Marie Antoinette a valuable diamond necklace originally made for Mme. du Barry. The Cardinal handed the necklace to the Countess, who sold it to an English jeweller and kept the money. When the time for payment arrived, the jeweller sent his bill to the Queen, who denied all knowledge of it. A trial followed, which lasted nine months and created an immense scandal. The Cardinal, though found innocent, was banished from the court; the Comtesse de la Motte was flogged and branded; but many suspected that the Queen was the real culprit in the case. She was widely supposed to have sold her favours to the Cardinal for the necklace and then to have refused to pay the price. The episode did much to turn general public opinion against her and so weaken the prestige of the monarchy.

In 1774 the accession of a young king and his tall, graceful queen in place of a dissolute old widower was naturally greeted with enthusiasm and loyalty in France. After Louis XV's long and inglorious reign, public opinion confidently hoped that the crown would lead the nation towards a better future; but the weakness of the King and the indiscretions of the Queen speedily brought disenchantment and steadily dissipated the national goodwill, and the seriously undermined prestige of the monarchy was to contribute towards the development of the situation which culminated in the outbreak of the Revolution.

From Reform to Revolt

Upon his accession, Louis XVI in his determination to break with the ways of the old court dismissed the Triumvirate, whom he regarded as being among Mme. du Barry's *protégés*. His own sense of inferiority led him to seek an adviser. He chose the Comte de Maurepas (1701–81), who had been a capable and successful Minister of Marine from 1723 to 1744, when the loss of the Marquise de Pompadour's favour had forced his retirement. Though technically only *Ministre d'Etat*, Maurepas was in fact *Premier Ministre*; but he was now a rather cynical old man, delighted to have attained supreme office so unexpectedly and only wished to remain there as long as possible with the minimum of effort. The *parlementaires* took advantage of Maupeou's dismissal to organize the Paris mob to demonstrate in favour of the exiled *parlements*, and the government yielded by reinstating them. This was a popular move, but disastrous for the future of reform and the authority of the crown.

Other new appointments included that of the Comte de Vergennes (1717–87), who was to be Foreign Minister until his death. Apart from French intervention in the American War of Independence, foreign affairs were relatively unimportant during Louis XVI's reign. Yet it was the sole aspect of politics which Louis really understood. In the words of Albert Sorel, '*Il connaissait les affaires de l'Europe infiniment mieux que celles de la France*'. It was through the opposition of Louis and Vergennes that the pro-Austrian party at court, despite Marie Antoinette's leadership, was unable to secure French support for the Habsburg cause on the Continent. Despite her internal difficulties, France continued to hold a strong position in European politics during these years.

The most important appointment in the new government was that of Anne-Robert-Jacques Turgot, Baron de l'Aulne (1727–81), who became *Contrôleur Général*, to the delight of the Physiocrats, for he was a disciple of Quesnay.[1]   Turgot had followed an administrative career, having been for the last thirteen years Intendant of Limoges, where on a small scale in this backward *généralité* he had obtained remarkable success in putting his reforming ideas into practice by improving the assessment and collection of the *taille*, replacing the *corvée* by a tax and developing roads, education and public assistance.   He hoped now that he would be able to rationalize the national administrative system and eradicate its abuses.

On his appointment Turgot declared in a letter that his policy included rigorous economy to save the State from being overtaken by bankruptcy as soon as the first cannon should fire in a war. So he attacked the extravagance of the administration, cutting down the list of pensions, abolishing several thousand useless posts and even trying to limit the expenditure of the court.   He could not touch the exemption of noble lands from the *taille*, but he sought to check illegal exemptions and insisted upon the payment of the *capitation* by everyone.   Among his reforms, the most important was the replacement of the *corvée* by an impost levied without exemptions on landed property.   He also tried to apply the principles of the Physiocrats in economic matters through the removal of interprovincial customs duties on corn and wine, to permit internal free trade in these commodities and the abolition of the guilds which still regulated urban industry in medieval fashion.   For the future he projected more far-reaching plans such as a system of schools staffed by lay-teachers, a measure of local government by elected councils, national provision for the poor and the recognition of the validity of Protestant marriages.

Both Turgot's actual reforms and his proposals inevitably aroused powerful opposition.   The nobility disliked his tax reforms and abolition of the *corvée*; the *financiers* and *rentiers* resented his financial economies; and the *dévot* party feared his projects for lay education and religious toleration.   Above all, the *parlementaires* were now determined, after their temporary defeat by Maupeou, to resist any further attacks on their privileges.   Turgot's first edicts were registered in March 1776 by the Parlement of Paris only after a *lit de justice*.   He had not the gift of maintaining his power by intriguing among the factions of Versailles.   His power could remain only as long as he had the King's support, and this was undermined by the Queen's hostility

[1] P. 62.

and the wish of Maurepas to avoid trouble. In May of that year Louis dismissed Turgot after less than two years in office. An attempt to establish an enlightened monarchy and efficient administration in France had been defeated by the weakness of the King and the opposition of the privileged classes.

Turgot's dismissal was followed by a time of reaction. The *corvée,* the guilds and the internal duties on corn and wine were restored. The new *Contrôleur Général* died before the year was out. His place was taken by Jacques Necker (1732–1804), a wealthy banker from Geneva. Since he was a foreigner and a Protestant, he could not actually be made *Contrôleur Général,* but was given the title of *Directeur Général des Finances.* Though he had been a successful *financier,* Necker had no administrative experience. He did not consider constitutional changes desirable, but believed that the necessary financial reforms could be accomplished without opposition from vested interests.

Necker's years of office corresponded closely with those of French participation in the American War of Independence, which increased so drastically the problems of royal finance.[1] During the War, he managed to avoid new taxation by raising loans at between eight and ten per cent interest. This inevitably produced desperate consequences for the treasury. The total interest on the royal debt, which Terray had reduced to 93 million livres in 1774, had grown to over 300 million by 1789, mainly through Necker's borrowing.

Necker's policy brought him much popularity, but he had serious critics, and to answer them he published early in 1781 his *Compte Rendu au Roi de l'Etat des Finances,* which endeavoured to show by unduly optimistic figures that the condition of the royal finances was completely satisfactory. He announced a surplus of revenue over expenditure amounting to 10,000,000 livres, but the deficit at that period was, in fact, probably well over 46,000,000 livres. Some 100,000 copies of the *Compte Rendu* were sold. It increased Necker's general popularity, but drew upon him the hostility of the privileged orders because it also contained criticisms of such taxes as the *gabelle* and *corvée* and the pensions paid to courtiers by the treasury. When, therefore, Necker asked the King for wider powers to enable him to introduce reforms, his enemies succeeded in getting Louis to refuse. Necker resigned amid widespread public dismay. With Turgot's dismissal

[1] P. 83.

and Necker's resignation, there did not now seem much chance of effective reform, and little was left of Louis XV's original popularity in the country.

Necker's successor as *Contrôleur Général* was Joly de Fleury, who tried to increase taxation and check expenditure. The court and the *parlements* secured his dismissal after a bare two years of office. He was followed by Lefèvre d'Ormesson, who retired in less than a year after his proposals to postpone paying interest on the national debt had aroused the hostility of the *financiers,* many of whom had made fortunes by subscribing to Necker's loans and were opposed, therefore, to such attempts at economy.

The failure of his predecessors guided the policy of the next *Contrôleur Général*, Charles Alexandre de Calonne (1734–1802), who was appointed in 1783 and had gained considerable administrative experience through being an *intendant* for fifteen years. Calonne has been called '*une sorte de charlatan politique*', but modern historians do not accept the general condemnation passed upon him after his fall from office. He wished first to secure the support of the *financiers* and the privileged orders and so for three years encouraged large-scale government expenditure. St. Cloud was bought for the Queen, gifts and pensions were widely bestowed, and public works were undertaken in many parts of France. The recovery of confidence achieved by this policy enabled Calonne to float new loans until by the summer of 1786 he had exhausted the treasury's credit and could obtain no more money.

Calonne was sufficiently intelligent and self-confident to come to the decision that there was nothing for him to do but make a fresh approach to the country's pressing financial difficulties. He now proposed, therefore, a new land tax from which there should be no exemptions. It was certain that the *parlements* would resist such a measure, while to summon the national representative assembly, the States-General, would generally be interpreted as a confession of national bankruptcy, and the alarm would increase the financial crisis. Calonne, therefore, procured the summoning of an Assembly of Notables, composed of representatives of the bishops, princes, great nobles, judges and other important persons in the realm, all nominated by the King. Such an expedient had last been used in the previous century under Louis XIII to avoid summoning the States-General. Calonne hoped that the Assembly would accept his programme and make registration by the *parlements* easier to secure, but he had gravely miscalculated. When it met in February 1787, its members, nearly all of whom belonged to the privileged classes, both rejected his scheme and censured him for financial mismanagement. Calonne's lack of political sense not only cost him his office, but also compelled him to flee to England to avoid legal proceedings against him by the Parlement of Paris.

Calonne's successor as *Contrôleur Général* was one of his leading critics in the Assembly of Notables, Cardinal Loménie de Brienne, Archbishop of Toulouse (1727–94), who had a considerable reputation as an administrator and enjoyed Marie Antoinette's support. To increase his authority, the title of *Principal Ministre* was shortly afterwards revived for him. Brienne, however, could not think of any better plan than to adopt, only slightly modified, Calonne's scheme which he had himself strongly opposed. The Assembly of Notables naturally resumed its opposition to this and was dissolved by the King in May 1787. Brienne now returned to the usual procedure, which Calonne had realized was likely to be useless, of calling upon the *parlements* to register his edicts. When Brienne presented these edicts to the Parlement of Paris, it rejected them and demanded the calling of the States-General. The King summoned the Parlement to Versailles and held a *lit de justice* to register the edicts. The Parlement declared the registration illegal and was exiled by the King to Troyes. Though the Parlement's purpose was to maintain and augment the power of the privileged orders, its opposition to the crown aroused great popular excitement in Paris and the provinces, stimulated by the belief that this was a struggle which concerned the rights of the whole nation.

Brienne still hoped for conciliation. A compromise was reached through him. The government withdrew the edicts, and the Parlement in return agreed to register further royal loans on the understanding that the States-General would meet. So in November 1787 the Parlement returned in triumph to Paris; but the reconciliation was short-lived. The government, alarmed by the popular excitement aroused by recent events, announced that the States-General would not meet until July 1792 and only if the required loans had been floated by then. This brought an immediate outcry from the Parlement, and when the King again held a *lit de justice* to register the loans, the Duc d'Orléans, the first *prince du sang* after the King's two brothers, protested that this was illegal. The King exiled the Duke to his country château and arrested two of the leading *parlementaires*.

Brienne was at last convinced that he must act firmly and imitate Maupeou. The provincial *parlements* had again joined in the resistance to the crown, hindering the work of the *intendants* and the collection of taxes, while the loyalty of many noble officers in the army was in doubt. In May 1788 the Parlement was again summoned to Versailles, where a *lit de justice* secured the registration of six edicts, which suspended the *parlements* throughout France, replaced them by forty-seven new provincial courts and established a *Cour Plenière*, consisting of great dignitaries appointed for life by the King, which was to register royal edicts.

The situation had altered, however, since the days of the Triumvirate. Years of royal weakness and ministerial ineptitude had now convinced the *parlements* as representatives of the privileged classes that they could resist the government openly. They were supported by the General Assembly of the Clergy, which in June refused Brienne's urgent request for an adequate *don gratuit* to stave off financial disaster and protested against the suspension of the *parlements*. That summer *parlementaires* and *noblesse* joined in stirring up popular demonstrations and riots in several parts of France, notably in Béarn, Brittany and Dauphiné. The bloodshed in these disturbances was small, but the danger of events in the provinces getting out of control was real, especially as the army was unreliable. At the same time, the financial situation was becoming rapidly more desperate.

The privileged classes triumphed. In August the King virtually surrendered by announcing that the States-General would meet on 1st May 1789. Brienne, soon after suspending all payments from the treasury for six weeks, resigned, and Necker came back into office. His prestige was sufficient to improve the credit of the government to the extent of enabling it to borrow a few million livres to satisfy its most urgent needs. Events now had to wait upon the meeting of the States-General, but already another development had worsened the situation in France. Louis XV's reign, despite its many political and military failures, had been a time of relative prosperity for much of the country, but his grandson was not so fortunate. The greater part of his reign had already been a period of economic depression, and the harvest of 1788 was very bad. Starving peasants flocked into Paris during the autumn and winter, adding to the poor of the city's slums. These economic difficulties intensified popular unrest during the month when representatives were being elected for the forthcoming meeting of the States-General.

The Eve of the Revolution

Meanwhile, the representatives of the privileged classes had thrown the political scene into confusion. In September 1788 the Parlement of Paris registered the edict convoking the States-General, but added that it must be called and composed '*suivant la forme observée en 1614*', which was the year when it had last met. This meant that the three estates would be organized with an equal number of representatives, and each order would vote separately, so enabling the clergy and nobility to outvote the third estate. This was a clear indication of the real aims of the *parlements*. It lost them at once the support of the middle-classes, who had increased so considerably in social and economic importance since the seventeenth century and were not prepared to be excluded from political power by a revival of the traditional constitutional forms. Public opinion now turned against the *parlements*.

Consequently, the closing months of 1788 brought controversy over the form of the States-General; it has been estimated that twenty-five new pamphlets appeared each week for a period of six weeks. The third estate wanted to be given double representation. Necker, ever anxious to retain his popularity, decided to summon another Assembly of Notables in the hope of persuading it to make concessions to public opinion on this question, but it also strongly supported the practice of 1614. The unpopularity of the privileged classes was further increased.

The popular indignation convinced Necker that he must secure from the government at least the principle of double representation. In December 1788 he persuaded the *Conseil du Roi* to declare, '*Le nombre des députés du tiers état sera égal à celui des deux autres ordres réunis*'. The other question, whether the voting in the States-General should be *par tête* or *par ordre*, was left undecided with the result that disputation between privileged and unprivileged grew in intensity as the meeting of the States-General approached.

The French Revolution was now very near at hand. It was to

bring about the destruction of both the monarchy and the privileged classes. Yet it was these classes which had started the chain of occurrences which was to produce the Revolution. The reappearance of the aristocracy in the political sphere, their determination to seize power in the State, gradually but inexorably undermined the royal absolutism under Louis XV and Louis XVI. They sought to assert themselves first through the short-lived system of councils during the Regency and then through the much more menacing revival of the claims of the *parlements*. The Revolution was precipitated by the events of 1787 and 1788 which attended the attempt of the privileged orders to increase their political power and uphold their privileges in the face of a financial crisis only to be solved by the abrogation of these privileges.

So far the privileged classes had enjoyed popular approval because their cause could be represented as a struggle against the whole privileged basis of the monarchy. This, in particular, gave them the support of the important and unprivileged middle-classes in the third estate. By the end of 1788, however, they had forfeited this support because the divergent interests of the two groups had been revealed. The resolve of the clergy and nobility to possess administrative authority and maintain their privileges was now in conflict with the wish of the third estate to share in governing the country and also to refashion society and destroy aristocratic privilege.

As the year 1789 opened, therefore, the French political conflict had assumed a different aspect. The *révolt nobiliaire* was over. The privileged classes suddenly found themselves faced with a new and menacing threat to their position. By the time the States-General met, they had abandoned their campaign against monarchical absolutism and wished to join with the monarchy in supporting the *ancien régime* against the attack of the third estate. In this way, it became almost inevitable that the States-General would usher in a period not of peaceful constitutional reform, but of discord and turbulence. For once the middle-classes had assumed the leadership of the movement; they also found they could not control it, and it grew into a violent destructive revolution.

XVII · THE FRENCH REVOLUTION

The States-General (1789)

It was traditional, before a meeting of the States-General, for assemblies of electors to draw up lists of grievances – *cahiers de doléances*. In each constituency these were merged into an address for presentation by its deputy to the crown. There were about 600 of these addresses finally presented at Versailles in 1789, while some 20,000 of the *cahiers* still survive. Generally speaking, the *cahiers* from the towns were drawn up by the fairly wealthy bourgeoisie and demanded equality with the privileged classes, while those from the country parishes came from the larger farmers and wanted the abolition of seigneurial dues. The *cahiers* of the clergy and the nobility, on the other hand, showed that both these estates wished to retain their distinctive advantages and immunities. In this way was illustrated the social and political rift between privileged aristocracy and unprivileged bourgeoisie which had now developed in France. The poorer peasantry, however, had been unable to express themselves; their grievances were not made known until the revolt of the rural population in the summer of 1789.

The States-General was formally opened by Louis XVI at Versailles on 5th May 1789. In numbers, those hostile to the system of the *ancien régime,* the bourgeoisie and the parish priests, had a majority over those now likely to defend it, the nobles and the bishops. At the opening session, Necker made an indeterminate speech. He dealt at length with the financial difficulties of the treasury, but as a solution for these he did little more than express confidence in the generosity of the privileged classes. On the crucial question of procedure, he showed that the government was not prepared to make any further concessions to the middle-classes. It was to be left to the three orders to decide separately which subjects they would be prepared to discuss and vote on together.

Disappointed and disillusioned by such a discouraging speech, the third estate determined to seize the initiative itself. On the next day, when the clergy and nobility began to verify their powers separately, the third estate would not follow suit. Its object was to secure a union of the orders so that it would have a majority and be able to pass the reforms it wanted; and it set out to secure this by deliberate inaction. For six weeks the States-General was paralysed since the third estate refused to conduct any business until its demand was granted. Soon it became clear that the third estate were united in policy, but the first and second estates were not. Many of the lower clergy shared the outlook of the third estate rather than that of the aristocratic bishops, while a small group of liberal nobles also sympathized with the idea of union. Encouraged by this, the third estate on 17th June resolved to call itself the National Assembly and invited the other orders to join it.

This transformation of the third estate into the National Assembly was made possible by both the disunity of the privileged orders and the evident support of the people of Paris. It was brought about through the leadership of a group of deputies among whom the Comte de Mirabeau (1749–91) was outstanding. The younger son of a marquis with Physiocratic interests, Mirabeau had led a restless, profligate and extravagant life until the events of the Revolution gave him at last the opportunity to use his energy and ability in public life. Though a member of the second estate, he was elected to the States-General as a deputy for the third estate. With his massive figure, strong, pock-marked face, unruly hair and stentorian voice, he soon forced himself to the head of his fellow-deputies. He was the first of the revolutionary leaders to form a policy, which included the abolition of privilege and inequality and also the establishment of a constitutional monarchy. Of him Lord Macaulay expressed the opinion, 'Resembling Wilkes in the lower and grosser parts of his character, he had, in his higher qualities, some affinity to Chatham.'

The Constituent Assembly (1789–91)

The illegal formation of the National Assembly was a clear challenge to the monarchy. 'If His Majesty once gives his decided approbation of the proceedings of the third estate,' wrote the British ambassador, 'it will be little short of laying his crown at their feet.' The royal ministers now decided that the King should preside over a special joint session of the three orders of the States-General, though they could not clearly agree what should be done at this. The great hall, used by the third estate, was closed on 20th June to prepare it for this royal session, but by an oversight the deputies were not informed. On finding themselves locked out of their meeting-place, they assumed that the government was about to dismiss their assembly and adjourned to the royal indoor tennis-court, where they swore not to separate until they had drawn up a constitution for France. This tennis-court oath was a revolutionary act, contrary to the royal prerogative of dissolving the States-General.

Two days later, the majority of the clergy joined the third estate. When the royal session was held, the King declared that the distinction between the three orders must be maintained completely and ordered the third estate to abandon its plans. Mirabeau made his dramatic reply that the deputies would only give way at the point of the bayonet; and a group of liberal noblemen now joined them. On 27th June, however, four days after the royal session, the King, probably provoked by news that a mob was about to march from Paris upon Versailles, surrendered and ordered the two privileged orders to unite with the third estate to form a single body known as the Constituent Assembly.

'The whole business is now over,' wrote Arthur Young that day, 'and the revolution complete'; but the court did not regard its capitulation as final. Several regiments of troops, mostly German and Swiss mercenaries, were moved from the provinces to Versailles and the region of Paris. The government stated that these measures were to protect the Assembly and prevent disorder in Paris, but rumour suggested otherwise. Soon the aristocratic delegates, who had unwillingly obeyed the royal order to join the third estate, ceased to attend the Assembly's debates; and on 11th July the King suddenly dismissed Necker, who had been advising concessions to the third estate. It was now believed that the dissolution of the Assembly and the repudiation of the national debt were imminent.

These events had a great effect in Paris, where demonstrations and riots were becoming increasingly common in the face of the apparent inability of the authorities to maintain order. Many revolutionary pamphlets appeared, while orators added to the excitement of the crowds they addressed. This situation produced the capture and destruction of the royal fortress of the Bastille by a mob in search of arms on 14th July. The Bastille was popularly supposed to contain many prisoners confined indefinitely without trial by royal *lettres de cachet*, but in it were only four forgers, two lunatics and a dissolute young nobleman kept there by the wish of his family. The taking of the Bastille was, however, a significant insurrection against the *ancien régime*. It also indicated that the King no longer controlled Paris and could not hope to regain it even with his mercenary troops.

The fall of the Bastille had other and unexpected consequences. In order to protect property in the city from pillage, the middle-class citizens of Paris organized a militia, known as the National Guard, which was commanded by the Marquis de Lafayette, the hero of French participation in the American War of Independence, and also the Commune, a committee at the Hôtel de Ville to manage municipal affairs, with a mayor at its head. Louis had no choice but to come to Paris three days later and recognize the city's new government and National Guard and wear in his hat its coloured cockade formed from the red and blue colours of Paris and the white emblem of the Bourbons. A similar municipal revolution occurred in other towns throughout France; everywhere the wealthier members of the third estate seized power from royal officials and organized detachments of the National Guard.

The fall of the Bastille also stimulated a rising among the peasantry, which brought about a development of the Revolution not anticipated by the bourgeoisie. Earlier in the year there had been agrarian disturbances because of the high cost of bread. Now there were numerous revolts in the countryside. The peasants broke down enclosures, occupied common-land, killed game and destroyed manorial records by burning châteaux. Late in July these risings were intensified and spread by a movement known as the *Grande Peur*. For some weeks a panic overran France, started by rumours of the approach of brigands who intended to attack villages and steal the harvest. The villagers armed themselves and waited for attacks which never came. When it was over, the peasantry were in control in many parts of the country.

The news of these rural happenings caused alarm in the Assembly at Versailles. Bourgeois control over Paris and the towns seemed to have been secured by the establishment of the new municipal authorities and the National Guard, but the countryside could not so easily be subdued. A number of deputies, at first mainly from Brittany, had formed themselves into a group, the Club Breton – later, upon the removal of the Assembly to Paris, they were to meet in a monastery of the Dominicans (locally nicknamed Jacobins) and become the Jacobin

Club. These deputies decided that the situation in the countryside could be saved only by the destruction of traditional privileges, and they persuaded the Assembly in an emotional meeting
on the night of 4th August to abolish *'tous les privilèges et les
droits particuliers des provinces et des villes'*. Though this was
far-reaching in its consequences, the Assembly wished only to
abolish aspects of the manorial system which might be held
onerous, such as the payments in kind, *droit de chasse* and *justice
seigneuriale*, and to retain the money dues; but the peasants
generally refused to pay these, and as no effective compulsion
could be brought upon them, the Convention finally in July 1793
abolished all feudal rights without compensation.

The disturbing news from the countryside had interrupted the
debates of the Assembly upon the production of a Declaration of
the Rights of Man to assert those individual liberties denied to the
people of France by the *ancien régime*, which it expressed in such
eighteenth-century assertions as that men by nature are equal,
the people are sovereign and should make the law as an expression
of the general will, liberty of person and speech are sacred rights
and rebellion against injustice is a holy duty. This was now
published on 26th August. The King, however, would not
approve either the decrees abolishing feudal privileges or the
Declaration; Marie Antoinette was thought to be responsible for
this, and she was now nicknamed *'Madame Veto'*. Moreover,
the arrival at Versailles of the loyal Flanders Regiment from
Douai suggested that Louis had again been persuaded to resort to
force.

There followed a fresh intervention by the Paris mob and the
last of the revolts of 1789. Discontent was still strong in the city,
the main cause again the high price of bread. Though the summer's harvest was good, little flour had yet reached the capital's
bakeries. In addition, the flight of noble and wealthy families
in alarm from their town houses had thrown domestic servants
out of work and ruined luxury trades. The King's intransigence
enabled popular orators again to inflame the crowds against the
court, where it was believed food was plentiful.

At the beginning of October an event occurred at Versailles
which further stimulated the orators. A banquet, at which the
King and Queen were present, was given in the court theatre to
the officers of the Flanders Regiment, and after the band had
played Blondel's song from *Richard Cœur de Lion*, *'O Richard!*

ô mon roi! l'univers t'abandonne!', the guests rose with enthusiastic demonstrations of loyalty and counter-revolutionary shouts. Early in October a crowd of women, who had been demonstrating before the Hôtel de Ville and demanding bread, began to march from Paris to Versailles. Lafayette and the National Guard followed them, arriving in time to save the royal family from violence, but the crowd now took up the cry, *'Le Roi à Paris!'*. Louis was in no position to resist. Together with the Queen and the Dauphin, he was escorted back to the Tuileries, the old royal palace which Louis XIV had deserted a century previously. Moreover, the Assembly, not wishing to be left in isolation at Versailles, voted ten days later to transfer itself also to the capital. The government of the country was to be under Parisian influence for the next five years.

The fact that the third estate had obtained its triumph through direct action by the Paris mob was to have grave consequences upon the course of the Revolution. The prevailing atmosphere in the city inevitably led the movement beyond an attack on privilege. Influence was increasingly gained by those who wished to exploit the victory of the third estate – the Patriots, as they called themselves. At the same time, the hostility of the defeated members of the aristocratic revolution intensified. A growing number became *émigrés,* taking flight to foreign countries where they hoped to obtain military help to recover their position. Since such developments left the monarchy mistrusted by the Assembly and quite unable to influence events and yet still able to control the royal ministers and their departments, it gradually appeared that the consequence was to be administrative deadlock.

The October Days ended the first period of revolutionary violence. There was not to be a successful insurrection for another three years. Beneath the surface, however, the struggle between the political groups was becoming ever more virulent; and this was the atmosphere in which the Assembly, after its removal to Paris, occupied itself during the next two years with the pressing tasks of constructing a new constitution and method of government in place of what had already been destroyed. The *ancien régime* had been a patchwork of monarchical and feudal survivals to which more recent institutions had been added with great variety in different parts of the country. Now an attempt was to be made to give the State a completely new and unified system of administration.

Local government urgently needed restoring. The old administrative authorities – *intendants*, law-courts, judicial and financial officials – had disappeared during the uprisings of July. The communes which had then been set up were retained as the basic unit of the new system. Above the communes were larger areas, the cantons, then the districts (the *arrondissements*) and finally the eighty-three departments which replaced the old provinces of the kingdom. In place of the monarchical nomination of local officials, these were now to be appointed by elected councils in the departments and communes. The departments were deliberately made approximately equal in size, but each commune comprised either an entire town or a rural parish, however great the difference in population, so that the method of administration was the same for the largest towns and the smallest villages. These divisions of local government were to survive all future political changes in France and continue to exist today.

At the same time, the *parlements* and the subordinate courts were abolished and with them private and privileged jurisdictions and the acquisition of magistracies by inheritance or purchase. Torture, already nominally discarded between 1780 and 1788, was finally made illegal. A new system of law-courts for the departments and districts was set up. Like the new local administrative officials, the judges were elected by popular vote for a definite period of office.

Together with local government and justice, finance presented an immediate and serious problem. Since the summer of 1789 the collection of payment of taxes, direct and indirect, had ceased, and all venal offices had been abolished. The fears aroused by Law's disastrous failure were still strong enough to prevent the establishment of a national bank. A voluntary 'patriotic levy' in September 1789 yielded a completely inadequate sum. The Assembly now decided to confiscate the lands of the French Church, and this was accomplished with the assistance of Charles de Talleyrand-Périgord (1754–1838), the secular-minded ambitious Bishop of Autun, on condition that the State supported the clergy. To secure the desperately-needed ready money, the Assembly both sold ecclesiastical estates and issued *assignats,* paper currency backed by land. The over-issue of these *assignats* in 1792, in an effort to meet wartime expenditure, was to lead to an inflationary crisis early the next year, but they certainly saved the State from immediate bankruptcy and made it possible for the

Assembly to proceed with its constitutional measures for the next two years.

The seizure of the ecclesiastical lands aroused little opposition, but it was very different when the Assembly turned its attention to the relations of Church and State and produced the Civil Constitution of the Clergy.[1] This first made counter-revolution a practical cause by giving it considerable popular support. It also started a conflict between Church and State which was long to continue and divide the French people.

The Assembly's political and administrative measures met with strong criticism from Mirabeau, who continued to believe that a constitutional monarchy would be the best form of government for France and condemned the revolutionary course taken by the Assembly since the summer of 1789. His attitude was dictated by both policy and ambition. He wished to restore power and authority to the executive by linking the ministry with the Assembly on the lines of the British constitution; he wished also to become a minister himself. In November 1789, however, the Assembly excluded deputies from office under the crown. Mirabeau took to political intrigue and established secret relations with the court, receiving money to pay his debts and the promise of a monthly allowance, but neither the King nor the Queen trusted him, and when he died of a fever in April 1791 he had achieved nothing.

For some time Mirabeau had been advising the King to leave the capital and go to Rouen which was in the centre of an area where royalist and ecclesiastical sympathizers were strong, but when he died Louis and Marie Antoinette resolved to adopt what they believed was a better plan. They would escape from the Tuileries to the north-eastern frontier and appeal to the monarchs of Europe for help against the Assembly. So was attempted the ill-fated flight in June 1791, which resulted in the capture of the royal fugitives at Varennes, within a short distance of the frontier. For the third time in two years Louis was brought into his capital as a prisoner.

The consequence of the death of Mirabeau and the flight to Varennes was a growth of active republicanism. Prominent in the republican movement was the Cordelier Club, composed of Paris artisans, which in July 1791 organized in the great open space of the Champ de Mars the signing of a petition calling for

[1] P. 114.

the King's abdication. The municipal council, to ensure the maintenance of order, sent along a detachment of the National Guard under Lafayette. When some stone-throwing began, Lafayette ordered his troops to fire on the crowd and killed about fifty of them. This incident brought Lafayette's popularity and political influence to an end, besides strengthening the republican cause by providing it with its first martyrs. It also split the Jacobin Club, for those among its members who had opposed the organization of the petition seceded and founded the rival Feuillant Club, while the Jacobins became thorough republicans.

Meanwhile, the Assembly was nearing the end of its activities. By September 1791 the new constitution was completed. Under it the legislature was to have the sole right of making laws and levying taxes, but the King retained the right of veto, and the Feuillants succeeded in fixing a fairly high property qualification for the franchise, which they hoped would make it a more conservative body. Louis formally accepted the constitution, and the Constituent Assembly dissolved itself at the end of the month. Before doing so, it passed a decree that none of its members should be eligible for the new Legislative Assembly set up under the constitution. This was the result of an alliance between republicans and royalists, both of whom disliked the constitution and wished to deprive those who had framed it of their power.

The Legislative Assembly (1791-2)

When the Legislative Assembly was elected in 1791, some 265 of its 745 members were Feuillants, while about 135 were republicans, chiefly Cordeliers, Girondins and Jacobins. The Girondins, later to become bitter enemies of the Jacobins, were so called because several of them represented the department of the Gironde in the south-west of France. The centre of the Girondin group at this time was the Paris salon of the intelligent, passionate Madame Roland (1734-93), wife of one of their leaders. They were never a united, integrated party, but were numerically quite a small group of politicians, highly individualist in their conduct, but brought together by common interests, local associations and mutual friendships, which enabled them to maintain a common political position. From the first they suffered from the disadvantage of a lack of organization and a concentration of strength in distant provinces. The Jacobins, on the other hand, not only had the support of the mob in Paris, but also had the advantage in organization, having formed some four hundred affiliated clubs in the provinces.

The coming of war in 1792 transformed the political situation. Since the flight to Varennes, the King and Queen had believed more firmly than ever that the monarchy could only be saved by foreign intervention. They intrigued, therefore, with the groups of *émigrés* scattered among France's neighbouring countries and encouraged them to appeal to the courts of Europe to attack France and restore the *ancien régime*. The European powers, however, had no intention of embarking upon such a venture, which would be risky and unlikely to serve their own interests. The Emperor Leopold and the King of Prussia issued the famous Declaration of Pillnitz in August 1791, declaring that French affairs were the common interest of all Europe and asserting their willingness to intervene to protect Louis if other rulers would join them; but this was intended to be no more than a gesture for they knew that the other powers would not support them.

The diplomacy of these two sovereigns and the activities of the *émigrés* were, however, taken seriously in France.[1] There was an increasing fear of an invasion by foreign armies, assisted by the *émigrés* and supported by a royalist rising in France, which led some to think of a preventive war to anticipate the attack. At the same time, the republican clubs in Paris were welcoming political refugees from abroad, particularly the Austrian Netherlands, who persistently urged the French to intervene in their own countries where they said the people were anxiously awaiting the opportunity to revolt against their despotic rulers and join with revolutionary France. Such an idea appealed to the crusading spirit of the French revolutionaries, and the possibility of war against Austria was not unpopular with many French people, who resented both the Austrian alliance and the half-century of French humiliation in foreign affairs. The passions of past events had already excited a resurgence of patriotic feeling which found its expression in September 1791 when French troops seized the papal enclave of Avignon after massacring those who resisted them.

The war's origins are to be found, therefore, in a situation which increasingly favoured its outbreak, especially among the supporters of the republican clubs. Of these, the Girondins soon set out actively to bring war about. Their motives were mixed.

[1] Pp. 317, 333.

They believed both that France should protect herself by attacking
her enemies and should assist the oppressed peoples of other
countries.   They also calculated that war would rally popular
support behind themselves as republicans, so enabling them to
achieve power and secure their political aims.   For months they
urged the Feuillant ministry and the Legislative Assembly towards war and won in the end.   In April 1792 the Assembly
almost unanimously vetoed for war against Austria; it was declared to be 'la guerre aux rois et la paix aux peuples'.

The War began badly for France.   As hostilities had become
more likely, an Austro-Prussian alliance had been made in
February and now Prussia soon joined her ally.   The Legislative Assembly had made no preparations for warfare.   The
army was still disrupted by the convulsions of the Revolution –
whole regiments had disappeared, émigré officers had not been replaced, discipline had been undermined and arms and warlike
stores were lacking.   The Austrians invaded France from the
north-east and the Prussians from the east.[1]   Girondin hopes that
the declaration of war by France would be the sign for a general
rising by the peoples of neighbouring countries in her favour were
falsified.

Other hopes rested upon the War.   'Tant mieux', wrote Marie
Antoinette at its outset; but her hopes that the monarchy would
now be saved by foreign intervention were also to be frustrated.
Rather the hopes of the republicans that the War would even
further discredit the monarchy were soon fulfilled.   The early
disasters of 1792 produced an immediate popular reaction in
Paris.   In June a crowd of about eight thousand, singing the new
revolutionary song, Ça ira, invaded the Tuileries, and penetrated
into the royal apartments, forcing Louis to drink to the health of
the nation and wear a red cap of liberty until they were dispersed
after several hours by the mayor.

The Girondins and their supporters were encouraged to use
the situation for their own ends.   Orators and agitators insisted
that France had been betrayed to her enemies by the treachery of
the court.   Among the most prominent of these was now
Georges-Jacques Danton (1759–94), one of the founders of the
Cordelier Club.   Hitherto pleasure-loving and lethargic, the
national crisis aroused him to ceaseless activity.   He was a tall,
brawny man with harsh and threatening countenance, beetling

[1] P. 335.

black brows and a voice of enormous power. Persistently he denounced '*la trahison des Tuileries*'.

Excitement mounted as the government summoned National Guards, the famous *fédérés*, from the provinces to Paris. The contingent from Marseilles marched into the city singing the *Chant de l'Armée du Rhin*, composed at Strasbourg by an artillery officer, and soon to be widely sung and known as the *Marseillaise*. A Prussian army was advancing steadily towards Paris, and late in July its commander, the Duke of Brunswick, issued a manifesto (which was drawn up by an *émigré*) stating that his purpose was to 'restore the King to the safety and liberty of which he has been deprived and enable him to exercise his legitimate authority' and threatening, if any violence were offered to the royal family to exact 'an exemplary and unforgettable vengeance by delivering up Paris to military execution and complete destruction'.

Danton and the revolutionary politicians were now ready for action. On the morning of 10th August, the bell of the Cordeliers tolled out the signal to the forces controlled by the clubs. They seized the Hôtel de Ville, ejected the members of the Commune by force and set up a new, insurrectionary Commune which had already been chosen. Then the forces, which included many *fédérés*, were directed to march on the Tuileries. The King with his family took refuge with the Legislative Assembly and ordered his Swiss guards to withdraw, but the attackers had already begun firing, and this soon became a massacre. Some six hundred Swiss guards and two hundred royalist sympathizers were killed, together with about ninety of the insurgents.

The Legislative Assembly had clearly lost control of events and had to recognize the new situation. It suspended the King from his functions instead of deposing him; but the new Commune insisted upon his imprisonment in the old fortified monastery of the Temple. The Commune also induced the Assembly to order the election by universal manhood suffrage of a new body, the Convention, which was to draw up a fresh constitution.

The weakness of the Legislative Assembly in its last days enabled the Commune and its revolutionary supporters to make full use of their power. The Prussians were still advancing on Paris, slowly but seemingly irresistibly. In August Lafayette went over to the Austrians. On 2nd September Danton uttered his famous words, '*Pour les vaincre, pour les atterrer, que faut-il? De l'audace, encore de l'audace et toujours l'audace'*; but fear and suspicion spread through the city. Jean-Paul Marat (1743–93) urged in his violent journal, *L'Ami du Peuple*, the punishment of all traitors and counter-revolutionaries. The Assembly yielded to the popular demand by arresting priests, aristocrats and other suspects. Soon the prisons of the capital were overcrowded, and rumours asserted that their inmates were plotting to break out and seize the city.

Such was the situation responsible for the 'September Massacres', which lasted sporadically from the 2nd to the 7th of the month and seem to have taken place without systematic preparation or organization. Mobs broke into the prisons of Paris and set up improvised tribunals, which sentenced the prisoners and handed them over to be murdered by groups of killers. Similar incidents occurred in the provinces. The impotence of the authorities ensured the continuance of the massacres until the popular frenzy had run its course. The most recent estimates suggest that about 1,200 people were killed in Paris, which was just under half of the total prison population of the city. Only a little more than a quarter of those who died had been imprisoned on political charges; the rest were common criminals, debtors and prostitutes. The popular fury, aroused by the tensions of the times, quickly forgot its original motives for slaughter.

The Convention (1792–5)

Meanwhile, the elections to the Convention had been proceeding. Though these were technically free, the Jacobin clubs succeeded in depriving most Feuillants and other conservatives of the vote. The Convention assembled on 20th September. Of its 750 members, a third had formerly sat in either the Constituent Assembly or the Legislative Assembly. The Girondins were now the largest party. The Jacobin deputies from Paris formed a group known as the Mountain because it took seats high up at the back of the hall. The majority of the deputies were called the Plain; they did not belong to either faction, though they usually supported the Girondins, whose names were familiar, rather than the Parisian extremists most of whom were unknown outside the city.

The very day when the Convention first met was also that on which the fortune of war suddenly changed. At Valmy in the Argonne, French artillery halted the Prussian advance. As the weather was bad and dysentery had broken out among his troops, Brunswick withdrew to the frontier. The French armies at once took the offensive. Within a few weeks that autumn they occupied the Austrian Netherlands, conquered at the Battle of Jemappes, and proceeded to cross the Rhine, while other French forces advanced into Italy. These victories induced the Girondins to proclaim the War a revolutionary struggle waged to liberate the people of every state from their tyrannical rulers. The Convention issued in November the Edict of Fraternity, declaring, '*La France accordera fraternité et secours à tous les peuples*', and ordered the abolition of tithes and feudal rights and the establishment of elective administrations in occupied territories.

Unfortunately these military successes and acts of defiance towards the powers of Europe occurred at the same time as the contest between the parties in the Convention was endangering national unity. The differences between the Jacobins and the Girondins largely resulted from a twofold rivalry which became intertwined in a struggle for power – the rivalry for political importance between Paris and the provinces and the personal rivalry of the political leaders. To the authority gained by Danton and Marat in the Mountain was now added the increasing influence of Maximilien Robespierre (1758–94), a provincial lawyer whose election to the States-General in 1789 had first brought him into politics. There he had soon revealed himself in his many speeches as a fanatical and unswerving follower of the ideas of Rousseau, whose *Contrat Social* lay always on his desk. This resolute radicalism, together with his honesty in financial matters, gradually made him important in the Jacobin Club, where he was soon known as the 'Incorruptible' (the additional epithet 'sea-green' seems merely to have been an invention of Thomas Carlyle). His outlook was limited and his intelligence small, but his invariably neat appearance, his solemn air and high-sounding phrases and his persistent championship of middle-class rights gained him the support of the bourgeoisie. He had proposed the motion disqualifying members of the Constituent Assembly from sitting in the Legislative Assembly. Though the result was that he himself was excluded from this body, he managed to keep before the public eye and was chosen to represent a Parisian constituency in the Convention. Here he rapidly gained a prominent place in the Mountain.

The Convention abolished the monarchy and henceforward dated its decrees from the first year of the Republic; but this was its only measure which met with general acceptance. The two factions engaged in a dispute over what was to be done with the royal family. The Jacobins agreed upon their policy from the start. To them Louis was a traitor because he had intrigued with foreign powers against France and should be brought to trial and punished. The Girondins, never a well-disciplined group, were badly divided. Most of them favoured moderation since they believed that most Frenchmen were still royalists. They wanted a direct vote by the people on the issue, but Robespierre opposed this vigorously. After long debates, Louis was brought to trial before the Convention and condemned to death by a small majority. He was executed on 21st January 1793 by the guillotine, the instrument named after the physician who had secured its adoption the previous spring as a painless means of decapitation.

The execution of the King was a triumph for the Jacobins. The Girondins might have regained their influence if the War had continued to go well for France, but the declaration of hostilities by Britain and Spain was followed by French reverses in the Netherlands and elsewhere in the early months of 1793.[1] The Convention ordered the levying of 300,000 men for the army; this provoked a rising by the peasants of the department of La Vendée, which was not finally to be subdued until 1796. And in April, the commander of the French forces, Charles François Dumouriez (1739–1823), who was a Girondin and constitutional monarchist, deserted to the Austrians. These disastrous events brought unpopularity upon the Girondins, which their opponents exploited, accusing them of feebleness and incapacity and demanding more energetic measures against the enemies of the Revolution.

The Girondins had to agree to such a course. In March the Convention set up a Revolutionary Tribunal for the summary trial of traitors. This was followed in April by the Committee of Public Safety of nine members, which was accountable only to the Convention and able even to override ministers; it was assisted by representatives on mission, who were sent into the provinces with full powers to enforce the orders of the government and proceed against suspected traitors. These measures were not, however, to save the Girondins. The Convention showed its mistrust of them

[1] P. 338.

by appointing Danton and other Jacobins to the Committee of Public Safety. Now the Jacobins were ready to strike at them. At the end of May, a huge crowd, composed partly of the organized National Guard, broke into the Convention and compelled it to send a number of Girondin deputies to prison whence they were sent by the Revolutionary Tribunal to the guillotine.

For the Jacobins, once they had overthrown the Girondins, proceeded to use the new 'revolutionary government' against their opponents. The Girondins and their leaders were immediately executed. This brought France to the verge of civil war. The Vendéan revolt was still uncrushed. Now Lyons rose, and Toulon received a British fleet. Both these ports were to be subdued by the end of the year, but their rebellion strengthened the hands of the extremists. So too did the murder of Marat – as he sat in a bath to obtain relief from a skin-disease contracted while hiding in the sewers of Paris from his opponents in the early days of the revolution – by the Girondin zealot, Charlotte Corday. The triumph of the extremists was shown by the ejection from the Committee of Public Safety of Danton, who had hitherto dominated it, on 10th July, the same day on which Robespierre became a member of it.

Mindful that the Convention had been elected to produce a new constitution, the Jacobins, as soon as they seized power, drew up an extremely democratic constitution, which included universal manhood suffrage and plebiscites on important questions, but since it was to be suspended for the duration of the War, it was deposited in a cedar box in the Convention and soon forgotten. Authority resided in the Committee of Public Safety, which controlled the Convention. In the course of three years, the Convention sanctioned 11,250 decrees without giving any one of them more than a first reading. Throughout the country the Committee used the local Jacobin clubs to administer its policy and sent down representatives on mission to enforce compliance with its decisions. This was the way the '*levée en masse*' and other military measures, which secured the salvation of the Republic, were so successfully applied under the direction of a member of the Committee, Lazare Carnot (1753–1823).[1]

The military situation was partly responsible for the organization of the Terror by the Jacobins from the autumn of 1793 to the summer of 1794. The grave dangers of the time enabled them to

[1] P. 338.

act on the principle that treachery must be destroyed ruthlessly. *'Le ressort du gouvernement populaire dans la paix est dans la vertu,'* said Robespierre, who rapidly acquired power in the Committee of Public Safety; *'en révolution, il est à la fois dans la vertu et la terreur.'*

The Terror was made possible by the passing of the Law of Suspects in September 1793, which allowed arrest and imprisonment without any proof of guilt. All over France men and women were thrown into prison, usually to face summary trial and execution. The victims were priests, noblemen, ladies of high birth and also republican opponents of the men in power and unsuccessful revolutionary generals. In fact, of those guillotined 85 per cent belonged to the third estate, some 6·5 per cent to the clergy and 8·5 per cent to the nobility. Among them were Marie Antoinette, Madame Roland and the Duc d'Orléans (who had supported the Revolution). The great majority of executions occurred in those western, southern and eastern frontier districts most directly affected by war and civil war. In Paris the Revolutionary Tribunal controlled the Terror with more moderation than in some places in the provinces, where the representatives on mission committed such excesses as the butchering of over 4,000 in four months at Nantes, some by drowning through the deliberate sinking of a boat, and the mass shooting by volleys of gunfire of 2,000 at Lyons. During the months of the Terror, 16,594 people are known to have been executed, 2,639 in Paris; and Donald Greer in a recent statistical survey has concluded: 'It is probable that between 35,000 and 40,000 persons, including those who succumbed in the prisons and those killed without any form of trial, lost their lives.'

The victory of the Jacobins brought into power those in the Convention who wished to proceed with further reforms in the Republic, though the events of the Terror frustrated much of their efforts. Plans were prepared for a system of education, and a start was made on the modernization and codification of the laws, which was to be completed by Napoleon as First Consul.[1] Their most durable achievement was the creation of the metric system of weight and measures, which was to secure adoption by most other countries.

A small group of fanatics also seized the opportunity to promote a campaign of *déchristianisation*. They succeeded in persuading

[1] Pp. 351–2.

the Convention to introduce a new republican calendar, which fixed 22nd September 1792 as its beginning and had months named after the appropriate weather or crops and a ten-day week. This, however, was widely ignored by the French people, and its use was mainly restricted to official announcements and legal documents; it was abolished in 1804, shortly after the establishment of the Empire. Throughout the country many local authorities closed churches, and a new 'cult of Reason' was proclaimed. In Paris, where the Commune was strongly anti-clerical, Notre Dame was converted into a Temple of Reason in which a festival of liberty, personified by an appropriately-clad actress enthroned in the choir, was celebrated; and all the churches in the city were closed.

Robespierre and his supporters were alarmed by this dechristianization, which seemed likely to alienate popular opinion in France. Nor did they like to see the Commune of Paris so powerful. The economic situation, however, seemed to be favouring these *enragés*, as they were commonly called. The outbreak of war had produced a rapid depreciation in the value of the *assignat*, which by July 1793 had lost 77 per cent of its face value. The *enragés*, ready like other political factions to exploit the economic distress of the Parisians, demanded that action should be taken against speculators whom they accused of raising the cost of living. The Committee of Public Safety had to answer the challenge. It introduced measures against hoarding, requisitioned certain foodstuffs and passed the two laws of the Maximum – that of May 1793 imposing a limit on the price of grain and that of September 1793 extending price-control to nearly all articles of prime necessity, including labour. These measures were successful. The value of the *assignat* rose to 50 per cent of its face value by the end of 1793. This strengthened the prestige of the Committee, as did also the military successes gained against both the revolts within France and the allied attacks on her frontiers during the later months of the year.

By March 1794 Robespierre felt strong enough to deal with the *enragés*. They were arrested, tried by the Revolutionary Tribunal and guillotined; Robespierrists were appointed to their places in the Commune. Next Robespierre struck at the other group challenging his power – the Dantonists, more dangerous to him than the *enragés*, who had never gained support outside Paris. Around Danton and Desmoulins had gathered many opponents of Jacobin rule.   These included friends and relatives of victims of the Terror, dismissed officials and speculators and profiteers.   They urged the ending of the Terror and the opening of peace negotiations with the allies.   At the end of March, Danton, Desmoulins and others were arrested, charged with complicity in a 'foreign plot' and executed within a few days.

The elimination of the Dantonists was followed by four months of dictatorship by Robespierre and the Committee of Public Safety.   Elaborate pageants were organized in an effort to build up popular support for the government, the most spectacular being the Fête of the Supreme Being, which expressed Robespierre's theistic ideas of religion.   At the same time, the Terror was strengthened by the passing in June of the Law of Prairial, so called from the revolutionary name for this month.   This deprived the Revolutionary Tribunal of the need to hear witnesses and permitted no verdict except acquittal or death.   The next fifty days produced nearly half the total number of executions in Paris during the Terror.

Robespierre's days of power, however, were nearly ended.   If its political and economic measures had saved the country from military defeat, the victories of the French armies threatened the Terror's continued existence.   As the danger of invasion receded, the bourgeois deputies of the Plain in the Convention increasingly desired its end and a relaxation of the Maximum of prices, while the *sans-culottes*, the small property-owners and wage-earners, had been estranged from Robespierre by their resentment at the Maximum of wages.   In addition, the unity of the Committee of Public Safety was undermined; the Law of Prairial alarmed a faction, who feared it might be used against them.   The Convention supported them against Robespierre, from whom the Parisians and the National Guard had now also been estranged by weariness of war and terrorism.   On 28th July (10th Thermidor) Robespierre was arrested, though not before his lower jaw was broken by a pistol shot; and the next day he was guillotined, to be followed by nearly ninety of his supporters in the Paris Commune.   A group of Parisian workpeople is said to have greeted the news with the cry, *'Et voilà le Maximum dans le panier!'*, and immediately asked for a $33\frac{1}{3}$ per cent increase in their wages.

The fall of Robespierre also marked the end of the Terror. To gain popularity, the new bourgeois rulers, once they had eliminated him and his supporters, destroyed the 'revolutionary government' – the Committee of Public Safety, the Revolutionary Tribunal, the Jacobin Club and the Law of Prairial. They also immediately released some 80,000 prisoners and soon cancelled all arrests made before Robespierre's fall. Moreover, the course of the Revolution was changed. The Convention abandoned the idea of a democratic republic in favour of one for the property-owners. In 1795 it drew up another new constitution in which the electorate was restricted to tax-payers and power was divided between an Assembly of two houses and a Directory of five men.[1] With the Directory there emerged a new ruling class of purchasers of national property, war-contractors, profiteers, speculators and politicians. This class was soon to accept the virtual destruction of the Republic by the dictatorial Consulate.[2] Its members did so because the social and economic victories of the Revolution were in this way preserved for those who had benefited most from it – themselves.

The Aftermath

The French Revolution witnessed to the power of the ideas of the Enlightenment of the eighteenth century. This witness was admirable as well as deplorable. Despite the political excitement and bitterness in the last years of the *ancien régime* which preceded the outbreak of the Revolution, it was not a blind uprising. The bourgeoisie of the third estate made use of the discontents of the lower urban and rural classes to defeat the privileged orders and divert the Revolution to its own ends. Both classes were opposed to privilege, and the revolutionary leaders in the Constituent Assembly sought to replace the rottenness and absurdity of the *ancien régime* by a better social order. Their reforms were lasting, and they represented the social and intellectual developments of the century. After the storming of the Bastille, the Revolution was remarkably peaceable and orderly; and it might have continued so but for the intrigues of the *émigrés* and the constant danger of foreign invasion, which was a major cause of the Terror.

The Revolution had its excesses. It also had its ironic aftermath. To Europe it brought general war and the conquests of Napoleon and inaugurated a period of nationalism, conscription and unrestricted hostilities in international relations. To France

[1] P. 347.   [2] P. 349.

it brought a legacy of national disunity and religious dispute which was to be long-lasting in its effects. Nevertheless, many of the achievements of the Revolution remained. Aristocracy and Church never regained their feudal privileges. The common people retained substantial political rights and religious freedom. The administration was conducted efficiently, and justice was open to all. The peasantry were much better off than before, and taxation was levied fairly. Still more, besides these benefits it brought to France, the French Revolution remained the inspiration of popular causes all over the world. A new ideal in politics was set by the phrase which it inherited from the radicals of the century – *Liberté, Egalité, Fraternité*. And Lord Acton described the Declaration of the Rights of Man as 'the triumphant proclamation of the doctrine that human obligations are not all assignable to interest or to force. This single page of print is stronger than all the armies of Napoleon.'

XVIII · THE REVOLUTIONARY WAR

The Coming of War (1792)

THE outbreak of the French Revolution did not seem likely to the governments of the European powers to produce a general war. On the contrary, it seemed likely that France would long be incapacitated by her internal dissensions and afterwards might be less aggressive than under the *ancien régime*.   Early in 1790 the British Prime Minister, William Pitt the Younger (1759–1806), said in the House of Commons, 'The present convulsions in France must sooner or later terminate in general harmony and regular order, and though the fortunate arrangements of such a situation may make her more formidable, they may also render her less obnoxious as a neighbour.'   Events at first did, indeed, suggest French incapacity in foreign affairs.   In 1789 when Spain became involved in a dispute with Britain through her seizure of British ships in Nootka Sound off Vancouver Island, she had to yield because the Family Compact no longer brought her French support.   Similarly, Turkey at war with Russia was deprived of assistance from her traditional French ally and had to make peace.   France's influence in Europe seemed to have disappeared.

Such a situation was very acceptable to the rulers of the other powers.   They did not yet consider that the effects of the French Revolution would be dangerous to themselves.   Towards the end of 1791, Kaunitz drew up some official 'reflections on the pretended dangers of contagion with which the new French constitution menaces other sovereign states of Europe'.   The idea of preventive action against revolution, such as the member-states of the Holy Alliance undertook after 1815, was not contemplated.   As Albert Sorel observed: 'The old Europe was incapable of it, and the French Revolution was necessary to give it such a notion.' The Declaration of Pillnitz, which Marie Antoinette's brother, the Emperor Leopold II, persuaded Frederick William II of Prussia to join with him in issuing in August 1791, was meant to be only a diplomatic gesture.[1]

[1] P. 321.

It was a move, however, which alarmed the French revolution-aries; and there were other factors which tended to lead France towards war. In 1791 the *émigré* princes and nobles formed an army in the Rhenish provinces of the Empire with its head-quarters at Coblenz. They were in active contact with the French court, while *émigré* agents toured France persuading noblemen to join their exiled relatives in the forces of liberation. Neither Austria nor Prussia intended to support them, but many in France believed that they would, and this belief strengthened the Girondins, who increasingly favoured war, while, at the same time, the royalists were now convinced that war alone would save the French monarchy.

Accordingly, the new Legislative Assembly in January 1792 decreed that the Emperor Leopold should be called upon to state whether or not he would agree to renounce every treaty directed against the sovereignty, independence and security of the French nation, and soon afterwards it ordered the sequestration of all *émigré* property. This was a challenge both to Europe and the *émigrés*. Catherine of Russia was anxious that Austria and Prussia should go to war with France – 'I cudgel my brains to embroil the courts of Vienna and Berlin in the affairs of France that I may have elbow room' – to assist her conquest of Polish territory. Leopold, however, still did not want war; he con-tented himself with making an alliance with Prussia in February. On 1st March, however, he died and was succeeded by his son, Francis II, who was less intelligent and more susceptible to domestic and foreign warlike pressure. When he rejected the French ultimatum, the Legislative Assembly declared war on 20th April, and Frederick William of Prussia the following July supported his Austrian ally.

Apart from these immediate causes which brought about the beginning of hostilities, there were also deeper reasons which would probably have made the outbreak of the Revolutionary War inevitable sooner or later. A novel society was coming into being in France which could hardly exist peacefully with the older society still persisting on the rest of the Continent. The new French rulers had overthrown the traditional institutions of royal absolutism, aristocratic feudalism and agrarian serfdom and new ideas of popular government and personal liberty and equality were already spreading and threatening to undermine the authority of neighbouring sovereigns. Such revolutionary principles were incompatible with the old-established order and too powerful to be ignored by nearby absolute monarchies.

The inexorable, ideological nature of the War was made clear in the manifesto issued by the Duke of Brunswick in July 1792 and the revolutionary manifesto put forward by the Convention the following November.[1]   The War itself was slow in opening. If the French army was disorganized and ill-equipped, the allies were restrained by suspicion of Russian policy in eastern Europe. Not until July did the Austrians invade France from the north-east and besiege Lille, while the Prussians advanced into Lorraine and captured the fortresses of Longwy and Verdun.

There followed in September the massacres in Paris and the French stand at Valmy against the Prussians, who abandoned their conquests and withdrew over the frontier.[2]   A French army followed them, captured Mainz and Worms and for a long time occupied Frankfort.   Before the end of the year, Dumouriez had relieved Lille and invaded the Austrian Netherlands, where the people had not long before revolted against the Emperor Joseph II.   The defeat of the Austrians at Jemappes enabled Brussels to be captured and the country overrun.   At the same time, another French army took Savoy and Nice from Piedmont which by now was also at war with the Republic.   The French successes were, however, to be the prelude to the rapid spread of the War to the greater part of Europe.

The Entry of Britain into the War (1793)

The opening stages of the French Revolution had been generally welcomed in Britain.   Her political struggles of the seventeenth century, her unique system of parliamentary monarchy and her early industrial development made her particularly sympathetic to the revolutionary ideas.   It was to be expected that active radical leaders, such as Tom Paine, Horne Tooke and Thomas Hardy, should acclaim the Revolution as the greatest blow struck for liberty since American independence. Societies which had just been established to celebrate the centenary of the Glorious Revolution of 1688 now welcomed the developments in France.   The Society for Constitutional Information, suspended since 1784, was revived in 1791, while the Corresponding Society, for the encouragement of constitutional discussion, was formed early in 1792.   So the movement for

---

[1] Pp. 323, 325.   [2] P. 324.

parliamentary reform received encouragement, and the Dissenters, whose ministers included many able men, naturally took the occasion to urge the abolition of all legal disabilities in public life.

Still more, Charles James Fox (1749–1806), the fiery leader of the large and influential Whig party, defended the Revolution in Parliament.   When he wrote of the taking of the Bastille, 'How much the greatest event that has ever happened in the world! and how much the best!', the majority of his party agreed with him.   Most Englishmen also felt something of his enthusiasm. France had been symbolized by 'wooden shoes and black bread', emblems of tyranny and poverty, but now events were occurring which might mean a new age for all.   Young William Words-worth acclaimed,

> France standing on the top of golden hours
> And human nature seeming born again.

These events had the opposite effect, however, upon another prominent Whig, Edmund Burke (1729–97), who published in 1790 his famous *Reflections on the French Revolution*.   Though he had demanded a wide liberty for the American colonies, Burke no more believed in the 'rights of man' than in the rights of kings and considered that any assertion of such rights savoured of atheism.   He mistrusted the enthronement of 'Reason' as the sovereign power and predicted that the resort to extremism and force would produce anarchy, tyranny and war – 'Good order is the foundation of all good things.'   Although published at five shillings, no fewer than seven thousand copies of the book were sold in six days.   George III was delighted and told everyone, 'Read it; it will do you good; it is a book which every gentleman ought to read.'   It had a rapid and marked effect.

Moreover, as the Revolution became more clearly republican and violent, public opinion became alarmed and increasingly accepted Burke's view of it.   Many of the Whigs deserted Fox's leadership, and the party was split.   The threat of disorder spread to England when in 1791 the mob at Birmingham attacked a reform banquet, wrecked Dissenting chapels and sacked the house of Joseph Priestley, the radical philosopher. Memories of the terrorizing of London by the Gordon rioters were revived.   The words, 'No King! Liberty! Equality!', were chalked on the walls in towns.   A government proclamation in

May 1792 urged magistrates to control rigorously riotous meetings or seditious publications.

Pitt took no part in the mounting controversy. He still believed that the French Revolution was not likely to involve Britain in war. As late as February 1792 he repealed taxes, reduced the naval estimates and said, 'Unquestionably there never was a time in the history of this country when from the situation of Europe we might more reasonably expect fifteen years of peace than at the present moment.' Hardly had he spoken than the situation changed. France declared war on Austria and Prussia and invaded the Austrian Netherlands. Pitt held that this did not call for British action, since the integrity of the Habsburg dominions was no longer an object of British diplomacy, but it caused widespread public uneasiness. The deposition of Louis XVI and the September massacres disillusioned many supporters of the Revolution. Opinion was fast hardening against France, though Pitt still wished to avoid war.

In November 1792, however, two actions by the French government made the situation worse. The first was the publication of the Edict of Fraternity, which was clearly an incitement to the discontented in England and elsewhere and, therefore, a challenge to the government. The second was the opening of the Scheldt estuary to the shipping of all nations on the grounds of natural rights, despite the provisions of the Treaty of Westphalia of 1648, which had assured the exclusive navigation of the river to the Dutch. Britain was the principal guarantor of the closing of the Scheldt and also Holland's ally. France now seemed to be preparing to invade Dutch territory, and Pitt let it be known that Britain would regard this as a hostile act. War was quickly accepted as inevitable in Britain. When news arrived of Louis XVI's execution, the French envoy was dismissed. France took the final step on 1st February 1793 by declaring war on Britain and Holland.

The First Coalition (1793–7)

Though events were soon to show that this was a war in which Britain fought for survival, Pitt entered upon it with very limited aims. 'It will be a short war,' he said, 'and certainly ended in one to two campaigns.' Like his father before him, he believed that Britain's true interest lay outside Europe; he envisaged a policy that would concentrate upon capturing French possessions overseas, while on the Continent allies would be sustained to enable Austria to recover the Netherlands, which both belonged to her and were a vital area of British concern.   French threats of aggression brought Spain into the War almost immediately after Britain, and so by the end of August 1793 Pitt had formed the First Coalition of fifteen states, the most important being Britain, Austria, Prussia, Holland and Piedmont.

Meanwhile, Dumouriez had unwillingly obeyed an order from Paris to advance into Holland, but had to retreat to protect his flank from the Austrians, who defeated him in the Battle of Neerwinden; soon afterwards he went over to the enemy.   The French threat to Holland had induced Pitt to send a British expeditionary force there under the Duke of York.   This now joined the Austrians in the Netherlands, drove the French back, invaded France and invested Dunkirk.   The Spaniards invaded Roussillon, in the south-west, and in the east the Prussians recaptured Mainz and invaded Alsace.   There were risings in La Vendée and Lyons, and a British fleet occupied Toulon.[1]

Defeat, however, stimulated the Terror in France and led her to adopt measures which both saved her from defeat and revolutionized contemporary warfare.   The *levée en masse,* ordered by the Committee of Public Safety in August 1793, on the advice of Carnot, the 'organizer of victory', introduced the principle of universal conscription for military service.   At first only bachelors and childless widowers between the ages of eighteen and twenty-five were called up.   The men were organized and equipped by Carnot into a force of about half-a-million, which changed the manner of war as fought by the older professional armies.[2]   The system, when permanent and developed, made possible first the victories of the French armies and then the military dictatorship of Napoleon.

Against the new unity, efficiency and military strength acquired by France, the allies suffered from the disadvantage of fighting on external lines.   Moreover, they were far from being a harmonious alliance; they had neither a common plan nor agreement in aims and interests.   The Second Partition of Poland in 1793, in which Prussia participated and Austria did not, produced crippling jealousies and tensions between these two powers. British naval supremacy had enabled the French coasts to be blockaded, but Pitt in his inexperience used sea-power to send in

1793 the best regiments of the British army on an expedition to the French West Indies, where they captured some islands of no great consequence and in a few years lost nearly 100,000 men by disease. As George III himself warned his ministers, 'The misfortune of our situation is that we have too many objects to attend to, and our forces consequently must be too weak at each place.'

Under these circumstances, the allied armies on the Continent suffered a series of disasters and reverses. In the autumn of 1793 the French relieved Dunkirk, checked the Vendéan revolt, forced the British to leave Toulon and forced the Austrians and Prussians back. The next year they drove the Spanish back across the Pyrenees and invaded Catalonia. Soon afterwards they overran the Austrian Netherlands and in the winter advanced into Holland, defeating her on land and capturing her fleet by a cavalry charge over the ice. The Dutch government had to sign a peace treaty which put its military forces at the disposal of France, and when the Stadtholder refused to agree to these terms, Holland was organized into the Batavian Republic, which was practically annexed to France.

Prussia was the next power to leave the Coalition, not as the result of defeat, but because Frederick William had lost all interest in the western war and was determined to gain territory in the final partition of Poland. In April 1795 France and Prussia signed the Treaty of Basel by which France was to remain in occupation of the left bank of the Rhine and in secret clauses undertook to compensate Prussia for the loss of this territory at the expense of other German states. Later in the year, Spain also withdrew from the Coalition, surrendering the island of San Domingo to France, and the next year made an alliance with the Republic.

Britain's part in the fighting had so far been uninspiring. The first important naval action of the War, the Glorious First of June, had been fought in 1794, and though the French grain convoy got through, the battle was decisive for it established a long-unchallenged British naval control of the Channel.[1] The use made of this in the next year was, however, disastrous. A force, consisting largely of French royalist refugees, was landed from British ships in Quiberon Bay in Brittany, only to be defeated and massacred by a revolutionary army. All hope of a successful insurrection in western France against the Republic was

[1] P. 147.

destroyed. The collapse of Holland enabled the British navy to
seize the Cape of Good Hope, Ceylon and other valuable Dutch
colonies, but it also drove the British army from the Continent.
In 1795 the Duke of York's expeditionary force came home from
a German port. Of the members of the First Coalition, only
Britain, Austria and Piedmont remained at war with France.

The Directory decided in 1796 to attack Austria in both Germany and Italy. Two armies were to cross the Rhine, while a
third was to invade northern Italy under the command of
Napoleon Bonaparte, who had already won attention for himself
at Toulon in 1793 and in the streets of Paris in 1795.[1] The
Italian campaign was the first great undertaking which proved
the worth both of his own genius and of the new French revolutionary forces.[2] The absence of baggage-trains and his reliance
upon the countryside for provisions enabled him to move rapidly
and make surprise attacks after long marches; his artillery-fire
and bayonet-charges demoralized the enemy in battle. His
successful tactics were made possible by his care and his ability to
appoint capable staff officers. In addition, the ideals of the
French Revolution were still strong enough to inspire the men of
his army. 'We were as men marching into the dawn,' said one
of them afterwards of the campaign. Unlike his opponents,
Napoleon could send his troops out as single scouts or in small
parties without fear of desertion. And in Italy many of the
people welcomed the French as liberators and were only gradually
disillusioned by plundering in the countryside and heavy taxation
in the towns.

Napoleon took command in the spring of 1796 of a French
army of about 36,000 men, distributed between Nice and Savona,
and opposing 20,000 Piedmontese and 38,000 Austrians. Four
days after entering Italy, he had defeated the Piedmontese and
forced them to sue for peace at the price of Nice and Savoy; and
within a month he had beaten the Austrians at the Battle of Lodi
and gained Milan, the capital of Lombardy. For some months
the Austrians resisted stubbornly in Mantua, but finally they were
scattered at the Battle of Rivoli early in 1797 and completely lost
their hold of northern Italy. Since the French armies in Germany had meanwhile been unsuccessful, Napoleon now marched
north-eastwards from Italy towards Vienna and forced Austria to
sue for peace.

[1] Pp. 347-8.   [2] P. 138.

The Treaty of Campo Formio was signed in October 1797 between Napoleon and the Austrians. The Emperor recognized the French annexation of the Austrian Netherlands and the west bank of the Rhine and the organization of the conquests in northern Italy into a French-controlled Cisalpine Republic. In return, the Venetian Republic, which the French had occupied, Napoleon assigned to Austria, though not before most of its works of art, including the great bronze horses of St. Mark, had been sent to Paris. Earlier in the year Genoa had become the Ligurian Republic. Napoleon had conducted the Italian campaign on his own initiative, and now he himself made the peace treaty. The First Coalition was destroyed. France dominated the Continent, with her boundary on the Rhine and effective control over the entire Netherlands and northern Italy.

The War against Britain (1797–9)

Only Britain remained in the War. France now had the fleets of Holland and Spain as well as her own. Should all be united, the threat to Britain would be great. There were other perils which made 1797 a critical year for Britain. At home there was a financial crisis, a corn shortage and simmering discontent. An attempted French invasion of Ireland at the end of 1796 had been scattered by storms, but the country remained on the verge of revolt. In India, the ruler of Mysore, Tipu Sahib, had made an alliance with France and threatened the British settlements in the sub-continent. Early in 1797 Sir John Jervis and Nelson routed the Spanish fleet at Cape St. Vincent; but in April and May there were mutinies in the Channel fleet at Spithead and the North Sea fleet at the Nore. Though the rising at Spithead was soon ended when grievances were redressed, the Nore fleet blockaded the Thames for six weeks until the mutiny collapsed, and then it defeated the Dutch fleet at Camperdown. The danger now seemed over, except in Ireland, and when the rebellion at last broke out there in 1798 it was effectively subdued.

Napoleon now realized that the invasion of Britain was unlikely to be a promising enterprise. Instead, he devised an expedition to Egypt (which belonged to Turkey) to cut off the British from India and their other eastern possessions. He sailed from Toulon in May 1798 with 40,000 troops in 400 ships and a number of scientists, antiquarians and officials for the French colony which was to be established in Egypt. At first all went well. He captured Malta from the Knights of St. John, avoided the British fleet in the Mediterranean and in July landed his army safely at Alexandria.   Before the end of the month this army was drawn up to fight the Battle of the Pyramids.   '*Soldats, songez que, du haut de ces pyramides, quarante siècles vous contemplent*', he said dramatically to them.   The Turkish troops, the Mamelukes, were defeated; all Egypt seemed to be about to pass under French control.

By now, however, Nelson and the British fleet had followed him and within a week of his victory in Egypt won the Battle of the Nile, in which the French fleet was destroyed at anchor in Aboukir Bay.   Napoleon's army had been deprived of its communications with France.   He tried to save his position in Egypt by marching north into Syria to meet the Turkish forces which were assembling against him, only to be checked at Acre which Sir Sidney Smith had hurriedly reinforced with a British naval brigade.   Plague broke out among his troops.   He had to retreat to Egypt without capturing the town.   There he defeated another Turkish army, which had been sent to Egypt by sea, but he realized the hopelessness of his position.   In August 1799, he sailed from Alexandria, evaded the watching British fleet and landed in France, leaving his army in Egypt to face eventual surrender to the British and Turks in 1801.   By then Malta, the one French conquest of the campaign, had been taken by the British.

Meanwhile, France had continued to expand in Europe.   In 1798 liberal reformers in both Switzerland and the Papal States appealed for French help.   The result was that France overthrew the Swiss government and replaced it by the Helvetic Republic and similarly attacked Rome, deported Pope Pius VI and set up the Roman Republic.[1]   Early the next year the French conquered Naples, abolished the monarchy and established the Parthenopean Republic.   By the beginning of 1799 France was consequently stronger than ever on the Continent, being enlarged and protected by six dependent republics formed in the Netherlands, Switzerland and Italy.   Nevertheless, Britain was still unsubdued, and the Battle of the Nile was the first great defeat France had undergone.   While Napoleon was still in Egypt, the Continental powers ventured to accept British support to form another alliance against France.

[1] P. 123.

The Second Coalition (1798–1801)

The events of the last years of the 1790's led to the spontaneous formation of the Second Coalition. The half-mad Czar Paul of Russia (1796–1801) shared his mother's desire to prevent the infiltration of French revolutionary ideas into his empire, and Napoleon's threatened dismemberment of the Turkish Empire was clearly inimical to Russian security, while the Emperor Francis II was easily persuaded to resume a conflict which might restore Austria's lost influence in Italy. The result was that at the end of 1798 a Second Coalition was being established with Britain, Russia, Austria and Turkey as its most important members.

The fighting, which began the next year, at first went in favour of the allies. The most complete victory was won by the great Alexander Suvorov (1729–1800), who commanded a Russian army sent to Italy to assist the Austrians against the French. He entered northern Italy, easily overran it and took Milan. The French abandoned Naples and Rome and were defeated by Suvorov at the Battle of Novi, not far from Genoa. The Ligurian Republic alone remained to the French of their conquests in Italy, while elsewhere – on the Rhine and in the Netherlands and Switzerland – they were in difficulties.

The Second Coalition was soon, however, distracted by the same differences which had contributed towards the ruin of its predecessor. Although there was now no longer the Polish question to paralyse joint action by the allies, suspicions and rivalries still told against their co-operation. Suvorov was ordered to move up to Switzerland to join another Russian army before Zurich. After a terrible journey over the Alps, he found that the army he was to join had already been defeated by the French and was forced to retreat into Austria with the loss of 13,000 men and every cannon and waggon in his force. This French victory really sealed the fate of the second Coalition, for Suvorov considered that lack of Austrian co-operation had been partly responsible for his difficulties, and the Czar soon afterwards withdrew from participation in the War.

When Napoleon returned from Egypt to France and established the Consulate in November 1799,[1] the Second Coalition was, therefore, already falling to pieces, and the newly-appointed

---

[1] P. 349.

First Consul proceeded to destroy it completely. He crossed the Alps and in June 1800 defeated the Austrians at the Battle of Marengo in northern Italy, thereby regaining Lombardy and relieving France of the threat of an Austrian invasion. Meanwhile, another French army had advanced through Bavaria, taken Munich and in the following December routed the Austrians at the Battle of Hohenlinden.

Since the road to Vienna once more lay open, Austria could only sue for peace. Napoleon agreed to this early in 1801 in the Treaty of Lunéville, the terms of which were much the same as the previous Treaty of Campo Formio. It recognized French territory on the west bank of the Rhine, ceded Tuscany and Elba to the Cisalpine Republic and confirmed the independence of the Cisalpine, Ligurian, Helvetic and Batavian Republics. The Parthenopean Republic was not reconstituted, but a French army of occupation was settled in the Kingdom of Naples.

The Treaty of Amiens (1802)

The destruction of the Second Coalition meant that Britain was once again alone in continuing to resist France, but the War was soon to come to a close. When he became First Consul, Napoleon had promised France that he would bring her peace. He knew that his countrymen, after nearly ten years of warfare, ardently desired this. He knew also that they expected him to give France a stable and efficient administration. His popularity depended upon this, and he himself needed peace in order to do it successfully. At the same time, he realized that in the last resort his power was based upon the support of the army, which wanted its battles and campaigns to be crowned with conquest and glory and would not be content with peace at any price. From his point of view, therefore, the War must be brought to an end in a manner likely to produce an atmosphere of achievement and contentment in France. The Treaty of Lunéville was a contribution towards this; so also was the concordat with the Papacy which he made the same year.[1]

Napoleon now needed, above all else, a pacification with Britain on as favourable terms as possible. To secure this, he set about isolating her in Europe. By clever flattery he persuaded the Czar Paul to pass from hostility to France into co-operation with his schemes. In blockading France during this war, Britain

[1] Pp. 354-7.

had asserted the same claim to search the vessels of all powers, including neutrals, on the high seas for contraband goods as she had done during the American War of Independence, and aroused the same resentment among a number of nations. In 1800 Russia persuaded Denmark, Sweden and Prussia to join with her in reviving the League of Armed Neutrality of 1780.[1] The threat of expulsion by such a hostile combination from the Baltic, which supplied Britain with corn and important naval stores, might have had serious consequences for her.

This plan was dislocated in 1801 by Nelson's action in crippling the Danish fleet at Copenhagen, and the murder of the Czar Paul by his courtiers; but by now Britain was as ready for peace as France. In February of that year Pitt had resigned office on the issue of Roman Catholic emancipation. His successor, Henry Addington, did not become Prime Minister merely because he opposed concessions to Roman Catholicism. He represented also the growing war-weariness in Britain which made many people feel that Pitt's dogged continuance of the War was mistaken. Though the War had stimulated industrial expansion and naval supremacy fostered overseas trade, Britain was facing economic difficulties at this time. The harvest of 1799 had been very bad; bread was scarce and dear; riots had taken place in several parts of the country. The War seemed to have reached a condition of stalemate. Pitt's system of alliances had collapsed again with the signing of the Treaty of Lunéville, and there seemed no possibility of renewing the onslaught upon the French military domination of the Continent.

Both sides made overtures for peace. The negotiations were difficult and protracted, but public opinion in Britain so strongly desired peace that Napoleon was able to obtain conditions which were favourable to France when the Treaty of Amiens was finally signed in March 1802. Addington called it 'a genuine reconciliation between the two first nations of the world', but Richard Sheridan described it as 'a peace which all men are glad of, but no man can be proud of'.

The most important terms of the Treaty were that Britain was to restore to the French the captured West Indian islands and to the Dutch the Cape of Good Hope, but she kept Trinidad, taken from Spain, and Ceylon, taken from Holland. She also agreed to restore Malta to the Knights of St. John. France was to

[1] P. 83.

withdraw her troops from the Papal States and Naples, while both British and French troops were to leave Egypt, which was to be restored to the Turkish Empire.

Napoleon would not consider any suggestion for a revision of the European settlement made by the Treaty of Lunéville. Britain had to accept French possession of the Netherlands and the west bank of the Rhine as well as the continued existence of the vassal republics in Holland, Switzerland and northern Italy. Napoleon was now free to devote himself to the establishment of his rule in France.

XIX · NAPOLEON'S RULE IN FRANCE

The Rise of Bonaparte

NAPOLEON BONAPARTE was born in Corsica in 1769. Though he was of Italian extraction, in the previous year France had purchased the island from the Republic of Genoa, so he was born a French subject. He was one of a large family, and his feeling for his family remained remarkably strong throughout his career. His father managed to have his claims to noble rank officially recognized, which meant that Napoleon was able to secure a scholarship at the age of ten to a military academy established under Choiseul's reforms.[1] During his military training, he read the writings of the *philosophes,* becoming an enthusiastic disciple of Rousseau, whose ideas he was later to detest. On the outbreak of the French Revolution he was a sub-lieutenant in an artillery regiment, and he welcomed it as an ardent republican, but he was in Paris in 1792 and saw the violent events attending the overthrow of the monarchy, which gave him a lasting dislike of anarchy and mob rule.

The next year Napoleon, now a major, took part in the capture of Toulon from the British, when he showed that he had an eye for key positions and used his batteries to their best advantage. The action which brought him prominence and gave him his supreme chance came in 1795. In that year the Convention drew up the constitution for the Directory.[2] Besides the Directory of five men, there was to be an Assembly of two houses – a Council of Five Hundred to propose legislation and a Council of Ancients to accept or reject it. One-third of each Council was to retire every year, but two-thirds of their first members were to come from the existing Convention. This 'Law of Two-Thirds' was unpopular in Paris, since it meant that the elections could not end the virtual continuance of the Convention's power. The Paris mob gathered to attack the Tuileries, where the Convention was sitting; but the Convention was ready to meet them, and General Bonaparte was in command of the troops and field-guns which were placed to guard the Tuileries. That he fired a 'whiff

---

[1] Pp. 137, 297–8.　　　　[2] P. 331.

of grape-shot' upon the mob seems to have been another of Carlyle's inventions, but the attack was certainly repulsed with casualties. The crowd dispersed, and the Convention was saved. This was the *coup d'état* of Vendémiaire, which brought the political importance of the Paris mob to an end.

From this time Napoleon became a celebrity in the capital. The next year he maried a widow, Josephine de Beauharnais, whose connexions with the rulers of France may have assisted her new husband's unresting ambition for influence and power. At any rate, when the Directory after the Treaty of Basel decided to attack Austria in both Italy and Germany, the command of the army which was sent to invade Italy was given to Napoleon.[1]

When the conclusion of his victorious campaign in Italy brought Napoleon back to Paris, the Directory was facing serious difficulties. In March 1797 the elections, held to return a third of the members of the two Councils, had resulted in a majority for the Constitutional monarchists, who wished to make peace with Britain. The army, however, wanted hostilities to continue, and the three republican Directors decided to appeal to Napoleon for support. Upon his orders the *coup d'état* of Fructidor was carried out in September 1797. The army occupied Paris, the two moderate Directors were dismissed, the recent elections were cancelled, and a number of the members of the defeated party were deported to Guiana or summarily executed by firing-squads. The army had now taken a decisive part in French politics, and Napoleon was rapidly gaining power.

Though Napoleon had saved the Directory, its members mistrusted his ability and ambition and welcomed, therefore, the idea of an Egyptian campaign in the spring of 1798.[2] It seemed to them an excellent means of removing him far from France, but it also brought about a renewal of fighting in Europe, and French defeats which gravely weakened their position in the nation which was already hostile to their power. When Napoleon arrived back in France from Egypt in October 1799, the people were despondent, and the government had almost collapsed. That he had suffered defeat and lost his army seemed to be forgotten. Rather he was received with immense popular enthusiasm as the man who would restore the situation and reconquer Italy.

[1] P. 340. [2] Pp. 341–2.

Napoleon was very ready to make use of these circumstances to enlarge his power in the country. He hoped that his popularity would enable him to persuade the Councils to vote away the constitution and end their own existence. When they refused to do so, Napoleon entered into a conspiracy with one of their number, the Abbé Siéyès, and called in troops to drive out the members who opposed him; an officer, replying to those who said that this was unlawful, said, *'La loi, c'est le sabre!'*. The remaining members elected three Consuls to form a new government. Napoleon was First Consul, and the two other Consuls were his supporters. Such was the *coup d'état* of Brumaire, which replaced the parliamentary republic by a dictatorship. When the new government submitted itself to a plebiscite, it was approved by an enormous majority. It was proclaimed that 3,011,007 had voted for it and only 1,562 against it.

The remaining steps in Napoleon's rise to power followed during the next few years. Plots against his life in Paris, the victories at Marengo and Hohenlinden, the settlements of Lunéville and Amiens, all enabled Napoleon to remove political opponents by deportation and exile and to increase his prestige with the French people. In 1802 he was declared First Consul for life and allowed to choose his own successor. The renewal of war with Britain in 1803 strengthened Napoleon's position still more, and in 1804 he was proclaimed Emperor of the French. Both of these two steps which transformed the Consulate into the Empire were followed by plebiscites, each of which again approved of Napoleon's actions by overwhelmingly large majorities.

The transition was, indeed, performed with surprisingly general acquiescence in France. The republican character of the government had been lost already. Most Frenchmen now wanted stability and order, which Napoleon's rule seemed to promise. Royalists were gratified by the revival of monarchical forms and observances. Jacobins considered the hereditary Empire a guarantee against a restoration of the Bourbons. Roman Catholics were reconciled by the religious sanction provided by the appearance of Pope Pius VII at the imperial coronation.[1] And Napoleon's assurance that he was Emperor *'par la grâce de Dieu et les constitutions de la République'* was accepted by many who wished to believe it either for religious or secular reasons.

[1] P. 356.

Government, Law and Finance

The cessation of continuous hostilities brought about by the Treaty of Amiens in March 1802 provided Napoleon with an opportunity to base his rule upon a reorganization of the government of France.   He had begun this work as soon as he became First Consul late in 1799, but the most important of his measures were inaugurated in the course of these few brief months of peace which only lasted until May 1803 when war broke out again, and they were given their final form under the imperial régime.   It is upon the institutions and reforms introduced by him during this time that the claim that Napoleon was equally great a statesman as a soldier must be based.

A month after the *coup d'état* of Brumaire, the constitution of the Consulate was set up.   Although it provided for government by three Consuls, all power, including military command, was effectively wielded by the First Consul.   Beneath him was established a sham system of representative institutions, which largely survived the transition to the Empire and were designed to mask the fact that, whether as First Consul or Emperor, Napoleon retained control over legislation and administration.   He was in as despotic a position as the old Bourbon monarchs, but was not hindered by the aristocratic and provincial privileges of the *ancien régime* and possessed a modern, efficient administrative machine.   The other two consuls were the Abbé Siéyès and Roger Ducos.

Most important to Napoleon was the Council of State, which consisted of experts appointed by himself to advise him in every matter of government.   It was also the real legislative body, for it drew up laws and administrative regulations and introduced them into the legislative bodies.   These, despite the possession of names derived from republican Rome, were virtually powerless. The Senate, whose members were partly appointed by Napoleon and partly co-opted, elected the members of the Legislative Corps and the Tribunate.   Legislation introduced by the Council of State was discussed by the Tribunate, but finally accepted or rejected by the Legislative Corps.   In the words of H. A. L. Fisher, 'the Tribunate could speak, but not vote; the Legislative Corps could vote, but not speak.'   In fact, they both merely represented a formal procedure for registering Napoleon's decisions, and soon after the creation of the Empire, the process was made speedier by the abolition of the Tribunate.

Napoleon's system of centralized administration also gained a control of local government which enforced its orders throughout France. Difficulties had already appeared in the system of nominating local officials by elected councils in the departments and communes set up by the Constituent Assembly.[1] Napoleon retained the revolutionary divisions of local government, but eliminated the elective principle from the appointment of all local officials. All administrative authority in each department was now to be exercised by a prefect (a name also taken from ancient Rome), while each district was to have a sub-prefect and each commune a mayor. All these officials were appointed by the central government in Paris. Paris itself was divided into twelve districts, each under a mayor, the whole city being under a prefect of police. Just as the revolutionary divisions of local government still exist in France today, so also does the system of government-appointed officials instituted by Napoleon.

Napoleon similarly reorganized the law-courts, abolishing the election of judges in favour of their nomination by the government; but his greatest judicial achievement was the remodelling of the law itself. Under the *ancien régime*, there had been no common law in France, but only a tangle of Frankish and Roman, royal and baronial, ecclesiastical and provincial laws. The events of the Revolution had completely changed property rights and civic rights. The revolutionary Assemblies had set up committees to produce a uniform, written law-code, but none had made much progress towards its accomplishment. In 1800 Napoleon appointed a committee of lawyers to perform the task, ordering them to complete it in five months. The drafts were discussed by the Council of State in eighty-four sessions, Napoleon himself presiding over thirty-six of them. The final result was the Civil Code or *Code Napoléon*, promulgated in 1804, which dealt with such matters as rights and duties, marriage, divorce, parentage and inheritance. Napoleon left most of the work of framing its clauses to the legal experts, which was fortunate, for the few provisions he insisted upon included the subjugation of married women to their husbands and the restoration of paternal authority in the family. Nevertheless, as a whole the *Code Napoléon* enshrined the basic principles of the Revolution –

[1] P. 318.

equality before the law, the principle of religious toleration, the abolition of feudal rights and the equal inheritance of property by all children at death. As such, it was readily accepted by countries which came under French sway, and from them its influence spread through the world, from Central and South Germany, Prussia, Switzerland and Spain to Central and South America. It was followed in France by a Code of Civil Procedure, a Commercial Code and a Criminal Code.

Finance represented another problem inherited by Napoleon from the *ancien régime* and the Revolution. All indirect taxes had been abolished by the Constituent Assembly, although the Directory had re-imposed them on tobacco and playing-cards. Napoleon had the land reassessed for taxation and reintroduced further indirect taxes on salt and wines and cider. He also established a new body of officials, appointed and controlled by the central government, to collect the taxes and transmit them to the treasury. In 1800 he gave France a national bank at last – the Bank of France – which was another Napoleonic institution destined to be of lasting importance in the life of the nation.

Napoleon succeeded in balancing the French budget in 1802 and tried hard to cut down government expenditure and encourage economy in subsequent years. The resumption of war in 1803, however, presented him with great difficulties. In contrast to the British financial system, his government never had sufficient credit to raise large loans, and, in any case, Napoleon suspected such means of obtaining money, thinking that large-scale indebtedness would threaten national bankruptcy. The longer war lasted, the more his financial policy became like that of the *ancien régime*, depending upon expedients and existing from hand to mouth. His most successful device was the special fund under his personal control, known as the Extraordinary Domain, into which were paid the heavy exactions he imposed upon conquered countries and subject states. He was able to finance even his most expensive military campaigns from its resources. Not until 1813 did he raise French taxation sharply, and when he abdicated in 1814 the country's national debt was only sixty million francs. To a great extent, therefore, French finance under Napoleon was geared to continual war.

During the ten years between 1804 and 1814, the reorganization of the government of France was accompanied by the formation of an imperial court in which much of the traditional etiquette

and trappings of monarchy were revived. Its officials and uni-
forms were new, but not their positions and functions. Survivors
of the old Bourbon court, however, found the atmosphere of
Napoleon's court dull and heavy, gloomy rather than dignified.
He himself was never at home in it. He wished the wives of his
generals and officials to attend it, but their society bored him, and
he terrified them by brusque remarks suggesting that they should
really be at home with their children.

To grace his court, Napoleon created a new imperial nobility,
whose members he provided with estates and ranks and with the
old feudal titles of duke, count and baron. In all he created 31
dukes, 452 counts and 1,500 barons. In 1810 he divorced
Josephine and married the Archduchess Marie Louise, daughter
of the Emperor Francis I of Austria and great-niece of Marie
Antoinette, to ally himself with the ancient house of Habsburg;
and, when his son was born in 1811, he created for him the title
of 'King of Rome', so reminiscent of the designation 'King of the
Romans' which the successors of Charlemagne had conferred on
their heirs.

Yet Napoleon wished to make it clear that he had no intention
of reviving the social system of the *ancien régime* which had been
destroyed by the Revolution. The *Code Napoléon* insisted upon
the principle of equality before the law. He invited the *émigré*
nobles to return to France, but they received back neither their
estates nor their financial privileges. He was also to preserve
from molestation the rights of the peasants and confirm them in
the ownership of their lands. Under his rule he insisted that all
Frenchmen had equality of opportunity. '*La carrière ouverte
aux talents*' was the way in which he expressed the ideal. It is
true that the Legion of Honour, which he founded in 1802 to
reward service to the State, was refashioned under the Empire on
the lines of the old feudal orders of chivalry with the traditional
titles of *chevalier, commandeur* and *grand'croix*, but he maintained that these awards were only to be obtained by ability and
merit. '*Tout soldat français porte dans sa giberne la bâton de
maréchal de France*' represented an ideal which he liked to think
applied, not just in the army, but throughout the State under his
rule. He maintained that he was the child of the Revolution,
who had not betrayed it but rather secured its aims for the people.

Such protestations, however, were accompanied by an increasing denial of political freedom in France. From 1804 the

police were efficiently organized by Joseph Fouché, a former terrorist and regicide. A decree of 1810 virtually restored the hated *lettre de cachet* since it established state prisons and permitted the Council of State to arrest and detain suspects without trial. A censorship of the press was set up, and fewer and fewer papers were allowed to appear. When Napoleon became First Consul in 1800, there were seventy-three journals in Paris; he immediately suppressed sixty of them and forbade the establishment of new ones. By 1810 only four remained, and none approached the size or circulation of the official journal, *Le Moniteur*, which was the mouthpiece of Napoleon's policy. Private correspondence was also censored, while numerous secret agents and spies kept Napoleon informed of any conspiracy or opposition, which he did not hesitate to destroy mercilessly if he considered circumstances made such action necessary.

Religion and Education

None of Napoleon's reforms would probably have brought stability and unity within France if he had not realized that an ecclesiastical settlement was a particularly urgent and important matter. The religious issue was, indeed, one of the most serious difficulties bequeathed him by the Revolution. The Civil Constitution of the Clergy of 1790 and the subsequent actions of republican governments had split France into hostile parties and contributed much to the failure of the revolutionary leaders to establish themselves securely in power. Most of the French people, and especially the peasantry of the countryside, remained firmly Roman Catholic. The clergy were now divided into three groups.[1] There were the *constitutionnels,* who had accepted the revolutionary reorganization of the Church and were disowned by the Pope and no longer paid their salaries by the republican government; the *soumissionnaires,* who were in communion with the Pope, but had agreed to take the oath imposed by the government and were, therefore, tolerated; and the *réfractaires*, who refused to have anything to do with the government and were strongly monarchical and so for the most part were in hiding or exile. Persecution, however, had not destroyed religious feeling in the country, but rather revived and strengthened it. Worship had by now been re-established in many cathedrals and churches with popular support throughout the country.

[1] P. 114.

Nevertheless, local piety and zeal could not do everything. There still remained three things which had to be done to settle the religious situation, and these the State alone could accomplish. The divisions between the different groups of the clergy and their supporters had to be healed; relations had to be restored between France and the Papacy; and the finances of the French Church had to be established on a permanent basis.

Napoleon shared the scepticism of the *philosophes* in matters of faith, but he had no sympathy with their violent anti-clericalism. He was prepared to override many of his supporters and use religion, as everything else, to supply him with a means which would assist him in the establishment of his own power. For him religion had a powerful political importance; it was '*un auxiliaire nécessaire au gouvernement*'. The support of the Roman Catholic Church would be very valuable for his newly-established position at the head of the consular régime. It would assist the complete pacification of La Vendée and Normandy, promote the assimilation of the Belgic provinces and other conquered territory where Roman Catholicism was strong and deprive the Bourbons of the support of 'the present leaders of the French clergy, fifty *émigré* bishops in English pay'.

The opportunity to obtain an ecclesiastical settlement came in 1800 with the election of a new pope, Pius VII, a simple and devout monk who had only a slight acquaintance with the world of politics and was not strongly hostile to the Revolution. The result was the signing of the Concordat of 1801 which restored to the French state very much the same powers as it had possessed before the Revolution.[1] Ecclesiastical patronage was to be exercised by Napoleon as it had been by the Bourbon kings previously. This new Concordat, the *mariage de convenance*, as some of its opponents called it, seemed to resolve the religious problem and at the same time produced the consequences desired by Napoleon. All the clergy were reconciled to the Republic, and the schism in the French Church was healed, while papal recognition of Napoleon's rule was conceded, and those who possessed ecclesiastical property had their titles to it validated.

The Pope wished the Concordat to describe Roman Catholicism as the *religion d'état*, but Napoleon would only agree that it should be acknowledged as the predominant religion in France. Moreover, the Concordat was followed by the supplementary

[1] Pp. 16, 107 ff.

Organic Articles by which Napoleon sought to subject the French Church to a new and more stringent Gallicanism.[1] These Articles also brought the Protestant Churches – Calvinist and Lutheran – under the control of the State, which henceforward paid their pastors and controlled their synods. The Jews in France also received from Napoleon both a guarantee of civil and religious liberties and a set of regulations governing their existence and activities.

Napoleon's next demand upon the Pope followed his proclamation as Emperor of the French. He desired him to come to Paris to officiate at the imperial coronation, which would give his new throne an immense prestige at home and abroad, for it would mean that the Papacy, after condemning the Revolution, now recognized him as the successor of the Bourbons and the equal of the Habsburgs. Pius VII was induced to come to Paris in December 1804, despite the combined protests of royalists, recalcitrant bishops in England and the Austrian court; he was ready to believe that his complaisance would serve the cause of religion in France. When Pius arrived in Paris, he was able to insist that Napoleon's civil marriage with Josephine should be completed by a religious ceremony before the coronation; but in Notre Dame, after Napoleon had received papal anointing, he placed the crown upon his head himself. He did not, as is often said, snatch it from the Pope's hands at the last moment; he had insisted beforehand that it should be recognized as part of the ritual of the service.

Pius VII, indeed, found it increasingly difficult to collaborate with Napoleon. He did not understand Napoleon's interpretation of the nature of the relationship established between them by the Concordat. Napoleon regarded it as something more than an agreement between the civil and ecclesiastical authorities on matters of concern to both of them, and he expressed his ideas in grandiose historical terms. 'So far as the Pope is concerned,' he wrote, 'I am Charlemagne.' When the Pope stood in the way of Napoleon's plans to make himself the ruler of all Italy, he threatened to reduce him to the position of Bishop of Rome by 'withdrawing from the Papacy the donation made by his illustrious predecessor, Charlemagne'. In 1809 the Papal States were annexed to the French Empire, and the Pope was arrested and taken away to captivity in France.[2] Now he refused to co-

[1] P. 115.   [2] P. 123.

operate with Napoleon, but with no apparent effect upon the subsequent course of events.

Napoleon's ecclesiastical settlement was not to be as endurable as some of his domestic achievements; it was to come to an end with the Law of Separation of 1905. The Concordat never proved acceptable to extreme sections of opinion. It alienated many devout Roman Catholics as well as the more violent anticlericals, and both of these uncompromising parties were strong enough to jeopardize its success as a final solution to France's religious problems. Unlike the legal codes, which were a successful synthesis, the Concordat had inevitably to be a compromise, and like so many compromises, it failed to satisfy the most active and sincere members of either side. The French religious divisions, older than the Revolution though acerbated by it, were to remain unresolved.

In giving the French Church a recognized position again in the State, Napoleon made no contribution towards the re-establishment of the religious orders, and one reason for this was that he had no intention of allowing the Church to regain the control over education which it had exercised in the days of the *ancien régime*. From the small village school to the college in a cathedral city and ultimately to the university, the education given in the French kingdom had been largely classical and semiclerical. Most of the lower and middle-class revolutionary leaders were taught in these schools and colleges; some had taken minor orders before deciding they would rather be lawyers or journalists. The Revolution had practically destroyed the old system of education. The members of the revolutionary Assemblies had believed strongly in popular education, but done little to implement it. Only in the last days of its existence had the Convention set up a small number of central secondary schools in the main provincial cities.

These new schools did not please Napoleon. They were not sufficiently authoritarian in their discipline or traditional in their curriculum for him. He was afraid that they would make their pupils liberals and ideologists (to use his own description) and not, therefore, suitable citizens for his state. He needed soldiers, administrators, magistrates and technical experts to carry out his policies. As J. M. Thompson has written, 'He did not believe in education for education's sake, but in education for the service of the State.' He wanted also education to be sufficiently military and religious to promote obedience and respect for authority, and to emphasize the old eighteenth-century classical culture in order to counteract the dangerous new liberal ideas of the Revolution.

Napoleon characteristically conceived a scheme for national, government-controlled education at all levels, but it was imperfectly put into practice. Primary education remained very much as it had under the *ancien régime,* being left to the initiative of the bishops and the teaching orders of the French Church; and such schools as were founded were still too few to provide even the most elementary education for more than a small fraction of the population. The country people as a whole remained illiterate and uneducated.

Much more was done for secondary education, which was a matter of the greatest interest both to Napoleon and to the French middle-classes. The revolutionary central schools were replaced by some forty-five *lycées*, boarding-schools for boys from the age of twelve, the majority of whom were destined for commissions in the army. The syllabuses and methods of these schools, which were scarcely to be altered until 1865, represented a return to those of the *ancien régime*; but religion, on Napoleon's instructions, was kept to the 'necessary minimum'. Most of the pupils had *bourses* or scholarships, which were usually granted to the sons of officers and officials. The *lycées* had much of the monastery and the barrack about them. The teaching staff were unmarried, while the boys wore a blue uniform with metal buttons, drilled twice a week, marched from dormitory to chapel and classroom to the beat of a drum and had to obey a set of rules.

In addition to the *lycées*, the Napoleonic government recognized other secondary schools, which the prefects' returns for 1805 put at over a thousand in number. Some of these were supported by the communes, some by the Church and some by private individuals. There were also some schools for girls, and Napoleon had his ideas about the way these should be conducted. 'Religion is an important affair in a public institution for the education of young ladies,' he wrote. 'Let them be brought up to believe and not to reason.' The discipline should aim at making them meek and obedient wives; they should be taught only reading, writing, arithmetic and elementary history and geography and spend most time learning sewing, cooking and nursing to prepare them for married life.

To provide the technical experts needed by the Empire, the

secondary schools led on to schools of law, medicine and pharmacy, the *école militaire spéciale* and the *école normale* established in 1808 to train teachers for the school and colleges. In 1808 also Napoleon established the Imperial University, which was to be a single university for the whole of France with seventeen subordinate provincial institutions under its control. Moreover, the whole educational system was to be directed by the University; every college and secondary school was to submit to its regulations, and only graduates in one of its faculties were to be allowed to teach. The University proved to be a durable institution and with it grew the tradition of strict bureaucratic control from the centre in the French national system of education.

At the same time, the demands of Napoleon's many military and political undertakings made it impossible for him to concentrate sufficiently upon education to achieve his aim. Despite all his efforts to enforce government supervision and uniform standards, most of the secondary education in the country was under private or clerical control. Moreover, many parents preferred to send their sons to schools managed by priests rather than to the state *lycées*. The way was already being prepared for the conflict between secular and clerical education, which was to cause so much dispute and disunity in nineteenth-century France.

Industry, Commerce and Public Works

The years of the Consulate and the Empire were an important period for French industry. The Revolutionary and Napoleonic Wars brought greater benefits to French manufacturers than has often been thought. Hostilities with Britain eliminated their most serious competitors, which was especially welcome to the large proportion of them who were beginning to make the costly and risky change to machine and power production. The advent of Napoleon to power brought them further encouragements. The Treaty of Amiens made it possible for him to initiate an economic policy designed to stimulate French industry very much on the lines of Louis XIV's able minister, Jean-Baptiste Colbert (1619–83). Napoleon's energetic efforts at first achieved considerable success. Technical schools were established, prizes awarded to inventors and industrial fairs and exhibitions arranged. The silk industry of Lyons was expanded through the adoption of the new Jacquard loom. Lavoisier and other French chemists had discovered improved methods of dyeing, tanning and bleaching.

Agents were sent to Britain, who imported new machines with government financial assistance, such as the spinning-jenny for the cotton industry. The pace of development, however, was not rapid. It has been estimated that by 1815 French industry had only reached the approximate level of mechanization attained in Britain in 1780. The domestic system still largely prevailed, and workshops were small.

Like Colbert himself, Napoleon thought of national prosperity as a means towards the attainment of power. His economic measures were, therefore, dictated by political objectives, and this was shown clearly in his commercial policy, in which his most extensive plan was the inauguration of the Continental System, the attempt to exclude British trade from the Continent.[1] This was something more than a method of waging economic warfare against Britain. It sought to gain not only British defeat, but also French economic supremacy, for it was an enormous system of economic protection and preference affecting the other countries of Europe as well as Britain.

Napoleon stated in 1810 that his aim was to promote the export of French goods and the import of foreign bullion. Consequently the economies of Continental countries were co-ordinated and subordinated to that of France. High customs barriers made Italy almost an economic dependency of France in which French manufactured products, especially textiles, captured the market, and French industry received Italian raw materials in return. The already growing industrial area of the Ruhr was compelled to send its goods to France instead of to its established markets in the Netherlands and the Baltic. Holland had to accept French imports without customs duties, but there was no corresponding freedom of entry for Dutch exports to France. While French industrialists were encouraged to introduce machinery, those in other countries were discouraged. The French cotton and sugar-beet industries enjoyed the protection of especially high tariffs. For a time such measures brought considerable economic prosperity to parts of France.

Nevertheless, Napoleon's industrial and commercial policies failed in the long run in France. His regulation of industry had the effect of hindering its development in some aspects, and high tariffs made many commodities expensive for both producers and consumers. Above all, the consequences of war with Britain

[1] Pp. 368–71.

ruined Napoleon's efforts. Before the Revolution, a third of France's imports and a fifth of her exports had depended upon her colonies. British command of the sea destroyed this colonial trade, and the great French ports from Marseilles to Rouen became almost derelict. To make good the deprivation of colonial raw materials, Napoleon promoted desperate efforts to develop effective substitutes, such as chicory for coffee and beet-sugar for cane-sugar, but these met with only a very limited success. He also tried to replace the lost colonial trade by European trade, but here the facts of geography told against him. Heavy goods like lumber could not easily be transported by land instead of sea in those days before the advent of railways, and the Continental rivers did not flow in the right direction to make France the dominant industrial nation of Europe. Despite all Napoleon's efforts, French foreign trade under the Empire never regained the level it had attained during the last years of the *ancien régime*.

Yet the Empire did bring France the permanent benefit of a vast series of public works inaugurated by Napoleon. Canals, bridges and roads, demanded by his commercial policy, provided the country with an improved system of communications. Napoleon wished the Empire to be as renowned for its patronage of the arts as the great age of Louis XIV. So museums were established, while the Louvre was completed and furnished with the invaluable works of art which had been brought from conquered Italy. Napoleon also supported painters and sculptors handsomely so long as they produced work which attracted his favour, such as huge neo-classical historical set-pieces or heroic statues of the Emperor himself; and though his motives and tastes were both questionable, his patronage did assist the artists of the time and gave its name to a style which took its place in the history of art.

Paris particularly felt the influence of Napoleon, for he wished to make the city, as the capital of his Empire, '*non seulement la plus belle ville qui existe, mais la plus belle qui puisse exister*'. Such a high ambition, which necessitated vast projects, inevitably meant the destruction of some fine and historical buildings. Though Napoleon admired old buildings, like Fontainebleau which he restored, he preferred plain, geometrical, classical buildings. He thought that the grandeur of the ancient world would best contribute to the glory of his reign. The edifice he most appreciated was the classical temple, which was adapted to several functions, such as the Church of the Madeleine and the Paris Bourse. He also favoured triumphal arches and columns. He expressed his architectural criterion in the words, '*Ce qui est grand est toujours beau.*' Some of his buildings in Paris do not seem to uphold the accuracy of this belief, but on the other hand, the planning of the great group of long straight roads centred upon the *Arc de Triomphe de l'Etoile* and the clearing of the Tuileries Gardens began the process of transforming it into a great modern city.

Such public works in the French capital may be said to symbolize the contribution of Napoleon to France, which ensured him the support of the people for so long. He brought order, efficiency and prestige, and few Frenchmen found his rule unbearably oppressive, for in the words of Professor Herbert Butterfield, 'Liberty comes to the world from English traditions, not from French theories.' In many ways, therefore, Napoleon's policies seemed to bring the people of France what they most wanted after the injustice and incompetence of the monarchy and the turmoil and excesses of the Revolution. Only from about 1808 onwards did the prolongation of war, the failure of his commercial policy and the increasing likelihood of defeat cause his popularity to decline at home.

XX · THE NAPOLEONIC WAR

The War against Britain (1803–5)

THE Treaty of Amiens had not been made in circumstances likely to produce a permanent peace. Napoleon was not willing to countenance a situation in which Britain enjoyed a superiority in naval strength and colonial empire over France, while Britain considered French military domination of the Continent as incompatible with her own safety. In other words, as long as Britain remained supreme at sea and France supreme in Europe, Napoleon could not obtain the absolute power that he desired, and the British people could not feel secure.

British alarm was increased by the way in which Napoleon continued to extend his power and influence over the Continent in the months following the Treaty of Amiens. The Treaty of Lunéville had recognized the independence of as many as six European republics set up by France, but Napoleon treated them as subordinate states and maintained French garrisons in them. Piedmont was annexed to France. The Cisalpine Republic was made a virtual French possession and renamed the Italian Republic with Napoleon as its President. The Helvetic Republic was remodelled as the Swiss Confederation and allied with France. To compensate German princes who had lost territory by the French annexation of the west bank of the Rhine under the terms of the Treaty of Campo Formio, a reorganization of the map of Germany was undertaken under French direction by which many of the small states and most of the free cities and prince-bishoprics were merged into the territories of the larger states. Finally, French troops were kept in the Batavian Republic and it was believed that Dutch ports might be closed to British commerce.

Though none of these acts, except the retention of a French garrison in Holland, infringed the terms of the Treaty of Amiens, they alarmed Britain. Other matters also worsened relations between the two countries. In pursuance of his economic policy, Napoleon refused to renew the commercial treaty between France and Britain, which had existed before 1793, and imposed a practically prohibitive tariff on British goods. For his part, Napoleon was as sensitive as any dictator to the strictures and cartoons published about him in the English newspapers; he also resented the refusal of the British government to expel the *émigré* Bourbon princes from its soil. The immediate cause of the renewal of war was the refusal of Britain, in view of the international situation, to deprive herself of a valuable Mediterranean base by handing back Malta to the Knights of St. John as she had promised in the Treaty of Amiens.

By May 1802 the two countries were at war with each other again, and France was soon joined by Spain after Britain had seized Spanish treasure ships taking a subsidy to France. The struggle had now assumed a different character. In the Revolutionary War Britain had been allied with the old monarchical absolutisms against a revolutionary nation whose ideals made its troops welcome as liberators to the people of the countries they invaded; but in the Napoleonic War Britain was fighting a despotic empire whose conquests and policies increasingly aroused other nations to revolt in the name of freedom and independence.

Upon the outbreak of war, Napoleon decided to attempt an invasion of England. Between May 1803 and May 1805 he assembled his Grand Army of over 100,000 men in camp at Boulogne. To transport them across the Channel, flat-bottomed barges were gathered from many European ports, but he never obtained as many as three-quarters of the 2,000 he estimated he needed, and extensions to the harbour of Boulogne failed to make it large enough to allow an embarkation of his troops on less than five or six tides. More serious for him was the problem of obtaining naval supremacy in the Channel to enable the invasion to take place. In 1805, therefore, Napoleon planned that the French fleet should escape the British blockade, join up with the Spanish fleet, entice the British fleet to the West Indies and then double back to afford the invasion barges protection across the Channel. The first part of the plan succeeded, but when the combined Franco-Spanish fleet set off back to Europe, Nelson was not deceived and defeated it in the Battle of Trafalgar.[1] Napoleon had already abandoned his invasion scheme and broken up the camp at Boulogne before the battle was fought.

[1] P. 149.

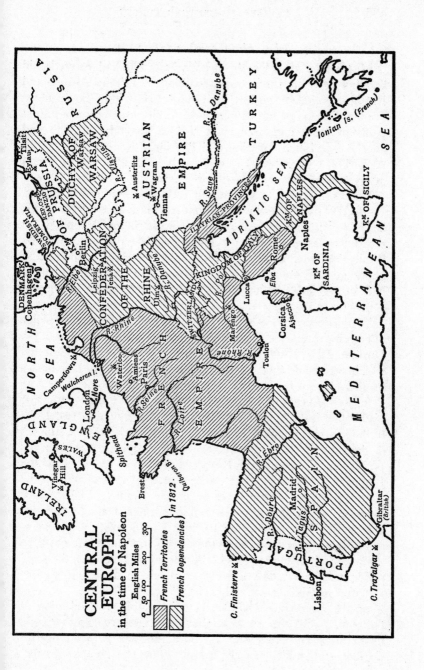

CENTRAL EUROPE
in the time of Napoleon

English Miles
0 50 100 200 300

░░ French Territories } in 1812
▨ French Dependencies }

The Third Coalition (1805–7)

Meanwhile, after lengthy negotiations, Pitt had succeeded in forming early in 1805 a new coalition of Britain, Austria and Russia. Napoleon rushed his Grand Army from Boulogne to Central Europe by forced marches.[1] Before the year was out an Austrian army had been compelled to surrender at Ulm and another combined Austrian and Russian army overwhelmed at Austerlitz. The news was a grievous blow for Pitt, who died soon afterwards at the early age of forty-seven.

Napoleon was now supreme in Italy and southern Germany. By the Treaty of Pressburg in 1805, Austria had to relinquish the last of her Italian possessions – Venetia, Istria and Dalmatia – to the Italian Republic, which Napoleon again renamed, converting it into the Kingdom of Italy with himself as King. Austria also had to give territory to both Bavaria and Württemberg, which she had to recognize as kingdoms, and her possessions in western Germany to Baden.

Napoleon also followed his victories by embarking upon a policy of creating a series of vassal states ruled by members of his family. Ferdinand IV, King of the Two Sicilies, was deprived of Naples, which was made into a separate kingdom, ruled by Napoleon's brother, Joseph Bonaparte. The Emperor's sister, Elise, became Princess of Lucca; his brother, Louis, was made King of Holland; his brother-in-law, Joachim Murat, was appointed Grand Duke of Berg; and his stepson, Eugène de Beauharnais, who was the son of the Empress Josephine by her former marriage, was given the position of Viceroy of the Kingdom of Italy in the name of the Emperor. This attempt to create a new dynastic system on the Continent was doomed, however, to failure. The junior branches of the dynasty were unable to make themselves acceptable to their new countries because Napoleon's policy was to subordinate these countries so thoroughly to French interests as to undo the advantages brought by the introduction of the legal codes and the establishment of a relatively uniform and efficient system of administration and justice.

At the same time, Napoleon continued his reorganization of Germany. His aim was to establish, as a counterpoise to Prussia in the north and Austria in the south and east, a third powerful German state under French control. This was done by the for-

[1] P. 139.

mation in 1806 of the Confederation of the Rhine, which consisted of sixteen states whose territory had been enlarged by the absorption of a number of smaller states. A diet was to meet at Frankfort to discuss matters of common interest, but it never functioned. The Confederation was bound, upon demand, to supply Napoleon with troops, and its armies were trained by French officers. Napoleon assumed the position of Protector of the Confederation, and his administrative and legal reforms were extended to it. As Protector, one of his first actions was to announce the withdrawal of the Confederation from the Holy Roman Empire. Francis II, who had already declared himself hereditary Emperor of Austria in 1804 when Napoleon became Emperor of the French, now renounced his old Imperial title, becoming the Emperor Francis I of Austria, and so after centuries of increasing weakness the thousand-year-old Holy Roman Empire at last came to an end.

The continual growth of French power in Germany alarmed Frederick William III of Prussia, who had come to the throne in 1797 and was well aware of the danger from the revived strength of France, but he was incapable of following a firm, consistent foreign policy. The war-party in Berlin had urged that the formation of the Third Coalition gave Prussia an excellent opportunity to strike at France, but Napoleon secured Prussian neutrality by ceding Hanover (which he had occupied on the renewal of war with Britain) to Frederick William. Yet again France had benefited from the disunity of her opponents.

The formation of the Confederation of the Rhine, however, led Frederick William to accept the Czar Alexander I's promise of Russian help and belatedly declare war on France. Twenty years after the death of Frederick the Great, the Prussian army had become antiquated and inefficient.[1] In October 1806 Napoleon at the Battle of Jena inflicted upon Prussia the most crushing defeat she had ever suffered. Two weeks later the French had occupied Berlin.

The next June Napoleon defeated the Russians so severely at the Battle of Friedland that the Czar decided to seek peace. The two emperors met in a pavilion built on a raft in the middle of the River Niemen, and Alexander accepted from Napoleon the terms of the Treaty of Tilsit, which concerned both Russia and Prussia. Russia had to accept an alliance with France and abandon the

[1] P. 198.

Turkish provinces of Moldavia and Wallachia; but Prussia lost nearly half her territory, and her population was reduced from ten to five millions. She lost almost all her Polish lands, which were formed into the Grand Duchy of Warsaw and given to the King of Saxony, and her provinces on the Rhine were made into another new state for the Bonapartist dynasty – the Kingdom of Westphalia, ruled by Napoleon's younger brother, Jerome. Finally, the Prussian army was restricted to 42,000 men.

The Treaty of Tilsit in 1807 saw Napoleon at the height of his power. He was still to make considerable additions to his conquests, which reached their furthest extent in 1811, when the territory of his empire and its allies covered the whole of the European mainland except the Balkans; but by then his position was being seriously challenged. In 1807 Russia and Austria were the only powers on the Continent not dominated by him, and he had inflicted military defeat on both of them. Only Britain remained at war with him, and he had already embarked upon a plan which he hoped would lead to her collapse.

The Continental System (1806–14)

As in the Revolutionary War, so in the Napoleonic War, British sea-power played a decisive part. After the Battle of Trafalgar in 1805, Britain's control of the seas remained unchallenged. The British navy kept the sea routes of the world open for her trade, blockaded the coasts of France and her subordinate states and made it possible for subsidies to be sent to her allies on the Continent. Above all, it enabled Britain to remain still unconquered and hostile to France. As long as this was so, there could be no permanent future for Napoleon's newly-established European empire. Yet French sea-power was weaker than ever. As Napoleon himself expressed it, 'the elephant could not fight the whale'; he adopted, therefore, a scheme which he hoped would make it possible that 'the sea should be subdued by the land'.

In 1806 he issued from Berlin after the Battle of Jena a series of orders known as the Berlin Decrees, and these were supplemented from Milan the next year by the Milan Decrees. These embodied the Continental system, his plan to defeat Britain by ruining her economically and to establish French prosperity.[1] His belief that British dependence upon commerce made it

[1] P. 360.

possible for her to be brought down in this way was expressed in his scornful words about this nation of shop-keepers – '*L'Angleterre est une nation de boutiquiers*'. British power seemed to be based upon her naval strength and her subsidies to allies, and both these were created from the profits she gained from trade. If, therefore, Britain were cut off from her markets, her financial supremacy would be destroyed and her power brought to an end.

The Berlin and Milan Decrees declared the British Isles to be in a condition of blockade, ordered every European port to be closed to British commerce, forbade France and her allies to trade with Britain, required neutral ships to cease calling at British ports upon pain of confiscation as prizes and ordered the seizure and destruction of all British merchandise upon the Continent. The British government replied to these decrees by Orders in Council issued in 1806 and 1807. These declared a blockade of France and her allies, forbade neutral ships to sail to the Continent and stated that those intercepted on their way would be diverted to British ports. In short, each combatant had now instituted a total blockade of the other, and the resultant commercial struggle lasted for the rest of the War with important consequences for its outcome.

The Continental System failed to have any significant effect upon Britain. The proportion of British exports to the Continent remained consistently high – from 25 to 42 per cent of her exports and from 71 to 83 per cent of re-exports – and her manufacturers were able to develop new markets overseas, especially in the New World. The French naval squadrons and privateers, which occasionally eluded the blockade, sank about 480 British merchant ships a year and ruined many rich shipowners; but nearly eight times that number of neutral vessels were seized by the British navy and added to the mercantile marine. In fact, Britain suffered most through the blockade from a shortage of imports, which included raw materials for industry, such as wool from Spain and Germany or timber from Scandinavia, and also corn from the Baltic ports, the absence of which was particularly felt during the bad harvest of 1812 when the price of wheat rose from 75s. to 130s. a quarter, and there were bread riots; but never was there any danger of the country being starved into surrender. Nor did the Continental System stop Britain from sending subsidies to her allies, though it was thought advisable that in the Peninsula and elsewhere these should consist partly of warlike and other supplies as well as gold. Indeed, during the years of the Continental System the British population continued to grow, and industry generally expanded, while the total revenue of the United Kingdom increased steadily from £103,000,000 in 1805 to £120,000,000 in 1808, £131,000,000 in 1811, and £162,000,000 in 1814, exceeding expenditure in each year but the last. Neither was the British war-effort ever seriously impeded nor the popular will to victory diminished. The difficulties that Britain had to face in this period arose from the Industrial Revolution, the inflationary currency-policy of the government and the existence of a state of war, as well as the Continental System.

Naval supremacy enabled Britain to enforce her blockade more effectively than ever France could do; and when it became known in 1807 that Napoleon was planning to seize the Danish navy, a British fleet was a second time sent to Copenhagen and bombarded the city until the Danes surrendered their warships. Neutral shipping inevitably suffered considerably from British measures, and once again the practice of searching the ships of all nations on the high seas caused resentment, so much so in the United States that in 1812 Congress declared war on Britain. Hostilities lasted until 1814, being inconclusive and hardly noticed in Europe amid the more important events of the retreat from Moscow and the War of Liberation. Though the Americans won some single-ship actions, their coasts were blockaded throughout the war, virtually without opposition.

It was impossible for Napoleon to keep British exports completely out of the Continent. Her Industrial Revolution had made Britain so much the 'workshop of the world' that Europe demanded the cheap manufactured goods which her new machines and factories could turn out in such vast quantities, while she was also the carrier of such important overseas products as cotton, tobacco, sugar and coffee. A huge establishment was erected at Malta as a base for the smuggling of British goods into the Mediterranean countries, and in 1807 Britain acquired Heligoland for the same purpose in the North Sea. Napoleon even relaxed prohibitions at times for the sake of obtaining revenue from customs-duties and also issued licences allowing French merchants to trade with the enemy, so great was the country's need for British manufactures. He himself shaved with a razor of Sheffield steel, and it has been said that 'the Grand Army which the Emperor took to Moscow was clad in greatcoats made at Leeds and in boots made at Northampton'.

The shortage of British manufactured goods and colonial products assisted the development of the backward industry and agriculture of some European countries, notably the Habsburg lands, but since it was designed both to defeat Britain and to ensure French economic supremacy, the French dependencies in Europe, particularly Germany and Italy, suffered from the operation of the Continental System more than France herself. To these countries it brought high prices, severe shortages and even occasional starvation. The contrast between these actualities and the French claim to be the promoters of independence and freedom on the Continent was a bitter experience which aroused growing popular resentment and helped to stimulate nationalist feeling against Napoleon's empire.

The success of the Continental System depended upon its universal application in Europe. Napoleon himself said that his purpose was to close to British shipping every port from the Sound to the Hellespont. This meant that he must try to exercise an increasingly rigid control of the Continental coastline. Between 1808 and 1812 Napoleon intervened in Spain, occupied Rome, compelled Louis Bonaparte to abdicate from the Dutch throne and annexed Holland, incorporated Hamburg and Oldenburg in his empire and invaded Russia; and in all of these actions he was strongly influenced by his desire to make his blockade more effective. In this way the Continental System became closely connected with the existence of his empire and was an important cause of its collapse.

The Peninsular War (1808–13)

The first country in which open and active revolt against Napoleon occurred was Spain. Since 1795, when Spain left the First Coalition, she had been virtually an ally of France, as a result of which she had been forced to pay heavy subsidies and had lost her fleet at Trafalgar. In 1807 Napoleon decided that Spain must close her harbours to British shipping and join in compelling Portugal to do the same. Spain was thus forced into a war with Portugal which gave Napoleon an opportunity to send French troops across the Spanish frontier. Portugal was invaded, but the royal family escaped, under the protection of British warships, to the Portuguese colony of Brazil.

Napoleon, however, doubted whether the Bourbon monarchy, which was beset by quarrels between the incapable King Charles IV and the equally worthless Crown Prince Ferdinand, would be likely to make Spain a satisfactory French ally.   In 1808 accordingly he compelled Charles to abdicate and Ferdinand to surrender all his rights to the Spanish throne to the Emperor of the French.   Joseph Bonaparte was then summoned from Naples and proclaimed King of Spain.

It seemed as if Louis XIV's ambition to make Spain a subordinate state to France was at last to be achieved.   Napoleon expected no resistance from this backward, badly governed and priest-ridden country which he now proposed to bring within the scope of French administrative reform and control.   Spain, however, differed from Germany and Italy.   Unlike them, it was a single kingdom, and though now far gone in decline, it had a great past in which the Spanish people felt a strong national pride. Moreover, the ideas of the French Revolution made no appeal to the conservative and only half-European character of the Spaniards.   Rather Napoleon antagonized the superstitious peasantry and powerful clergy by abolishing the Spanish Inquisition and closing two out of every three monasteries in the country. The Spaniards, therefore, regarded him as the enemy of their religion, the destroyer of their monarchy and the invader of their country.

Even before Joseph reached Madrid, a spontaneous, sporadic rising broke out all over the country, which received immediate British assistance; and so the Peninsular War began.   At first Spanish resistance was led by local groups or *juntas*, but in 1810 popular demand led to the summoning of the Cortes, which proceeded to draw up a new constitution modelled upon the French revolutionary constitution of 1791.   This provided for a single legislative assembly elected by universal manhood suffrage, freedom of the press and universal liberty.   This constitution of 1812 was of little importance for Spain, since the country was not yet liberated, and when Ferdinand was placed on the throne he refused to accept it; but it was to be taken as the embodiment of their demands by liberal movements in several countries of southern Europe during the years after 1815.   Only in granting Roman Catholicism an exclusive position in Spain and not allowing religious toleration did it fall short of the democratic ideals of the nineteenth century.

The Peninsular War presented the French with extreme difficulties which they could not overcome. The barrenness of the rocky central plateau, the location of all the mountain chains across the line of advance from Bayonne to Cadiz, the river system which impeded rather than assisted travel, the bad state and scarcity of the roads, the scattered, impoverished villages, all these circumstances made it impossible for the French armies to fight as they had been accustomed to in Italy, Germany or even Egypt. They could not live on the countryside nor concentrate their forces in overwhelming numbers nor win decisive victories by superior strategy. On the other hand, the nature of the country, the length of French communications, especially in Portugal, and the enforced dispersal of their forces, with the assistance which Britain could give through her naval supremacy, offered ideal conditions for the fighting of a defensive and guerrilla war by the determined, implacable Spaniards.

There were other circumstances which contributed toward the defeat of the French in Spain. Napoleon himself spent only a brief two months in the country during the winter of 1808. For the remaining five years, while his army fought there, his attention was demanded elsewhere by the events which led up to the still more calamitous campaign in Russia. The orders which he sent from Paris or Vienna or Moscow to the generals whom he left in command were often more of a hindrance than a help, especially as they sometimes arrived only when the situation to which they applied had changed completely; and in his absence the generals quarrelled among themselves and treated King Joseph with contemptuous insubordination. Scattered in different parts of the country, the French garrisons found it extremely difficult to maintain their communications. A force of two hundred cavalry might be needed to protect a messenger from attack by villagers. French commanders sometimes only heard of one another's movements from Napoleon in Austria or Poland, and he got his information, as he had done in Egypt, from the English newspapers; but the British found that the parish priests provided a system of espionage, which told them of every French move. It was not surprising, therefore, that the French forces were frequently surprised by bands of the Spanish *juntas* and were unable to contain the successive raids and retreats of the small yet well-disciplined British contingent, which was centrally placed on an almost unapproachable plain and continually supplied from the sea.

When the fighting began in 1808, the French army was dispersed throughout Spain.   In July one force was defeated by the Spaniards at Baylen in Andalusia and in August another by a British expeditionary force which had hastily been sent to Portugal under the command of Sir Arthur Wellesley (afterwards Duke of Wellington).   Joseph and the remaining French troops withdrew north of the Ebro.   Napoleon came from Central Europe with veteran French troops, reoccupied Madrid and then turned upon the British forces, now commanded by Sir John Moore. The British retreated to Corunna and were safely evacuated by sea, though Moore was killed.   Napoleon was now obliged to hurry back to France, aware that he had overcommitted himself, for Moore's campaign had diverted the French from occupying the whole peninsula.   As soon as Napoleon was gone, the British returned to Portugal, and in 1810 Wellington protected Lisbon with the lines of Torres Vedras, an elaborate series of defensive earthworks protected by hundreds of guns.   Behind these, Wellington received men, supplies and equipment and frequently emerged to support the Spanish guerrillas until in 1812 he was able to take the offensive and invade Spain.   That summer he captured Madrid, and a year later he defeated the French at Vittoria and forced them to retreat across the Pyrenees.   Early in 1814 he invaded France.

Napoleon afterwards described the Peninsular War as the 'Spanish ulcer', which had seriously sapped his strength.   Certainly it kept large French forces permanently engaged there. When the rising began, there were 150,000 French troops in the peninsula; Napoleon had over 300,000 during his winter campaign of 1808; by the spring of 1810 the number had further risen to 370,000; during 1812, the critical year of the Russian campaign, there were 290,000; and in 1813 still 224,000.   The fighting was savage and disease frequent.   Perhaps half of the French troops never returned.   The loss to Napoleon was not fatal, but it was expensive, and it meant that in his last years he had to fight on two fronts.

Apart from the French entanglement and the losses it involved, the Peninsular War had other valuable consequences for the allied cause.   It was the first national rising of a people against the French invader.   The surrender of 20,000 French troops at Baylen in 1808 to Spanish irregulars made a vivid impression throughout Europe, and the perpetual failure of the French to crush the rising encouraged resistance to Napoleon elsewhere. Still more, the war provided Britain at last with an opportunity for successful military intervention on the Continent. This time the British forces were not wasted upon unimportant colonial expeditions. Wellington was able to create a first-rate army in the peninsula, gain useful military experience and invade France from the south at the moment she was also facing invasion from the north.

The War against Austria (1809)

Before going himself to Spain with the intention of crushing the revolt, Napoleon in October 1808 invited the Czar Alexander, and commanded the kings and princes of the Confederation of the Rhine, to meet him at Erfurt in Saxony. Outwardly it was to be a display to impress Europe, but it was also to make diplomatic arrangements to ensure that Napoleon would be free to campaign next year in Spain. The parades and receptions, the balls and banquets, were very successful. Alexander, however, refused to give an assurance that he would resist a renewal of Austrian aggression, while the astute Talleyrand, who had long been Napoleon's trusted foreign minister, now sensed the instability of the French Empire and took the opportunity of offering his services to Austria and Russia in any action they might take to oppose the future plans of the Emperor.

Austria had been re-arming since the Battle of Austerlitz and had introduced reforms in her military organization. When it seemed that Napoleon was likely to have to keep a considerable army in Spain for some time, the Emperor Francis I declared war yet again on France. Napoleon, however, on his return from Spain, advanced into Austria with a large force, occupied Vienna and defeated the Austrians under the Archduke Charles at the Battle of Wagram in July 1809. The victory was nevertheless gained at great cost. Napoleon's opponents were now beginning to study and copy his tactics. His armies, too, no longer possessed their former qualities. The strain of his campaigns was beginning to tell on French manpower, and the unity and national spirit of his forces was weakened by the need to enrol soldiers from Italy, the Confederation of the Rhine and other countries.

Russia had taken no active steps to implement her alliance with Napoleon in the fighting of 1809; but neither had the rest of Germany given Austria any support. Britain, indeed, attempted to divert Napoleon by occupying the Isle of Walcheren for an attack on Antwerp, but the expedition was so mismanaged that it lost many men through the swamps and fevers of the island without ever doing any fighting. The Emperor Francis, therefore, resolved to make peace rather than risk further defeat by continuing the war. By the Treaty of Schönbrunn, Austria had to cede western Galicia to the Duchy of Warsaw, Salzburg and the Tyrol to Bavaria and the Illyrian provinces of Trieste, Croatia, Carniola and part of Carinthia (because of the requirements of the Continental System) to direct French rule. In all, Austria lost 3,500,000 subjects. She also had to pay a large indemnity and reduce her army to 150,000 men. This treaty was followed in 1810 by the marriage of Napoleon to Marie Louise, daughter of Francis I.[1]

The Recovery of Prussia (1807–12)

Though German disunity had contributed to the downfall of Austria in 1809, Prussia – still the most important wholly-German independent state – had already entered upon a programme of reforms which was to enable her to take an active part in the final overthrow of Napoleon. The Prussia which had been defeated so disastrously in 1806 at Jena was the Prussia of Frederick the Great, a state still organized along the lines of the old ideas of the eighteenth century, which had been destroyed in France by the Revolution and elsewhere were succumbing to its influence. Military defeat now stimulated the introduction into Prussia of reforms which expressed the aims and methods of the *philosophes*. An administrative and military reorganization was carried out between 1807 and 1814 by a group of statesmen and soldiers, who were aided by an increasing national spirit expressed in poems and songs, popular leagues and societies. They were also aided by Queen Louise, who convinced the cautious Frederick William III that reform was needed.

The old Prussian military system had failed so completely in the war against Napoleon that there could be little opposition to the reorganization of the army, even by those most adversely affected. The task was carried through by Gerhard von Scharnhorst (1755–1813) and August von Gneisenau (1760–1831). Under their direction, privileges were abolished, and the officers were no longer appointed solely from the nobility. Conditions of

[1] P. 353.

service in the ranks were improved, flogging was abolished as the normal means of punishment, and promotion was to be partly at least on merit. Arms, methods and tactics were revised according to the new ideas. Although Napoleon had restricted the Prussian army to 42,000 men, Scharnhorst devised a system of short service by which recruits were rapidly trained and then passed into the reserve. This enabled Prussia by 1814 to put in the field an army of 270,000 men, which gained prestige in the last battles against France. Moreover, the introduction of conscription in that year placed Prussia once again in the position of being able to establish for herself the strongest and most efficient army on the Continent.

Even more important was the political and social reorganization in Prussia, undertaken simultaneously mainly under the direction of two statesmen, Heinrich von Stein (1757–1831) and Karl von Hardenberg (1750–1822). Stein had been born a citizen of Nassau, one of the smallest German states, but came to Prussia when the Napoleonic reconstruction of western Germany destroyed its old divisions. By the Emancipating Edict of 1807, he freed the serfs, so that they no longer had to perform forced labour for their landlords and could work for wages anywhere they chose; permitted nobles to engage in trade and burgesses to buy the land of nobles; and abolished the trade barriers between the towns of Prussia and the rest of the country. Stein, however, was a Prussian minister for little more than a year. He met with strong opposition in Prussia, especially from the nobility who hated him as a revolutionary; and in 1808 Napoleon ordered him to be exiled. Frederick William dared not do otherwise. Stein went first to Vienna and then to St. Petersburg, where he played some part in bringing about the Czar's open breach of his alliance with France. Stein's work was continued by Hardenberg, who reformed the financial system, liberated industry from the control of the guilds and in 1810 completed the abolition of serfdom by a land law which gave the peasants two-thirds of their lands as freehold, assigning the other third to their lords as compensation for the loss of dues and rents from their serfs.

At the same time, important educational measures were undertaken by another Prussian minister, Karl von Humboldt (1767–1835). The foundation of the University of Halle in 1694 by Frederick I, the first King of Prussia, had given the state an influential centre of German culture, but Prussia had now been deprived of Halle by the Treaty of Tilsit. Through Humboldt's efforts a new University of Berlin was established in 1810. At first it had only four professors, but it was soon housed in a royal palace and given a considerable grant from the government, which enabled it to exercise an increasingly important influence. Humboldt also introduced reforms in the schools which were the first steps in the establishment of a system of state education in Prussia.

The effect of these military, social and educational reforms, together with the patriotic movement which had originally helped to bring them into being, was to make Prussian popular sentiment grow more and more in favour of resistance to Napoleon. Frederick William viewed with alarm the prospects of renewed war with France, but he had eventually to make an alliance with Russia.[1] Even so, this did not occur until Napoleon had suffered disastrous defeat in Russia.

The Invasion of Russia (1812)

By 1812, now that Austria had again been defeated by Napoleon and accepted a dynastic alliance with him, Russia remained the only Continental power really independent of French control. Nominally France and Russia were united by the Treaty of Tilsit, but suspicion and enmity were fast developing between them. Alexander resented Napoleon's annexation of the Duchy of Oldenburg in 1810, since its ruler was his uncle, and this action strengthened the French position in the Baltic contrary to the terms of Tilsit. Alexander also regarded the continuance of the Grand Duchy of Warsaw as an ever-present threat to his retention of his own Polish territories. More serious as a cause of friction between the two countries was Alexander's attitude towards the Continental System. To meet the economic distress and consequent discontent from which Russia, like most other European countries, was suffering, Alexander placed heavy duties on French imports and allowed the importation of British colonial products in neutral ships. British trade with Russia was very small indeed, but the Czar's defiance of the blockade angered Napoleon and alarmed him by its possible effect upon the policy of other countries. It became the ostensible reason for his attack on Russia.

Behind these developments, however, lay the real reason for

conflict between France and Russia, which was the irreconcilable hostility between these two rival empires, each of which desired supremacy in the Mediterranean and the Near East. As Napoleon himself wrote in 1808, 'At bottom the great question is – Who shall have Constantinople?' Napoleon and Alexander each suspected with considerable reason that the other was prepared to attack him when possible. Napoleon feared that the opportunity had come for Russia in May 1812 when she brought to an end the war she had been fighting with Turkey since 1806. In 1812 also, Alexander signed the Treaty of Abo with Charles Bernadotte, formerly one of Napoleon's marshals whom the Swedes had chosen in 1810 as Crown Prince on the failure of their own royal line. In return for Swedish help to Russia, she was promised Norway, then ruled by Denmark, an ally of France, at the end of the war, though Russia was to retain Finland, which she had conquered from Sweden in 1808.

Napoleon made his preparations to attack Russia. Estimates of the size of the army he gathered in East Prussia vary. It may have amounted to 675,000 men of whom he perhaps took some 430,000 with 1,350 guns into Russia. It is certain that the Grand Army now was not an entirely French force; possibly as many as two-thirds of its members were conscripts levied from Poland, Prussia, Austria, Italy, Holland, Switzerland and even Spain.

Napoleon crossed the River Niemen on 24th June 1812, planning to defeat the Russian army which opposed him with considerably less than half his numbers and then win the campaign by capturing Moscow, some five hundred miles from the Niemen. As in Spain, however, he was defeated by the improvised tactics of his opponents and the particularly difficult nature of the country and its extremes of climate; his army was destroyed by sheer starvation of men and horses. The persistent withdrawal by the Russians under their commander-in-chief Prince Kutuzoff and their destruction of crops and stores, the inability of his transport, through climate and terrain, to keep pace with the troops, the loss of horses unable to live on the rough pasturage of the Russian plains, the sickness among his men, the indiscipline and large-scale desertion particularly among his foreign troops, all these combined to disrupt his communications and consume his provisions.

As the Russian forces retreated and avoided battle, the Grand

Army toiled forward through the heat and dust of the summer, and by September death and desertion had lost it two-thirds of its men. Now, outside Moscow, the Russians at last stood and fought the Battle of Borodino, but it did not give Napoleon the decisive victory he wanted. The French lost some 30,000 men and as many horses, and though the Russian casualties were heavier, they retreated in order. A week later, the exhausted Grand Army entered Moscow, which was abandoned and empty and soon largely destroyed by fire. Napoleon waited for five weeks in vain for the Russians to ask for peace. As the Russian winter set in, there was no alternative for the army, now reduced to about 100,000 men, except retreat through a snow-covered, already desolate region, laden with booty, inadequately provisioned and continually harassed by Cossack cavalry. Perhaps some 50,000 men eventually crossed the River Niemen, and not more than a thousand of them were fit for further military service.

The disastrous losses of the Russian campaign were the culmination of the heavy price that France had been compelled to pay for Napoleon's policy. In 1802 he had said that he could draw upon an annual 'income' of 100,000 men, and for ten years he had lived up to this 'blood levy'. Now he had exceeded it terribly.[1] A growing war-weariness and desire for peace was to spread in the army itself.

The Fourth Coalition (1813–14)

Back in Paris, Napoleon applied himself with all his ruthless will and energy to raising a new army. This time it had to come from France alone; the rest of Europe would send no more recruits. He proceeded to call up conscripts before their time and enrol home-service militia. There were stories of Frenchmen who fled or mutilated themselves to escape military service, but the resolve to defend the frontier of the Rhine ensured that the nation as a whole still rallied behind him. By great efforts Napoleon succeeded within four months in raising a force of 226,000 men and 457 guns, but many of his new troops were young and untrained who could not be compared with the veterans of the Grand Army.

Meanwhile, during the first weeks of 1813, the Russians had followed the remnants of the Grand Army into East Prussia, but a successful offensive in northern Germany required the co-

[1] P. 139.

operation of Prussia. Frederick William's unwillingness to turn against France was overridden by the growing nationalism of his people, and in January he signed the Treaty of Kalisch with the Czar by which he became an ally of Russia and agreed not to make a separate peace in return for a promise that Prussia would regain her former boundaries. So began the War of Liberation in Germany. The armies of the two countries drove the French west of the Elbe. Then Napoleon brought up his new forces. He established control over half of Germany, including Saxony, and defeated the Russians and Prussians at Lützen and Bautzen.

To maintain the fight against Napoleon, Lord Castlereagh induced Russia and Prussia to accept British financial help and form the Fourth Coalition. Prince Metternich (1773–1859), the Foreign Minister of Austria since 1809, suggested an armistice as a preliminary to a general peace conference. Napoleon accepted this in June, but negotiations collapsed, and Austria joined the Coalition. With nearly a million men, the Allies now had larger forces than Napoleon. By anticipating their attack, Napoleon won yet another victory at Dresden, but it was his last. Metternich's diplomacy had now won over all the important states in the Confederation of the Rhine except Saxony. In October Napoleon suffered an overwhelming defeat in the Battle of the Nations at Leipzig; he lost 50,000 men and retreated to the Rhine.

On the last day of 1813, for the first time for twenty years, France was herself invaded. In March 1814 the Allies entered Paris at the same time as Wellington was advancing into France from Spain. Faced with the refusal of his marshals to continue fighting, Napoleon abdicated the next month and was granted the sovereignty of the small island of Elba by the Allies; but this was not quite the end of his story. The Allies decided to restore the French monarchy. The young Dauphin, who died in prison in 1795, had been regarded by royalists as Louis XVII, so Louis XVI's younger brother was brought from a country house in Buckinghamshire to become Louis XVIII. After ten months Napoleon escaped from Elba to France. The loyalty of the old army to him and the political passivity of most of the nation enabled him to regain power; but the 'Hundred Days' ended with the Battle of Waterloo on 18th June 1815 and Napoleon's final exile to St. Helena, where he died in 1821.

Though the twofold invasion of France in 1813 was made

possible by the Peninsular War and the War of Liberation, it must
not be thought that these national risings were prime factors in
the defeat of Napoleon. The 'Spanish ulcer' would not have
been significant if it had not provided an opportunity for Wellington's forces to fight on the Continent, and the war in Germany
would not have occurred without Napoleon's retreat from Moscow. Rather, as Professor Geoffrey Barraclough has written,
'Napoleon was defeated, not by an uprising of the Continental
peoples, but by powers which drew their strength from outside
Europe, Russia from its vast Asiatic reserves beyond the Urals,
England from the wealth of the New World'.

In fact, Napoleon was faced with the same situation as Hitler
130 years later. Both men found that they could not impose
their will on the Continent because of the opposition of these two
powers upon the edge of Europe. Failing an agreement with
one of them, Napoleon tried to break out of this deadlock, as
Hitler did later, by taking the step natural for a Continental land
power with a great army. He accepted naval inferiority in the
west and made a desperate effort to gain military supremacy in
the east. The consequence was that Napoleonic France, like
Nazi Germany, aroused an alliance of east and west and was overwhelmed by the double attack which followed.

The Vienna Settlement (1815)

After Napoleon's abdication in April 1814, peace was made
with France the next month by the First Treaty of Paris, which
restored to her her boundaries of 1792. This gave her half a
million more inhabitants than in 1790, but it meant the loss of her
great Belgian, Dutch, German and Italian conquests. She was
not to be occupied or made to pay an indemnity and was to be
allowed to keep most of her looted works of art. After the Battle
of Waterloo, this was replaced by the Second Treaty of Paris in
November 1815. France was now reduced to her boundaries
of 1790, which involved the loss of further strategic territory on
her north-eastern frontier. She was to be occupied by an allied
army until 1820 and pay a large indemnity; she was also to return
all the works of art she had taken from the European countries
she had conquered.

Meanwhile, the Congress of Vienna had met to consider a
general European settlement. Its work was interrupted by
Napoleon's return from Elba, but the Treaty of Vienna was

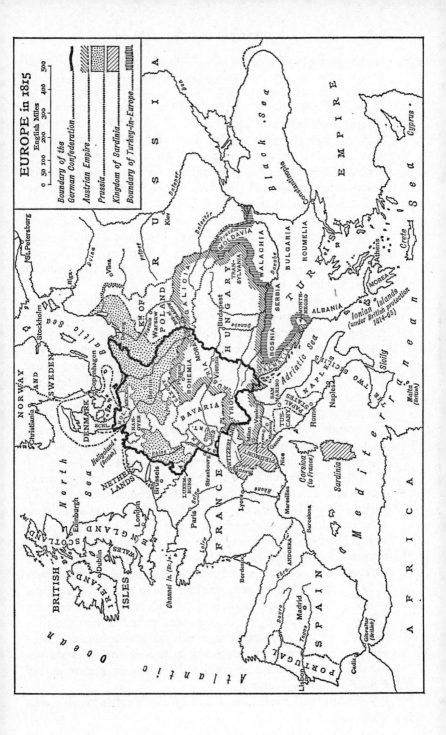

EUROPE in 1815

English Miles
0 50 100 200 300 400 500

Boundary of the German Confederation
Austrian Empire
Prussia
Kingdom of Sardinia
Boundary of Turkey-in-Europe

signed a few days before the Battle of Waterloo. Although almost every state in Europe was represented at the Congress, the greatest influence was exercised by Castlereagh for Britain, Metternich for Austria, Alexander I for Russia, Hardenberg for Prussia and Talleyrand for France. Each of these great powers had its own interests. With her world-wide commitments, Britain wanted a peaceful, settled Europe which would afford her security and commercial opportunities. Russia, despite her czar's enigmatic idealism, still followed the traditional aims of her diplomacy in the Balkans, the Baltic and Poland. Metternich's consistent conservatism was coupled with Austria's wish to uphold her influence in Germany and Italy. Prussia wanted to increase her own territory and also her power in Germany. Talleyrand ably used every opportunity to secure a settlement as favourable as possible for France.

Despite the inevitable differences produced by these varying and often conflicting objectives, the great powers did agree upon certain general aims. They wanted to make, after twenty-two years of war, a permanent European settlement, which would include safeguards against renewed French aggression. They also wanted to restore social stability in Europe; this they did through the principle of 'legitimacy', the restoration of 'rightful' sovereigns to their thrones. Finally, they desired to reward and compensate states which had fought on the allied side, generally at the expense of those which had supported France, and in some cases they were already bound by wartime agreements.

In the end, the Vienna settlement, like all such arrangements, was achieved as the result of negotiation and compromise. To make a ring of barrier states around France, the Austrian Netherlands and Luxembourg were combined with Holland to form a united kingdom; Prussia was given the Rhineland; and Piedmont obtained Genoa and part of Savoy. Prussia also secured the northern part of Saxony and Swedish Pomerania, though most of her Polish territory was left under Russian rule; so Saxony was punished and Prussia considerably strengthened, especially as the German territory she gained was more valuable than the Slav territory she lost. In accordance with previous agreements, Norway was transferred from Denmark to Sweden and Finland from Sweden to Russia, who also got Bessarabia and the greater part of Poland, including Warsaw.

Germany was made into a loose Confederation, which contained thirty-nine states, including Prussia and Austria, and was to have a diet meeting at Frankfort to discuss common affairs under the presidency of Austria. Italy was restored nearly to its condition before Napoleon's campaign of 1796. Austria's power in the peninsula was strengthened, for she received back Lombardy and was given Venetia as compensation for the loss of the Netherlands. The Pope regained the Papal States, and the Bourbons were restored to Naples. The small duchies of Parma, Modena and Tuscany were placed under Austrian princes.

Britain's share in the settlement was in accordance with Castlereagh's policy. 'It is not the business of England,' he wrote, 'to collect trophies but to restore Europe to peaceful habits.' To give strength to the new Kingdom of the Netherlands, he relinquished to it the Dutch East Indies, despite the protests of British traders; and, similarly, to give stability to the Bourbon monarchy in France, he restored to her most of her colonies. Yet the conquests which Britain retained were important for the future development of her empire. St. Lucia, Tobago, Trinidad and Guiana in the western Atlantic; Mauritius and Ceylon in the Indian Ocean; the Cape of Good Hope at the junction of the two oceans; Malta and the Ionian Islands in the Mediterranean – all these were of great strategic value and ensured her undisputed control of the world's seaways. As compensation for the loss of the Cape, Holland received £6,000,000, which was to be spent on the fortification of the Belgian frontier against France, an arrangement typical of the way Castlereagh tried to make colonial questions assist European situations.

The Vienna settlement was strongly criticized by nineteenth-century liberals. It is true that much of it was made in the interests of the great powers, that the future of territories such as Belgium, Norway, Finland and Poland was arranged without regard to the wishes of their inhabitants, that aspirations for unity in Germany and Italy were ignored and that the principle of 'legitimacy' often meant a restoration of reaction. Wordsworth was angry that the Italians were 'transferred to Austria, to the King of Sardinia and the rest of those vile tyrants'; and Lord Byron wrote still more sweepingly, 'Here we are retrograding to the full, stupid old system – balance of Europe – posing straws upon Kings' noses, instead of wringing them off'.

It must be realized, however, that the aim which most united the Congress was the restoration of stability, order and peace in

Europe. The long years of war had followed the outbreak of revolution, and so the upholding of legitimist monarchs, especially in France, Spain and Italy, was an effort towards the establishment of tranquillity. Similarly, an attempt was made to prevent any one power dominating an important area of Europe. In Germany, for instance, the Prussian demand for the whole of Saxony and Alsace-Lorraine was refused, and the new German Confederation included both Prussia and Austria as members. And for the future, a system of periodic congresses of the great powers was planned to settle peacefully any further international disputes. The new forces and rapid developments of the nineteenth century told against the permanence of the Vienna settlement, but it did achieve the considerable success of bringing Europe almost half a century of comparative peace.

BIBLIOGRAPHY

GENERAL HISTORIES

The Cambridge Modern History: vol. VI, *The Eighteenth Century* (1909); vol. VIII, *The French Revolution* (1907); vol. IX, *Napoleon* (1907).

The New Cambridge Modern History: vol. VII, *The Old Régime 1713–1763* (1957); vol. VIII, *The Revolution in America and Europe 1763–1792* (in preparation); vol. IX, *The New Régimes and the Industrial Revolution 1793–1830/2* (in preparation).

Peuples et Civilisations (edd. L. Halphen and P. Sagnac): vol. XI, P. Muret, *La Prépondérance anglaise 1715–63* (3rd ed. 1949); vol. XII, P. Sagnac, *La Fin de l'Ancien Régime et la Révolution américaine 1763–89* (3rd ed. 1952); vol. XIII, G. Lefebvre, *La Révolution française* (3rd ed. 1951); vol. XIV, G. Lefebvre, *Napoléon* (4th ed. 1953).

The Rise of Modern Europe (ed. W. L. Langer): vol. VIII, P. Roberts, *The Quest for Security 1715–40* (1947); vol. IX, W. L. Dorn, *The Competition for Empire 1740–63* (1940); vol. X, L. Gershoy, *From Despotism to Revolution 1763–89* (1944); vol. XI, C. Brinton, *A Decade of Revolution 1789–99* (1934); vol. XII, G. Bruun, *Europe and the French Imperium 1799–1814* (1938).

M. S. Anderson, *Europe in the Eighteenth Century 1713–1783* (1961).

M. Beloff, *The Age of Absolutism 1660–1815* (1954).

A. Hassall, *The Balance of Power 1715–89* (5th ed. 1950).

A. H. Johnson, *The Age of the Enlightened Despot 1660–1789* (1921).

F. M. H. Markham, *Napoleon and the Awakening of Europe* (1954).

R. Mousnier and E. Labrousse, *La XVIIIe siècle: Révolution intellectuelle, technique et politique 1715–1815* (1953).

W. F. Reddaway, *A History of Europe 1715–1814* (1936).

J. M. Thompson, *Lectures on Foreign History 1494–1789* (1945).

THE ENLIGHTENMENT

H. N. Brailsford, *Voltaire* (1935).

A. Cobban, *In Search of Humanity* (1960).

P. Hazard, *The European Mind 1680–1715* (1953).

P. Hazard, *European Thought in the Eighteenth Century from Montesquieu to Lessing* (1954).

H. J. Laski, *The Rise of European Liberalism* (1936).

K. Martin, *French Liberal Thought in the Eighteenth Century* (1929).

R. R. Palmer, *The Age of the Democratic Revolution 1760–1800* (1959).

B. Willey, *The Eighteenth Century Background* (1946).

RELIGION

The Pelican History of the Church: vol. IV, G. R. Cragg, *The Church and the Age of Reason 1648–1789* (1960); vol. V, A. R. Vidler, *The Church in an Age of Revolution 1789 to the Present Day* (1961).

K. S. Latourette, *A History of the Expansion of Christianity:* vol. III, *Three Centuries of Advance 1500–1800* (1947).

K. S. Latourette, *A History of Christianity* (1954).

L. Pullan, *Religion Since the Reformation* (1923).

J. W. C. Wand, *A History of the Modern Church* (1952).
R. A. Knox, *Enthusiasm* (1950). [Jansenism.]
E. E. Y. Hales, *Revolution and the Papacy 1796–1846* (1960).

ECONOMIC HISTORY

H. Heaton, *Economic History of Europe* (2nd ed. 1948).
A. Gray, *The Development of Economic Doctrine* (1931).
E. Roll, *A History of Economic Thought* (3rd ed. 1954).
T. S. Ashton, *The Industrial Revolution 1760–1830* (1948).

INTERNATIONAL RELATIONS

P. Rain, *La Diplomatie française d' Henri IV à Vergennes* (1945).
H. W. V. Temperley, *Frederick the Great and Kaiser Joseph* (1915).
J. H. Clapham, *The Causes of the War of 1792* (1899).
R. B. Mowat, *The Diplomacy of Napoleon* (1924).
H. Nicolson, *The Congress of Vienna* (1946).
C. K. Webster, *The Congress of Vienna* (1934).

ARMIES AND NAVIES

G. A. Craig, *The Politics of the Prussian Army* (1955).
H. S. Wilkinson, *The French Army before Napoleon* (1915).
B. H. Liddell Hart, *The Ghost of Napoleon* (1933).
G. Davies, *Wellington and his Army* (1954).
G. Callender and F. H. Hinsley, *The Naval Side of British History 1485–1945*
        (1952).
M. Lewis, *The Navy of Britain* (1948).
C. Lloyd, *Ships and Seamen* (1961).
C. Oman, *Nelson* (4th ed. 1954).
O. Warner, *A Portrait of Lord Nelson* (1958).
O. Warner, *Trafalgar* (1959).

COLONIAL HISTORY

R. Muir, *The Expansion of Europe* (6th ed. 1939).
The Cambridge History of the British Empire, vols. I and II (1929).
A. P. Newton, *The British Empire to 1783* (1935).
J. A. Williamson, *A Short History of British Expansion*, 2 vols. (1943).
G. S. Graham, *Canada* (1950).
C. H. Philips, *India* (1948).

FRANCE

A. Cobban, *A History of Modern France 1715–1945*, 2 vols. (1961).
Albert Guérard, *France* (1959).
J. Lough, *An Introduction to Eighteenth Century France* (1960).
R. L. G. Ritchie, *France* (1953).
F. C. Roe, *Modern France* (1956).
C. Seignobos, *A History of the French People* (trans. C. A. Phillips, 1933).
H. See, *Economic and Social Conditions in France during the Eighteenth Century*
        (trans. H. H. Zeyder, 1927).
F. L. Ford, *Robe and Sword: The Regrouping of the French Aristocracy after
        Louis XIV* (1953).
D. Dakin, *Turgot and the Ancien Régime in France* (1939).
G. P. Gooch, *Louis XV, the Monarchy in Decline* (1956).
Lord Elton, *The Revolutionary Idea in France* (1923).
A. Goodwin, *The French Revolution* (1953).

G. Lefebvre, *The Coming of the French Revolution 1789* (trans. R. R. Palmer, 1947).
A. Mathiez, *The French Revolution* (1928).
G. Rudé, *The Crowd in the French Revolution* (1959).
J. M. Thompson, *The French Revolution* (3rd ed. 1947).
J. M. Thompson, *Robespierre and the French Revolution* (1952).
J. M. Thompson, *Leaders of the French Revolution* (1929).
E. L. Woodward, *French Revolutions* (1934).
H. Butterfield, *Napoleon* (1939).
H. A. L. Fisher, *Napoleon* (1912).
J. M. Thompson, *Napoleon Bonaparte, His Rise and Fall* (1952).
A. Duff Cooper, *Talleyrand* (1932).

GERMANY

R. Flenley, *Modern German History* (1959).
J. Haller, *The Epochs of German History* (1930).
W. H. Bruford, *Germany in the Eighteenth Century* (1959).
G. P. Gooch, *Germany and the French Revolution* (1920).
J. A. R. Marriott and C. Grant Robertson, *The Evolution of Prussia* (1915).
S. B. Fay, *The Rise of Brandenburg-Prussia to 1786* (1937).
R. Ergang, *The Potsdam Führer* (1941).   [Frederick William I.]
G. P. Gooch, *Frederick the Great* (1947).
C. de Grunwald, *Baron Stein* (1936).

RUSSIA

R. D. Charques, *A Short History of Russia* (1956).
J. Lawrence, *Russia in the Making* (1957).
B. Pares, *A History of Russia* (2nd ed. 1955).
B. H. Sumner, *A Survey of Russian History* (2nd ed. 1948).
G. P. Gooch, *Catherine the Great and other Studies* (1954).
I. Grey, *Catherine the Great* (1961).
G. Scott Thomson, *Catherine the Great and the Expansion of Russia* (1947).

SPAIN AND PORTUGAL

W. C. Atkinson, *A History of Spain and Portugal* (1960).
L. Bertrand and C. Petrie, *The History of Spain* (2nd ed. 1952).
R. Herr, *The Eighteenth Century Revolution in Spain* (1958).
M. A. S. Hume, *Spain, its Greatness and Decay 1749–1788* (1925).

THE HABSBURG LANDS

G. P. Gooch, *Maria Theresa and other Studies* (1951).
S. K. Padover, *The Revolutionary Emperor: Joseph II* (1938).
A. Cecil, *Metternich* (1933).

ITALY

L. Salvatorelli, *A Concise History of Italy from Prehistoric Times* (1940).
J. P. Trevelyan, *A Short History of the Italian People* (4th ed. 1956).
H. Acton, *The Bourbons of Naples 1734–1825* (1956).
A. Herrot, *The French in Italy 1796–99* (1957).

POLAND

The Cambridge History of Poland, vol. II (1950).
O. Halecki, *A History of Poland* (2nd ed. 1955).
G. Slocombe, *A History of Poland* (1939).
Lord Eversley, *Partitions of Poland* (1915).

INDEX